Purchasing Power Parity
and Exchange Rates:
Theory, Evidence and
Relevance

CONTEMPORARY STUDIES IN
ECONOMIC AND FINANCIAL ANALYSIS, VOLUME 35

Editors: Edward·I. Altman and Ingo Walter, Associate Dean
   Graduate School of Business Administration, New York University

CONTEMPORARY STUDIES IN ECONOMIC AND FINANCIAL ANALYSIS

An International Series of Monographs

Series Editors: **Edward I. Altman and Ingo Walter**
Graduate School of Business Administration, New York University

To My Wife
Sue Anne Officer

Purchasing Power Parity and Exchange Rates:
Theory, Evidence and
Relevance

by LAWRENCE H. OFFICER
Department of Economics
Michigan State University

Ai JAI PRESS INC.

Greenwich, Connecticut *London, England*

Library of Congress Cataloging in Publication Data

Officer, Lawrence H.
  Purchasing power parity and exchange rates.

  (Contemporary studies in economic and financial
analysis; v. 35)
  Bibliography: p.
  Includes index.
  1. Foreign exchange.   2. Purchasing power.
I. Title.   II. Series.
HG3821.035   332.4′5   81-81650
ISBN 0-89232-229-2   AACR2

Copyright © 1982 JAI PRESS INC.
36 Sherwood Place
Greenwich, Connecticut 06830

JAI PRESS INC.
3 Henrietta Street
London WC2E 8LU
England

ISBN NUMBER: 0-89232-229-2
Library of Congress Catalog Card Number: 81-81650
Manufactured in the United States of America

CONTENTS

vii

Part IV: Selected PPP Studies

Part V: Conclusions

List of Tables

Preface

My interest in purchasing power parity (PPP) as an exchange-rate theory began in 1961, when Hendrik S. Houthakker presented a PPP analysis when serving as a guest lecturer in Jaroslav Vanek's class in international economics at Harvard University. A year later, Houthakker committed his ideas to print, but it was not until more than a decade thereafter that I wrote a paper elaborating on Houthakker's approach. The paper was published in 1974, and apparently induced the International Monetary Fund to offer me the opportunity to continue work on PPP as a resident consultant in 1975. The stimulating professional atmosphere at the Fund led to a permanent interest in the PPP approach on my part.

This volume presents a complete statement of the PPP approach in all its aspects. I am grateful to Kyklos, the Canadian Economics Association, the International Monetary Fund, and the North-Holland Publishing Company for permitting the use of my previously published material on the subject. The book can be viewed as a survey of the entire PPP literature, an extension of a much shorter review published as Officer (1976a). However, except for Part Four, which reprints some of my existing specific studies of PPP (with the only changes the result of minor editing), the volume is fundamentally new; it extends and updates the previous survey, introducing much new material in the process.

I wish to thank my colleague Warren J. Samuels for encouraging me to produce a volume of this nature. I also thank Mr. Stephan W. M. Schoess for assisting in the translation of non-English material. The work was completed when I was Visiting Professor of Economics at the Graduate School of Business at the University of Chicago. I am grateful to the School for providing the support facilities that enabled me to complete the volume in good time.

Lawrence H. Officer

Part I

INTRODUCTION

Chapter I

Introductory Comments

"Our willingness to pay a certain price for foreign money must ultimately and essentially be due to the fact that this money possesses a purchasing power as against commodities and services in that foreign country." (Gustav Cassel, 1922, p. 138)

The purchasing-power-parity theory asserts that the exchange rate is determined by the level of prices in the domestic country compared to that abroad, that changes in the exchange rate are determined by changes in these price levels, and that the percentage change in the exchange rate per month, quarter, or year is determined by inflation at home relative to that abroad over these time intervals. The theory is based on the intuitively appealing idea that money, whether domestic or foreign, is valued—and therefore demanded—for the goods and services it can purchase in the country to which the money pertains.

In this volume all aspects of the purchasing-power-parity (PPP) theory are explored, and in as comprehensive a manner as space permits. Part I deals with methodological issues—the conceptual ingredients of the theory and the different forms the theory can take. Part II provides a complete history of the development of the PPP theory from its beginning to the First World War. The episodic resurgences of interest in the theory over historical time indicate those circumstances under which the theory may be expected to be valid. Part III offers a survey of the modern PPP approach, with attention paid to the types of PPP analyses, criticisms of PPP, practical uses of the theory, and tests of the validity of the theory. Part IV presents a group of complete PPP studies, mainly empirical in nature, undertaken by this author. The volume closes in Part V, which sets forth the conclusions that can be drawn from the entire study.

3

Chapter II

Methodology of Purchasing Power Parity

"To define the equilibrium rate formally is one thing; to determine its height or probable behavior in a given situation, another." (Howard S. Ellis, 1936, p. 27)

This chapter provides a methodological foundation for the PPP theory that underpins the entire study. The PPP theory of exchange rates involves a relationship between a country's foreign-exchange rate, on the one hand, and its price level or price movement compared to the foreign price level or movement, on the other. We consider the price and exchange-rate ingredients of the theory in turn. The price concept provides us with a definition of PPP itself (as distinct from the PPP theory).

I. CONCEPTS OF PURCHASING POWER PARITY

Purchasing power parity may be expressed in either absolute or relative terms. The absolute PPP of the domestic country's currency is the ratio of the foreign price level to the domestic price level. A price level is an average (generally a weighted average) of *absolute* (money) prices; so its dimension is number of units of currency per physical quantity. Absolute PPP then, as the ratio of the foreign to the domestic price level, has as dimension number of units of foreign currency per unit of domestic currency.

Relative PPP pertains to price movements rather than levels, with movements measured by price indices. A base period must be selected, and indices are measured in a current period relative to the base period.

Then relative PPP has two alternative definitions: either the ratio of the foreign to the domestic price index or the product of this ratio and the base-period exchange rate.

We define the exchange rate here as the price of domestic currency in terms of foreign exchange, that is, the number of units of foreign currency per unit of domestic currency.[1] Also, it is the actual or "market" or "current" exchange rate, thus distinct from and not necessarily equal to the "equilibrium" exchange rate defined in any manner. Further, the exchange rate pertains to "spot" transactions, where delivery of currency is immediate or nearly so, rather than to "forward" or "future" transactions, where delivery is to take place at a determinate time in the future though the price (the forward exchange rate) is known and accepted now. The base-period rate, therefore, is the spot exchange rate.

What are the dimensions of the relative-PPP concepts? A price index is an average (again generally a weighted average) of price relatives, where a price relative is the ratio of a particular individual price (the price of an individual commodity, for example) in the current period to the price of the same item in the base period. So a price index is dimensionless. Therefore, the first relative-PPP concept, as the ratio of two price indices, is also without dimension. The second concept, though, is the product of the first and the base-period exchange rate. It has the same dimension as the exchange rate, that is, number of units of foreign currency per unit of domestic currency. That happens to be also the same dimension as absolute PPP.

Symbolically, the variables for the PPP concepts are as follows:

L_j = price level in domestic country in period j
L_j^f = foreign price level in period j
P_j = price index in domestic country in period j
P_j^f = foreign price index in period j
R_j = actual exchange rate in period j, number of units of foreign currency per unit of domestic currency
PPP_j^{abs} = absolute purchasing power parity in period j
$PPP_j^{rel\ 1}$ = relative purchasing power parity, first concept, in period j
$PPP_j^{rel\ 2}$ = relative purchasing power parity, second concept, in period j

Let "t" be the current time period and "o" the base period (with respect to which the price indices are measured). Of course, the current time period can vary, while the base period is fixed. The respective PPP concepts are defined as follows for current period "t".

$$PPP_t^{abs} \equiv L_t^f/L_t$$
$$PPP_t^{rel\ 1} \equiv P_t^f/P_t$$
$$PPP_t^{rel\ 2} \equiv (P_t^f/P_t) \cdot R_o$$

The rationale behind the PPP definitions is that the purchasing power of a currency, its command over domestic goods and services, can be measured by the inverse of the country's price level. Changes in the currency's purchasing power are given by the inverse of the country's price index. The purchasing power *parity* of the domestic currency with respect to the foreign currency is the domestic/foreign relative purchasing power, that is: (i) the foreign/domestic relative price level (absolute PPP), or (ii) the foreign/domestic relative price index (relative PPP, first concept), or (iii) the product of the foreign/domestic relative price index and the base-period exchange rate (relative PPP, second concept).

II. CONCEPTS OF THE EQUILIBRIUM EXCHANGE RATE

Thus far, the only exchange-rate concept encountered is the spot exchange rate in the base period, needed for the second relative-PPP measure. That rate is the actual, the then current, exchange rate. The PPP theory also involves a concept of the equilibrium, as distinct from actual exchange rate. Rather, two such concepts are involved, one for the short run, the other for the long run. As will be seen, these time frames ("runs") are different from the conventional use of the terms.

There is a distinct body of literature concerning the appropriate definition of the long-run equilibrium exchange rate, so we consider that concept first. Writers simply refer to the "equilibrium exchange rate;" the designation "long run" is understood. Also, implicitly, the equilibrium refers to the spot, rather than forward, exchange rate.

It is not generally known that John Maynard Keynes was the first to propose a definition of the equilibrium exchange rate; nearly all discussions of the topic begin with the work of Ragnar Nurkse (1945). Yet Keynes (1935, p. 528) had the following passage in print a full decade earlier:

> The first condition, which must be satisfied before it is worth while to discuss permanent policy, is that the *de facto* rates of exchange, from which we start out, should be in reasonable equilibrium. . . . We have to consider, on the one hand, a country's balance of payments on income account on the basis of the existing natural resources, equipment, technique and costs (especially wage costs) at home and abroad, a normal level of employment, and those tariffs, etc., which are a permanent feature

of national policies; and, on the other hand, the probable readiness and ability of the country in question to borrow or lend abroad on long term (or, perhaps, repay or accept repayment of old loans), on the average of the next few years. A set of rates of exchange, which can be established without undue strain on either side and without large movements of gold (on a balance of transactions), will satisfy our condition of equilibrium. This does not mean that a set of rates can be found which can be relied on to persist indefinitely without strain. It will be sufficient if a set can be found which the various Central Banks can accept without serious anxiety for the time being, provided that there is no substantial change in the underlying conditions.

A number of aspects of Keynes' definition are noteworthy. First, the equilibrium rate is fixed or pegged at a certain level. This treatment of the equilibrium rate as fixed rather than floating or flexible in some manner is a feature of all later writings on the topic. Second, this rate keeps the balance of payments not far from equilibrium over a certain time period, where the imbalance is measured by gold flows. Later writers were to insist on a zero balance over the given time period, and the measure of financing the imbalance would be more inclusive, incorporating gains or losses of all reserve assets (not just monetary gold, to which Keynes was presumably referring) plus some or all short-term capital movements.

Third, the time period over which payments imbalances are to be limited is not precise. The exchange rate need not "persist indefinitely;" it is to be accepted "for the time being," with "the next few years" mentioned as a time interval. Keynes' views here are consistent with much of the later discussion of the concept.

Fourth, a "normal" level of employment is not to be subject to "undue strain." Subsequent authors would specify the employment criterion more precisely.[2] Fifth, only those trade restrictions ("tariffs, etc.") which are "a permanent feature of national policies" are permitted under the definition. Keynes is emphatic about this criterion:

> The test of success will be found in the voluntary removal of all those exchange restrictions, import quotas, exceptional tariffs, etc., which are not desired for their own sake as a permanent feature of national policy, but are acts of desperation and an expression of the extreme anxiety of the authorities, either to make both ends meet, or to alleviate the unemployment inflicted by deflation.

Later authors, knowingly or unknowingly, had been anticipated by Keynes in this aspect as well.

Finally, the rate is to hold for no structural changes in the domestic and foreign economies, or at least "without undue strain" brought on by structural changes. Included under given structural conditions are natural resources, factor supplies, costs, and portfolio preferences. The hypothesis of no structural changes was to be adopted by all later writers, though sometimes only implicitly.

Though not specifically concerned with the long-run equilibrium exchange rate, some of Keynes' followers in effect refined the employment criterion of the equilibrium concept in the process of extending Keynes' *General Theory* to an open economy. Joan Robinson (1937) notes that the balance of trade (and therefore implicitly the balance of payments) is improved when effective demand falls, because of the induced decline in imports. She states in particular that balance-of-payments equilibrium might be attained only at the cost of unemployment in the domestic economy.[3]

A similar analysis is provided by R. F. Harrod (1939), who shows that the exchange rate that yields a balance on trade account varies with the assumed level of employment. He considers the case of an autonomous decline in exports. The more that income falls as a result, the greater the induced decline in imports, and so the smaller the depreciation of the currency required to preserve balance (by improving the competitive position of domestic producers at home and abroad). It is interesting that neither Robinson nor Harrod makes reference to Keynes' 1935 article.

In two studies, (1944; 1945), Ragnar Nurkse began the mainstream literature on defining the equilibrium exchange rate. He devotes only a small passage to the issue in the first work, yet provides some essentials of the concept. He begins with what has come to be the standard statement: "the equilibrium rate of exchange, that is the rate which, over a certain period, maintains the balance of payments in equilibrium without any net change in the international reserve" (1944, p. 124). The basic balance (though the term did not become current until the 1950s) is Nurkse's preferred measure of the balance of payments. He includes in the balance the current account and "normal" capital movements, excluding "in most cases" short-term capital movements, whether the latter are disequilibrating "hot money" flows or equilibrating flows substituting for transfers of official reserves.

Nurkse goes on to make the point that Robinson and Harrod had made earlier, either without his knowledge or ignored by him. "A country may have a rate of exchange such that its balance of payments can be kept in equilibrium only by a contraction of total domestic income and demand; and if wages and prices are rigid, such a contraction must operate through unemployment" (1944, p. 126). The British experience in 1925–1930, with the overvalued pound reflected in unemployment rather than a payments imbalance, is cited as an example. Nurkse concludes:

> Thus balance-of-payments equilibrium alone is not a sufficient condition; at different levels of income and employment, equilibrium in the balance of payments can be secured at different rates of exchange. It may be better therefore to define the true equilibrium rate as one that maintains the balance in equilibrium without the need for mass unemployment at home, or at any rate without a degree of unemployment greater than in the outside world.

Both Gottfried Haberler (1944a) and Alvin H. Hansen (1944) cite, and approve of, Nurkse's views on the equilibrium exchange rate. Haberler, however, redefines the imbalance to be something less than that of the basic-balance concept. Specifically, it is the change in official reserves (gold, foreign exchange, and credit facilities at the International Monetary Fund) plus equilibrating or accommodating capital movements. The latter are not to be identified with short-term capital movements; for disequilibrating flows (hot money) and "spontaneous" capital movements (from capital-rich to capital-poor countries) are short-term movements lacking the equilibrating function. Also, some long-term capital flows might be equilibrating. This motivational concept of a payments imbalance was to be further developed by J. E. Meade (1951).

Nurkse (1945) refined his concept of the equilibrium exchange rate in a work that to this day is the authoritative reference on the topic. The equilibrium rate is again considered to be that which preserves balance-of-payments equilibrium over a certain period of time and the basic-balance concept is now used without reservation.[4] Also, Nurkse elaborates on his earlier discussion of the relationship between the equilibrium exchange rate and unemployment. He now writes: "balance-of-payments equilibrium is not a sufficient criterion of an equilibrium exchange rate. . .in the presence of a special or additional depression necessitated by the maintenance of the actual rate. At given levels of national income and employment in a given country, equilibrium in the balance of payments can be secured at different rates of exchange. It would seem better therefore to define the true equilibrium rate of exchange as one that maintains a country's external accounts in equilibrium without the need for wholesale unemployment at home" (1945; 1950, pp. 11–12).

Nurkse also discusses two matters absent from his 1944 study: the length of the time period and the role of trade restrictions. What is that certain period of time over which the balance of payments is to be in equilibrium? To eliminate seasonal fluctuations, the time period cannot be less than a year. Nurkse also wishes to eliminate cyclical fluctuations in the balance of payments and suggests a period of 5 to 10 years as sufficient for this purpose. For countries the balance of payments of which exhibits "no very marked cyclical behavior," a period of 2 or 3 years is suggested.

Regarding trade restrictions, Nurkse notes that payments equilibrium can be achieved by means of "artificial restrictions on imports," or "artificial stimulation of exports by means of subsidies." The structure of trade barriers at the beginning of the period is the one applicable to the equilibrium exchange rate. The case of Germany after 1934 is mentioned, with the overvalued reichsmark supported "only by means of additional import restrictions, which took mainly the form of drastic exchange controls. . . . The true equilibrium rate is the rate at which payments and receipts are equalized without additional restrictions on trade" (1945; 1950, pp. 10, 9).

Frank M. Tamagna (1945, p. 69), apparently writing independent of Nurkse's work, defines the equilibrium exchange rate as "the rate which, under prevailing conditions of national income and flow of foreign investments, achieves and maintains a state of equilibrium in a country's balance of payments." Like Nurkse, the basic balance is the payments concept adopted; but, unlike Nurkse, trade restrictions are not incorporated and the prevailing level of income is specified rather than the absence of large-scale unemployment to maintain the rate.

Raymond F. Mikesell (1947) mentions Nurkse and Haberler, and does not go beyond them conceptually. In contrast, John Parke Young (1947) does not refer to preceding authors but breaks some new, or at least different ground. He defines the equilibrium exchange rate as "a rate which in the light of prospective conditions, including governmental policies and programs (fiscal policies, tariffs and other restrictions on trade), gives promise of yielding an approximate balance in a country's foreign accounts over a period of several years (in so far as a rate by itself can do this), and which will at the same time provide cost and income relationships with foreign countries which will permit a maximum flow of trade in both directions at high levels of domestic activity and employment" (1947, p. 589).

"Unless a prospective flow of capital in predictable amounts is fairly clear," Young would measure the payments balance by the current account alone. The period over which the payments balance is to be sought is 3 to 4 years in practice, though a longer period is probably necessary to achieve the balance. This longer period is related to economic fluctuations, including the business cycle.

Young's definition of the equilibrium exchange rate involves the concept of maximum international trade. Extensive import restrictions and/or low levels of income and employment are excluded because they would reduce the volume of trade. In addition, the definition specifies a high level of economic activity and "prospective conditions" of government policies on the restriction of trade. In contrast, Nurkse is content merely to exclude large-scale unemployment (for the purpose of preserving payments balance) and takes as fixed, the pre-existing structure of trade restrictions. Also, the criterion of maximum trade is lacking.

In the same volume, Haberler (1947) and Robert Triffin (1947) consider not the equilibrium exchange rate, but rather its obverse, a disequilibrium rate or "fundamental disequilibrium" in a country's balance of payments.[5] The authors agree that a balance-of-payments deficit avoided by low levels of income and employment or by extraordinary trade restrictions, such as tariffs and exchange control, constitutes a fundamental disequilibrium, in other words, a disequilibrium exchange rate. This assessment is consistent with the Nurkse definition of exchange-rate equilibrium.

One of the rare citations to Keynes' antecedent work on the equilibrium exchange rate is provided by Arthur I. Bloomfield (1947). Indeed, he accepts Keynes' definition, amending it only by incorporating equilibrating short-term capital flows together with gold (and presumably other reserve) movements as financing items in the balance of payments. Nurkse is criticized for including also disequilibrating short-term capital flows in the measure, on grounds that "capital flight" in large amounts vitiates the very concept of an equilibrium exchange rate.

Bloomfield presents a definition of the equilibrium exchange rate along the lines provided by Keynes: "that which keeps the country's international accounts in equilibrium over a period of several years (on the average) without having caused undue deflationary (or expansionist) pressures, or necessitated additional import restrictions" (1947, p. 303). He specifically rejects full employment as a criterion. It is interesting that Keynes' definition also does not involve full employment as such; rather, the term used is "normal" employment.

Ellsworth (1950) presents a discussion of the equilibrium exchange rate, following Nurkse very closely. Ellsworth's refinements are that the period involved be equal to the average length of a business cycle (indicating that this criterion is consistent with Nurkse's 5–10 year period) and that balance-of-payments equilibrium require neither large-scale unemployment (as Nurkse stated) nor domestic inflation (considering now the case of a currency undervaluation).

Nurkse's concept of the equilibrium exchange rate is also followed by Eugenio Gudin and Jorge Kingston (1951), while Meade (1951) develops the related concept of a "potential" balance-of-payments disequilibrium. This concept is the payments imbalance during a given period required "in order to avoid any depreciation in the exchange rate without the employment of exchange controls, import restrictions, or other governmental measures specially devised to restrict the demand for foreign currencies" (1951, p. 15). Domestic deflation is mentioned as an example of these other measures. Meade's measure of financing the imbalance is based on a motivational criterion; included transactions are those that take place because of the state of the balance of payments. In principle, any item could be thus accommodating.

Basing his analysis on that of Nurkse, W. M. Scammell (1961) makes a number of amendments. To remove the influence of the business cycle and other forces making for "periodic recurrent fluctuations" in the balance of payments, a decade would be needed. During so long a period, many structural changes may occur. So two to three years is a preferred period. Nurkse's period of five to ten years is criticized for industrial countries, which are less subject to cyclical influences on the balance of payments than are primary-producing countries. While Nurkse's period "satisfies intellectually in that it eliminates all recurrent influences on the rate," he implicitly assumes mild effects of the cycle.

Scammell states his definition as follows: "An equilibrium rate is that rate which, over a standard period, during which full employment is maintained and there is no change in the amount of restriction on trade or on currency transfer, causes no net change in the holdings of gold and currency reserves of the country concerned" (1961, p. 56). The full-employment criterion is a definite break with the literature to date, replacing the condition of a normal level of employment (Keynes) or the absence of domestic deflation or of large-scale unemployment (the Nurkse tradition).[6] In a footnote, Scammell remarks that it is interesting to compare his definition of exchange-rate equilibrium with that of Keynes, and quotes Keynes (1935) without comment. Apart from Bloomfield (1947), this is the only reference to Keynes' work that I could find in this literature.

Robert M. Stern (1973) points out that Nurkse's criteria for an equilibrium exchange rate are based on the experience of the interwar (1919–1939) period. The time period of 5–10 years corresponded to what was thought to be the major business cycle. The decision to include short-term capital movements in the imbalance measure emanated from the substantial capital flight and "hot money" flows in the 1930s. Also, the conditions regarding unemployment and trade restrictions were imposed in light of Britain's deflationary policies in 1925–1930 and the widespread adoption of exchange control in the 1930s.

These features of the economy have changed. Stern notes that fluctuations in economic activity have been relatively minor in the postwar period (1946–) with downturns of short duration. Also, short-term capital movements are now very large, and (as Stern might have gone on to say) such large flows are a regular feature of balances of payments. Stern, however, does not reject the concept of an equilibrium exchange rate.

Though sparse, there does exist literature asserting that the equilibrium exchange rate is a false or non-operational concept. Joan Robinson (1937) states that no one equilibrium rate corresponds to a given state of demand and technology (that is, to given structural conditions). "The notion of *the* equilibrium exchange rate is a chimera. The rate of exchange, the rate of interest, the level of effective demand and the level of money wages react upon each other like the balls in Marshall's bowl, and no one is determined unless all the rest are given" (1937, p. 208).

Some thirty years later, Bela Balassa and Daniel M. Schydlowsky (1968) criticized the equilibrium-rate concept on two grounds. First, the suggested criteria regarding trade restrictions are not operational. If additional restrictions on trade are excluded (Nurkse's condition), there is the problem of separating "basic" from "additional" restrictions. If trade restrictions on balance-of-payments grounds are excluded (Meade's criterion), this neglects the fact that restrictions have various purposes and the original motivation (even if oriented to a single purpose) is not relevant. In fact, it is not possible to define a single exchange rate for a given level of protection; for various combinations of trade restrictions, trade subsidies, and the exchange rate can result in the same degree of protection.

Second, the general point made by Robinson is repeated: "for given demand and supply conditions, there are an infinite number of 'equilibrium' exchange rates, each corresponding to a different configuration of trade, monetary, and fiscal policies" (1968, p. 357).

An exposition of the equilibrium exchange rate in the Nurkse tradition is provided by Giancarlo Gandolfo (1979). He amends Nurkse's concept in two respects: the imbalance measure and the time period. Nurkse had chosen the basic balance because short-term capital movements are volatile and reversible; but the same properties might also apply to long-term capital flows. So Gandolfo sees no one measure as appropriate; the basic balance, trade balance, current-account balance, and balance on goods and services should all be considered.

Regarding the time period, Nurkse chose a five to ten year period to eliminate cylical fluctuations, while Scammell had warned that over so long a period structural changes can take place. Gandolfo agrees with

Scammell that a shorter period is warranted; but sees any *a priori* specification of the time period as arbitrary. The length of period should depend on the data availability and limitations faced by the researcher. In his own empirical study, Gandolfo uses a one-year period.

In the light of the literature just surveyed, how should the equilibrium exchange rate be defined for the purpose of expositing the PPP theory? First, the equilibrium exchange rate is the fixed exchange rate that yields balance-of-payments equilibrium over a certain time period. This basic component of the definition is a feature of all writers dealing with the concept. Second, an inclusive measure of the balance of payments should be used, namely, the basic balance or official-settlements balance. These measures have a minimum of transactions financing the imbalance: the change in official reserves plus either all short-term capital flows or government short-term capital movements, respectively.

Third, the length of period should incorporate not only seasonal fluctuations (and hence be no less than a year) but also any cyclical fluctuations in the balance of payments, including those related to business cycles at home and abroad. There is no need to fix the length of the period precisely, for a conceptual definition of the equilibrium exchange rate. The period would depend on the duration of any recurrent fluctuation in the country's balance of payments. However, such fluctuations—if they exist at all—are not of long duration, if only because of the automatic and/or policy mechanisms that act to adjust the balance of payments. It is for this reason that an inclusive concept of the balance of payments is used. If the period were truly long run, spanning decades, the balance on goods and services or the current-account balance would be appropriate. These measures have all capital movements, both short-term and long-term, financing the imbalance, along with changes in official reserves (both measures) and unilateral transfers (balance on goods and services).[7]

Fourth, the equilibrium rate is predicated on the absence of special policies to avoid balance-of-payments disequilibrium, such as the use of monetary and fiscal restraint or trade and payments restrictions to prevent or suppress a deficit. Nurkse's criterion of no additional trade restrictions beyond those existing at the start of the period is too strict, as is Scammell's condition of full employment.

The arguments of the critics of the equilibrium-rate concept are rejected. It should not be difficult to establish whether trade and/or payments restrictions are imposed for balance-of-payments reasons. What of the argument that the equilibrium exchange rate is indeterminate because of the large number of variables that affect the rate and the interrelationships of the equilibrium rate and these variables? Such reasoning amounts to a refusal to make abstractions and thus a refusal to theorize in a meaningful way. While the equilibrium exchange rate can be criticized as a partial-analytical concept, to move to a world in which "everything depends on everything else" is to throw up one's hands in despair!

The four conditions stipulated above define the long-run equilibrium exchange rate for the purpose of this study. Generally called simply the equilibrium exchange rate in the literature, the designation "long run" is used to distinguish the concept from its short-run analogue. There is only one logical definition of the short-run equilibrium exchange rate: the rate that would exist under a freely floating exchange-rate system. Under this definition, there is no exchange-market intervention by the government at home or of that abroad; the exchange rate is completely unmanaged. Of course, as for the long-run concept, the short-run equilibrium pertains to the spot, rather than forward, exchange rate.

There can be no objection to the definition of the short-run equilibrium exchange rate offered here, except perhaps that some observers might consider a freely floating rate to be dynamically unstable. For example, Nurkse (1945) takes this position on grounds that destabilizing speculation would exist. Scammell (1961) asserts that even the most ardent advocates of freely floating rates envision short-run movements in the rate being eliminated by exchange-rate management. It is fair to say that Scammell's statement is certainly incorrect today and an exaggeration at the time of writing.

As for the general issue of dynamic instability, to allow for this phenomenon would negate a good deal of the PPP literature. Therefore, for purposes of the present study, the definition of the short-run equilibrium rate is accepted.

Symbolically, we have:

RS_j = short-run equilibrium exchange rate in period j, number of units of foreign currency per unit of domestic currency

RL_j = long-run equilibrium exchange rate in period j, number of units of foreign currency per unit of domestic currency

III. PROPOSITIONS OF THE PURCHASING-POWER-PARITY THEORY

Purchasing-power-parity theory consists of two basic propositions and a third, derivative, proposition. Each hypothesis can take two or three alternative forms, corresponding to the alternative definitions of PPP.

The first proposition relates the long-run equilibrium exchange rate to PPP; the second relates the short-run and long-run equilibrium exchange rates; and the third relates the short-run equilibrium rate to PPP.

Proposition One: PPP is the principal determinant of the long-run equilibrium exchange rate. Specifically, the long-run equilibrium rate is a function of PPP such that the former variable, in any current period (t), tends to equal the latter. In symbols:

$$RL_t = f_1(PPP_t^{abs}, \dots)$$
$$RL_t/RL_o = f_2(PPP_t^{rel\ 1}, \dots)$$
$$RL_t = f_3(PPP_t^{rel\ 2}, \dots)$$

The symbols f_1, f_2, f_3 denote arbitrary increasing functions with respect to the explicit independent variable, with the ellipses indicating space for additional explanatory variables and a random error term. The dependent variable in the f_2 function, RL_t/RL_o, is an exchange-rate index in the current period (t) with respect to the base period (o), specifically, the index of the long-run equilibrium exchange rate.

Proposition Two: The short-run equilibrium exchange rate in any current period (t) is a function of the long-run equilibrium exchange rate in the sense that the latter variable is the principal determinant of, and tends to be approached by, the former. So we have:

$$RS_t = g_1(RL_t, \dots)$$
$$RS_t/RS_o = g_2(RL_t/RL_o, \dots)$$

where g_1 and g_2 have the same significance as f_1, f_2, and f_3. Again, RS_t/RS_o is an exchange-rate index, that of the short-run equilibrium exchange rate.

Proposition Three: The short-run equilibrium exchange rate in any current period (t) is determined principally by the PPP, with the former variable tending to equal the latter. Thus:

$$RS_t = h_1(PPP_t^{abs}, \dots)$$
$$RS_t/RS_o = h_2(PPP_t^{rel\ 1}, \dots)$$
$$RS_t = h_3(PPP_t^{rel\ 2}, \dots)$$

where h_1, h_2, h_3 have the same meaning as the f and g symbols.

Clearly, proposition three is derived from propositions one and two by substituting each f function into the appropriate g function, that is:

$$h_1 \equiv g_1 \circ f_1$$

$$h_2 \equiv g_2 \circ f_2$$

$$h_3 \equiv g_1 \circ f_3$$

It is propositions one and three—either or both—that are generally considered to constitute the PPP theory. The existing literature classifies the theory into two alternative hypotheses: the absolute PPP theory, which involves the absolute PPP concept, and the relative or comparative PPP theory, based on one or other of the relative PPP measures. So the functions f_1 and h_1 are classified under the absolute PPP theory, while f_2, f_3, h_2, and h_3 pertain to the relative version of the theory.

Far from being a single theory, PPP consists of many alternative theories.[8] One can consider a four-way classification of these theories. First, the absolute form of the PPP theory is distinguished from the relative form. Second, a variety of product-price or factor-cost concepts may be used to construct the PPP (the parity measure). Those concepts that have been used in the literature, whether in theoretical analysis or empirical work, are as follows (for absolute or relative PPP, respectively): (i) the gross-national-product (GNP) price level or the GNP deflator, (ii) the gross-domestic-product(GDP) price level or the GDP deflator, (iii) a retail price level (cost-of-living, COL, level) or retail price index (COL index; consumer price index, CPI), (iv) a wholesale price level or wholesale price index (WPI), (v) the export price level or export price index (EPI), (vi) a cost (average-cost or unit-cost) level or index, (vii) a wage-rate level or index, (viii) unit-factor-cost (UFC) level or index, and (ix) unit-labor-cost (ULC) level or index.

The third dimension of any PPP theory is the form of the f and/or h functions. To simplify the exposition, one function, say H, can represent all six of the f and h functions. One ordered triple, (E, H, P), is defined to be any of six ordered triples, thus:

$$(E, H, P) \equiv (RL_t, f_1, PPP_t^{abs}) \text{ or } (RL_t/RL_o, f_2, PPP_t^{rel\ 1})$$

$$\text{or } (RL_t, f_3, PPP_t^{rel\ 2}) \text{ or } (RS_t, h_1, PPP_t^{abs})$$

$$\text{or } (RS_t/RS_0, h_2, PPP_t^{rel\ 1}) \text{ or } (RS_t, h_3, PPP_t^{rel\ 2})$$

Further, for ease in discussion, the term "exchange rate" will be used to denote any or all of the four exchange-rate variables in the six triples: the current-period, or current/base-period, short-run or long-run equilibrium exchange rate (all denoted by E); and "PPP" or "parity" will represent the corresponding PPP variable or variables (any or all of the three concepts, all denoted by P).

Then the most general form of the PPP theory is, as already stated:

$$E = H(P, ...)$$

with H an arbitrary increasing function with respect to P, with the ellipsis indicating possible other explanatory variables as well as a random error term. The central tenet of all PPP theories is a tendency for the exchange rate (E) to equal the parity (P).[9] Factors, if any, that are recognized as inhibiting this tendency (and space for which in the function is indicated by the ellipsis) may be either short-run or long-run in nature, with the classification in certain cases depending on one's time horizon. As examples, a possible short-run inhibiting influence might be exchange-market speculation (for proposition three); possible long-run factors are productivity (for proposition one) or a persistent unidirectional flow of long-term capital (for proposition three).

What is the strictest form of PPP theory? Obviously it involves H as the identity function, with the ellipsis removed, that is:

$$E = P$$

In this formulation, the exchange rate cannot deviate even temporarily from the PPP. This relationship is the most extreme form of the PPP theory; but it has never been advocated by a proponent of the theory. Yet Paul A. Samuelson (1964) has attacked the PPP literature on the grounds that it posits an unqualified equality between E and P. Considering the equation:

$$\text{"}R \text{ [exchange-rate] index} = \frac{\text{American Export Price Index}}{\text{European Export Price Index}} \cdot (10)\text{"}$$

he comments: "Obviously, a point-of-time equality like (10) is complete nonsense, since $R = P_3/p_1$ is like saying that the $2.80 price per £ must equal the ratio of the price of a California sherry to the price of a European Volkswagon" (1964, pp. 148, 149). More generally, Samuelson (1964, p. 153) concludes:

> Unless very sophisticated indeed, PPP is a misleadingly pretentious doctrine, promising us what is rare in economics, detailed numerical predications. Few doubt that long-run wheat prices are determined by supply and demand equations rather like the one above; but who ever expects from this analysis detailed numerical predictions based upon simple historical calculations?

Fifteen years later, this position was supported by Louka T. Katseli-Papaefstratiou (1979), who ends her study with the observation: "In conclusion, I am afraid there is an important element of truth in

Samuelson's (1964, p. 153) statement that 'unless very sophisticated indeed, PPP is a misleading, pretentious doctrine, promising us what is rare in economics, detailed numerical predictions. . .'" (1979, p. 29).

Samuelson's assertion that PPP theory is generally devoid of an error term is incorrect. Rather, the strictest form of the theory postulated by proponents is:

$$E = P + \epsilon \qquad \text{or} \qquad E = P \cdot e^{\epsilon}$$

where ϵ is a randomly distributed error term (with value ϵ_t in period t, represented by ϵ). The error term does not necessarily have the same value in its additive (first-equation) and multiplicative (second-equation) versions. In the latter equation, e is the exponential; so that taking logarithms to that base, the equation becomes:

$$\log E = \log P + \epsilon$$

True, advocates of strict PPP do not generally state the error term in mathematical symbols; a literary acknowledgment of a random error in the relationship might suffice. Even if a verbal discussion of an error term is absent, it is unfair to project the absurdity of an *exact* theory on PPP theorists. Unless a statement is made to the effect that $E = P$ in any time period, always and everywhere, a random error term should be viewed as implicit in the relationship.[10]

A less-strict PPP theory, still without explanatory variables other than the parity itself, is:

$$E = H(P, \epsilon)$$

Now E is an arbitrary increasing function of P, including a random error term but no other variables. A PPP relationship of this form is sometimes said to be "unbiased."

Returning to the original, general, form of the PPP theory, we have:

$$E = H(P, \epsilon, \ldots)$$

where the ellipsis represents other explanatory variables. In this form, that is, with at least one independent variable in addition to P, the theory is sometimes called "biased." More pointedly, is the relationship still legitimately designated as a PPP theory?

Consider the most general case of such a theory: a multivariable multiequation explanation of the exchange rate, but a model in which the PPP is but one variable with no overriding importance in determining the rate.[11] Obviously, this formulation cannot be considered as falling within the rubric of the PPP theory.

The criterion for a PPP theory in the present study is that PPP be the most important determinant of the exchange rate. The parity need not be the *only* systematic variable explaining the exchange rate; the general H function permitting other systematic influences on the exchange rate applies. However, only H functions in which the parity, *P*, is the *most important* explanatory variable, are considered to be in the PPP-theory domain.[12]

To complete the schemata of PPP theories, the foreign country and currency underlying the parity and exchange-rate measures (*P* and *E*) may be specified in two alternative ways: either as a single country and currency or a group of countries with associated currencies. In the first case, one speaks of the "standard country" for the PPP measure. Often (though not always) in empirical work, the United States plays this role.

In the second case, the concept of the "effective exchange rate" (EER) is applied to the PPP theory. The EER is in the nature of an index number; so it can be used only for the first-concept, relative form of PPP (that is, only for the functions f_2, g_2, h_2). In effect, the standard country's currency (rather, its exchange-rate index with respect to the domestic currency) and price index are replaced by weighted averages of the currencies (rather, their exchange-rate indices with respect to the domestic currency) and price indices of the domestic country's main partners in trade and payments.

When I first recommended, in Officer (1976a), that the EER concept be used to replace the standard country in the PPP approach, it was thought that the suggestion was an original one.[13] I have since discovered that 40 years previously, long before the development of the EER concept, Seymour E. Harris (1936, p. 42) expressed dissatisfaction with the standard-country approach of the PPP theory:

> It must by now be clear that authorities who are intent upon discovering whether a currency is over- or under-valued or upon determining a proper rate of stabilization will be confronted with almost insuperable obstacles. A comparison of price movements between two countries (say the United States and Great Britain) is a popular method of tackling the problem. Yet in theory much more is to be said for a comparison between one country and *all* countries. [italics in original]

These various elements of the PPP theory will be developed further in later chapters. The classification scheme for the PPP approach will itself be a reference point in examining both the theoretical and empirical PPP literature.

NOTES

1. Of course, the exchange rate could be defined alternatively as the price of foreign exchange in terms of domestic currency. In that case, for symmetry, the PPP concepts would be respecified in terms of the ratio of the domestic to the foreign price level or price index. The exchange-rate definition in the text equates the exchange value of a country's

currency with the exchange rate; the alternative definition would measure it as the inverse of the exchange rate.

2. It might be noted that Keynes' *General Theory* had not yet been published at the time that he wrote the passage on equilibrium exchange rates.

3. Robinson's concept of payments imbalance is the gold flow plus non-recurrent capital movements. For practical purposes, she would measure the latter by short-term capital flows. Extending gold movements to incorporate the change in all reserve assets would yield the basic balance, the measure adopted by Nurkse and some other later writers on the equilibrium exchange rate.

4. Balancing items are the "transfer of gold or other liquid reserves" and all short-term capital movements.

5. The term "fundamental disequilibrium" was used but not defined in the recently released Articles of Agreement of the International Monetary Fund.

6. Stern (1973) wrongly asserts that Nurkse and Meade postulate that full employment without inflation is a condition for balance-of-payments equilibrium. What may have confused Stern is Meade's concern with the attainment of both external balance and internal balance, the latter defined as full employment without inflation. However, the criteria for external and internal balance are independent of one another. The projection to Nurkse's view is entirely without justification.

7. An excellent outline and assessment of the various concepts of balance-of-payments equilibrium or disequilibrium is provided by C. P. Kindleberger (1969).

8. To avoid labored expression, the term PPP may denote the PPP *theory*, as in this sentence, rather than parity itself. Which meaning applies will be made clear from the context.

9. Although only the current-period value of the PPP is included explicitly in the function, P may be interpreted more generally as representing a distributed lag of this variable over past periods and the current period.

10. Typically in economic analysis, relationships—whether functional or equilibrium—are presented void of an explicit error term. (This is not true for econometric work, of course.) The question of whether a random error term is implicitly incorporated in the relationship is never raised because an affirmative answer is so obvious! It is strange that of all economic theories, only PPP has been attacked for established practice.

11. Perhaps the earliest suggestion of this view can be ascribed to G. W. Terborgh: "A satisfactory theory of the exchanges must include every important element in the problem. This the purchasing-power-parity doctrine fails to do. As a self-sufficient and independent explanation of exchange phenomena it is scarcely entitled to serious consideration. It must be reduced from the rôle of an independent theory to that of a component element in a comprehensive synthesis, where it has a proper and permanent place" (1926, p. 208).

12. In an earlier study, I used the same criterion for distinguishing the PPP group from the entire set of exchange-rate theories. I wrote there, Officer (1976a, p. 5): "Following Cassel, the criterion for a PPP theory adopted in this review is that the PPP be the most important determinant of the exchange rate." Yet one author, Peter Isard (1978, p. 3), ascribes to me a much broader definition of PPP theories: "In contrast, Officer (1976a) applies the term PPP more broadly to all theories that include a relative-price index among the variables on which the exchange rate is assumed to depend."

Isard would have me classifying *all* H functions that include the variable P as a PPP theory. This interpretation is clearly incorrect, both for my previous work and the present study.

13. For example, Goldstein (1979) gives me credit for this suggested modification of the standard-country procedure.

Part II

EVOLUTION OF PPP THEORY

Chapter III

The Beginnings through the Tudor Period

"The most noteworthy achievement of our Spanish writers, and the most original, was their formulation of the basic principles of the purchasing-power parity theory of exchange, a doctrine not usually associated with the sixteenth century." (Marjorie Grice-Hutchinson, 1952, pp. 52-53)

Over the centuries, the PPP theory has been discovered, fallen into disuse, and rediscovered—with this pattern repeated several times. Gustav Cassel, writing in the 20th century, is the most famous proponent of the theory; but he had a good number of antecedents. In this and the following several chapters, the pre-Cassel literature on the PPP approach is reviewed. Attention will be paid to the historical contexts in which the theory was (or was not) proposed. Each episodic support for the theory was associated with a traumatic economic development—inflation following price stability and/or a floating exchange rate breaking with a fixed-rate tradition.

I. ANCIENT PERIOD

The origins of PPP theory are not to be found in the ancient literature. Paul Einzig, the noted historian on foreign exchange, writes: "Neither Greek nor Roman writers gave any indication of having discovered even the most rudimentary form of purchasing power parity theory" (1970, p. 44). What is the reason for this neglect? To a large extent, no doubt, it reflected a general lack of analytical interest in foreign exchange. A. R. Burns (1927) comments that: "Contemporary pronouncements on monetary administration are almost entirely wanting. The Greek philosophers made passing references to money in their treatises on politics and ethics, to which the Romans added little or nothing" (1927, p. 314). Within that sphere, scant attention was devoted to issues of foreign exchange and none at all to the PPP theory.

There is also a practical reason for the absence of the PPP approach in the Roman writings: the nature of the Roman Empire's foreign trade. The goods imported were luxuries rather than necessities; they were for purchase only by the minority, wealthy segment of the population. What were the source countries and specific commodities involved? Edward Gibbon (1900), writing in 1776, mentions valuable furs from Scythia, amber from Prussia, carpets from Babylonia, and silk, precious stones and aromatics from Arabia and India. These goods were not produced in the Roman Empire and they were all luxuries in ancient times.[1]

One reason why only luxuries were imported was the tremendous difference between the c.i.f. and f.o.b. prices of traded commodities. Einzig declares: "Cost of transport and profit margins amounted to a much higher proportion of the sale price of goods than in modern times" (1970, p. 45). Of course, the high transportation and commission charges were in large part due to the resources required for the transportation of goods across vast expanses of ocean or land, as well as to the risks involved. Gibbon notes that 40 days were required for the ocean voyage from Egypt to Ceylon. The latter country was established as the market to which merchants of the Far East brought their products for trade. While this central market increased the efficiency of exchange, it nevertheless meant that transportation charges, including commissions and profits, were incurred in moving the Eastern goods from the source of production to the market place. Then, after the voyage, additional charges were incurred in moving the goods from Egypt to Rome itself.

Another reason for vast price differences between the Roman Empire and its trading partners (always, of course, with prices expressed in Roman currency both at home and abroad) may have been monopoly elements in foreign trade. Gibbon writes of a fleet of 120 trading vessels that sailed yearly between Egypt and Ceylon. He does not mention individual voyages or smaller fleets in the trade. Of course, the Roman Emperor himself had the power to encourage or discourage foreign trade. Gibbon reports of Nero sending an official to what later became Prussia to purchase great quantities of amber.

High transport and related charges meant that even with unlimited arbitrage there would be a large difference in traded-goods prices between Rome and the Far East. Possible monopoly elements restricting trade—and no doubt a limited number of individuals with the entrepreneurial spirit required for providing trading services over vast distances with all the dangers that travel in ancient times entailed—left some arbitrage opportunities unfilled, further widening price differences. Gibbon writes: "The labour and risk of the voyage was rewarded with almost incredible profit. . . ." (1900, p. 55).

Some indication of the incredible price differences is provided by citations from ancient writers. Concerning Roman purchases of amber, Gibbon refers to Tacitus and Pliny for the observation that "the barbarians were astonished at the price which they received in exchange for so useless a commodity" (1900, p. 54). He cites the *Historia Augusta,* a composite work, as authority for the Roman price of silk, ". . . a pound of which was esteemed not inferior in value to a pound of gold. . . ." (1900, pp. 54–55). Einzig writes that: "According to Pliny (A.D. 23–79), merchants importing Indian goods sold them in Rome at a hundredfold of what they had paid for them" (1970, p. 45).

What of Roman exports? Gibbon writes: "As the natives of Arabia and India were contented with the productions and manufactures of their own country, silver, on the side of the Romans, was the principal, if not the only, instrument of commerce" (1900, p. 55). Einzig restates this observation as follows: ". . . the countries of the East were largely self-sufficient and did not want to buy any goods that Rome would have been in a position to supply" (1970, p. 45). J. B. Bury, an editor of Gibbon's work, is more cautious on this point: "Silver was not the only, though it seems to have been the chief, commodity sent to the east. . . . Yet. . . the spirit of his observation is right" (Gibbon, 1900, p. 55, fn. 111, editor's note). He cites a 19th-century authority, Charles Merivale, who observed that the Far Eastern nations "cared little" for wines and oils, "still less" for goods manufactured from wool and leather, all of which constituted the Empire's potential exports.

The result of this structure of trade was that exchange rates bore no relationship to purchasing power parity. There were four reasons for the inapplicability of the PPP theory. First, Roman imports, as luxuries for the very rich, were demanded for income, not price considerations. The own-price demand elasticity was effectively zero. Second, as these goods were not produced in the Empire and had no close domestic substitutes, relative price could not have been a significant determinant of demand even if the imports had been consumed by a large proportion of the population. Third, arbitrage imperfections left large price differences for these commodities between Rome and Asia. Fourth, Roman exports were largely silver, to finance the Empire's balance-of-payments deficit. With trade in non-monetary commodities so one-sided, there was no empirical foundation for construing the concept of a Roman/Asian price-level ratio, that is, PPP. One can hardly blame Roman writers for letting the PPP theory escape their notice when actual exchange rates were far from PPP and one-sided trade militated against a concept of relative price levels.[2]

An interesting, contrary view is offered by Burns, who sees a relatively high Roman price level—itself caused in part by overvalued Roman coins in terms of PPP—as the reason for the one-sided trade. He writes: "Thus the reason for the produce of the West not finding a ready sale in the East whence came the Roman luxuries was a high price level in Rome which raised the cost price of exports and offered good prices for imports. This high price level was due to the inflation caused by the issues of base coins and the failure of the exchange to represent the purchasing power parity between Roman and foreign coins" (1927, pp. 416–417). This argument is rejected by Einzig.[3]

II. MEDIEVAL PERIOD

The PPP theory was not discovered in the Medieval period, as well as the ancient period. Einzig points out that ". . . the notion of price levels was non-existent in the Middle Ages. What is perhaps even more important, exports and imports were largely inelastic and unresponsive to changes in prices or exchanges" (1970, p. 99). Price inelasticity would be an empirical reason justifying the absence of PPP analysis; but Einzig does not state the reasons for this inelasticity. One can surmise that in the early Middle Ages, the feudal economy, with its self-sufficient nature and associated structured society, might have resulted in purely luxury imports, as in Roman times. Of course, there was also a general contraction of trade, both within Europe (the former Empire) and with the outside world—again inhibiting a PPP (or any) theory of the foreign exchanges.

However, by the later Middle Ages many currency areas, and some countries, had arisen in Europe. Trade among these entities took place both directly and through the intermediary of fairs. What used to be intra-Empire trade was now foreign trade, with distances and uncertainties far less than in ancient Rome's trade with the Far East. Under this favorable situation, did the PPP theory arise?

Einzig writes that "Scholastic writers may conceivably have had an inkling of the purchasing power parity theory in its most rudimentary form. The view that exchanges were determined by the difference between the 'common estimation' of money in two countries may possibly indicate anticipation of the view that purchasing power parities were capable of affecting exchanges. . . ." (1970, p. 99). Laurentius de Rodolphis, a Florentine writing in 1403, is cited by Marjorie Grice-Hutchinson (1952) as the originator of the "common estimation" theory of foreign exchange.

However, as both Grice-Hutchinson and Einzig are aware, neither Laurentius nor his followers went beyond a demand-and-supply theory of foreign exchange.[4] (Of course, this theory was itself a definite contribution to the evolution of exchange-rate analysis.) Grice-Hutchinson notes: "Laurentius mentions, as factors that helped to determine the price of money, . . . the purity, weight, and market-value of its metal content, and the conditions of supply and demand 'according to which gold is worth more at one time than another, or florins are more sought after than ducats or vice-versa'" (1952, pp. 37–38). Einzig observes that Laurentius condemned as usurious exchange transactions taking place at rates other than the current market rate. "This rule suggests by implication that the free play of supply and demand necessarily produced the correct rate" (1970, p. 91).

A theory of exchange-rate determination that stops with "common estimation" or demand and supply is not a PPP theory. Price levels would have to enter the analysis, possibly through demand and supply—an extension that Laurentius and his followers did not make.

There remains a second route through which Medieval authors might have anticipated PPP analysis. Enzig writes: "Scholastic writers noted the effect of the scarce or plentiful money supplies on exchange rates. . . . Outstanding among them was Pegolotti's book, written about 1340, and Uzzano's book, written about a century later. Both of them were aware of the influence of the monetary scarcity (*strettezza*) or ease (*larghezza*) on exchange rates" (1970, p. 94).

Again, a statement of the PPP theory would have to involve going beyond the money-supply influence on exchange rates to that of the price level. A quantity theory of money, even in rudimentary form, would be required, which these and other writers of the time failed to have. Perhaps the Medieval writers can be excused for lacking the quantity theory; for, according to Raymond De Roover (1948), the correlation between the amount of money and the level of prices could as well be negative as positive in the Middle Ages: "Credit contraction, or an acute scarcity of money, as it was called in the technical parlance of the Middle Ages, was often the prelude to a depression and was accompanied by a drastic fall in prices, forced sales, and business failures. . . . An easy money market, however, was by no means an unmistakable sign of prosperity. Often money was plentiful because it failed to circulate, because trade was dull, and because prices were generally depressed" (1948, p. 76).

III. SALAMANCA SCHOOL

The originators of the PPP theory were Spanish scholars of the 16th century, the Salamanca School. As will be shown below, there can be no doubt about this assertion. Yet the Salamancan accomplishment went unnoticed in the English literature until Margorie Grice-Hutchinson (1952) authored a description of Spanish monetary theory in the 1544–1605 period, while providing translated excerpts from the writings of the scholars involved. Later, basing his comments on Grice-Hutchinson's work, Einzig (1970) also attributed the origins of the PPP theory to these 16th and 17th century Spanish writers.[5]

It was a confluence of diverse circumstances that led these scholars to develop the PPP theory. First of all, by the middle of the 16th century the University of Salamanca, in western Spain, was a great center of learning the seventy chairs of which, according to Grice-Hutchinson (1952, p. xi), were "filled by the best scholars of the age." Second, these scholars, as theologians and jurists, were well acquainted with the earlier, scholastic work on foreign exchange. Indeed, Grice-Hutchinson views the Salamancan analysis of foreign exchange as a development of the theories of the Florentine theologians Laurentius and St. Antonio.

Yet, and third, the men of the Salamanca School could not help but be interested in secular issues, among which was international commercial activity, for which Spain had become a leading center. This role of Spain was closely related to its conquests in America and the resulting flow of gold and silver to the home country. Fourth, Medieval analysis of foreign exchange had included the idea that ease (scarcity) of a money gave it a low (high) value against foreign exchange. As mentioned above, the missing link to reach the PPP theory was the quantity theory of money. The empirical impetus for the quantity theory was provided in 16th-century Spain, the first country in Europe to receive large inflows of precious metals from the New World, with resultant conspicuous increases in the money supply and in prices.

It should be noted that the true contribution of New World treasure to the 16th-century "price revolution" is beside the point for our purposes here. No doubt, other factors were involved, including those on the real side. The *perception* of substantial increases in the coined money supply and in prices led to the formulation of the quantity-theory relationship between the two, and earliest in Spain; that is the relevant point.

Fifth, it was also clear empirically that exchange rates had become unfavorable to Spain. If exchange rates themselves were not recorded, nevertheless, according to Grice-Hutchinson, the Salamancan economists observed that the ratio of the amount of money repaid to the amount delivered was much higher for initial delivery of money to Spain from abroad than this two-way transaction beginning in the opposite direction. This relationship required an explanation, and relative supplies of money or relative price levels in Spain and foreign countries were obvious candidates.

Sixth, premiums on exchange transactions incorporating a time element (that is, on bills of exchange) had long been used as a way of escaping the Catholic Church's prohibition of usury. The Salamancans had a theological benefit in developing a theory such as PPP; variations in exchange rates could then be interpreted as non-usurious in nature and so quite consistent with Church doctrine. Grice-Hutchinson writes: "This early version of the purchasing-power parity theory. . . removed the taint of usury that had formerly accompanied even the most genuine exchange transaction. . . ." (1952, p. 58). Indeed, she explains the demise of the PPP theory in the late seventeenth century as reflecting a final full toleration of exchange transactions, irrespective of their nature:

> The last traces of the medieval objection to exchange transactions (though not, of course, the dislike of usury itself) seems to have died away towards the end of the seventeenth century. . . . the old purchasing-power parity theory, which had been framed to show that the premium on a bill of exchange was not necessarily a disguised form of interest on a loan, lost its *raison d'être* and presumably died a natural death after performing a useful function for close on 150 years (1952, p. 77).

In spite of these common circumstances, not all the Salamancan writers on exchange-rate determination put forward the PPP theory. To some extent, this may have been due to the natural development of the PPP approach from antecedent theories in an atmosphere in which the scholars had access to, and commented on, each other's work. Another reason, no doubt, is that some Salamancans preferred to profess alternative theories of foreign exchange even while aware of the PPP approach. These other theories amounted to sophisticated treatments of the demand-and-supply and money-supply theories that developed in the Middle Ages.

Our concern here is with those Spanish writers that proposed the PPP theory itself. The earliest of these, and certainly a forerunner if not the actual founder of the PPP approach, is Azpilcueta de Navarro, writing in 1556. In any event, he is without doubt the founder of the quantity theory of money; for he writes:[6]

> . . .other things being equal, in countries where there is a great scarcity of money, all other saleable goods, and even the hands and labour of men, are given for less

money than where it is abundant. . . And even in Spain, in times when money was scarcer, saleable goods and labour were given for very much less than after the discovery of the Indies, which flooded the country with gold and silver. (Quoted by Grice-Hutchinson, 1978, p. 104.)

The PPP theory is presented in a less direct fashion. Navarro states: "We cannot know whether an exchange transaction be just unless we know the value of both monies; since. . . the money must be changed at its proper value if the transaction is to be a just one." He then presents various reasons why "the value of the two moneys may diverge," among which "because of scarcity and need." Concentrating on this reason, he declares that "money, in so far as it may be sold, bartered, or exchanged by some other form of contract, is merchandise and therefore also becomes dearer when it is in great demand and short supply."[7] He then proceeds to make the connection between the scarcity or abundance of money and the high or low level of prices, via the quantity theory of money in the passage quoted above. The result is the relative PPP theory.

The Salamancan writers are considering coined, not paper, money. When Navarro states that "the value of the two moneys may diverge," his standard of reference must be the mint parity between the monies. The "proper value" of the exchange rate is not the mint parity, but the PPP. It is PPP that explains deviations of exchange rates from mint parities.

Though Navarro thus formulates the PPP theory in an indirect fashion, it is a complete statement of the theory in that the discussions of monetary ease and scarcity and of the quantity theory are general in nature, therefore applicable to both the domestic and foreign country. In 1594, Domingo de Bañez stated the PPP theory quite directly:

In places where money is scarce, goods will be cheaper than in those where the whole mass of money is bigger, and therefore it is lawful to exchange a smaller sum in one country for a larger sum in another. . . . one party may lawfully agree to repay a larger sum to another, corresponding to the amount required to buy the same parcel of goods that the latter might have bought if he had not delivered his money in exchange." (Cited in Grice-Hutchinson, 1952, pp. 57–58.)

Again, sums of money in different currencies can be compared only via some standard, implicitly the mint parity. The exchange value of a country's money can legitimately exceed its mint parity when the money's purchasing power over commodities exceeds that of money abroad. This is a theory of absolute PPP in which currencies exchange with each other in their respective amounts that are required to purchase the same bas-

ket ("parcel") of goods. A similar presentation of PPP theory was made
by Juan de Lugo in 1642:

> . . . the excess of this unequal value which money has in different places . . . may also
> be caused by diversity in its extrinsic value. Thus, in the place to which the money is
> sent there may be a general scarcity of money, or more people may require it, or
> there may be better opportunities for doing business with it and making a profit.
> And, since money will there be more useful for satisfying human needs, more goods
> will be bought than elsewhere with the same sum of money, and therefore money
> will rightly be regarded as more valuable in that place. (Quoted by Grice-
> Hutchinson, 1978, p. 106.)

Once more, a Salamancan scholar is presenting the absolute PPP
theory. The exchange rate between two currencies, expressed as a deviation from their metallic parity ("the excess of this unequal value which
money has in different places"), is determined by the relative purchasing
power ("extrinsic value") of the monies. (In the unquoted part of the
passage, de Lugo points out that another determinant of the exchange
rate is differing "intrinsic value," metallic content, of monies.)

At first consideration, it seems surprising that the PPP theory was
developed not under a freely floating exchange rate, with unconstrained
exchange-rate movements, but rather under a metallic standard, with
the exchange rate confined within specie points. Yet, to repeat, the latter
situation applied. Gold and silver coins (or bills of exchange payable in
coin) were the usual medium of foreign-exchange transactions. An unconstrained floating rate for Spain would have involved paper money
irredeemable in gold or silver.

However, upper and lower parity points were much wider than in
later periods, providing scope for substantial exchange-rate variations.
The Salamancan economists were quite aware of non-PPP influences on
the exchange rate as determinants of the spread between parity points,
citing such matters as differences among coins in metallic weight or
fineness and costs of transporting coin or bullion. As was suggested
above, the depreciation of Spanish currency against foreign exchange in
the absence of (or correcting for) changes in these non-PPP influences
provided an impetus for Salamancan development of the PPP theory.

IV. TUDOR PERIOD

Gerrard de Malynes, writing in England at the end of the Tudor period,
in 1601, presented a PPP theory of foreign exchange not unlike that of
Navarro. The Salamancan had published his treatise 45 years earlier, but

Malynes apparently was unaware of any Spanish predecessors. Two modern authors, Schumpeter (1954) and Kalamotousakis (1978), trace the origins of the PPP theory to Malynes.

Like Navarro, Malynes has all the ingredients of the PPP approach and leaves it to the reader to put them together. He begins with the quantity theory of money:[8]

> ...plentie of money maketh generally things dear, and scarcitie of money maketh likewise generally things good cheape. . . . According to the plentie or scarcitie of the monie then, generally things become dearer or good cheape, whereunto the great store or abundance of monie and bullion, which of late years is come from the west Indies into Christendom hath made euery thing dearer according to the increase of monie. . . .(1601; 1924, p. 387).

This clear exposition of the quantity theory is at variance with the comments of Angell (1926, p. 13) that Malynes "has no clear idea of the quantity theory of money" and that "his lack of any form of the quantity theory led him into numerous errors. . . ." Even Schumpeter is unduly restrained in his acknowledgement of Malynes' accomplishment: ". . . Malynes . . . tried, I think, to convey the genuine quantity-theory idea—though in a quite rudimentary form. . . ." (1954, p. 314).

Malynes then presents the money-supply theory of foreign exchange:

> ...plentie of money beyond the seas maketh the price of the exchange to rise, and scarcitie of money likewise beyond the seas maketh the price to fall: and so on the contrary with vs here in England, plenty of money maketh the price to fall, and scarcity of money maketh the price to rise. . .(1601; 1924, p. 397).

Malynes goes on to state the obvious but rarely expressed pedagogical point that, for this rule, "the head of the exchange resteth with vs. . . ," where " . . . the head of the exchange is taken to bee at such a place or places where the price doth not alter" (1601; 1924, pp. 390–91). In other words, the exchange rate is defined as the number of units of foreign currency per English currency. The inverse definition, he notes, would reverse the direction of price movements in the theorem.

The quantity theory of money and the money-supply theory of foreign exchange together imply the PPP theory. The question arises whether Malynes was at all aware of this connection.

During the Tudor reign in England, exchange controls of various degrees of severity were periodically adopted and then removed.[9] It was part of Malynes' genius as a mercantilist that, though he recommended officially fixed exchange rates supported by exchange control, he was concerned with the proper *level* at which an exchange rate should be fixed. He asserts that ". . . the exchange for all places ought to be kept at a certaintie in price, according to value for value. . ." (1601; 1924, p. 397).

It would be pleasing for the PPP theory if Malynes meant by "value for value" simply PPP. However, what he seems to mean, rather, is the true *mint* parity. Yet the PPP theory may be deemed reached by another route; for Malynes has in mind a theory of price-level changes in response to exchange rates differing from the mint parity. As Schumpeter states: ". . . he [Malynes] nicely explains how, if a country's currency falls below its mint par and coin flows out in consequence, then prices will fall in that country and rise abroad. . ." (1954, p. 345). It is reasonable to project that the level at which Malynes recommended that the exchange rate be fixed was not only the mint parity but also (ultimately if not initially) the purchasing power parity, since specie flows and price-level changes (the price specie-flow mechanism) at home and abroad would make the PPP equal to the mint parity. This interpretation of Malynes' theory is certainly that of Schumpeter:

> When countries are in monetary equilibrium with reference to one another, then . . . gold is distributed between them in such a way that there is no profit in transferring any part of a country's holdings to any other country. We may express this by saying that the purchasing power of gold is internationally at par and also, from the standpoint of the inflation theory of foreign exchange, that this parity and its variations are the (immediately) determining factors in the foreign-exchange market. This Purchasing-Power Parity theory, or some rudimentary form of it, goes far back and can . . . certainly be attributed to Malynes (1954, p. 737).

By the "inflation theory of foreign exchange," Schumpeter means precisely the PPP theory; for he writes: "We may label as Relative Inflation the variations in the value of a country's monetary unit, in relation to the value of other countries' monetary units, and speak accordingly of an Inflation Theory of Foreign Exchange" (1954, p. 736).

Malynes can thus be interpreted as seeing a role for the PPP theory whether the exchange rate is floating or fixed. Under a floating rate, PPP determines the exchange rate via the quantity theory of money and the money-supply theory of foreign exchange. Under a fixed rate, that is, one confined within specie points, the price specie-flow mechanism operates to change countries' price levels until countries' relative price levels (absolute PPP) equal the mint parity.[10]

Malynes does not draw the conclusions himself for either proposition, probably because of his overconcern with defects in the international payments mechanism, to the neglect of completing his basic arguments. For example, Wu (1939) points out that Malynes sometimes seems to assume price inelasticity of demand for England's exports, while

Schumpeter (1954) sees Malynes as observing (unhappily) an unfavorable terms of trade for his home country.

NOTES

1. Gibbon mentions, referring to Pliny: "The latter observed, with some humour, that even fashion had not found out the use of amber" (1900, p. 54).

2. Some of these reasons are indicated by Einzig, who also excuses the Roman writers: "Amidst the then prevailing conditions it would be clearly absurd to entertain any notions that purchasing power parities had any influence on exchange rates" (1970, p. 44).

3. He writes: "The attempt made by Burns to apply the purchasing power parity theory in retrospect to conditions between the 1st and 4th centuries A.D. appears to me quite unconvincing" (1970, p. 45).

4. The most notable of Laurentius' followers was St. Antonio of Florence (1389–1459). According to Grice-Hutchinson, he added only minor elaborations to the work of Laurentius.

5. Yet recognition of the Spanish accomplishment remains sparse in the literature. All else that I could find are one-sentence acknowledgements by Myhrman (1976), Isard (1978), and Officer (1976a). The only subsequent analysis of the Salamancan contribution is provided by Grice-Hutchinson herself (1978) in a study of Spanish economic thought over a much longer time period.

Grice-Hutchinson notes that the School of Salamanca had been discovered earlier in the non-English literature, notably by J. Larraz (Spanish), writing in 1943. She mentions as his predecessors A. E. Sayous (French) in 1928 and Alberto Ullastres Calvo (Spanish) in 1942.

6. Historians of economic thought generally attribute origination of the quantity theory to Jean Bodin, who published his work in 1568. Schumpeter (1954) is apparently unaware of de Navarro, though he refers to later Salamancan writers on the topic.

7. All quotations are from Grice-Hutchinson's translation (1952, pp. 91–94).

8. Quotations are from Malynes' *A Treatise of the Canker of England's Commonwealth* (1601), as excerpted in Tawney and Power (1924).

9. A history of these exchange controls is provided by Einzig (1970, ch. 14).

10. With a spread between upper and lower parity points, there is no tendency for the exchange to settle mid-way, at the mint parity itself. While Malynes did not state this point, the Salamancan writers understood it; for them, PPP is the exchange-rate determinant within the spread.

Chapter IV

Swedish and French
Bullionist Periods

"Assuming that there really was a Christiernin and that he wrote what Eagly has attributed to him, we are genuinely in debt to our host for making a review and assessment of this work available to a much wider audience." (William R. Allen, 1968, p. 32)

After Malynes, two full centuries were to pass until English economists rediscovered the PPP theory early in the 19th century, during the so-called bullionist period. In fact, however, there was not only a bullionist period in England (and contemporaneously in Ireland) but also two prior bullionist periods elsewhere, in Sweden and France. These earlier experiences, too, witnessed a resurgence (albeit temporarily) of the PPP theory. Interestingly enough, the PPP discoveries in the later periods appear to be independent of those made earlier.

I. SWEDISH BULLIONIST PERIOD

At least one economist in Sweden postulated the PPP theory in the mid-18th century. He was Pehr Niclas Christiernin, writing in 1761. Like the Spanish economists of the 16th and 17th centuries, Christiernin's work was unknown to English-speaking economists until the pioneering studies and translations of one person, in this case, Robert V. Eagly (1963; 1968; 1971). Indeed, before Eagly's translation (1971) of Christiernin's treatise occurred, there was room for skepticism as to whether his life and work were fact or fiction. William R. Allen (1968, p. 32) commented:

Professor Eagly has told us of the remarkable intellectual achievements of one P. N. Christiernin, a supposed Swede in the middle of the 18th century. Christiernin is not mentioned in Schumpeter or in other encyclopedias I have consulted. I am aware of only one item in English literature on Christiernin—and that is an article by Eagly!

Perhaps in response to such skepticism, Eagly (1971) produced a photograph of the title page of Christiernin's study, which happens to include the date of publication (1761). In fact, there had been one other English-language reference to the Swedish contribution to PPP analysis in Christiernin's time, although his name is not mentioned. Sven Brisman, a 20th-century Swedish economist, claims: "That theory [PPP] originated and was first developed in Sweden, where it was already fairly well known before the devaluation of Swedish currency in 1777. . .(1933, p. 72). This statement suggests that other Swedes of the period might also have articulated the PPP theory; but we have translations only of Christiernin's publications.[1]

According to Eagly, Christiernin was the only "trained" economist participating in the Swedish monetary discussion of that period, and the one who made by far the most important contribution to economic analysis. Christiernin was "trained" as an economist in that he had read, and obviously mastered, much of the important non-Swedish literature available. Among the many foreign authors cited is Malynes; but Christiernin's formulation of the PPP theory differs from that of Malynes.[2]

Why did the PPP theory arise in Sweden in the 18th century? One reason, of course, was the existence of an unusually competent and well-read economist (Christiernin) interested in issues of money and foreign exchange. A second reason was that Sweden had a floating exchange rate.[3] The country was off a specie standard for over 30 years, from 1745 to 1777. A floating regime, allowing greater fluctuations in the exchange rate than under a metallic standard, can stimulate theorizing on the cause of exchange-rate fluctuations.

At first, the Swedish government attempted to keep the exchange rate stable by means of exchange-market intervention. By 1757, however, the attempt at a managed float had broken down and subsequent efforts to restrain exchange-rate movements were unsuccessful. So by the time Christiernin prepared his treatise, he had several years' observations of a freely floating exchange rate.

Third, Christiernin wrote during a period of unusually high inflation in Sweden and a greatly depreciated external value of the country's currency. The dominant form of money was the paper daler, irredeemable in specie, as has been mentioned. Circulation of these bank notes increased annually from 1755 to 1762, amounting to a total increase of nearly 300% over the seven-year period. During this time, inflation proceeded at a rapid pace and the daler depreciated greatly in the foreign-exchange market against other currencies and, of course, also against bullion. Those that saw a causal connection running from the increased money supply, on the one hand, to inflation and depreciation of domestic currency against foreign exchange and bullion, on the other, may be called "bullionists." This was the terminology of the similar British experience that was to occur half a century later, and Christiernin was a bullionist according to this definition. The entire period of the irredeemable paper daler may be called the Swedish bullionist period, by the same analogy with the British experience.

Fourth, in addition to the analytical opportunity offered by the above macroeconomic circumstances, there was the chance to make a contribution to an ongoing political debate. The party then in power in Parliament, and its supporters on the outside, professed a balance-of-payments explanation of the exchange rate. They blamed an adverse balance of trade for the currency depreciation, asserting further that inflation was caused by the consequent increase in import prices which led to general price inflation. In contrast, the opposition political party saw the expansion in the money supply as the reason for inflation and currency depreciation. In this matter, Christiernin aligned himself with the second group. There was considerable writing of books and pamphlets on both sides. Eagly comments: "The social rewards to authors of economic tracts were sufficient to attract the energetic response of the talented—as well as the untalented" (1968, p. 14).

What of Christiernin's thesis itself? One feature of clear relevance to the PPP approach is that, for the first time in the literature, the concept of the price level—crucial for the PPP theory—is made explicit. Christiernin recognized the role of money as a unit of account. The value of the unit of account is seen to vary in terms of commodities, factors of production (labor is specified), and coined money. Thus Christiernin explicitly states and uses the concept of the price level (the real value of the unit of account) and changes in the price level (variations in this real value). This distinguishes him from all other pre-20th-century proponents of the PPP theory, who, of course, had to understand the price-level concept in order to present the PPP theory, but did not formulate the concept in as explicit terms. As Christiernin (1761; 1971, p. 53) writes:[4]

But the "imaginary" money or unit of account designates no certain metal of a specified weight and fineness. Rather, it is used only as a method of counting in order to name the real gold, silver, and copper monies . . . the pound sterling, *livre*, *sols*, and our Swedish *daler* and *mark* . . . are never coined but are used only as an understood concept in terms of which we count the value of goods, labor, and minted coins.

Christiernin also states: "The value of the daler is not higher than that quantity of goods, effort and metals which correspond to it" (1761; 1971, p. 78). From the context, it is apparent that "not higher than" is to be interpreted as "equal to" or "given by" rather than as expressing an upper-bound relationship.

A similar interpretation of these passages is presented by Eagly: "Christiernin thus spoke of changes in the value content of the monetary unit in the same sense as his modern counterparts speak of changes in the general price level" (1761; 1971, p. 26).

As was the case with earlier expositors of the PPP approach, Christiernin offered a quantity theory of money linking prices (in his case, explicitly the price level) to the money supply (in his case, the paper daler):

When we double the supply of our bank notes through bank loans, the effect must be the same as if the face value of each bank note was doubled . . . higher nominal values of goods in terms of the monetary unit (*daler*) . . . . Thus, when the circulating money is increased and the quantity of goods remains unchanged, more money is required to purchase the same amount of goods and labor. . . . the prices of goods and labor is in a constant proportion to the quantity of circulating money for which they exchange. . . . (1761; 1971, pp. 76, 77, 78).

Christiernin went beyond a simple quantity theory. He noted employment effects associated with changes in the velocity of circulation of money and emphasized downward price rigidity: "It is easier for prices to adjust upward when the money supply increases, but to get prices to fall has always been more difficult" (1761; 1971, p. 90). He warned that reducing the money supply from whatever level would result in unemployment.

What was Christiernin's theory of the exchange rate? His interpreters to date have ascribed something other than the PPP theory to him. True, the money supply is viewed as the ultimate influence on the exchange rate; but the effect is not via the quantity theory (changing the domestic price level). Instead, domestic-price and exchange-rate changes are viewed as *co-determined* by the change in the money supply. The exchange rate itself is affected not directly by changing domestic prices but rather by changes in the demand for domestic goods spilling over into imports. Exchange-rate changes are determined by an income rather than price (PPP) effect.

Such an interpretation is made by Eagly (1963; 1968; 1971), Myhrman (1976), and Humphrey (1978). For example, Eagly (1971) sees Christiernin as declaring: "... the main reason for the rise in the price of foreign exchange in Sweden prior to 1761 was the excessive issue of bank notes ... the price of all goods and services rose ... The general increase in money demand for domestic goods was accompanied by an increased demand for imports, which, in turn, caused a rise in the exchange rate" (1971, p. 32).

Humphrey's interpretation is even clearer:

> Christiernin maintained that the chief cause of currency depreciation was an over-issue of banknotes by the Riksbank and that causation flowed from money to spending to all prices including the prices of commodities and foreign exchange. He saw monetary expansion as stimulating demand. Part of the demand pressure falls on domestic commodity markets raising prices there. The rest spills over into the current account balance of payments in the form of increased demand for imports. (1978, p. 149)

Neither Eagly nor Myhrman nor Humphrey mentions the term "purchasing power parity" in connection with Christiernin's theory of exchange-rate determination. Yet a good case can be made that Christiernin's theory is one of PPP. He writes: "But general high prices that affect all products, labor wages, house rents, real estate prices, and the price of foreign exchange, etc., cannot be caused by other than the increase in the money supply" (1761; 1971, p. 65). It is "general high prices" that affect the price of foreign exchange. True, they also "affect" (rather than "pertain to") commodity and factor prices, but the price of foreign exchange is mentioned last.

Is the stated sequence of price changes implicit recognition of a causal chain (and therefore of the relative PPP theory) or is the sequence merely accidental? The rise in the price of foreign exchange is again mentioned last, following other prices, in Christiernin's account of recent Swedish monetary history. Then he writes: "When, for example, our bank notes come into the hands of foreigners they are valued not in terms of a specified number of *daler* but in terms of the supply of bank notes relative to the availability of goods and coin which are exchanged for bank notes in our country" (1761; 1971, pp. 74–75). This sentence has foreigners valuing Swedish currency in terms of its purchasing power (over commodities and coined money) in Sweden—clearly a PPP argument.

The last quotation from Christiernin is a statement of the absolute PPP theory. He also expresses a corollary of the relative PPP theory, namely, the proposition that changing the exchange rate and all domestic prices in the same proportion (holding foreign prices constant) would have neutral effects: "Even if it were possible to lower the exchange rate to the preinflation level while at the same time all prices and wages fell by the same proportion, there would still be injurious consequences" (1761; 1971, p. 91).

It is interesting that Christiernin rejects the neutrality of proportional changes in the exchange rate and the domestic price level. His main reason is the adverse distributional effect of the price deflation on debtors. He also points out that foreigners holding Swedish bank notes would benefit.

A deficiency of Christiernin's expression of the PPP theory is that the commodity prices considered pertain only to the domestic country (Sweden). In this respect his analysis is inferior to that of Malynes, who incorporated price changes both at home and abroad.

II. FRENCH BULLIONIST PERIOD

Paper currency inconvertible into specie came to France just before the 1789 Revolution. These were the notes of the Caisse d'Escompte, given currency status in August 1788. A second type of inconvertible paper money, the assignats, were first issued at the end of 1789, though assignats were not accorded legal-tender status until 1790, with subsequent issues. In 1796, a third kind of inconvertible currency was issued, the mandats territoriaux. One year later, all paper money in circulation was demonetized.[5]

With the issuance of inconvertible paper money, especially the assignats, a situation ensued similar to that in Sweden more than a century earlier. The increased money supply led to price inflation, and a depreciating exchange value of domestic currency in terms of bullion and foreign currency occurred. A controversy arose over the cause of the falling external value of the domestic currency. Just as in Sweden, some observers took a "bullionist" viewpoint, others ascribed the depreciation to changes in the balance of payments.

The question arises as to whether any of the French "bullionists" of the early 1790s offered a PPP explanation of the depreciation. Seymour E. Harris (1930) notes that several "bullionists"—he does not use the term—asserted that over-issuance of paper money was the cause of the depreciated exchange value of the currency. He mentions Mosneron, Boislandry, Solignac, and an unnamed speaker before the "Society of 1789" as having this view. Incidentally, according to Harris, this group was in a minority in relation to the "anti-bullionists." Returning to the bullionists, only Mosneron's analysis is clearly a PPP approach. The relative PPP theory is obtained by applying the quantity theory of money:

The Government has issued too much money, and its value has fallen in terms of commodities and silver, said Mosneron; and since the foreign exchanges merely enable us to exchange our money for the money of the foreigner, our exchanges are depreciated accordingly. (Harris, 1930, p. 236)

Mosneron's PPP analysis has the same deficiency as that of Christiernin. Only domestic, and not foreign, commodity prices are incorporated in the analysis. Mosneron's treatment, though, was almost certainly independent of the Swedish literature. No modern commentator on the Swedish or French episodes mentions any connection at all between the two debates. Indeed, until now, the two experiences together have not even been discussed by any one observer.

The other "bullionists" mentioned by Harris might also have let the money supply influence the exchange rate via commodity prices and therefore adhered to the PPP approach, but this is not clear from Harris' description as far as other individual bullionists are concerned. He does seem to ascribe a PPP viewpoint to the group, however: "A few attributed it [the depreciation] to changes in the internal value of the paper money" (1930, p. 236). It is interesting that the term "purchasing power parity" is not used by Harris, though it was common in economists' vocabulary at the time of his writing.

Referring to Mosneron's view, Einzig (1970, p. 203) writes: "Here we have the rudiments of the purchasing power parity theory. Mosneron was not the only Frenchman to hold this view . . . " (Einzig, 1970, p. 203). I have not been able to find any other English-language reference to these French writers of the 1790s as harbingers of the PPP theory or indeed as "bullionists."

NOTES

1.   Brisman's comment on the 18th-century Swedish contribution to PPP apparently went unnoticed until it was reported by Officer (1976a). Eagly's pioneering discovery of Christiernin, and hence Christiernin's work itself, was not recognized in the PPP literature until Johan Myhrman (1976) provided a useful summary and analysis. References since then have focused on Myhrman's treatment.

2.   It is not surprising that Christiernin's treatment of PPP should be distinctive, because the work of Malynes that he cites is *The Maintenance of Free Trade*, not the treatise in which Malynes exposited the PPP theory.

3.   The historical material in what follows is based on the work of Eagly.

4.   All quotations from Christiernin (1761) are as translated by Eagly (1971).

5.   Histories of the French currency and exchange-rate experience of 1788–1797 are provided by Harris (1930) and Hawtrey (1950, ch. XIV).

Chapter V

English/Irish Bullionist Period

"The purchasing power parity theory finds full expression in the Bullion Committee's Report." (Paul Einzig, 1970, p. 206)

A third bullionist period—generally named *the* bullionist period in the English-language literature—occurred in England and, for the separate Irish currency, in Ireland from 1797 to 1821. This episode is also called the Bank Restriction Period, because the Bank of England's obligation to pay cash (gold) for its note issue was restricted. England and Ireland had legally been on a bimetallic standard, but the mint ratio between gold and silver overvalued gold compared to the world price ratio between the two metals. Therefore it was economically unsound for private parties to provide silver for coinage, and the countries were effectively on the gold standard.

I. HISTORY OF THE BULLIONIST PERIOD

It was principally gold drainage arising out of war with revolutionary France, the so-called first French War of 1793 to 1802, that led the British government to suspend the pound's convertibility into gold in February 1797. Subsidies to allied nations in the war, heavy military expenditure, gold hoarding at home accompanying invasion fears, and the coincidental occurrence of a poor harvest, all contributed to the decision. The Irish decision to suspend had a different basis. Ireland's situation alone involved no pressures to suspend specie payments. It was British pressure that induced the Irish government to suspend convertibility of Bank of Ireland notes. Andréadès (1966, p. 24) sees the Irish decision as "prompted solely by a mania for uniformity."

45

At first the suspension was short-run in nature. Several times, however, Parliament extended the restriction, and it was not until 1819 that the Resumption Act was passed, with specie payments for notes resumed in 1821. Shortly afterward, the Bank of Ireland Restriction was also terminated. Just as for the earlier Swedish and French bullionist experiences, the history of the period is of interest only in setting the stage for contributions to the PPP literature.[1]

Yet the histories of these three bullionist periods (the British and Irish may be considered together) exhibit strong parallels. All the periods involved, of course, a prior specie standard followed by paper money made inconvertible into specie. On the international side, this meant that a fixed exchange rate (or rather one constrained within a band around an effective mint parity) gave way to a floating rate. All three episodes included wars fought by the domestic country—the Seven Years' War for Sweden, the Revolutionary Wars for France, and the First French War and Napoleonic Wars for England. In each case, further, there was a sharp expansion in the money supply (via issuance of paper currency), unusually high inflation, and a depreciation of the domestic currency in the foreign-exchange market and against bullion. Finally, the return to a specie standard and fixed exchange rate in each episode involved a period of deflation.

II. THE BULLIONIST DEBATE

The similarities among the three periods in economic thought are even more striking. Just as in the Swedish and French episodes, the British case gave rise to heated debate in the legislature, the popular press, and (intermixed with the two) among economists. Again, the British Bank Restriction Period involved a separation of commentators into two groups, bullionists and anti-bullionists. Indeed, it is the British experience that gave rise to this nomenclature.

A variety of issues divided the English (and Irish) bullionists and non-bullionists.[2] This was so in the Swedish, and presumably French, experiences as well. For our purposes, the explanation of the drop in the exchange value of the domestic currency is the relevant issue. (As a parenthetical note, the English bullionist controversy concerned the exchange value of the British pound against Continental currencies or bullion, while the Irish debate centered on the depreciated Irish pound with respect to the British pound.) As twice before, the anti-bullionists explained the depreciated currency in terms of changing components in the balance of payments: in the British case, increased imports of grain due to poor harvests, and British military expenditure abroad and subsidies to allied countries in connection with the war effort. Again, in this third episode, the bullionists blamed expansion of the money supply—specifically, excessive issue of paper currency by the Bank of England—for the currency depreciation.

Now, as in the Swedish and French debates, not all bullionists made the connection between the expanded money supply to the externally depreciated domestic currency via the enhancement of commodity prices. Only those bullionists who saw a causal relationship running from price levels to the external value of a country's currency were using a PPP argument. As with the Swedish and French episodes, these are the writers whose theories and explanations we wish to examine.

Were the English bullionists in general, or advocates of the PPP theory in particular, aware of the previous bullionist debates? The answer must be negative, because in none of their written work do the English bullionists refer to their Swedish or French predecessors.[3] Also, there is no reason to believe that they were aware of the contributions of the Salamancan scholars in the 16th and 17th centuries. While their country's own economic literature extending over the past several centuries was available to the English bullionists, apparently they did not read much of it. Schumpeter (1954, p. 706) asserts that: "The Englishmen who started writing on monetary policy around 1800 knew very little about the English work of the seventeenth and even eighteenth centuries and still less, almost nothing in fact, of the non-English work of these centuries. . . ."

Only one pre-19th-century English author, Gerrard de Malynes, had developed a PPP theory—and his work is not cited by the bullionists. There is also no evidence from the context of their writings that the bullionists built on Malynes' approach.

III. THORNTON

The first English bullionist to present a PPP theory was Henry Thornton, writing in 1802.[4] In fact, over the years, many 20th-century economists have credited Thornton with originating the theory. The first such attribution was made by Silberling (1924, p. 410), who writes: "Nevertheless, Thornton did present (altho not in a context definitely specifying his assumptions) a striking statement of what has come to be called the 'purchasing-power-parity' doctrine relating to conditions of irredeemable paper—a doctrine which ought in justice to be associated with his name."

Angell (1926, p. 49) declares that ". . . Thornton must be credited with developing at least half of the present-day 'purchasing-power-parity' doctrine . . . ." Bresciani-Turroni (1934, p. 433) states that: "Thornton was the first economist who developed the theory known now as the 'purchasing power parity doctrine'." This view is reiterated by Wasserman (1936, p. 73), who refers to ". . .the famous theory of purchasing power parities first discovered in 1802 by Henry Thornton . . ." Thirty-five years later, Wasserman, with co-authors Hultman and Ware, (1971, p. 217) again commented that ". . . the purchasing power parity theory, was probably first stated by Henry Thornton in 1802."

Hayek (1939, p. 48) declares that Thornton's exposition ". . . already contains practically all the doctrine which, one hundred and twenty years later, was 'rediscovered' as the purchasing power parity theory." Wu (1939, p. 26) states that Thornton's ". . . doctrine concerning a depreciated currency . . . is substantially what is now known as the 'purchasing power parity doctrine'." Finally, Humphrey (1979) traces the origin of the PPP theory to Thornton and John Wheatley, whose writing appeared later.

In contrast, I have shown that the PPP theory was originated by 16th-century Spanish writers and was also developed by the English writer Malynes at the turn of the 17th century, the Swedish author Christiernin in the mid-18th century, and at least one Frenchman shortly before the Bank Restriction Period. Of course, many of these predecessors were subject to rediscovery in the second half of the 20th century. The question remains as to the extent of objective originality in Thornton's work on PPP—granted that his analysis is subjectively original in the sense that he was unaware of the contributions of his precursors.

To begin with, although his formulation is less sophisticated than that of Christiernin, Thornton has a clear concept of the price level:

> Gold must be considered as dear, in proportion as goods for which it is exchangeable are cheap; and as cheap, in proportion as goods are dear. Any circumstance, therefore, which serves to make goods generally dear, must serve to make gold generally cheap, and *vice versa;* and any circumstance which serves to make goods dear at any particular time or place, must serve to make gold cheap at that time or place, and *vice versa* (1802; 1939, p. 148).[5]

This price-level concept is also extended to paper money. Also, while the term "price level" is itself not used, in a parliamentary speech nine years later, Thornton (1811) adopts the equivalent expressions "general prices" and "general price of commodities."

Thornton also accepts the quantity theory of money, but the relationship between the money supply (specifically, paper money) and the price level is not one of simple proportionality:

... paper fluctuates in price on the same principles as any other article, its value rising as its quantity sinks, and *vice versâ*, or, in other words, that an augmentation of it has a general tendency to raise, and a diminished issue to lower, the nominal cost of commodities, although ... an exact correspondence between the quantity of paper and the price of commodities can by no means be expected always to subsist (1802; 1939, p. 197).

Like Christiernin before him, Thornton pointed out that expansion of the money supply can have real effects, thus obviating the simple quantity theory. In particular, and as did his predecessor, he emphasized the adverse employment effects of monetary contraction in the face of downward price rigidity.

Turning to Thornton's PPP theory, there is yet another correspondence with Christiernin in ignoring the foreign price level, which is assumed constant (though sometimes only implicitly so). However, Thornton's analysis goes beyond that of all previous PPP theories in recognizing that the increase in domestic prices (which causes a depreciation of the country's currency in the foreign-exchange and bullion markets) need not arise solely from an expansion of the money supply. Any other cause of an increase in the domestic price level also leads to the PPP result of currency depreciation:

... a general rise in the price of commodities, whether proceeding from an extravagant issue of paper, or from any other circumstance, contributes to produce an excess of the market price above the mint price of gold (1802; 1939, p. 198).

The process of the decline in the exchange value of the country's currency begins with the increased domestic price level leading to a reduced demand for the country's commodity exports and an enhanced demand for its commodity imports *at the initial exchange rate*. These changes turn the balance of trade against the domestic country (Great Britain). The resulting excess supply of domestic currency causes the currency to depreciate on the foreign-exchange market. In Thornton's words:

This disparity between the number of individuals wanting to draw, and of those wanting to remit [bills on Great Britain] ... must produce a fall in the price at which the overabundant bills on England sell in the foreign market ... The fall on our exchange will ... in a great degree, prevent the high price of goods in Great Britain from producing that unfavourable balance of trade, which, for the sake of illustrating the subject was supposed to exist (1802; 1939, p. 199).

Unlike the imprecise exposition of Christiernin's argument, Thornton is quite clear that an expanded money supply increases the price of foreign exchange only *through* a higher domestic price level. In his parliamentary speech of May 7, 1811, Thornton again states this chain of causation:

> He would now proceed to prove, that quantity of paper had an influence on the price of Bullion and the Exchanges. There were two steps in this argument, First, he had to shew that quantity of paper influenced its value, or, in other words, the relative value of commodities exchanged for it.
>
> ... he had, in order to establish the second and concluding part of his argument, merely to prove ... that supposing an increase of paper to take place, and to augment the general price of commodities in exchange for that paper, it must influence also the state of the Exchanges, and raise the price of Bullion (1811; 1939, pp. 328, 329).[6]

He goes on to make explicit the assumption of an unchanged foreign price level:

> Supposing, then, the circulating medium (the gold or silver coin, for example) of other countries to remain as before, that is, to bear the same price as before in exchange for commodities, while the value of our currency, in exchange for commodities, has been altered, it follows that our currency must exchange for a new quantity of such foreign coin (1811; 1939, pp. 329-330).

Thornton states the neutrality proposition of the relative PPP theory, namely, that an increase in the domestic price level (holding the foreign price level constant) combined with a compensating decreased exchange value of the domestic currency has no real effect:

> The fall in the selling price abroad of bills payable here, will operate as an advantage to the foreign buyer of our commodities in the computation of the exchangeable value of that circulating medium of his own country with which he discharges the debt in Britain contracted by his purchase. It will thus obviate the dearness of our articles; it will serve as a compensation to the foreigner for the loss which he would otherwise sustain by buying in our market (1802; 1939, p. 199).

A restatement of the neutrality proposition is noteworthy because the constancy of the foreign price level is again made an explicit assumption:

> This general augmentation, however, of the price of our articles, unattended by a similar rise in the price of the commodities of other countries, obstructs ... the exportation of our goods; since it renders them less able to stand the competition to which they are subject in foreign markets, unless a compensation for the rise is afforded to the foreigner in the computation of the exchange between the two countries (1802; 1939, p. 220).

Unlike Christiernin, Thornton accepts the neutrality hypothesis without reservation. The former author had noted the effects of domestic price changes on the real value of existing assets and liabilities.

IV. HORNER

Thornton's book was reviewed by Francis Horner (1802), who provided a useful summary, corrected some ambiguities or errors, and presented Thornton's teachings to a wider readership. It is as an expositor that Horner is remembered.[7] Yet, as regards the PPP theory, Horner makes a distinct contribution. He is the first writer to distinguish between, or at least use the terms, "real" and "nominal" exchange rates:[8]

> But it is not the bullion price of goods that is raised by an increase of paper-money; which only occasions a rise in the *paper* or *currency* price, and occasions that sort of rise in the price of bullion as well as in that of all other commodities.... The proportion, therefore, of the bullion value of our currency to the bullion value of foreign currency, is altered; and, in order to preserve the same apparent rate of exchange, there ought to be a corresponding alteration of the numerical tables in which that rate is expressed. As long as the ancient mode of computation remains still in use, the apparent or computed rate of exchange will be different from the real one ... When the local rise of the price of goods consists in an actual increase of their bullion price, a real fall of the foreign exchange will generally take place .... But when an excessive issue of paper money produces a nominal rise of prices, a nominal fall of the foreign exchange will always take place ... (1802; 1957, pp. 39, 40).[9]

It is important to note that Horner is *not* using the bullion price of domestic currency as conceptually equivalent to the foreign-exchange rate (against countries with a specie standard). Rather, the bullion value of a country's currency is the reciprocal of the (paper) price of bullion in the country, and the latter price measures the general price level.[10] Then absolute PPP, the ratio of the foreign to the domestic price level, is represented by Horner as the ratio of the bullion value of domestic to that of foreign currency. So the nominal exchange rate is determined by, and equal to, absolute PPP, the ratio of the foreign to the domestic price level. The real exchange rate, in contrast, is the exchange rate that would exist in the absence of a mere monetary change (inflation or deflation induced by variations in money supplies). In Horner's example of domestic monetary expansion, there is no change in the real rate but the nominal rate (price of domestic currency in terms of foreign currency) has fallen.

Horner uses the term "apparent" or "computed" exchange rate to denote the actual (market) rate. What is the relationship among the three exchange-rate concepts? Consider Horner's first passage in the above quote. Before the domestic price inflation, the market and real rates were equal. Also, the market rate changes in proportion to the nominal rate. Horner is considering the market exchange rate as the product of two components: (i) the real exchange rate and (ii) the ratio of the nominal exchange rate (absolute PPP) in the current period to its value in the base period (before expansion of the domestic money supply).

It should be noted that modern usage is only partially consistent with Horner's terminology. Today, the market (actual) and nominal exchange rates are synonymous terms. The real exchange rate is obtained by dividing the nominal exchange rate by the PPP, thus correcting the rate for monetary influences. So Horner's concept of the real exchange rate remains. What he called the nominal exchange rate is the PPP in today's usage.

In the second passage of the above quote, Horner states a condition for a real exchange-rate decline, namely, that the *bullion* price of goods increase. Now, the bullion price of goods is the ratio of the paper price of goods (the price level) to the paper price of bullion (representative of the price level). For the bullion price of goods to fall, that is, for a real exchange-rate decrease, the increase in the paper price of bullion must exaggerate the price-level change. Horner does not state the reason for this distortion. An increase in the ratio of the price of tradable to that of nontradable goods accompanying the over-all price rise would be one explanation of this phenomenon.

The last sentence of the quote is a clear and succinct statement of the relative PPP theory. It involves the continuation of Thornton's assumption of an unchanged foreign price level (made explicit by Horner elsewhere). In this statement and the earlier quoted passage, Horner is considering the case of pure price inflation, that is, inflation with no change in relative prices. Presumably, this is the situation brought on by an expansion of the money supply. The pure price inflation would involve a fall in the nominal exchange rate but no change in the real rate.

It is not unreasonable to project that, in Horner's model, a real exchange-rate change would result from (or be associated with) non-uniform price movements, that is, relative-price changes (possibly accompanying general inflation). A fall in the real rate would then be associated with a rise in the tradable/nontradable price ratio. So there is some (though admittedly weak) justification for this interpretation of the first point of the latter quoted passage.

Horner correctly points out that a real exchange-rate change is associated with movements in commodity trade, whereas this is not so for a mere nominal exchange-rate change. Therefore a change in the real rate implies changes in real behavior, not so for a change in the nominal rate unaccompanied by a real-rate change.

The neutrality hypothesis involved in a mere nominal exchange-rate change is also recognized by Horner via a clever analogy:

> ... the operation of an excessive paper-currency, upon prices and upon the course of exchange, must be the same as that of a debasement of the coin, either by waste, or by the recent fraud of government (1802; 1957, p. 40).

It is characteristic that Horner's contribution of the real versus nominal exchange-rate distinction is within the context of a correction of a passage in Thornton's work.

V. WHEATLEY

Another prominent bullionist who played an active role in the development of the PPP theory was John Wheatley. As with his contemporaries, it is his contribution to the PPP literature rather than his position in the bullionist controversy that is our concern.[11] Assessments of Wheatley's role in the development of PPP analysis fall into two categories.

First, some 20th-century writers see Wheatley as the sole or joint originator of the PPP theory. Bresciani-Turroni (1937, p. 107) asserts that: "Thornton and Wheatley ... were the originators of the Purchasing Power Parity Theory." One notes that Thornton published his treatise a year before Wheatley's first work (1803) appeared in print. Whittaker (1940, p. 656) states: "John Wheatley ... suggests the *purchasing power parity* theory of the exchanges, which was developed by Cassel under similar conditions over a century later ..."

Frenkel (1978, p. 170) lists Wheatley and David Ricardo as "originators of the PPP doctrine." Here Wheatley was first chronologically. Ricardo did not publish any economic writing until after Wheatley had written two of his three treatises (1803; 1807; 1819), all of which devote attention to the PPP theory. Humphrey (1978, p. 150) describes "the famous purchasing power parity doctrine" as "First enunciated by Wheatley in 1803." In print a year later (1979, p. 8), considering "the key propositions of the PPP theory," he claims to have "traced their origin to Thornton and Wheatley in the early 1800's."

We have shown that various writers prior to the English bullionist period adopted PPP reasoning; so it is incorrect to ascribe to Wheatley origination of the PPP theory. However, a second group of commentators claim only that Wheatley provided either the earliest complete formulation of the theory or the clearest PPP exposition to his time.

The first writer with this view is Silberling (1924, pp. 415–416), who states: ". . . Wheatley formulated the 'purchasing-power-parity' idea relating to irredeemable paper in remarkably clear and cogent form." Angell (1925, p. 268) writes: "The first complete formulation of the purchasing-power-parity doctrine seems to have been made by an English writer of the early Bullion-Controversy period, Wheatley." A year later, Angell (1926, p. 52) affirmed his statement: ". . . Wheatley turned to the problem of inconvertible currencies, and at once formulated the purchasing-power-parity doctrine in its entirety."

Ellsworth (1938, p. 244) declares that: "The theory of purchasing power parity was first developed in the opening years of the nineteenth century by a group of English writers, its clearest statement being provided by John Wheatley (1803)," and repeats the statement in a later publication (1950). Finally, Einzig (1970, pp. 204–205) states: "It was in John Wheatley's writings—the first of which appeared in 1803—that the purchasing power parity theory first emerged really clearly and articulately."

To assess the clarity and thoroughness of Wheatley's PPP analysis compared to that of his predecessors requires an examination of his theory.

To begin, Wheatley had in mind a firmer concept of the price level than did any other developer of PPP, indeed possibly any economist at all, up to and including his time. It is true that his exposition of the concept is quite similar to that of Thornton: "Money can be of no greater value than the produce for which it will exchange . . ." (1803, p. 15); ". . . an advance in the price of produce, and a reduction in the value of money, are synonymous terms . . ." (1803, p. 17). However, Wheatley goes further and clearly demonstrates understanding of an *index-number* representation of the price level. In this respect he is superior to all his predecessors and contemporaries.

Jacob Viner (1937, p. 380) declares that ". . . the purchasing-power-parity theory . . . differs substantially from any version of the classical theory known to me." He includes the economic analysis during the Bank Restriction Period as within the confines of the classical theory. The English bullionist economists did not have the PPP theory, according to Viner, because they lacked the concept of the price level. The main reason is that index numbers representing price levels were not being computed on a current basis and, in fact, the price index as a statistical measure had, coincidentally, just been invented in England a year after the start of the Bank Restriction Period:

> The notion of an index number was still in its infancy. Evelyn had published his crude index number of English prices for the preceding two centuries in 1798, and Wheatley had commented on it in laudatory terms. But no current index number yet existed for England, and there was but little information as to the prices prevailing in other countries . . .

> Even after 1798, the leading economists until the time of Jevons either revealed no acquaintance with the notion of representing, by means of statistical averages, either a level of price, or changes in such level, or found it unacceptable for various reasons, good and bad. While a number of crude index numbers were constructed during the first half of the nineteenth century, none of the classical economists, with the single exception of Wheatley, would have anything to do with them (Viner, 1937, pp. 126, 312–313).

Viner's argument that the classical economists as a group lacked the concept of a price level because of the absence of index numbers is rejected by Gottfried Haberler (1961, pp. 47–48) as follows: ". . . one can have a clear idea of a phenomenon before it has been measured and one can vaguely refer to something before anyone has given a precise definition." In this study I adopt Haberler's viewpoint and have ascribed a price-level concept (implicitly or explicitly) to all proponents of the PPP theory. Indeed, as Viner correctly indicates, the absence of a price-level concept negates classification of an exchange-rate theory within the PPP domain.

In the case of Wheatley, though, even in Viner's terms the price-level concept is apparent, because Wheatley shows acquaintance with Evelyn's work on index numbers. What was Evelyn's work and how does Wheatley acknowledge it? Viner provides a full reference to Evelyn's (1798) study, but does not provide further details than those given in the above quotation.

Sir George Shuckburgh Evelyn (1798) wrote a 50-page paper only the last paragraph of which, together with one table, is concerned with index numbers. With this obscurity, it is perhaps surprising that notice was taken of his work on the subject. Evelyn's interest is ". . . the prices of provisions and of the necessaries of life, etc. at different periods of our history, and, in consequence, the depreciation of money" (1798, p. 175). He proceeds to construct a price index from 15 absolute price series, 14 of which are commodities, and the other a wage rate. Viner is correct in describing Evelyn's index number as crude. In Evelyn's words, the technique involves taking ". . . a mean rate of the price of each article, at the particular period, and afterwards combining these means, to obtain a general mean for the depreciation of that period; and lastly, by interpolation, reducing the whole into more regular periods, from the Conquest to the present time . . ." (1798, p. 176). The result is a price index running from 26 in the year 1050 to 562 in 1800.[12]

Although he constructed a price index from individual price series pertaining to a variety of products (and to labor), Evelyn does not use the term price level or even price index to describe his resulting series. Rather, the series measures "the depreciation of money." The terminology of the bullionists is consistent with this usage. Both Thornton and Wheatley state an inverse relationship between the price of goods and the value of money.

Wheatley refers to Evelyn's index number in two separate passages in his first book and in fact closes the treatise with a tabulation of the index-number series. In so doing, Wheatley not only demonstrates an understanding of the concept of an index number, but also makes the judgment that changes in the price level (value of money) are better measured by an index number than by individual commodity prices. He writes:

> In the construction of his table, the learned author [Evelyn] has taken the price of many other commodities as well as corn for the direction of his judgment, and has formed a more accurate conclusion on the depression of money, by the mean appreciation of all, than could have been formed by an exclusive attention to the particular value of a single article. The table exhibits, in a comprehensive view, the value of money, in arithmetical proportions, from the conquest to the present times . . . But, important as it is to the historian in the review of past events, it is still more important to us, at the present period, for the direction of our future policy.
>
> If the arithmetical proportions of this table be examined, it will be seen that the value of money depreciated to a greater extent from 1750 to 1800 than from 1550 to 1600, in the reign of Elizabeth . . . . But a reduction in the value of money and an advance in the price of produce are synonimous terms; one effect cannot take place without the other; and if paper depreciate money, it must advance in a similar proportion the prices of the articles of subsistence and luxury (1803, pp. 178–180).

One notes that Evelyn's data show, according to Wheatley, that the 16th-century price revolution involved less inflation than in the most recent half-century (culminating, of course, in the Bank Restriction Period). Wheatley closes his treatise, just before presenting Evelyn's index-number series, with the observation:

> . . . the plan adopted by Sir George Schuckburgh, in taking the medium from the price of various articles, is preferable to the price of any particular produce; and should the ascertainment of the comparative value of money at different periods be necessary for any political measure, this mode will be found least objectionable (1803, pp. 260–261).

Wheatley advocates a strict quantity theory of money, with the price level proportionate to the money supply and no real effects associated with changes in the money stock:

> The greater the quantity [of money] in circulation, the lower will be its standard as a measure of equivalency, the greater will be the quantity given in exchange between produce and produce, and the higher will be the price of all things. But as an advance in the price of produce, and a reduction in the value of money, are synonimous terms, an increase of money has no other effect than to cause its own depression . . . (1803, p. 17).

> It is imagined by some, that an increase of currency gives a stimulus to industry by a partial advance of prices, but it appears to me to have no such effect (1803, pp. 18–19).

> . . . the circulation of a country . . . can never be excessive for the transaction of exchanges, as it may be absorbed to any extent by a proportionate elevation of prices (1807, p. 26).

In the first passage, we see another indication of the sophistication of Wheatley's price-level concept. He is aware of the role of money as a unit of account, and emphasizes it throughout his writings. The standard of value ("measure of equivalency") can change, meaning that the price level has changed. As Wheatley considers the price-level concept from several perspectives, he must be credited with a firmer understanding of it than any of his predecessors (and contemporaries) in the PPP literature, including even Christiernin.

Wheatley presents a complete two-country formulation of the PPP theory in that he does not (implicitly or explicitly) take the foreign price level as constant. Indeed, he often considers the two countries symmetrically rather than distinguishing the one as the domestic, the other as the foreign country. In operating without the assumption of a constant foreign price level, Wheatley goes beyond his immediate predecessors—Christiernin, Mosneron, Thornton, and Horner. In effect, Wheatley reverts to the less restrictive, two-country formulation of the earliest writers on PPP—the Salamancans and Malynes.

The absolute PPP theory is stated by Wheatley in several ways:

> A bill of exchange is an order for the receipt of a given sum of money in a foreign country, and must therefore be estimated according to the value of money in the country, upon which the order is given, and the value of money in the country where it is presented for sale (1807, p. 60).

Of course, the value of money, for Wheatley, is the inverse of the price level. The ratio of the countries' price levels, absolute PPP in our terminology, is called "par of produce."[13] In Wheatley's words:

... the exchange comes to a variation in its rate correspondent with the variation of prices, and causes so much more moneyworth of produce belonging to the dear country to be given for so much less moneyworth of produce belonging to the cheap country as the difference in their prices makes necessary—there being no other reason for the fluctuations of exchange than to maintain the par of produce ... (1819, p. 21).

A numerical example of the absolute PPP theory holding is provided:

... between whatever nations, it will be uniformly found that the variation of their exchange is the variation of their prices ... the exchange between London and Hamburgh is at any given moment five per cent. against London, only because the general prices at Hamburgh are at that time five per cent. lower than the general prices of London ... the exchange is at any given moment five per cent. in favour of London, only because the general prices of Hamburgh are at that time five per cent. higher than the general prices of London ... (1807, p. 63)

It is fair to say that the above passage is the clearest exposition of the PPP theory that was made prior to the 20th century. One notes that the term "general prices" is used, yet another expression of the price level. As has been mentioned, Thornton was to use this phrase four years later.

The version of the PPP theory held by Wheatley is quite strict.[14] It is emphatically stated that "Nothing can alter the state of the exchange that does not alter the state of prices ..." (1819, p. 27). Also, the direction of causation is one-way only, from PPP to the exchange rate: "The variation in the state of the exchange, therefore, is the effect, not the cause, of the variation in the value of money" (1807, p. 88). Further, over time, Wheatley became an extreme bullionist regarding exchange-rate determination, eventually seeing no way at all for components of the balance of payments to influence the exchange rate, not even through prices.[15]

In spite of his extreme PPP belief, it is unfair to declare that Wheatley—or indeed any other proponent of the PPP theory—adopted the unitary H function: $E = P$, in the symbols of Chapter II. Yet, in effect, this position is asserted by Humphrey (1979, p. 7): "Regarding temporary deviations from PPP, he [Wheatley] flatly denied they could occur. In his view, the exchange rate is always at its equilibrium level and thus it is impossible for currencies to be temporarily over- or under-valued on the market for foreign exchange. In particular, according to Humphrey, Wheatley ruled out any effect, even a temporary one, of real disturbances on the exchange rate.[16] Of course, monetary disturbances—changes in the money supply at home or abroad—affect the exchange rate, and do so by altering price levels, that is, via the quantity theory of money.

Wheatley's numerical example showing an exact PPP relationship notwithstanding, he does allow for an error term in the H function. Following an exposition of his arithmetical example, he writes: "I do not mean to contend, that the course of exchange, in every instance of a partial increase of currency, will adjust the difference with so much correctnes, but that it will ever possess sufficient influence to prevent any material alteration in the measure of equivalency."

An outline of Wheatley's adjustment mechanism that leads to the PPP result shows that he recognizes other influences that inhibit an exact relationship. He begins by stating that there cannot be a divergence in prices, whether of individual commodities or price levels, between different regions of the same country. Commodity arbitrage would correct any price differences. Another force is at work to equalize interregional price levels. The area with higher prices would experience a reduction in its money stock, through payment for commodity imports from the area with lower prices. The quantity theory of money, applied locally, then operates to equalize commodity price levels.

The same forces to equalize prices and price levels are at work internationally:

> But immediately that any one nation should collect to itself such a quantity of currency, as to have a tendency to circulate its produce at a higher price than others, foreign produce would be attracted by the advance in its market, and take off the surplus currency . . . (1803, p. 21).

The emphasis internationally is on domestic inflation or deflation via the price specie-flow mechanism rather than on commodity arbitrage:

> . . . it follows . . . that no one nation can possess a greater or less currency than its due proportion, than that proportion which is competent to circulate its produce at par with other countries; that in whatever instance it should be augmented above this proportion, foreign produce would be attracted by the advance in its market, and take off the surplus currency; that in whatever instance it should be reduced below this proportion, foreign bullion would be attracted by the cheapness of its market, and supply the requisite addition; and that no permanent variation can be effected in the value of money to prevent its universal agency as a common measure of equivalency (1807, pp. 47–48).

Again, in this passage, Wheatley acknowledges temporary deviations from the strict PPP relationship, as his adjustment mechanism corrects "permanent" variations from international price-level equalization; by implication, temporary divergences may not be eliminated.

In another statement of price-level equalization, the theorem is held to be approximate, with no restriction to a short-run perspective:

The facility with which the reciprocal communication of nations, is carried on, has a necessary influence on the markets of all, and approximates the price of their produce to a general level (1803, pp. 25–26; 1807, p. 45).

Wheatley states two reasons why individual commodity prices and price levels are not equalized internationally: transport costs and trade restrictions. Then these two factors also inhibit the strict PPP relationship.

Wheatley's international price-equalization theorem is the earliest systematic formulation of the "law of one price," though Hume (1742) certainly had the concept.[17] In terms of price levels, the law asserts that (abstracting from an error term and inhibiting influences):

$$R \cdot L = L^f$$

where, consistent with the symbology in Chapter II, R is the exchange rate (price of domestic currency in terms of foreign currency) and $L(L^f)$ the domestic (foreign) price level. This equation is nothing but the reexpressed strict absolute-PPP relationship. However, no causal relationship among R, L, and L^f is imposed. The law of one price may be brought about by changes in any of the three variables in the equation. In contrast, the PPP theory asserts that the exchange rate is *determined* by the PPP (L^f/L). Causation runs primarily (although not exclusively) from price levels (PPP) to the exchange rate, rather than in the opposite direction.

While the PPP theory implies the law of one price, the reverse is not true. Thus far, in fact, Wheatley's mechanism involves a tendency toward the law of one price, but not the PPP theory. The reason is that deviations from equalization are brought about by variations in prices and price levels at an unchanged exchange rate. Wheatley must have in mind a fixed exchange-rate system, a specie standard, in this part of his analysis. So Wheatley sees the PPP result as holding even for a fixed exchange rate, though here price levels adjust to accommodate the given exchange rate.

Suppose that the country has an inconvertible paper currency, so the exchange rate is free to float (or that the exchange rate is between the gold points, under a fixed rate). Then it is the exchange rate that varies in order to maintain the law of one price in the face of divergent price-level changes in countries (itself a consequence of differing movements in national money supplies). The PPP theory is thus operative. Commodity arbitrage and associated flows of money need not occur, because the exchange rate is so quickly adjusting. National price changes result in compensating exchange-rate changes even without arbitrage, because traders anticipate the induced exchange-rate movement and bring it about immediately in their transactions. Traders' behavior is based on rational expectations:

> The course of exchange, by pointing out the respective value of money in the two countries, between whom the exchange is negociated, . . . gives to the merchants of each a practical standard, by which the minutest difference is distinguished. By means of this standard all nations are enabled to continue their intercourse without the smallest interruption from the fluctuation, which the constant alteration in the relative amount of their currencies is constantly effecting in the value of their money, as the instant that the variation occurs it is announced by the exchange, and a credit given in conformity to the difference (1807, p. 64).

It is true that Wheatley occasionally confuses the cases of a specie standard (fixed exchange rate) and inconvertible paper currency (floating rate) and so does not clearly distinguish the respective methods of adjustment to the law of one price. However, the main thrust of his argument is crystal clear:

> If paper be not convertible into specie at the option of the holder, and a relative excess of currency ensue from its over-issue, the course of exchange will prevent the interruption, that would otherwise be effected in the general level, by maintaining the specie at the same value with the value of money in other countries, and reducing the paper to a discount in proportion to its excess, in proportion as it elevated the paper prices of the country, where it circulated, above the prices of other countries (1807, p. 68).

The assessment that Wheatley provided the first complete formulation of the PPP theory has been verified.

VI. FOSTER

John Leslie Foster was a bullionist writer whose principal concern was the Irish currency and who asserted the PPP theory.[18] He states the following proposition: ". . . if the currency of any country becomes less valuable than formerly, it becomes exchangeable for a less quantity of the currency of any other country, which continues as valuable as formerly" (1804, p. 88).

What can cause money to have less internal value? For coined money, the reason is an altered nature of the coin itself, a reduction in the precious-metal component due to factors such as seigniorage or adulteration.

In the case of paper money, reduced value results from excessive issuance, as the money supply rises faster than real output (called "the commerce and demands" of the country). Foster's quantity theory of money is not strict, unlike that of Wheatley. Following Thornton, Foster allows for real effects of money-supply changes.

VII. BLAKE

Another bullionist writer, William Blake, is noteworthy for his emphasis on real and nominal exchange rates.[19] Indeed, his entire treatise (1810) centers on this distinction. With all exchange rates measured as percentage changes from parity, the computed (that is, market) exchange rate is the sum of the real and nominal exchange rates. This relationship between the three exchange-rate concepts is different from that of Francis Horner, the originator of the nominal/real exchange-rate distinction, and who receives no credit from Blake for his earlier treatment of the issue.[20]

Assessments of Blake's contribution to exchange-rate theory are favorable for his exposition rather than his originality. Haberler (1936, p. 32) writes that the PPP theory "was also extremely well set out by William Blake." Angell (1926, pp. 61–62) declares that Blake's treatise "would have been a remarkable performance had it been published ten years earlier." It is fair to say, though, that Blake's treatment of real and nominal exchange rates is much more elaborate than that of Horner and does exhibit flashes of originality.

For Blake, analysis of the real exchange rate requires assuming that the ratio of the money supply to real output is unchanged in each country.[21] The money supply must also be unchanged in a qualitative sense; for example, coins must be non-adulterated. Then: "The *real* exchange . . . depend[s] upon the proportion between the foreign payments which a country has to make, and the payments it has to receive" (1810, p. 86). In other words, it is the state of the balance of payments that determines the real exchange rate, and this rate is at par when there is balance-of-payments equilibrium.[22]

Now, the real exchange rate is self-correcting in the sense that any deviation from parity would induce changes in commodity trade that restore it. The volume of exports and imports depends on *real* prices at home and abroad (prices net of inflation or deflation and converted to foreign currency using the real exchange rate). A rise (fall) in the real exchange value of the domestic country's currency would make its products less (more) competitive. This price effect would decrease (increase) exports and increase (decrease) imports until real-rate parity is restored. Blake ignores the issue of "elasticity pessimism," implicitly assuming that the volume and value of trade flows move in the same direction. In allowing the correction process to take time, he (perhaps unwittingly) provides scope for larger elasticities. In modern concept, the time horizon goes beyond the initial segment of the "J curve," corresponding to low trade elasticities.

Irrespective of domestic deflation or inflation, and therefore of the level or change in the nominal exchange rate, the real exchange rate ultimately returns to parity: "The *real* exchange rate cannot be permanently favorable or unfavorable, whatever be the state of the currency" (1810, p. 87).

Turning to the nominal exchange rate, Blake has the two concepts requisite for applying a PPP explanation of that rate: the price level and the quantity theory of money. Regarding the price level, he writes: "If the value of currency is diminished, the prices of all commodities must advance . . ." (1810, p. 51). With the real exchange rate assumed to remain at parity, application of the quantity theory of money results in the relative PPP theory: "An augmentation of currency that affects prices cannot take place without a corresponding alteration in the *nominal* exchange" (1810, p. 46). An x-percent rise in domestic prices, the foreign price level remaining the same, results in an x-percent depreciation of the nominal exchange value of the domestic currency.

Blake also asserts the absolute PPP theory: "The *nominal* exchange depends upon the comparative value of currencies" (1810, p. 86). The "comparative value of currencies" is the ratio of the two countries' price levels, that is, absolute PPP.

Real behavior, including the demand for imports and supply of exports, does not depend on the nominal exchange rate. The neutrality theorem of relative PPP applies: ". . . nominal prices and the nominal exchange being alike dependent upon the depreciation of currency, whatever apparent advantage might be derived from the former, would be counterbalanced by a loss on the latter, and vice versa" (1810, p. 51).

Unlike the real exchange rate, there is no corrective mechanism to return the nominal exchange rate to its parity (where currencies are "in their due proportions," presumably as in a base period before monetary expansion or contraction).

As mentioned earlier, the percentage deviation of the computed (market) exchange rate from parity is identically equal to the sum of the percentage deviations of the real and nominal exchange rates from their respective parities. Blake correctly points out, however, that traders need know only the computed exchange rate and nominal prices of commodities in order to make rational decisions. The real/nominal distinction is important, according to Blake, because the nominal—and not the real—exchange rate is under governmental control, through the government's determination of the money supply. (The assumption is that the foreign government behaves passively in this respect.)

Blake points out that changes in the computed rate, even if due solely to nominal-rate changes, do have income-distribution effects as well as altering the exchange-rate cost of capital transfers (government foreign spending is the case considered). In these respects, changes in the nominal exchange rate are non-neutral. So Blake's analysis is similar to that of Christiernin in providing qualifications to the neutrality theorem of relative PPP.

How can one summarize Blake's view of PPP in exchange-rate determination? In the short run, both PPP (as determining the nominal exchange rate) and real factors affecting the balance of payments (for example; unilateral transfers made to foreign countries, poor harvests at home) determine the market (computed) rate. Blake takes Wheatley to task for ignoring changes in the real exchange rate and asserting, in effect, a purely PPP theory of the exchange rate (variations in the computed rate emanating solely from changes in relative values of currencies, that is, changes in the nominal exchange rate).

In the long run, though, Blake is a true believer in the PPP theory. The real exchange rate returns to its parity and the nominal exchange governs the computed rate. Blake does not recognize the possibility of an *altered* parity for the real exchange rate. If real changes in economies could be permanent and the corrective mechanism via real trade flows provided incomplete compensation even in the long run, then changes in the real parity could occur. It is instructive that the examples of real changes provided by Blake are inherently temporary; for example, variations in output due to seasonal factors, and remittances made abroad by government or private citizens.

Even if real changes could be long-lasting and the corrective mechanism were partial, the PPP theory would hold in the long run if the effects of real changes tended to cancel themselves out. With many real effects independent of one another, one could have recourse to the law of large numbers: a random (normally distributed) net effect would result. Such residual net effects conjoined with incomplete adjustment could be incorporated as a random error term in the PPP theory. This justification of his long-run PPP theory is not recognized by Blake.

VIII. RICARDO

Although his first writings on the bullionist controversy—which happened to be his first publications in economics itself—did not appear until a dozen years after the Bank Restriction Period began, David

Ricardo became the most influential of all the bullionists.[23] As always, it is the man's PPP theory in which we are interested and here there is some controversy as to whether Ricardo actually subscribed to the PPP theory. Many commentators do assert Ricardo's exchange-rate theory is one of PPP.[24]

On the other side, Silberling (1924), Angell (1926), and Viner (1937) claim that Ricardo did not have the PPP theory. The two former authors take the view that Ricardo related a depreciated exchange value of the country's currency (fall in the exchange rate) to a rise in the paper-currency price of bullion rather than a rise in the price level (the paper price of commodities). Silberling (1924, p. 425) declares that: "Ricardo did not deduce the exchange deviations *from* domestic price elevation . . .;" and Angell (1926, p. 59) notes that Ricardo's alleged PPP theory ". . . amounts simply to the evident proposition that the exchanges and the specie premium move fairly closely together."

Viner states a fundamental reason why Ricardo's exchange-rate theory cannot be one of PPP: the concept and measurement of index numbers to represent price-level movements were at a primitive stage, as discussed above in the section on Wheatley. Also, according to Viner, Ricardo rejected the very idea of a price level or index. "To Ricardo, moreover, it seemed an absurd notion that the trend of prices in general, or of the general purchasing power of money, could be measured . . . . He refused to acknowledge that there was any satisfactory way of comparing the value of money, or of bullion, in different countries" (1937, pp. 126–127, 313). Schumpeter (1954, p. 701) also notes Ricardo's "refusal to recognize the price level as a meaningful, or measurable, concept."

It is true that Ricardo writes: "It has indeed been said that we might judge of its [money's] value by its relation, not to one, but to the mass of commodities . . . . when we consider that commodities are continually varying in value, as compared with each other; and that when such variation takes place, it is impossible to ascertain which commodity has increased which diminished in value, it must be allowed that such a test would be of no use whatever. . . . Commodities generally, then, can never become a standard to regulate the quantity and value of money . . ." (1816; 1951, pp. 59, 61)[25]

However, in other writings, Ricardo shows both understanding and acceptance of the price-level concept. He sees the value of money and the price level as inverse equivalents: ". . . the value of the whole currency would be diminished, or, in other words, the prices of commodities would rise . . ." (1811a; 1951, p. 210). He also states: "The currency must, I apprehend, be considered as a whole and as such must be compared with the whole of the commodities which it circulates. If then it be in a greater proportion to commodities after than before the scarce harvest, whilst no such alteration has taken place in the proportions between money and commodities abroad, it appears to me that no expression can more correctly describe such a state of things than a 'relative redundancy of currency'" (1811c; 1952, p. 36).

A balanced view is that Ricardo accepted the concept of the price level, but was skeptical of index-number representations of it. Even Viner acknowledges Ricardo's use of the price-level concept in his correspondence. A complementary assessment is provided by Sayers (1953), who asserts that it was a matter of interest (and not fundamental principle) that led Ricardo to concentrate on the reduced value of British money in terms of gold rather than commodities: "... like everyone else Ricardo was ultimately interested in the commodity value of money..." (1953, p. 31).

There is no dispute concerning Ricardo's adherence to the quantity theory of money. He affirms belief in this theory throughout his writings. The only question is the extent to which Ricardo qualified the strict quantity theory. In some passages, Ricardo states the theory in extreme form, allowing for no real effects of a money-supply change. For example: "The currency has been augmented 2pc^t. Consequently, the price of all commodities, more or less, both inland and foreign, would rise 2 pc^t'" (1811b; 1952, p. 30). Elsewhere, the theory is presented in mild form, as a long-run result and/or allowing for non-proportionality between money supply and prices. For example: "Reduction or Increase of the Quantity of Money always ultimately raises or lowers the Price of Commodities..." (1819a; 1952, p. 445).[26]

Wheatley and Ricardo are often linked together as "extreme bullionists." Are their views on PPP also similar? Wheatley had asserted the law of one price. Ricardo follows him in applying the price specie-flow mechanism to obtain international price equalization under a fixed exchange rate (specie standard). If the countries' money supplies increased proportionately: "The prices of commodities would every where rise, on account of the increase of currency, but there would be no exportation of money from either. But if these proportions [of money supplies] be destroyed by England alone doubling her currency... part of our excess would be exported till the proportions... were again established" (1810–1811; 1951, pp. 56–57).

On the basis of passages such as the above, Keleher (1978) declares that Ricardo adopted the law of one price for the convertible-currency case, with the quantity theory of money inapplicable (replaced by the price specie-flow mechanism). Ricardo, however, in a contradictory passage, denies the law of one price: ". . . the value of money is never the same in any two countries, depending as it does on relative taxation, on manufacturing skill, on the advantages of climate, natural productions, and many other causes" (1817–1821; 1951, p. 143). Viner (1937) and Wu (1939) declare that Ricardo applied the law of one price not to general price levels but only to tradable commodities. If their interpretation is correct, then Ricardo's analysis of the fixed-rate case is hardly in the PPP tradition. Both proponents and opponents of PPP would acknowledge the law of one price for tradable goods, allowing only for market imperfections.

In the case of a floating exchange rate (inconvertible paper currency), though, there can be no doubt that Ricardo holds the PPP theory to be true; for he applies that theory consistently. In commenting on Horner's review of Thornton's book, Ricardo states the relative PPP theory (relying on the quantity theory of money) and shows himself aware of the real-versus-nominal-rate distinction: "When the circulation consists wholly of paper, any increase in its quantity will raise the *money* price of bullion without lowering its *value,* in the same manner, and in the same proportion, as it will raise the prices of other commodities, and for the same reason will lower the foreign exchanges; but this will only be a *nominal,* not *real* fall . . ." (1810–1811; 1951, p. 64).

Ricardo states the neutrality theorem of relative PPP: The effect of an increased money supply ". . . on prices will then be only local and nominal, as a compensation by means of the exchange will be made to foreign purchasers" (1810–1811; 1951, pp. 91–92). The causal sequence runs from the money supply to the exchange rate via prices. A 2 percent expansion of the money supply increases the price level by 2 percent. The resulting loss of competitiveness by domestic industry, fostering imports and discouraging exports, ". . . would be speedily counteracted by the demand for bills which would raise the price of them, or in other words lower the foreign exchange, 2 pc^t" (1811b; 1952, p. 30).

The exchange rate quickly adjusts to the PPP: ". . . if . . . there should be a slight alteration in the value of the currencies of any two countries it will speedily be communicated to the exchange . . ." (1811c; 1952, p. 39). The rate has no self-corrective process (this being the nominal exchange in the Horner-Blake real-nominal model).

Ricardo's relative-PPP theory is not the "unitary H function" of Chapter II; allowance is made for factors other than relative price levels: "The exchange in my opinion is, even in these turbulent times, rarely operated upon but by two causes: one, and that by far the most common is an alteration, or an apprehended alteration, in the relative prices of commodities in the two countries between which the exchange is estimated . . ." (1812; 1952, p. 79). The money supply is, "in most cases," the cause of the commodity-price movements, indicating that Ricardo's PPP theory is general and not merely a conduit for a money-supply theory of the exchange rate.

Actual or anticipated changes in the severity of exchange control ("difficulty and expense . . . attending the transmission of money") are mentioned as the second cause of exchange-rate fluctuations. In effect, Ricardo is proposing the change in the severity of exchange control (at home or abroad) as an inhibiting influence on the strict PPP relationship, that is, as a second variable (after the PPP itself) in the H function. The example given by Ricardo is the restrictions imposed by the Continent on the export of money to England. The correct directional effect is presented—a depreciation of the British pound beyond that accounted for by relative PPP—and Ricardo expresses the belief that the quantitative impact of Continental exchange control is large indeed, an exchange-rate change of 10 to 15 percent against the pound.

It is true that Ricardo can contradict this analysis by asserting a strict PPP theory: "The supply of bills and the demand for them must depend on the previous purchases and sales of goods in the two countries, and these are entirely influenced by relative prices. But relative prices are determined by relative value or quantity of currencies" (1819b; 1952, p. 87). In this passage, the exchange rate—the market, not just the nominal rate—is determined solely by monetary forces. More often, however, scope is given to real influences on the exchange rate. In response to a question as to whether exchange-rate depreciation might be due in part to causes other than money-supply variations, Ricardo answers "very frequently" (1819a; 1952, p. 448). He points out, though, that a reduction in the domestic money supply can always correct a currency depreciation irrespective of cause, carefully adding that such a policy may not be advisable.

Finally, Ricardo sets a quantitative limit on the effect of England's balance-of-trade deficit (implicitly viewed as due to real factors) on the exchange rate: "That limit is probably four or five percent" (1810–1811; 1951, p. 83). This bound is contrasted with an actual depreciation of 15 to 20 percent. In the long run, Ricardo says, there is balance-of-trade equilibrium; so a persistent exchange depreciation, the case in hand, must be entirely due to monetary influences.

Ricardo made many original contributions to economics, but his treatment of PPP went little beyond that already reached by his contemporaries. Recognition of the inhibiting influence of exchange control was the most important novel element in Ricardo's PPP theory. There is no doubt, however, that Ricardo was a firm believer in PPP. In view of

Ricardo's fame, he was perhaps the most conspicuous—if not the most original—proponent of the PPP theory prior to the 20th century. It is not surprising that Gustav Cassel (1922), who resurrected the PPP theory after World War I, credits Ricardo with the first "scientific" theory of the foreign-exchange market and recognizes his anticipation of Cassel's PPP theory. We now realize that Cassel was unfair not only to other English bullionists, who had prior claim on the theory, but also to earlier writers in England (Malynes), Sweden (Christiernin), and Spain (the Salamancans).

IX. PARLIAMENTARY BULLIONIST COMMITTEES

During the Bank Restriction Period, the British Parliament (House of Commons) established two committees that played an important role in the bullionist controversy and are also focal points for the PPP literature. Each committee was established by the House of Commons upon a resolution by a bullionist and PPP proponent, who thereupon became chairman of the committee. The first committee was concerned with the Irish bullionist controversy, the second with the English controversy.

In March 1804, John Leslie Foster successfully moved the appointment of a committee to investigate the causes of the depreciated Irish currency against the British pound and the state of the currency in Ireland. Six years later, in February 1810, upon a resolution by Francis Horner, the House appointed a committee to investigate the cause of the high price of gold, considering the state of the currency and the exchange between Britain and foreign countries.

The committees acted quickly to fulfill their mandates, the first presenting its report in June 1804, the second in August 1810. In addition to Foster, Henry Thornton was a member of the 1804 committee; and both, along with Horner, were members of the 1810 committee. Thus, illustrious names in the PPP literature were well represented on both committees.

Furthermore, a report strongly on the bullionist side of the respective controversies was prepared by each committee. Indeed, the 1810 Committee is commonly known in the literature as "the Bullion Committee." Not surprisingly, officials of the Bank of Ireland and Bank of England, appearing before the respective committees, took anti-bullionist positions, in particular blaming the depreciated exchange on the state of the balance of payments rather than on expansion of the inconvertible money supply. Finally, in neither case was the committee's report favorably received by Parliament. The 1804 report was never even discussed in the House, while Horner's resolutions emanating from the

1810 report were all voted down by substantial margins.[27] Some of these parallel experiences were to be expected, because six individuals, including Foster and Thornton, were members of both committees.

What influence did the PPP proponents have on the reports of the committees of which they were members? John Leslie Foster, as originator and chairman, must have played a strong role on the 1804 committee. Also, both Hayek (1939) and Fetter (1965) see Henry Thornton as an influential member of the committee. Concerning the 1810 committee, Hayek quotes a letter written by Francis Horner ascribing authorship of the committee report to Henry Thornton, William Huskisson (a bullionist, though not a contributor to the PPP literature), and himself. This authorship is also asserted by Silberling (1924), Angell (1926), and Fetter (1965), although the latter observer declares that the report was written only "in large part" (rather than exclusively) by the threesome.

Then one would expect the PPP theory to be embodied in the reports. Fetter (1955, p. 46) refers to the 1804 committee's "tacit assumption that the exchange situation was the result of relatively higher prices in Ireland than in England." However, the only statement that could be in the PPP tradition concerns:

> ... the over-abundant issue which has caused the depreciation of Paper in general, enhancing thereby the price of the necessaries of life, and of all manufactures, ... and above all, keeping up high and unexampled Rates of Exchange against the Kingdom, unwarranted in their height and continuance by any other great or adequate cause than that depreciation which such an extravagant issue had assisted (Report from the Committee, 1804; 1955, pp. 73–74).

The statement is ambiguous in the sense that it does not clearly specify whether the expanded money supply works through a higher price level to depreciate the country's currency on the foreign-exchange market (a true PPP argument) or whether the price and exchange-rate effects have no such link (an unrelated quantity theory of money and money-supply theory of the exchange rate). In contrast, the Bullion Report (the report of the 1810 Committee) presents a precise statement of the relative PPP theory:

> ... in the event of the prices of commodities being raised in one country by an augmentation of its circulating medium, while no similar augmentation in the circulating medium of a neighbouring country has led to a similar rise of prices, the currencies of those two countries will no longer continue to bear the same relative value to each other as before. The intrinsic value of a given portion of the one currency being lessened, while that of the other remains unaltered, the Exchange will be computed to the disadvantage of the former (Report from the Select Committee, 1810; 1925, p. 17).

In the English bullionist period, the PPP theory reached a peak that it was not to achieve again for a full century.

NOTES

1. There exist many histories of the English bullionist period. Among them are Cannon (1925), Hawtrey (1950, ch. XV), and Andréadès (1966). Useful accounts of the episode are also made by Silberling (1924), Viner (1937), Fetter (1965), and Einzig (1970), among others.
   Much less literature exists on the parallel Irish experience. Perhaps the only comprehensive work is Fetter (1955).

2. The bullionist debate in England has been described in a number of incisive studies. Classic treatises that deal in whole or in part with this issue are Hollander (1911), Silberling (1924), Angell (1926), Viner (1937), Wu (1939), Mints (1945), and Fetter (1965). A good summary of the bullionist position is offered by Humphrey (1980).

3. Eagly (1968, p. 24) writes: "No evidence exists which would suggest in any way that Christiernin's *Lectures* were known in England at the turn of the nineteenth century—or, for that matter, at any other time." It should be noted, though, that the writers during the Bank Restriction Period were well aware of the French (though apparently not the Swedish) bullionist *experience,* if not the associated economic debate.

4. Expositions and assessments of Thornton's views in the bullionist debate are provided by Hollander (1911), Silberling (1924), Angell (1926), Hayek (1939), Wu (1939), Mints (1945), Eagly (1968), O'Brien (1975), and Humphrey (1979). Eagly's study is unique in comparing Thornton's economic analysis and policy prescriptions with those made by Christiernin some 40 years earlier.

5. All quotations from Thornton's (1802) work are in the reprint edited by Hayek (1939).

6. Again, quotations from Thornton's parliamentary speech (1811) are from the Hayek (1939) reprint.

7. Hollander (1911, pp. 453–454) writes: "Much of the obscurity and all of the prolixity that clouded Thornton's work were eliminated in the version in which it attained its largest influence—Francis Horner's expository review in the first number (November, 1802) of the Edinburgh Review." Silberling (1924, p. 411) notes that Horner "composed a concise summary and appreciative review" and "carried the analysis forward at a number of points." Schumpeter (1954, p. 707) declares: "My impression is that Horner may be, to some extent, considered a pupil of Thornton." Fetter (1957), in his essay on Horner's professional life and contributions, concludes: "It was not primarily a systematic body of theory that Horner presented, but an orderly exposition of a problem, that gave to the reader the feeling that economic problems were fit topics for the educated man to discuss in the light of reasoned analysis" (1957, p. 19).

8. According to Angell (1926, p. 50), Horner provides "the first clear example of that distinction between 'real' and 'nominal' exchange rates which Blake was later to make so much of."

9. Quotations from Horner (1802) are taken from the collection of his writings edited by Fetter (1957).

10. Humphrey (1978, p. 151) comments, "Due to the unavailability of realiable general prices indexes, the classical economists also used the paper money price of bullion as an empirical proxy for the commodity price level."

11. Wheatley's bullionist views are outlined and discussed by Hollander (1911), Silberling (1924), Angell (1926), Viner (1937), and Wu (1939).

12. Viner is incorrect in describing the index as constructed only for the previous two centuries.

13. Quite correctly, Paul Einzig (1970, p. 205) notes that Wheatley "was the first to find . . . a name for ratio between the price levels, calling it the 'par of produce'."

14. Wheatley's theory of PPP is discussed by Wu (1939), Einzig (1970), and Humphrey (1979).

15. Einzig (1970) traces, through Wheatley's three treatises, his ever more negative attitude toward the balance-of-payments theory.

16. In contrast, Louka T. Katseli-Papaefstratiou (1979, p. 9) declares that, for Wheatley, "the effects of real disturbances, such as food shortages, changes in emigrant remittances, or military expenditures could only be temporary. . . ."

17. One can agree with Angell (1926, p. 52), who writes that "Wheatley was the first writer to develop so explicit a doctrine of price equalization, and for many decades was the only one." Yet, though his formulation was not as precise, Hume (1742) asserted price-level equalization, both domestically and internationally: "money . . . has brought itself nearly to a level. . . the difference between one Kingdom and another is not greater in this respect than it is often between different provinces of the same kingdom. . . . whenever I speak of the level of money, I mean always its proportional level to the commodities, labour, industry, and skill, which is in the several states . . ." (1742; 1963, p. 322). Transport costs are cited as the reason for incomplete price equalization. In fact, Wheatley recognized Hume as a predecessor with respect to both the quantity theory of money and the price-level equalization theorem.

18. Foster's views on the Irish bullionist controversy are discussed by Wu (1939).

19. Discussions of Blake's real versus nominal exchanges-rate dichotomy are provided by Wu (1939), O'Brien (1975), and Humphrey (1980).

20. It is true that Horner's article on PPP was anonymously written; but Blake does refer to it in connection with the quantity theory of money.

21. In modern terminology, one could, alternatively, correct for monetary effects.

22. One notes, with approval, that this parity concept is not necessarily the *mint* parity, although the par value of the real exchange rate, under a specie standard (fixed exchange rate), would fall between the gold points.

23. For outlines and assessments of Ricardo's bullionist views, see Silberling (1924), Angell (1926), Viner (1937), Wu (1939), Sayers (1953), Fetter (1965), and O'Brien (1975).

24. These commentators include Cassel (1922), Keynes (1923), Angell (1926), Bunting (1939), Wu (1939), Wijnholds (1947), Schumpeter (1954), Haberler (1961), Meinich (1968), Einzig (1970), Frenkel (1978), Humphrey (1978), Keleher (1978), and Katseli-Papaefstratiou (1979).

25. In quotations from Ricardo, the first year refers to the original work, the second to the publication to which the citation relies.

26. Among the 20th-century commentators on Ricardo's work, only Angell (1926) sees Ricardo as having a loose quantity theory. Fetter (1965), Humphrey (1978), and Keleher (1978) ascribe a strict version of the theory to Ricardo, as do Sayers (1953) and Schumpeter (1954). The two latter observers take note of Ricardo's qualifications to the extreme quantity theory, but view them either as unimportant or as not applied by Ricardo to the Bank Restriction Period.

27. Discussions of the history of the 1804 report and its bullionist views and recommendations are provided by Hollander (1911), Andréadès (1966), Wu (1939), and Fetter (1955). Analogous treatments of the 1810 report are found in Silberling (1924), Cannan (1925), Angell (1926), Hayek (1939), Fetter (1965), Andéadès (1966), and Einzig (1970).

Chapter VI

Modern Demise of the Theory

"The purchasing power parity theory was virtually forgotten by 1914."
(Paul Einzig, 1970, p. 210)

Following the tumultuous PPP literature of the English bullionist period, nearly a full century was to pass before PPP analysis was again to be in the forefront of theories of exchange-rate determination. In the meantime, the PPP approach was confined to the work of three pre-eminent English economists—John Stuart Mill, Viscount Goschen, and Alfred Marshall—and, at the end of the period, a leading Austrian economist, Ludwig von Mises.

I. MILL

The PPP theory is considered by Mill both in the context of a fixed exchange rate (a metallic standard) and a floating rate (a paper standard). He clearly has the concept of the price level; as his interest, under a fixed rate, is "the value of money, estimated in commodities" (1848; 1929, p. 609).[1] Is this value the same across countries, that is, does the law of one price prevail?

As did Wheatley and Ricardo before him, Mill applies the price specie-flow mechanism to obtain the law of one price. "The efflux [of coined money from a country increasing its money supply] would continue until the currencies of all countries had come to a level." This appears to be the law of one price; but Mill goes on to add: "... I do not mean, until money became of the same value everywhere, but until the differences were only those which existed before, and which corresponded to permanent differences in the cost of obtaining it" (1848; 1929, p. 631).

It is not fair to assert that Mill rejected the law of one price, as Angell (1926, pp. 88–89) seems to conclude: "It therefore seems probable that Mill... regarded the value of gold... as being permanently different [between countries] in terms of *commodities*; the differences being determined by relative differences in the comparative (labor) costs of obtaining the precious metals themselves." Rather, Mill's position follows that of Wheatley in accepting the mechanism that produces the law of one price but also recognizing inhibiting forces that prevent full price-level equalization. For Wheatley, these forces were *commodity* transport costs and trade restrictions. What are they for Mill?

> The countries whose exportable productions are most in demand abroad, and contain greatest value in smallest bulk, which are nearest to the mines, and which have least demand for foreign productions, are those in which money will be of lowest value, or, in other words, in which prices will habitually range the highest (1848; 1929, p. 609).

The value-to-bulk ratio for commodities and the proximity to mines refer to transport costs. Unlike Wheatley, though, Mill mentions transport costs of both commodities and bullion: "The expense of transport is partly that of carrying the goods to the bullion countries, and partly that of bringing back the bullion..." (1848; 1929, p. 609).

Because Mill's concern is with the process by which "gold and silver diffuse themselves from the mining countries into all other parts of the commercial world," (1848; 1929, p. 608) he limits himself, in this context, to trade between countries that produce precious metals and non-producing countries.

It is not clear why the domestic and foreign demand for imports should be a factor working against the law of one price. Mill is involved in an inconsistency here, for his analysis of international trade involves price equalization of traded goods.[2] Indeed, Keleher (1978) views the latter result as confirming Mill's adherence to the law of one price. However, as mentioned in the discussion of Ricardo's work in the previous chapter, a price equalization theorem restricted to traded commodities cannot differentiate between supporters and opponents of PPP, as both groups can legitimately subscribe to it.

We have seen that, traditionally in the literature, an important step in a PPP analysis of a floating exchange rate is provided by the quantity theory of money. Mill, too, propounds the quantity theory, but is ambivalent as to whether the relationship involves strict proportionality between the money supply and price level or whether the link is weaker, allowing for real effects of monetary disturbances. Wu (1939, p. 144) writes: "The form that he [Mill] gave to the quantity theory was, in general, a very rigid one, because he emphasized that *general* prices varied in *proportion* to the changes in the quantity of money." Indeed, Mill declares: ". . . the value of money, other things being the same, varies inversely as its quantity; every increase of quantity lowering the value, and every diminution raising it, in a ratio exactly equivalent" (1848; 1929, p. 493). For a paper currency inconvertible into specie, the statement is made without qualification: ". . . with an inconvertible currency . . . The issuers may add to it indefinitely, lowering its value and raising prices in proportion; they may, in other words, depreciate the currency without limit" (1848; 1929, p. 544). For future reference, one notes that, for Mill, depreciation of the currency, and increase in the price level, are synonymous expressions.

In his exposition of the quantity theory, Mill exhibits a clear concept of the price level as an average of individual commodity prices. "If the whole money in circulation were doubled, prices would be doubled. If it were only increased one-fourth, prices would rise one-fourth. . . . Even if some prices were raised more, and others less, the average rise would be one-fourth. . . . *General* prices, therefore, would in any case be a fourth higher" (1848; 1929, pp. 492–93). (Italics are in the original.)

Mill does point out qualifications to the strict quantity theory. Most important, only money that is spent affects prices; ". . . money hoarded does not act on prices" (1848; 1929, p. 496). Schumpeter (1954, p. 705) sees Mill's quantity theory as sophisticated indeed: "J. S. Mill's conceptual arrangement achieved the same end that others achieved by making velocity an economic variable. For to make the relevant quantity of money a variable in the purchasing-power problem by defining it as the quantity that is actually being spent evidently comes to the same theory as to start from a given quantity of money (however defined) and to make average velocity an economic, and in particular a cyclical, variable."

With paper money inconvertible into specie, prices rise as the issuance of currency increases. Following in the Horner-Blake tradition, Mill has the nominal exchange rate falling in proportion to the rise in the price level (the latter called the currency depreciation). "When, therefore, the *real* exchange is at par, there will be a *nominal* exchange against the country, of as much per cent as the amount of the depreciation" (1848; 1929, p. 635). The neutrality theorem of relative PPP applies: ". . . a depreciation of the currency does not affect the foreign trade of the country; this is carried on precisely as if the currency maintained its value" (1848; 1929, p. 635). Mill means here the *internal* value of the currency, that is, its purchasing power against domestic commodities.

A later observer, John H. Williams (1922, p. 493), wrote: "Indeed, in J.

S. Mill's chapter on "The Influence of the Currency on the Exchanges," written over seventy years ago, there is a striking passage which contains practically the whole of Cassel's doctrine of purchasing power parity." One cannot agree with this statement. Mill's exposition of the PPP theory is less advanced than even some earlier literature. Mill presents only the relative PPP theory, saying nothing about absolute PPP. He considers a change in the price level in only the domestic, and not also the foreign country. The real-versus-nominal exchange-rate distinction is implicitly assumed rather than developed or extended. Finally, no explicit attention is paid to inhibiting influences making the H function non-unitary or amending the neutrality result of relative PPP. In all these respects, previous writers on PPP accomplished what Mill did not do, as was outlined in Chapters III to V.

II. GOSCHEN

Writing in the 1860s, Viscount Goschen emphasized a balance-of-payments approach to exchange-rate determination. Yet he presents the PPP theory for an inconvertible paper currency (floating exchange rate) through the usual mechanism—the quantity theory of money leading to a relative-PPP result. Goschen declares ". . . when, through the over-issue of paper money, a general rise of prices ensues, the price of gold, as measured by paper money, rises with the rest" (1864; 1932, p. 62).[3] What happens to gold happens also to the currency of a country on the gold standard: "Thus, supposing the Austrian Government to be constantly depreciating the Austrian currency by issues of paper money, the value of gold in Austria will be constantly rising, and one hundred English sovereigns will be worth so many more Austrian paper florins" (1864; 1932, p. 62).

For Goschen, as for Mill, a rise in the price level and depreciation of the currency are equivalent terms. This internal depreciation of the florin is offset by an external depreciation (fall in its value in the foreign-exchange market), and no real effects on trade ensue. Again, like Mill, Goschen notes that the price rise need not be uniform; temporarily, some commodity prices can increase more than others.

Goschen observes that when an exchange-rate change is due to an altered balance of trade, real effects do occur; the greater amount of foreign money obtained for a given amount of domestic currency has more purchasing power. "But where the cheapness of the bills is caused by the depreciation of the foreign currency, he has no advantage; for the purchasing power of the nominally larger sum is not greater than that of the smaller" (1864; 1932, p. 64). Goschen is pursuing the logic of the real-versus-nominal rate distinction, although the terminology is not used.

In two respects Goschen's discussion of PPP does go beyond that of Mill. First, he recognizes an amendment to the neutrality result of relative PPP. The country with the falling exchange value of its currency has its creditors lose and debtors gain. Goschen points out that if the foreign assets of the country are equal to its foreign claims, then again no gains or losses arise from the exchange-rate change; so the neutrality result holds. Second, Goschen contrasts the small variation in exchange rates from non-PPP influences with the large changes arising from the internal depreciation of currencies. He observes that non-PPP factors—he mentions as examples interest rates, the balance of indebtedness, panic, and distance—can affect the exchange rate by only a few percent. "A variation of ten per cent owing to all these circumstances combined, is considered something extraordinary, and only occurs under rare circumstances" (1864; 1932, p. 63).

In contrast, monetary factors (working through relative PPP) can lead to much greater exchange-rate changes: "But as soon as the element of currency is introduced, we have had at once an instance before us in the Vienna exchange of a variation of fifty percent."

III. MARSHALL

In testimony before Royal Commissions in the late 19th century, Alfred Marshall presented both the PPP theory, in absolute form, for a floating exchange rate and its weaker variant, the law of one price, under a fixed exchange rate. More than a quarter-century later, Marshall (1923) saw fit to reprint verbatim that part of his testimonies relating to PPP. It is intriguing that he does not take the opportunity to mention the intervening work of Gustav Cassel (to be discussed in the next chapter). Of course, Marshall was toward the end of a long life and career. Perhaps he had not kept up with the literature. Possibly the issue of PPP was deemed too obvious and/or too unimportant to warrant more than reprinted testimony in an appendix in a new book. The unfairest speculation is that Marshall was reciprocating Cassel's neglect to mention Marshall's antecedent work on the PPP theory.

Marshall begins with the case of a gold-standard country (England) and a paper-standard country (Russia). In this connection, he states the absolute PPP theory in the most emphatic terms to date: ". . . when trade is in equilibrium, the gold price of the rouble will be fixed just at the ratio which gold prices in England bear to rouble prices in Russia" (1888; 1926, p. 170).[4] Then he considers a disturbance from equilibrium, the exchange rate (gold price of the ruble) falling below the PPP (ratio of the English to the Russian price level). The depreciated ruble in the foreign-exchange market provides extraordinary profits to Russian exporters and losses to English exporters to Russia. Instead of selling their ruble earnings for gold, the latter traders will buy Russian goods and export them to England. The decreased demand for gold causes the ruble to appreciate against gold in the foreign-exchange market, and the PPP equilibrium is restored.

Several features of the adjustment process are noteworthy. First, causation runs from the PPP to the exchange rate, the required direction for a true PPP theory under a floating rate. In the same vein, Marshall writes: ". . . the balancing of exporters' and importers' bills compels the gold price of the rouble to equal the ratio which average gold prices in A bear to average gold prices in B, allowance being made for carriage" (1888; 1926, p. 192). Second, commodity arbitrage is the essential ingredient in the adjustment process. Third, because the foreign-exchange market quickly corrects any disequilibrium involving a floating rate, adjustment is virtually without lag: ". . . the gold price of the rouble would rise almost instantaneously until it was equal to the ratio in which gold prices in England stand to rouble prices in Russia" (1888; 1926, p. 173).

A unitary H function is not imposed. Transport costs are mentioned several times as one factor inhibiting a strict PPP relationship. Also, non-PPP elements can cause fluctuations in the exchange rate. One such force is changes in the balance of trade ("relative supplies of importers' and exporters' bills"). Marshall deserves credit for being the first to impose balance-of-trade equilibrium as a condition for the absolute PPP theory to hold. Then the exchange rate will vary, independently of PPP, with any disequilibrium in the balance of trade. Changes in "other international obligations" also cause variations in the exchange rate. Capital flows are mentioned, both positive lending and withdrawal of capital. Again, Marshall is the first economist to place international capital flows in the H function, that is, as an inhibitor of a strict PPP determination of the exchange rate.

Eleven years later, Marshall (1899) weakened his PPP theory by redefining the PPP so it is composed of "prices at ports" rather than general price levels: ". . . the Indian exchange . . . has indicated the proportion between rupee prices at Indian ports and sterling prices at English ports . . ." (1899; 1926, p. 293). If Marshall means to replace general price levels by prices of traded goods, then the resulting "PPP theory" can be subscribed to by all who believe in simple commodity arbitrage internationally, that is, arbitrage involving goods that actually move between countries.

It could be, however, that Marshall was simply allowing for the fact of incomplete price equalization between regions of the same country. His justification for the restriction to prices at ports is that, "India is so large that prices at her ports differ widely from up-country prices; and partly for this reason, much of the produce of India is very little connected either as cause or effect with the course of trade" (1899; 1926, p. 293).

It is not unreasonable to conclude that Marshall restricted prices in England at ports purely for reasons of symmetry and that he would apply his original PPP theory, based on general price levels, to countries with sufficiently integrated internal markets. Large countries—both India and America are mentioned—would not be in this category. Presumably, the country's stage of economic development and the quality of internal transport and communication facilities are also relevant, although not mentioned by Marshall in this connection.

Marshall considers two cases of both countries on a specie standard. The first case involves England with a gold currency and India with a silver currency. Again, ". . . the gold price of silver is determined by the ratio between the prices of commodities in gold and in silver countries" (1888; 1926, p. 177). However, the correction of a disequilibrium takes longer than when one country is on a paper standard. Suppose the exchange rate (gold price of silver) is lower in England than in India. The latter country's exporters will use their bills of exchange on England to export silver to India. Commodity prices will fall in England and rise in India, and also the exchange rate may increase, until the PPP relationship is re-established. Thus the price specie-flow mechanism is the main part of the adjustment mechanism to yield the law of one price. Inherently, then, the speed of adjustment is slower than when the sole mechanism is via an exchange-rate change.

When both countries are on a gold standard, again the law of one price applies: "Then trade tends so to adjust the supplies of gold relatively to the demands for gold in the two countries as to bring gold prices at the sea-boards of the two countries to equality (allowance being made for carriage)" (1888; 1926, p. 191).[5] The fact that the exchange rate is confined within specie points is made explicit. The exchange-rate adjustment takes place until the applicable specie point is reached, after which the price specie-flow mechanism applies. If prices are higher in A than in B, the exchange value of A's currency will drop to its gold-export point. Then gold will flow from A to B, lowering prices in A, raising them in B, until the PPP relationship is restored.

This careful analysis of the adjustment to the law of one price under a "fixed" exchange rate, that is, a rate constrained between specie points, is another contribution of Marshall to the PPP literature.

IV. MISES

Just before World War I, Ludwig von Mises (1912), writing in German, presented a PPP approach to the exchange rate. He begins with a non-restrictive quantity theory of money in which the relationship between the money supply and the price level is positive, but not proportionate (although in certain passages he defends the restrictive form of the theory). He is aware that changes in velocity can occur, though pointing out (in Ellis' words) "that it [velocity] does not depend upon the supply of money" (1934, p. 162). So, more important for Mises, as an amendment to the theory, is his view that a money-supply change will not affect all individual prices in the same proportion. In this way, Mises indicates awareness of the price-level concept as a index number.

The contribution of Mises to PPP analysis is the proposition that exchange-market adjustment to an altered PPP can be either delayed or immediate. He writes: "Changes in the domestic purchasing power of one money will affect the exchange rate between this currency and other currencies at the time that these changes are reflected in goods that either are traded between these two countries or will be traded because of small price changes" (1912, p. 234). In this argument Mises is suggesting a conventional relative-PPP chain of causation in which an increase in the domestic money supply increases the price level. When the price increases spread to traded goods (including those now tradable because of the price change), then there is a fall in the exchange value of the country's currency. Prices of tradable goods can be affected either early or late in the process of adaptation of prices to the enhanced quantity of money.

However, this entire process can be circumvented. In a passage reminiscent of Wheatley (but going beyond him), Mises declares: "The speculators in exchange markets will activate the exchange-rate change when the change in the purchasing power of the currency has not yet been completed, perhaps not even begun, at any rate before it has reached tradable goods" (1912, p. 234). Rational expectations of market participants can bring about the exchange-rate change not merely before, or without, international commodity movements in response to the price change (Wheatley's position), but even before the price change has taken place or is completed. Mises also points out that the depreciation of the country's currency on the exchange market encourages exports and discourages imports as long as commodity prices are not fully adjusted.

Ellis (1934, p. 216) sees Mises as having the absolute-PPP theory, quoting him as saying that the normal exchange rate "makes it a matter of indifference whether a person buys goods directly with a unit of money or whether he first buys a unit of foreign money and then makes his purchases with it." Contrary to Ellis' reference, I could not find this sentence in Mises' original work (1912). However, the second edition, published in 1924, does contain the passage. It is possible that Ellis, whose bibliography includes both German editions of Mises' treatise, misdirected the reference.

It should be noted that at the time Ellis produced his masterful treatise (1934) on German monetary theory, none of Mises' writings on PPP had been translated into English. To this day, the first edition of Mises' (1912) study has not been so translated, but the second edition, Mises (1936), was released in English two years after Ellis' study appeared. It should be emphasized that our concern here is solely with Mises' pre-war work on PPP; a full appreciation of his contribution to the subject would require assessing his postwar writings. A useful English-language compilation of these writings is in Mises (1978).[6]

V. DEMISE OF THE PPP THEORY·

In spite of the acknowledgements to the PPP theory made by Mill and Goschen and also in spite of Marshall's important developments of the approach, the PPP theory remained dormant in the literature except for the work of Mises. From the end of the Bank Restriction Period to World War I, there was little, if any, attention devoted to the PPP theory by authors other than the four mentioned.

In fact, I could find direct or indirect references to only three other authors writing during this time period whose work touched on the PPP theory. Yeager (1969) mentions Wilhelm Launhardt (1894) as, like Marshall, a believer in the PPP theory. However, a reading of Launhardt's work shows that the reference to PPP is, at best, incomplete. Launhardt writes:

"The appreciation or depreciation of the rouble [with respect to the mark] is connected to changes in market prices" (1894, p. 30). (The context indicates that he means market prices of commodities.) He also states: "The international-trade relations between countries determine world market prices and at the same time the exchange rates of currencies of these countries. The changes in exchange rates are, however, not cause, but effect of this international market price determination" (1894, p. 31).

These statements are certainly consistent with the PPP theory. However, Launhardt does not specify the nature of the price variable in exchange-rate determination. In particular, he does not state or imply that relative price levels in the two countries are the relevant concept.

What about the case of prices or the price level in one country as influencing the exchange rate? Not even this model is considered. One must conclude that Launhardt's PPP-like statements are unsupported by a conceptual model. He writes only of the direction of causation postulated by the theory; all other aspects of the theory are neglected.

Einzig (1970, p. 210) speaks of "further contributions to the purchasing power theory after Goshen," with Marshall's work the only one of possible major importance. However, the other authors he cites seemingly in this connection, namely Augustin Cournot (1838) and Guillermo Subercaseaux (1912), did not present PPP theories. Einzig (1970, p. 210) writes that: "He [Cournot] endorsed the view that exchange rates depended on relative price levels, on the ground that goods must flow from the cheaper to the dearer market until the discrepancy between prices is reduced to transport costs." As for Subercaseaux, he is said to consider parities "based on relative note circulation."

A reading of Cournot (1838; 1927) shows that he considered the case only of an individual tradable commodity—what he calls "an article capable of transportation" (1927, p. 117)[7]—and that he presents only a statement of arbitrage for this commodity, with local prices (expressed in a common currency by means of the exchange rate) differing by, at most, the cost of transportation. The case of a floating exchange rate is not considered and "the law of one price" under a fixed rate refers not to general price levels, not even to price levels of tradable goods, but only to individual commodity prices. Clearly, Cournot's contribution—though a good statement of the commodity arbitrage supportive of the law of one price—is not in the PPP domain.

Turning to Subercaseaux, the statement that equilibrium exchange rates are determined by relative money supplies is not a PPP theory unless the effect is via price levels. So we are left with Mill, Goschen, Marshall, and Mises as perhaps the sole expositors, let alone proponents, of the PPP approach during the near century preceding World War I. Certainly they are the only well-known writers who presented the theory. Even periods of a paper standard and floating exchange rate—for example, the United States in 1862–1878—did not give rise to controversies in which the PPP theory played a role on the "bullionist" side.

What were the reasons for this neglect of the PPP approach? Einzig declares that it was Goschen who shifted attention from the PPP theory to the balance-of-payments theory of exchange-rate determination. He writes: "This was possible because the principal exchange movements remained within specie points—and there was no obvious call for theoretical explanations based on price differentials" (1970, pp. 209–210). It is true that by 1880 the international gold standard was in full swing.[8] Also relevant is the suggestion that the alleged exchange-rate stability of specie standards in the 19th century may have occurred only after the early 1870s.

The empirical work of Davis and Hughes (1960) indicates that, at least for the gold-dollar/sterling exchange rate, the gold points around the mint parity were either much wider, or more often violated, until about 1875 than in the last quarter of the 19th century.[9] Einzig sees a gradual narrowing of the spread between specie points for exchanges generally (not just the British/U. S. exchange). He ascribes the phenomenon to "a gradual lowering of transport costs, interest charges, and insurance" (1970, p. 172). This narrowing of the spread began after the Napoleonic Wars; in the last decades of the 19th century the spread became comparably narrow to exchange-rate bands that existed between the World Wars.

With a much narrower spread in which unconstrained floating occurred by the last 20–25 years of the 19th century, the impetus provided to the PPP theory by substantial exchange-rate movements even under a specie standard vanished.

There remains the question of why the PPP theory did not arise during the periods of floating exchange rates between the English bullionist period and World War I. Certainly such periods existed—the floating U.S. greenback in 1862–1878, the Austrian gulden and Russian ruble during much of the second half of the 19th century, the Italian lira as well as several Latin American currencies during various parts of the century, and the Indian and Japanese currencies in the latter part of the 19th century and (for Japan) into the 20th century. After relating these histories, Einzig concludes that: ". . . even during what has now come to be regarded as the Classical Period of exchange stability under the gold standard, a large number of exchanges were anything but stable" (1970, p. 198).

A plausible reason is that theories of speculation in the foreign-exchange market became dominant. Einzig writes: ". . . speculation was often held, rightly or wrongly, responsible for abnormal exchange movements" (1970, p. 211). Concerning explanations of the gold premium over the greenback during the U. S. Civil War, Mitchell (1903, pp. 187–88) writes: "Perhaps the simplest theory was that a nominal advance of gold had been produced by the nefarious acts of disloyal speculators, who took advantage of the fact that 'gold had become a mere commodity' to monopolize the supply and raise the price."

Interestingly enough, Mitchell does refer to contemporary views ascribing the U. S. price rise to over-issuance of currency (via the quantity theory of money) and also explaining the gold premium by means of monetary expansion. However, apparently the two theories were not linked and the money-supply theory of the exchange rate was not considered to work through prices, that is, via the PPP theory.

Perhaps for all these reasons—the role of Goschen in the 1860s in switching attention away from the PPP theory, the dominance of the gold standard by 1880, the narrowing of specie points during the century, the emergence of theories of speculation to explain variations in floating exchange rates—the PPP theory became dormant. By the time of World War I, the economic literature had ceased to incorporate the theory. Not for the first time in its history, the PPP theory awaited rediscovery.

NOTES

1. All quotations from Mill (1848) are as found in the version edited by Ashley (1929). Although based on the seventh edition of Mill's *Principles*, published in 1871, the quotations and arguments ascribed to Mill in the text of the present work appeared also in the first edition (1848). (Differences between editions are so indicated by Ashley.)

2. One cannot legitimately argue that Mill's international equalization of prices of imports and exports is based on his barter model of reciprocal demand and hence inapplicable to the real world of monetary economies. Mill is emphatic that ". . . the law of international values, and, consequently, the division of the advantages of trade among the nations which carry it on, are the same, on the supposition of money, as they would be in a state of barter" (1848; 1929, p. 622).

3. Goschen's *Theory of the Foreign Exchanges,* first published in 1861, was revised in 1863 and (only slightly) in 1864. Quotations are from the so-called fourth edition (actually a reprint of the third edition), published in 1932.

4. All quotations from Marshall's testimonies before the Royal Commissions (1888; 1899) are taken from his *Official Papers* (1926).

5. It is strange that Marshall here restricts prices to be at the sea-boards, a harbinger of the "prices at ports" to be specified 11 years later. Elsewhere in the same passage, general price levels are used in the PPP theory for the exchange rate both between a gold and paper currency and between a gold and silver currency.

6. Mises' views on PPP are discussed by Ellis (1934) and Humphrey (1979).

7. The quotation is from the English translation (1927) of Cournot's work originally published in 1838.

8. Bloomfield (1963) lists 15 major countries as adhering to gold in 1880.

9. This property of the Davis-Hughes exchange-rate series remains even after it is modified by Perkins (1978).

Chapter VII

The Contribution of Cassel

"If these critics, who express themselves in such vague general terms, were allowed to have their own way, the entire theory of the purchasing-power parity would have to be thrown to the winds, and we should be left in as much doubt as ever as to the real basis of the rates of exchange." (Gustav Cassel, 1924, p. 68)

Purchasing power parity and Gustav Cassel: the names are inextricably linked. We know from the discussions in Chapters III to VI that a considerable number of economists had propounded the PPP theory during various periods in the 16th to 19th centuries. Yet it is Cassel, writing as late as World War I, whose name is almost invariably the first connected to the theory. Indeed, the PPP theory is sometimes called, simply, "Cassel's theory."

I. THE IMPACT OF CASSEL

Einzig (1970, p. 264) states the reason for the association of Cassel's name with PPP:

> ... neither Ricardo nor any of the earlier economists had succeeded in developing the purchasing power parity theory sufficiently, or in making a strong enough impression with their exposition of that theory, to ensure its adoption by textbook-writers before the first World War. Cassel succeeded in doing so to a remarkable degree ...

One should go further than Einzig's statement. The impact of Cassel on bringing about the economic profession's awareness of PPP analysis was greater than that of any other person in the history of PPP development. No predecessor of Cassel, no contemporary, no later individual implanted the PPP theory so broadly and firmly in the economic profession's domain and also the public domain. Cassel was the supreme publicist of the PPP approach. Indeed, it is fair to describe that successful propaganda effort as perhaps his most important contribution to the PPP literature. After Cassel, the PPP approach was sometimes neglected, but never forgotten.

What were the reasons for the success of Cassel's publicity work on behalf of PPP? First of all, no other author—again, neither before Cassel, contemporaneously, or after him—wrote so prolificly on the topic. Cassel devoted a total of at least 25 English-language publications, in whole or in part, to the PPP approach. This list includes 15 articles: seven in the *Economic Journal* (1916a, 1916b, 1917, 1918, 1919, 1920a, 1928c); five in Skandinaviska Kreditaktiebolaget *Quarterly Report* (1923a, 1924, 1925b, 1925c, 1925d); and one each in *Annals of the American Academy* (1920b), *Economica* (1923b), and the *Encyclopedia Britannica* (1926). Also included in these writings are eight books authored by Cassel (1916c, 1921, 1922, 1925a, 1928a, 1932a, 1932b, 1936) and two volumes in which he served as a contributor (1925e, 1928b).

The second reason for Cassel's success as a PPP propagandist is that he disseminated all his PPP writings in the English-language mainstream of economics. His works on PPP were either published directly in English or translated into that language. Third, Cassel exposited the PPP approach in an extremely forceful and assertive style of writing. It is apparent to the reader that Cassel is both exuberant about the explanatory power of the PPP hypothesis and determined to carry out a mission of replacing other exchange-rate theories with the PPP theory in the professional and public domains. This tone of Cassel's writings on PPP contrasts with the matter-of-fact or coldly analytical treatment of his immediate predecessors, that is, Mill, Goschen, Marshall, and Mises. Even the English bullionist economists did not exhibit anything like Cassel's verve, excitement, and sense of mission in their PPP writings.

Fourth, Cassel's wartime and postwar publications on the subject stimulated a controversy on the merits of PPP analysis that was much more powerful than the bullionist controversies of earlier centuries. Unlike the several bullionist debates, the reaction to Cassel in the economic literature was international in scope—with publications not only in England (the place of Cassel's earliest writings on PPP), but also in several European countries and the United States. This controversy also differed from the previous debates in its exclusive focus on PPP analysis.

Furthermore, the sheer number of the publications involved far exceeded the world total of all previous writings on PPP. It is not surprising that following this chapter—devoted to Cassel's contribution to the development of PPP theory—I must abandon the approach of considering, chronologically, each and every publication dealing with PPP. For surveys of the decade or more of literary conflict between critics of PPP analysis and its proponents, the followers of Cassel, the studies of Angell (1926), Ellis (1934), and Einzig (1970) may be consulted.[1]

Fifth, Cassel wrote at a time of *international* ferment in foreign-exchange markets. The Swedish, French, and English/Irish bullionist experiences, in contrast, were purely domestic events. The background to Cassel's publications was the First World War and the early postwar period, with inflation and large-scale exchange-rate movements spanning a large number of economies.

Sixth, Cassel gave the PPP theory its name. He did not do this until his fourth article (1918) on the topic, where the term "purchasing power parity" was used for the first time. In his first article (1916a), the equivalent term "theoretical rate of exchange" was employed. As a descriptive device, "purchasing power parity" explains the theory precisely and it immediately was adopted by the economics profession. The nominal-versus-real-exchange-rate terminology invented by Horner and Blake a century earlier was entirely supplanted and, in fact, had never been fully incorporated in the literature.

Finally the substantive contributions of Cassel to PPP analysis cannot be overlooked as a powerful reason for his successful implantation of the theory firmly in the economic consciousness. There were many predecessors to Cassel in developing the PPP approach, but he was the first to place PPP within so systematic a framework that a clearly operational theory resulted. He distinguished carefully between the absolute and relative versions of the theory, although he did not provide them with names.[2] Also, Cassel was the first to express the theory formally in terms of statistical averages of prices. Not only did Cassel make PPP an operational theory, but also he was the first to use PPP to obtain estimates of exchange-rate disequilibria and the first to test the theory empirically. In this chapter only theoretical aspects of Cassel's work on PPP are considered; his empirical use of PPP and his testing of the theory are discussed in Part III. Further specific contributions of Cassel to PPP theory are discussed in later sections of this chapter.

II. MOTIVATION FOR CASSEL'S PPP THEORY

As far as Cassel was concerned, the motivation for his theory was the dislocations of exchange rates during the World War combined with his disagreement with the general view that prewar exchange values of currencies (mint parities under the gold standard) would be reestablished after the war. In one of his earliest works, he writes: "All the combatants wish the world to believe that after the war their currencies will resume their normal value. But, in all probability, this problem will possess far different features from those it now presents" (1916c, p. 57).

This situation occurred, according to Cassel, in an atmosphere of ignorance concerning the determination of exchange rates. "The discussion on the variations in exchange rates and their true explanation, which has been going on the whole world over since the outbreak of the War, has been chiefly characterised by a remarkable lack of clearness on the question as to what really determines the exchange rate between two independent currencies" (1922, pp. 137–138). Twelve years after his initial publication on PPP, Cassel reflected on the background for his theory.

> During the War it was generally believed, and even officially preached, that exchanges were only disturbed by the obstacles which the War put in the way of international trade, and that exchanges must therefore be expected to revert to their normal pre-War levels as soon as peace was in sight. The fundamental wrongness of this view was made manifest by the Purchasing Power Parity theory. (1928a, p. 24)

There is evidence, though, that Cassel had developed the PPP theory even before the war. Meinich (1968, p. 159) declares: "Cassel says that he got the principal ideas of this theory [PPP] during his lectures at Stockholms Högskola in 1905." The reference is to a footnote in the Swedish (but not the English) edition of Cassel's *Theory of Social Economy*. In beginning his first article on PPP, Cassel confirms that he possessed the theory in the prewar period, for he presents "the theory of the foreign exchanges which I have given for some years in my lectures" (1916a, p. 62). If Cassel's lecture notes, perhaps as taken by a student, were found, they might indicate the precise timing of his development of the PPP theory.

Was Cassel influenced by his antecedents in the PPP literature? In only one of his 25 publications on PPP does he allude to any predecessors; only Ricardo, Mill, and Goschen are acknowledged. It is strange that Cassel does not mention the PPP discovery during the Swedish bullionist controversy of the 18th century; for his fellow Swede, Sven Brisman, noted that fact during Cassel's lifetime.[3]

Cassel (1922, p. 170) credits Ricardo with "the first theory of exchanges of a scientific character." He acknowledges that Ricardo applied the relative PPP theory to a floating exchange-rate situation and also sees him as having the law of one price (subject to transport costs) under a fixed-rate, metallic system. His reference to Goschen indicates that Cassel sees him as having a PPP-like theory only for a metallic standard, with the exchange rate under a paper standard determined by the demand and supply of foreign exchange. This interpretation is incorrect; Goschen did apply the PPP theory to a paper currency.[4]

As for Mill, Cassel does not appear to credit him with any PPP theory at all. Mill is correctly viewed as having the "nominal" exchange rate determined by the amount of currency depreciation. However, quite unfairly, the latter is interpreted by Cassel as referring to depreciation with respect to the metal parity and not (or not also) the rise in the price level.

So Ricardo is considered by Cassel to be his true predecessor. Cassel writes: ". . . Ricardo finally draws various conclusions which in reality contain much of what a true theory of exchanges should contain" (1922, p. 172). Perhaps other bullionist proponents of PPP, such as Wheatley and Blake, were ignored by Cassel because Ricardo was the most prominent English economist of that time.

III. QUANTITY THEORY OF MONEY

According to Schumpeter (1954, p. 737), Cassel's PPP theory (as that of Ricardo) appeared ". . . in characteristic association with a strict (and crude) quantity theory." It is true that Cassel adhered to the quantity theory of money throughout his writing. In fact, he was regarded as a quantity theorist of Irving Fisher's stature. However, Cassel never expounded a simple quantity theory. Even his first article on PPP qualifies the theory: "Now, according to the quantitative theory of money the general level of prices varies, other things being equal, in direct proportion to the quantity of the circulating medium in a country" (1916a, p. 62).

In his subsequent writings, Cassel explained what "other things" are kept equal. Changes in output affect the price level (in the opposite direction), but money-supply changes are by far the more important factor. Changes in the demand for money (sometimes taking the form of changes in the velocity of circulation, in Cassel's later work) are explicitly considered, including effects on the price level as well as on real output. Also, causation can move in the opposite direction, with velocity affected by changes in the price level or the money supply.

Even the essence of the quantity theory admits of a two-way causation, as the demand for money increases proportionately to the rise in prices and the supply of money passively adjusts to the demand. However, Cassel is emphatic that the initiating cause of any inflationary process is always increases in the money supply, what he calls "the creation of artificial purchasing power." Continually increasing the money supply results in inflation as distinct from a once-and-for-all change in the price level. It is always within the power of the government to restrict the money supply and thereby stabilize the price level.

Cassel states the unqualified quantity-theory relationship only as a long-run proposition: "In the long run, of course, the internal purchasing power of a currency must, after all, always be determined by the amount of money in circulation" (1925d, p. 56).

In summary, far from being a believer in a crude quantity theory, Cassel was a sophisticated monetarist ahead of his time. As Holmes writes: "The idea that changes in the monetary sector would cause changes in the non-monetary sector is expressed so often in Cassel's writing . . . that it is amazing that one could think of him as a naive theorist—quantity or otherwise" (1967b, p. 688).

IV. PRICE-LEVEL CONCEPT

Cassel is well aware of the index-number problems involved both in computing a domestic price index and in constructing relative price levels (absolute PPP). Relative price changes and movements in the general price level, he notes, are commingled. A price index seeks to measure "how far a shifting of the centre of gravity of the price-level has taken place" (1932b, p. 463). Cassel notes that in constructing a relative PPP measure, the index-number problem is compounded.

In constructing absolute PPP, one can obtain a precise comparison of price levels in the two countries only in the limiting case of all individual prices in one country differing from corresponding prices in the other by the same multiplicative factor; that is, all relative prices are the same in the two countries. In that case, Cassel correctly points out, there will be no international trade. With differing relative prices in the countries (the realistic circumstance), only "an approximate comparison between the purchasing power of the one currency and the other" (1928b, p. 8) is possible.

What price measure should be used in the PPP theory and for PPP computations? The issue is discussed mainly in terms of price indices (with reference to the quantity theory of money and relative PPP), rather than in terms of price levels (absolute PPP). In forming a price index, price relatives of individual commodities may be weighted according to their importance. Cassel suggests that the weighting pattern reflect either production or consumption of commodities.

In particular, price indices limited to traded goods (exports and imports) are emphatically rejected. Several reasons for this decision are provided. First, such indices "are limited to a small class of commodities, and are therefore subject to variations" (1922, p. 47) that presumably would not be present in a broader-based price measure. Second, traded and nontraded goods are not unvarying collections of commodities. "There is never a definite group of commodities that can be exported. Even a small alteration in the rate of exchange may widen or restrict the group of exportable goods" (1928a, p. 33).

Third, Cassel hints that the "law of one price" applies to traded-goods prices, so that they tend to move together in different countries irrespective of the amount of deviation of exchange rates from their purchasing power parities. He writes: ". . . if export commodities have risen in relative value in the exporting country, they have probably in the importing country also risen in desirability, and therefore in value, as compared with other commodities. The higher price of the export commodities, therefore, need not necessarily cause the value of the exporting country's exchange to be reduced on a like scale" (1922, p. 155).

Cassel contends that a *general* price level is required to define absolute PPP and a *general* price index is needed for relative PPP. He writes: ". . . the height of the general price level in different countries . . . [is needed] to make a real calculation of the purchasing power parities. . . " (1922, p. 182); and: "The whole theory of Purchasing Power Parity essentially refers to the internal value of the currencies concerned, and variations in this value can be measured only by general index figures representing as far as possible the whole mass of commodities marketed in the country" (1928a, p. 33).

The most logical interpretation of the general price index envisaged by Cassel for relative PPP would be the gross-domestic-product (GDP) deflator and its analogue—the GDP price level—for absolute PPP. Certainly, the very concept of the internal purchasing power of a country's currency implies that Cassel means to exclude import prices from the measure and to include export prices. National accounts had not yet been developed at Cassel's time of writing, so the precise concept of a GDP price measure was alien to him. He declares that one must consider all available general price indices: the wholesale price index, retail price index, cost-of-living index, and wage-rate index.

At one point, Cassel suggests that the wholesale price index is most suitable to measure long-run price movements, the reason being: "We must confine ourselves to typical standard commodities of a practically fixed quality" (1932b, p. 463). This passage is clearly an aberration.

Elsewhere, Cassel notes: "An index for wholesale prices may be based on statistics of general prices or else on statistics of the prices of import and export goods" (1922, p. 47). The latter-type index is rejected.

Ultimately, Cassel leans in favor of a cost-parity concept. He writes: "Only when prices have adjusted themselves to one another so as to make prices of products correspond to their cost of production, can we regard the usual index number of wholesale prices as a fairly reliable index of the movements of the general level of prices" (1921, p. 110). This statement is supported elsewhere: "The level of wages in the country, therefore, is always a very important factor—in the long run may be the predominating one—in determining the international value of the country's currency" (1922, p. 144).

V. ABSOLUTE PPP THEORY

Cassel's theory of PPP is appropriately named; for its foundation is the idea that the value of a currency—and therefore the demand for it—is determined fundamentally by the amount of goods and services that a unit of the currency can buy in the country of issue, that is, by its "internal purchasing power." The internal purchasing power of a currency is sometimes called simply its "purchasing power" or—as in Cassel's early writings—its "buying power" or "paying power." Irrespective of the term used, the domestic purchasing power of a country's currency is defined as the inverse of the price level.

One of Cassel's many contributions to PPP analysis is that he was the first author to formulate his theory in terms of the schemata outlined in Chapter II of this study. The long-run equilibrium exchange rate—called by Cassel the "equilibrium rate of exchange," "normal rate of exchange," "equilibrium position" of the exchange rate, "normal position" of the rate, or the "normal parity"—is defined as the value of the exchange rate that yields balance-of-trade equilibrium. It is fair to interpret Cassel's balance-of-payments concept more broadly so that he means equilibrium in the current account. He writes: "The main reason why we pay anything for a foreign currency is of course that this currency represents in the foreign country a purchasing power which can be used for acquiring the goods or for paying for the services of that country" (1926, p. 1086). For simplicity, Cassel sometimes assumes that trade consists entirely of "commodities," that is, goods rather than services. This procedure justifies use of the trade rather than current account as the balance-of-payments concept in the definition of the equilibrium exchange rate.

Cassel points out that if the actual exchange rate (price of B-currency in terms of A-currency) exceeds (falls below) the equilibrium rate, then country A would have a trade surplus (deficit). Only when the actual rate is at equilibrium is there a trade balance. Now, the principal—though not the sole—determinant of the equilibrium exchange rate is the ratio of the internal purchasing powers or price levels of the two countries, that is, the absolute PPP. Though Cassel does not use the adjective "absolute," he defines and uses the absolute-PPP concept correctly and consistently.

Why is the PPP the main determinant of the equilibrium exchange rate? Since the value of a given currency is basically determined by its domestic purchasing power (inverse of the price level), the equilibrium value of one currency (relative to another) is fundamentally determined by, and in a limiting circumstance equal to, the ratio of the internal purchasing powers of the currencies, that is, the (absolute) PPP. As Cassel writes: "Obviously, in the state of equilibrium a certain sum of money must have about the same purchasing power if converted into the one currency or into the other" (1928b, p. 7).

In Cassel's most thorough analysis, there is both an f and a g function, in the terminology of Chapter II of the present study. The equilibrium exchange rate tends to equal the PPP (the f function)—"The internal purchasing power of the two currencies contemplated determines only the equilibrium of the rate of exchange" (1926, p. 1086)—and the actual exchange rate under a paper standard (floating exchange rate) tends to equal the equilibrium rate (the g function). In each case (f function, g function) there may be deviations of the dependent variable (equilibrium rate, actual rate) from its principal determinant (PPP, equilibrium rate). These deviations are discussed in a later section of this chapter.

As a short-cut in his analysis, Cassel equates the PPP with the equilibrium exchange rate. "In order to emphasize this dominating influence of the internal purchasing power in fixing the equilibrium rate of exchange, we call this rate, as here defined, the purchasing power parity between the two currencies" (1926, p. 1086). He combines this simple f function with the g function to obtain an h function in which the exchange value of a floating currency is a function principally of the PPP and, in the limiting case, equals the PPP. As Cassel writes:

Thus the rate of exchange between the two countries will be determined by the quotient between the general level of prices in the two countries. (1916a, p. 62)

Thus the price of the bill on country B must, as an expression of the value of the currency of country B in terms of the currency of country A, be directly determined by the relation existing between the value of money in countries B and A respectively. This relation is the purchasing power parity of the two currencies (1932b, p. 513).

Cassel states a neutrality theorem for the absolute PPP theory. High prices within a country will not encourage imports or discourage exports, as these prices will be counterbalanced by a low exchange value of the domestic country's currency, and the equilibrium balance of trade is maintained. Similarly, the level of the exchange rate is irrelevant for real behavior, providing only that the exchange rate reflects the PPP. So Cassel can comment: "In reality the purchasing power parity represents an indifferent equilibrium of the exchanges in the sense that it does not affect international trade either way" (1922, p. 157). "But as soon as this parity [PPP] has been established at a certain level it is of no importance whether this level is high or low" (1920b, p. 262).

An effective adjustment mechanism preserves the tendency of the exchange rate to equal the PPP. Cassel uses the term undervalued (overvalued) exchange rate to denote an exchange value of a country's currency below (above) its PPP. An undervalued (overvalued) exchange rate encourages (discourages) exports and discourages (encourages) imports, thus increasing (decreasing) the demand for the country's currency in the foreign-exchange market and restoring the equality of the exchange rate with the PPP. At this time, what Cassel calls the "artificial" stimulus or hampering of trade, ceases and equilibrium in the balance of trade is restored.

Though not formally using the elasticity concept, Cassel is an "elasticity optimist," believing in high price elasticities for exports and imports and, therefore, in a relatively large response of the balance of trade to a change in the exchange rate. His belief is especially strong for countries at a high level of development engaged in close commercial relations. Not only will a small deviation of the exchange rate from the PPP significantly affect the amount of trade in existing commodities, but also previously untraded commodities will become exported or imported (and some kinds of previously traded commodities will cease to be imported or exported). High elasticities imply a great stability to the exchange rate at the equilibrium (PPP) level. Cassel declares: ". . . the rate of exchange in its equilibrium position—always on the assumption of a constant value of money—possesses a great stability, that is, a great power of resistance against changes in the real conditions of international trade which tend to shift the rate in one direction or the other" (1932b, p. 661).

The ability to use currency to purchase goods and services in the country of issue is the foundation of Cassel's PPP theory. So he notes that the theory works best, that is, that the short-run equilibrium exchange rate is expected to have minimum deviation from the PPP, under conditions of free international trade. Cassel also states that the theory holds when trade restrictions have equal impact in both directions, that is, on both imports and exports of a country.

Under normal conditions, Cassel's theory involves a strict direction of causation, from a country's money supply to its price level and thence (given the foreign price level) to the exchange rate. "The sequence of cause and effect is incontestable . . . " (1924, p. 68). In particular, a rise in the foreign price level cannot affect the domestic price level, providing the exchange value of the domestic country's currency appreciates in the same proportion as the PPP (ratio of the foreign to the domestic price level) rises.

However, Cassel mentions several exceptions to the strict chain of causation. First, if the domestic currency is undervalued (overvalued) on the foreign-exchange market with respect to the PPP, then imports are made more expensive (cheaper) domestically and exports encouraged (discouraged) because of their lower (higher) price in foreign currency. The higher (lower) price of import goods spreads to the general price level, and the increased (reduced) exports also acts to increase (decrease) the price level. Cassel notes that it is still within the power of the country to prevent the stimulating (depressing) effect on the domestic price level by suitably controlling the money supply, restricting or expanding it as the case may be.

Second, in a period of moderate and relatively stable inflation, the valuation of the exchange rate will anticipate the future currency depreciation over, say, the next year or several months (rational expectations). In principle, notes Cassel, the PPP theory still holds; as the exchange rate is affected by the expected domestic (relative to foreign) price level.

The third case of reverse causation occurs under hyperinflation.[5] In this situation ". . . the causal connection between the rise of prices and the rate of exchange is reversed, that is to say, the falls in the rate of exchange now become the basis for new rises of prices" (1924, p. 69). The reasons are that the domestic currency becomes subject to adverse speculation by foreigners and that the currency becomes replaced by foreign currencies in its domestic roles of medium of exchange and unit of account. When the currency loses its domestic functions, Cassel observes, one cannot reasonably expect the PPP theory to be applicable.

It goes without saying that Cassel rejects the balance-of-payments approach to exchange-rate determination, in particular, "the popular fallacy that the movements of the exchanges could be explained by the balance of trade" (1920a, p. 44). The adjustment mechanism that makes

PPP a stable equilibrium value of the exchange rate would correct any undervaluation (overvaluation) engendering a balance-of-trade surplus (deficit).

Another argument Cassel employs against the balance-of-payments theory involves, in effect, expanding the concept of payments balance underlying the equilibrium exchange rate from the trade or current account to the basic (or perhaps official-settlements) balance (though these payments terms are, of course, not used). He declares that a deficit or surplus on current account would be fully compensated in the capital account. Cassel believes in a well-functioning transfer mechanism; so that a current-account deficit (surplus) is balanced by a surplus (deficit) on autonomous capital account: "For if a country buys more from another than it sells to it, the balance must be paid in some way; say, by export of securities or by loans in the other country. Thus the balance of payments must on the whole equalize itself, and there is no reason for a definite alteration in the rates of exchange" (1921, p. 47).

In the language of the transfer problem, Cassel states: "... a real transfer of capital will not affect the equilibrium of the rate of exchange, which will continue to be determined by the Purchasing Power Parity" (1928b, pp. 17–18). He writes: "... an export of capital is always counterbalanced by an export of goods to the same value. Goods may, of course, be replaced by services... " (1928b, p. 20). This statement is a good indication that Cassel had a basic-balance payments concept in mind.

What if there is a fixed exchange rate (for Cassel, taking the form of the gold standard) rather than a floating rate? Purchasing power parity remains the principal determinant of the exchange rate. If PPP represents the long-run equilibrium exchange rate, then it must be contained within the gold points. Otherwise, over time, the country will either gain or lose international reserves without limit. In a passage vaguely anticipated by Malynes, Cassel writes:

> The purchasing power of each currency has to be regulated so as to correspond to that of gold; and when this is the case, the Purchasing Power Parity will stand in the neighborhood of the gold parity of the two currencies. Only when the purchasing power of a currency is regulated in this way will it be possible to keep the exchanges of this currency in their parities with other gold currencies. If this fundamental condition is not fulfilled, no gold reserve whatever will suffice to guarantee the par exchange of the currency (1928a, pp. 31–32).

Cassel argues that what caused an exchange-rate change under a floating rate now brings about a corresponding change in the domestic price level under a fixed rate. This maintains the law of one price, though not the strict direction of causality postulated by the PPP theory for a floating rate. Ultimately, though, even under the gold standard, the country can determine its price level by controlling its money supply. Cassel rejects the modern monetarist view that a country completely loses the ability to determine its money supply under a fixed rate. He writes:

> But it would be impossible to keep up the gold standard if the purchasing powers of the currencies were not maintained at a corresponding level and if the supply of means of payment in both countries were not regulated to that end (1926, p. 1086).

VI. RELATIVE PPP THEORY

Cassel justifies a theory of relative PPP on the empirical grounds that measures of price levels—required to apply the absolute PPP theory—are virtually impossible to obtain. It is much easier to use a relative-PPP approach since the only price data required are measures of inflation, price index numbers, in the countries considered. He writes: "We have no trustworthy measure for the absolute purchasing power of a currency in its own country. With index numbers, we are only able to determine the relative changes in this purchasing power from time to time" (1932b, p. 660).

Cassel's theory of relative, like that of absolute, PPP is consistently presented throughout his writings. A succinct statement of his theory is "... the rates of exchange should accordingly be expected to deviate from their old parity in proportion to the inflation of each country" (1918, p. 413). A comprehensive description of his theory begins with the actual exchange rate in a base period, which must be a "normal" period. This exchange rate is multiplied by the ratio of proportionate changes in price levels in the countries concerned. The result is the (relative) PPP in the current period.[6] The ideal base period for Cassel is one in which the exchange rate is at its equilibrium level, best of all when that level is the absolute PPP in the base period. He writes that one must:

> ... start from a given equilibrium at a time when the exchange rate is presumed to be known, and on the basis of this rate calculate that rate which corresponds to the same equilibrium if an inflation of the currencies has taken place without any change having otherwise occurred" (1922, pp. 175-76).

The question arises as to whether the PPP so calculated, that is, the relative PPP in the current period, is equal to the absolute PPP newly calculated for this period, presumed to be the new equilibrium exchange rate. The answer is affirmative, according to Cassel, only if the changes in the economies that occurred since the base period were purely monetary in nature. Cassel notes that real changes may occur in this connection: "Strictly speaking, one must take into consideration the possibility that the normal levels [of exchange rates] might be altered somewhat as a result of changes in the entire economic situation of the countries in question, and also in the conditions of trade between them" (1932b, p. 515).

Cassel correctly points out that real changes in an economy will be associated with changes in relative prices. Only under a uniform inflation, where all prices change proportionately, is the calculated relative PPP necessarily equal to the new absolute PPP. This is a neutrality hypothesis for relative PPP. As Cassel writes:

> If in each country prices are unaltered in their relation to one another, but have only undergone a common rise, then there is nothing to prevent our supposing the balance of trade between the countries to be unaltered. The equilibrium of the exchanges must, then, have been dislocated in the manner shown by the ratio of the deterioration of money in the two countries. If, on the other hand, the different prices have moved in their relation to one another, this circumstance may possibly in itself have affected the equilibrium of international trade and have caused some dislocation of the equilibrium of the exchanges (1922, pp. 141–142).

VII. RECOGNIZED LIMITATIONS OF PPP

Cassel's form of the H function (in the symbology of Chapter II) involves the PPP not as the only systematic variable explaining the exchange rate but rather as the most important such variable. He allows room both for random influences and for other (though less important) explanatory variables in the H function. There are many ways in which Cassel makes clear that his PPP theory takes a less restrictive form than the strict "unitary H function."

First, throughout his writings the effect of the PPP on the exchange rate is described in terms suggestive of a nonrestrictive influence. Cassel states that the exchange rate is "determined essentially" or "governed essentially" or determined "in the main," "principally," "approximately," "in a rough sense," or "broadly speaking" by the PPP. He writes that PPP is the "essential factor" or "fundamental factor" or "dominating influence" on the exchange rate. The PPP theory is said to hold "broadly speaking" or in a "rough sense." Holmes (1967b, p. 692) notes that "Cassel *always* had such qualifying phrases. . . ." While this statement is an exaggeration (note the quotations from Cassel in the above section on the absolute PPP theory), it is true that it is difficult, if not impossible, to find entire passages in Cassel's work in which no qualifying language appears.

Second, there are two intriguing passages in Cassel—one relating to absolute, the other to relative PPP—in which the theory is described in weak terms indeed. He writes that absolute PPP ". . . presents a solution of the exchange problem in only a first and quite rough approximation" (1922, p. 139). Ten years later, he argued that relative PPP is ". . .- satisfactory for a first rough calculation of the new equilibrium level of the rates of exchange after big monetary changes have occurred" (1932b, p. 661).

Third, Cassel allows for a random error term in the H function, so that the exchange rate does not equal the PPP even if no other systematic influence is present. It is true that Cassel does not express his equations, and therefore their error terms, in mathematical language; Holmes (1967b, p. 693) argues convincingly, however, that Cassel "did discuss random fluctuations in a literary context" and so included "randomly distributed error terms in the equations of his operational theory."

Cassel speaks of "small fluctuations in the rate of exchange . . . caused by fluctuations of demand and supply of bills on the exchange market" (1928a, p. 32). He declares that even if non-PPP variables that systematically influence the exchange rate are absent or dormant, there may be divergences (described as small and/or temporary) of the exchange rate from the PPP. For example, abstracting from non-PPP factors, he argues that "the rate of exchange . . . cannot show more than small and quite temporary deviations from this level [PPP]" (1928b, p. 17). These are all allusions to a random error term.

Fourth, Cassel acknowledges that there are lags in the adjustment mechanism that corrects an undervaluation or overvaluation of a country's currency with respect to the PPP. In this context he writes: "In reality, however, this restoring of the equilibrium may take a long time, especially if the forces which keep the rate down are powerful and are continually at work" (1922, p. 158).

Fifth, Cassel makes the general qualification that, in principle, any real change in the economy can affect the exchange rate. "Theoretically, any change in the economic conditions in the two countries or in the trade relations between them may cause an alteration in the rate of exchange" (1928c, p. 589). He argues that real changes ("the effects of economic causes on the rate of exchange") are generally dominated by monetary changes ("those of monetary causes, i.e., of alterations of the price levels"):

> . . . alterations of the price level in one country may easily cause the rate of exchange to rise ten or a hundred times or even much more above its former height; whereas, if the general levels of prices in both countries remain constant, only extraordinary perturbations of the economic conditions are likely to call forth movements of the rate of exchange of any practical importance (1928c, p. 590).

Sixth, Cassel explicitly discusses the non-PPP variables in the H function. He provides a large number of reasons why a floating exchange rate may systematically diverge from the PPP. These reasons may be summarized as follows:[7]

1. Trade restrictions may be more severe in one direction than in another. For example, if a country's imports are more restricted than its exports, the exchange value of the country's currency may exceed the PPP.

2. Differences in countries' situations regarding transport costs may also cause the exchange rate to diverge from the PPP.

3. It is possible that speculation in the foreign-exchange market is against a country's currency and therefore reduces the currency's exchange value below the PPP. However, speculation usually plays a stabilizing role in the exchange market, moderating fluctuations in the exchange rate.

4. Anticipated future inflation in a country may lower the exchange value of its currency below the PPP. Similarly, the expectation of domestic deflation—for example, in order to restore a prewar gold parity of the currency—may lead to a currency overvaluation.

5. While the PPP is the primary determinant of the equilibrium exchange rate, a secondary influence is the pattern of relative prices in each country (domestic and foreign).

6. The equilibrium exchange rate is also affected by structural variables in the countries, that is, by the demand and supply of factors of production and by production functions.

7. Changes in relative prices within a country are an indicator of real changes in the economy from a base period, and so involve a divergence between relative PPP and the exchange rate. In particular, if its export prices increase more than prices in general, a country's currency will become undervalued with respect to the PPP.

8. Long-term capital movements can drive the exchange rate away from the PPP. For example, a net long-term capital outflow may depress a country's currency below the PPP. This effect can occur only until the transfer of financial capital is fully effected in real terms, that is, in a corresponding change (in this case, an improvement) in the country's current account.

9. A private short-term capital outflow induced by the desire to evade taxation at home will cause an undervaluation of the country's currency in relation to the PPP.

10. There may be a situation in which a country cannot readily obtain capital inflows to finance a balance-of-trade deficit, and yet the

commodity imports are price-inelastic (perhaps because imports of necessities are involved). In this circumstance both the private sector and government will bid up the price of foreign exchange above the PPP by demanding a specified amount of foreign currency irrespective of price. Here the short-term capital outflow depressing the exchange value of the domestic currency is both private and official in nature.

11. The case of a managed float is recognized. The domestic government, possibly supported by credits from abroad, can intervene in the foreign-exchange market and peg the exchange value of the country's currency above the PPP.

VIII. POLICY IMPLICATIONS

Cassel draws a number of policy implications from his PPP analysis. These guides to government policy may be summarized as follows.

1. The PPP is the ideal rate of exchange from the standpoint of good international relations. For example, if a country's currency is under-valued with respect to the PPP, its exports are effectively subsidized and its imports hindered, much to the annoyance of traders abroad.

2. Direct measures to improve a country's trade balance are an ineffective means of increasing the exchange value of a country's currency. Given stable monetary conditions abroad, the external value of a country's currency will be largely determined by its internal value.

3. Similarly, exchange control should not be used to counter adverse speculation against a country's currency. First of all, speculation has little influence on the exchange rate. Second, exchange control can have deleterious effects and is ineffective insofar as it attempts to prevent a falling internal value of the country's currency from manifesting itself on the foreign-exchange market.

4. Writing in the early and mid-1920s, Cassel warns against countries returning to the gold standard at the prewar parities (referring not to the PPP but to the rate of exchange or mint parity). If countries are to revert to a gold standard, they should do so by fixing the exchange rate (or mint parity) at the level of the current PPP. Otherwise, for countries that have experienced large-scale increases in their price level since 1913, a severe deflationary process will be required to drive the price level down to support an exchange rate set at the prewar parity. This deflation will involve a substantial decline in output and serious unemployment. Again, Cassel is recognizing real effects of a monetary change, in this case, a severely restrictive monetary policy.

5. If the gold standard is re-established, the spread between buying

and selling points should not be reduced. A narrower band would restrict the scope of the adjustment mechanism that counteracts deviations of the exchange rate from the PPP.

6. Instability in exchange rates and in internal values of currencies should be avoided. To stabilize their exchange rates, each country must select an internal value for its currency, that is, a particular price level, and support it by suitable control of the money supply.

7. Because purchasing power parities represent equilibrium exchange rates, they should be computed and placed in the public domain regularly on a monthly basis. To this end, suitable price indices measuring the extent of inflation in different countries and calculated on a uniform basis should be provided.

In tribute to Cassel's great accomplishment of making the PPP theory fully operational, this chapter closes with his plea for more and better data for use in applying the theory.

NOTES

1. Of course, not all participants in this discussion can be readily classified into one group or the other. More interesting, only one writer apparently moved from one camp to the other. John Maynard Keynes was editor, later co-editor, of the *Economic Journal,* at the time that Cassel's first writings on PPP were published, principally in that journal. As editor, Keynes presumably played an important role in accepting Cassel's articles for publication. He also commented favorably on Cassel's theory, both in two editorial notes—one appended to Cassel's first article (1916a), the other independently written by Keynes (1919) in the same issue as Cassel's fifth article (1919)—and in Keynes' *Tract on Monetary Reform* (1923). By the time of his *Treatise* (1930), however, Keynes had become a severe critic of PPP theory.

2. The first to do so was A. C. Pigou (1922), who used the terms "positive" and "comparative." These terms came to be replaced with "absolute" and "relative," respectively.

3. See Chapter IV.

4. See Chapter V.

5. The term is not used by Cassel; he refers to "cases where inflation proceeds with great violence and is so irregular that its progress cannot be foreseen" (1924, p. 69). The experiences of Germany and Austria after World War I are used as empirical examples.

6. The second concept of relative PPP exposited in Chapter II is used.

7. Summaries of Cassel's acknowledged non-PPP influences on the exchange rate are also provided by Angell (1926), Bunting (1939), Sadie (1948), Holmes (1967b), and Myhrman (1976).

Part III

MODERN PPP THEORY AND PRACTICE

Chapter VIII

Exposition and Analysis of PPP

"Under the skin of any international economist lies a deep-seated belief in some variant of the PPP theory of the exchange rate." (Dornbusch and Krugman, 1976, p. 540)

A comprehensive account of the development of PPP theory from (and even before) the beginnings to World War I, in fact, to the time of Gustav Cassel's first published work on PPP in 1916, was provided in Part II. Also exposited was a complete account of Cassel's contributions to PPP analysis. The enormous impact of Cassel caused an explosion of the PPP literature so that any survey of developments since World War I must of necessity be incomplete. It is unmanageable even to attempt a description of all contributions to the PPP approach by author; instead, resort must be had to highlighting the main points in the literature after World War I and providing a review of a sample of the studies of specific writers.

This limited objective is pursued in this Part of the volume, beginning in the present chapter with a treatment of PPP analysis since the work of Cassel. The topic naturally falls into five parts—(i) absolute PPP and (ii) relative PPP, both with reference to price parities, that is, levels or indices of prices as the concept underlying the parity; (iii) cost parity, in which the concept refers to production costs rather than prices; (iv) expressions of the theory with reference to the forward rather than spot exchange rate; and (v) reformulation of the theory in terms of expected exchange rates and expected inflation at home and abroad.

I. ABSOLUTE PRICE PARITY

Cassel's presentation and justification of the absolute PPP theory has not been superseded to the present day.[1] Both critics[2] and supporters[3]—as

105

well as those expressing no personal views regarding the theory's validity[4]—exposit the theory in terms virtually indistinguishable from those of Cassel. Thus Yeager writes, with approval: "People value currencies primarily for what they will buy and, in uncontrolled markets, tend to exchange them at rates that roughly express their relative purchasing powers" (1958, p. 516). Batchelor (1977, p. 45), without taking a stand on the theory, describes it again in a Casselian way:

> ... units of each currency initially derive their real value within the issuing countries in terms of the volume of domestically produced goods against which they can be exchanged. When trade is opened between two countries, their domestic goods compete as exports or import substitutes and so the prices they command in local currency terms and in terms of the foreign country's currency must be equalised. This determines the rate of exchange as the ratio of output prices expressed in each currency. Equilibrium external currency valuations are, in this *purchasing power parity* theory, derived ultimately from their real internal values ...

Some critics, however, use a *reductio ad absurdum* to destroy the theory:

> Of course, under perfect competition, free trade without tariffs, quotas, or exchange controls, relative prices of one good could not deviate regionally if transport costs were zero. In that case only, *each* competitive good's international price ratio ... would have to equal the official free exchange rate *exactly,* as a result of quick acting competitive arbitrage; and what is true for each and every good, must be true for the average index number of price (Samuelson, 1974, p. 602).

Under the extreme conditions outlined by Samuelson (and others before him),[5] the existing exchange rate—whether freely floating, managed floating, or pegged—cannot deviate even infinitesimally from the PPP, except to the extent that there are imperfections in the arbitrage process. This removes all operational content from the theory.

In contrast, the absolute price parity theory in the tradition of Cassel does not rely on the unrealistic assumption that *all* commodities are traded and without transport costs, tariffs, or quantitative restrictions. In particular, the theory accepts the fact that there are nontraded goods, but notes that the prices of traded and nontraded goods are closely related through links such as transportation and communication facilities, technological developments (for example, the invention of synthetic materials), the international diffusion of technologies, interindustry production relationships, the use of common factors of production, and the ability of different commodities to satisfy the same consumption demand more or less equivalently. These links all serve to connect markets of even seemingly disparate commodities both within a country and between countries.[6]

Some opponents of the theory, such as Katseli-Papaefstratiou (1979, pp.6,7), correctly note the implication of these market interconnections for the PPP theory: a high degree of *domestic* substitution in consumption and production between internationally traded and nontraded commodities. This phenomenon combines with the "law of one price" for traded commodities (of course, subject to imperfections in the arbitrage process) to yield the PPP theory in operational form, involving price levels for all commodities, tradables and nontradables. Haberler, also critical of PPP, describes its basis correctly: "The proposition that general price levels in different countries are connected through the prices of internationally traded goods is the foundation of the purchasing-power parity doctrine" (1975, p. 24).

Furthermore, although acknowledging the existence of both traded and nontraded goods, proponents of PPP emphasize that these two groups are not unvarying collections of commodities. Cassel himself had noted that the set of traded goods can expand or contract with an alteration in the exchange rate. This view is supported by Yeager: "Actually, the line between domestic and internationally traded goods is a fuzzy and shifting one" (1958, p. 522).

An alternative justification of a PPP theory applying to nontraded as well as traded commodities is provided in the section on "cost parity" below.

With the PPP theory thus based on general price levels, the assumption must be made that the ratio of the price of tradables to the price of nontradables is relatively invariant to real changes in the economy. Skeptics of the theory, such as Haberler (1975, p. 25) and Isard (1978, p. 5), stress this assumption. Cassel himself was aware of this limitation of the theory, though he discussed it in terms of export prices rather than prices of all traded goods.

Two other modern developments of the absolute PPP theory should be mentioned. First, Yeager (1958; 1968; 1976), in all his theoretical writings on PPP, stresses the "stabilizing pressures" aspect of the theory. As did Cassel before him, Yeager emphasizes that the adjustment mechanism that makes exchange rates tend toward their PPP equilibria involves high price elasticities in commodity markets. He writes: "So far as the parity doctrine holds true, supply and demand in international trade respond sensitively enough to prices not to require extreme divergent shifts in the prices of domestic and international goods to correct balance-of-payments disequilibriums" (1968, p. 75).

Second, often in the most recent literature the PPP theory is stated in the form of the "law of one price."[7] In terms of symbols used earlier in this volume:

$$L = L^f/R$$

where $L(L^f)$ is the domestic (foreign) price level and R the exchange rate (price of domestic currency in terms of foreign currency). Of course, the equation is abstracting from an error term and variables systematically inhibiting the strict relationship.

Under a fixed exchange rate, the domestic price level is determined by the foreign price level, assuming that the home country is relatively small. Alternatively, L^f may be interpreted as the world price level, and any effect of domestic macroeconomic policy on its own price level occurs through influencing the world price level. The PPP theory (in the form of the law of one price) thereby accounts for the international transmission of inflation. Under a floating exchange rate, the domestic economy regains control of its monetary policy and thereby its price level. The law of one price now determines the exchange rate in accordance with the standard PPP theory. Again, this analysis of fixed versus floating rates can be gleaned from Cassel's writings.

II. RELATIVE PRICE PARITY

Even more than Cassel's theory of absolute PPP, his theory of relative PPP remains essentially unchanged in the modern literature. Only Cassel's neutrality theorem for relative PPP has received elaboration. It is recalled that the issue is whether the relative PPP in the current period equals the absolute PPP for that period, where relative PPP is the product of the foreign/domestic price-index ratio and the base-period exchange rate (price of domestic currency in terms of foreign currency), the latter assumed equal to base-period absolute PPP. Cassel's answer was that the equality holds subject that only monetary changes, and no real changes, occurred in the economies since the base period.

In his answer, Cassel is at one with his critics. Viner writes: "The one type of case which would meet the requirement of exact inversely proportional changes in price levels and in exchange rates would be a monetary change in one country . . . which would operate to change all prices and money incomes in that country in equal degree, while every other element in the situation, in both countries, remained absolutely constant" (1937, p. 384). Similar discussions of the case of proportionate changes in exchange rates and price levels with no real changes are provided by Samuelson (1948, p. 399), Vanek (1962, p. 84), Stern (1973, pp. 144–146), Dornbusch and Jaffee (1978, p. 157), Girton and Roper (1978, pp. 222–224), Humphrey (1979, p. 5), and Officer (1978, pp. 562–563). Perhaps the most rigorous discussion of the neutrality theorem is that of Michaely (1980).

The assumptions required for the neutrality theorem to hold have been carefully presented in the post-Cassel literature. One assumption underlying the theorem is that there be no money illusion, that is, all commodity demand and supply functions in each country must be homogeneous of degree zero in all nominal prices. This assumption has been pointed out by Lee (1976, pp. 1–2) and Stockman (1980, p. 675), among others.

A second assumption is that monetary changes or disturbances do not in themselves involve real changes in the economy; that is, real variables are invariant with respect to nominal variables. In other words, the real exchange rate, defined in the Horner-Blake tradition as the ratio of the nominal (market) exchange rate to the PPP (relative, second concept, in the terminology of Chapter II), is unaffected by monetary changes.

Even the monetarists would acknowledge that changes in the nominal money supply can systematically affect real variables in the short run, except in the limiting case of inflationary expectations that are both "rational" and fully incorporated into current behavior, with instantaneous reflection in wages and prices.[8] The relative-PPP neutrality result is founded on the neutrality of money, which in general occurs only in the long run. Therefore the PPP neutrality theorem pertains, strictly speaking, only to the long run.[9]

In the short run (and also in the long run unless ideal conditions are fulfilled), real changes will take place in economies either as autonomous shocks or as a consequence of monetary disturbances. Then the relative PPP theorem will not hold exactly. However, if the monetary changes dominate the real changes, relative PPP still applies, although in an approximate fashion. This is certainly the position of Cassel. A good recent statement in this spirit is made by Stockman (1980, p. 675):

> . . . a change in the stock of money will, other things the same, be associated with a corresponding increase in all nominal prices including the nominal price of foreign exchange. . . . The purchasing power parity hypothesis, which states that there is a proportional relationship between the exchange rate and a ratio of foreign and domestic prices or price indexes, can be thought of as stating that other things *are* approximately the same.

III. COST PARITY

Arguments in favor of cost over price parity theories have been presented even by critics and evaluators of PPP, and are outlined as follows. (1) Costs of production are less subject to adjustment to exchange-rate changes than are prices of traded goods.[10] (2) Costs exclude the volatile component profits and so are more likely than product prices to represent long-run prices (for absolute parity) and to reflect permanent rather than temporary changes in prices upon inflation or deflation (for relative parity).[11] (3) A country's exporters may sell at world prices, with currency overvaluation reflected not in prices but in losses incurred or markets lost. In this situation, cost levels or indices may indicate the overvaluation.[12] These arguments, however, do not justify a cost parity as such, only its superiority in certain respects over a price parity.

Most recently, Artus (1978, p. 287) offers two further points in favor of the cost parity concept. First, the structure of factor prices (in particular, wage rates) within a country changes less over time than the structure of commodity prices. In other words, relative factor prices are more stable than relative product prices. Second, wage rates in the tradable sector of the economy are less susceptible to direct foreign influences than are commodity prices. One can interpret this statement to mean that the "law of one price," while necessarily holding for traded goods at any current exchange rate (subject only to arbitrage imperfections) applies far less to factors of production in these industries. Again, these are arguments in favor of a cost parity over a price parity, rather than establishing the cost-parity concept in itself.

The earliest proponent of cost parity is Sven Brisman (1933). He rejects price parities mainly on the grounds that they do not measure a country's competitiveness ("ability to compete") on the world market. In their place, he proposes an absolute cost parity calculated from the "effective cost of production" at home and abroad. It is clear that Brisman has a unit-factor-cost (UFC) concept in mind; for he explicitly states the elements of effective cost as wages, interest, rent (which can be ignored because of its small magnitude), and changes in productivity. Brisman notes that his parity concept cannot generally be employed in a quantitative fashion, because UFC is impossible to calculate statistically, owing to the unavailability of data.

Hansen (1944) also proposes an absolute cost parity, but in vaguer terms than Brisman. He calls it a "cost structure parity" and does not discuss its component cost measures. Further, unlike Brisman, Hansen does not reject the price-parity concept outright. Rather, he indicates that "cost structure parity" is a preferred way of stating the PPP theory. The cost structure parity provides the correct exchange rate that assigns factors of production to those export industries, and only those export industries, where the country has a comparative advantage.

A cost-parity theory that reduces to a price parity is offered by Houthakker (1962a; 1962b; 1963). He begins with an absolute-parity theory that is founded on UFC, which (he states) may be approximated by unit labor cost (ULC), since labor is the most important factor of production.

Again, the justification is in terms of competitiveness. Houthakker mentions, however, that the existence of long-term capital movements and unilateral transfers may cause the long-run equilibrium exchange rate to differ from the UFC parity. A net outflow would require greater competitiveness for the country's exports, that is, a lower exchange value for the currency than that given by the parity. He notes that this modification is not required to the extent that the capital flows are themselves caused by the deviation of the current exchange rate from the UFC parity.

Officer (1974) interprets Houthakker's theory as follows. Abstracting both from factors of production other than labor and from labor costs other than wages, the UFC parity (number of units of B-currency per unit of A-currency) is given by

$$\frac{W^B}{W^A} \cdot \frac{PR^A}{PR^B}$$

where W^i = wage rate in country i
PR^i = productivity in country i

Officer's justification of the ULC parity theory is that, to retain long-run balance-of-payments equilibrium, a rise in the wage rate relative to that abroad, if not compensated by an increase in productivity, requires a reduced exchange value of the country's currency.

Houthakker (1962a, p. 296) demonstrates that his ULC parity is equivalent to a COL price parity. His argument, however, is highly condensed and involves stronger assumptions than he recognizes. Relying on Officer's interpretation (1974, pp. 868–873), let

MPL^i = marginal product of labor in country i
P^i = price level in country i

Assume that (i) aggregate production functions of the two countries differ only by a neutral and constant efficiency factor, namely, PR^A/PR^B, so that

$$MPL^A = \frac{PR^A}{PR^B} \cdot MPL^B \tag{1}$$

and (ii) there is long-run pure competition in factor markets, so that the marginal-productivity theory of wages applies, that is,

$$W^i = P^i \cdot MPL^i \qquad i = A, B \tag{2}$$

Then, in the long run, factor-price equalization would exist at the aggregate level except for the efficiency factor; this factor is carried over into the international relationship of real wage rates:

$$\frac{W^A}{P^A} = \frac{PR^A}{PR^B} \cdot \frac{W^B}{P^B} \tag{3}$$

Reordering Equation (3),

$$\frac{W^B}{W^A} \cdot \frac{PR^A}{PR^B} = \frac{P^B}{P^A} \tag{4}$$

Thus, the absolute UFC parity is equal to an absolute price parity, but what kind of price levels (P^A and P^B) compose the latter parity? Each country's price level is a production-weighted average of commodity prices in that country, where the weights are specific to each country, that is, they refer to the country's own production pattern. The reason is that the intercountry relationship of marginal products of labor [Equation (1)] and the marginal-productivity theory of wages [Equation (2)] both refer to *production* within each country. Thus, the price levels pertain to the GDP in each country, and the result is an absolute GDP price parity theory.

What are the additional requirements to transform the ULC parity further, into a COL price parity? In other words, what are the conditions under which household consumption weights (again specific to each country) can be substituted for production weights in the computation of the price levels without altering the value of the GDP price parity?

First, there must be international equalization, at the parity rate, not only of the GDP price *level* but also of individual prices for all commodities. For traded commodities, international arbitrage guarantees this result at *any* current exchange rate, whether or not it is equal to the parity rate, providing that one abstracts from trade restrictions and transportation costs. For nontraded commodities, either pure competition or "equal degrees of monopoly" in domestic product markets are necessary for price equalization. The former assumption ensures that price is equal to ULC, the latter that the same percentage deviation between price and ULC occurs in each country. Second, production and household consumption patterns must be the same both within each country and between countries. Only then can one be assured that the calculated parity is invariant with respect to the choice of production or household consumption weights for the price levels.

Obviously, these additional assumptions are unlikely to be fulfilled, so that Houthakker's switching from production to household consumption weights in computing the price levels for absolute price parity entails some index-number problems, at the least—given that one begins with the absolute ULC parity theory. In fairness to Houthakker, it should be noted that it was lack of data on UFC or ULC parities and, presumably, also on GDP price parities that induced him to re-express his theory in terms of the COL price parity. It should also be stated that Houthakker (1978), while still considering the PPP theory as best expressed in terms of wage rates and relative productivity, has become much more skeptical of the theory.[13]

Friedman and Schwartz (1963, pp. 62–63, fn. 66) offer the unique viewpoint of rejecting price parity on the grounds that product price indices include the effect of changes in productivity. They argue that the logic of PPP is that the indices used to compute the parity should refer to monetary changes alone and not incorporate changes in productivity, which are real (nonmonetary) in nature. Implicitly, Friedman and Schwartz are also rejecting a UFC or ULC parity, and indeed they advocate that the parity be constructed from indices of factor prices weighted by employment (and with no allowance for changes in productivity). As a second best, a price parity may be calculated from product price indices, where the prices of individual commodities are weighted by the volume of domestic production "as a proxy for volume of resources employed."

IV.   FORWARD EXCHANGE RATE

Two authors have proposed a PPP theory of the forward exchange rate, applying to a situation in which the domestic currency is overvalued or undervalued with respect to the PPP. Syrett (1936) argues that when the domestic currency is overvalued, commodity imports are stimulated and traders cover open positions in foreign exchange for fear of a depreciation of the domestic currency. The result is an enhanced demand for forward exchange and a fall in the forward exchange rate (price of domestic currency in terms of foreign currency) to a discount with respect to the spot rate, that is, closer to the PPP than the (overvalued) spot rate. An analogous argument applies to an undervalued currency.

Why is the domestic currency overvalued or undervalued in the spot market? The reason may be that the currency is pegged, either to a par value under a fixed-rate system or via exchange-rate management under a managed float.

A quarter-century after Syrett wrote, Einzig (1962) refined his analysis by making it complementary with, rather than a substitute for, the interest-rate parity theory of forward exchange. Several reasons for a discounted forward rate in the presence of an overvalued spot rate are offered—an adverse movement in the trade balance, with forward selling of the domestic currency exceeding foreign buying on commercial account, higher interest rates at home, capital flight, leads and lags, hedging against exchange risk on assets located in the domestic country, and anticipation of a devaluation. The first and last reasons are essentially in Syrett's analysis.

Suppose that one defines the theoretical forward rate as that predicted by the interest-parity theory, that is, the product of the spot exchange rate and the ratio of unity plus the foreign interest rate to unity plus the domestic interest rate. Then Einzig argues that when the spot exchange rate is overvalued or undervalued with respect to the PPP, (i) the theoretical forward rate tends to be between the spot rate and the PPP, and (ii) the actual foward rate tends to be between the theoretical forward rate and the PPP. An overvalued (undervalued) spot rate with reference to PPP involves an undervalued (overvalued) forward rate in terms of the theoretical rate.

V. EXPECTATIONS

The Syrett-Einzig model has the defect that no attention is paid to inflationary expectations. Inspired by the pioneering work of Irving Fisher (1907; 1930), a PPP model integrating parity conditions in the commodity and financial (bond) markets has developed. In this approach, expectations of inflation at home and abroad play the key role. Further in contrast to the Syrett-Einzig model, the forward exchange rate is not an essential element in the theory. Consider the following notation:

R (F) = spot (forward) exchange rate, number of units of foreign currency per unit of domestic currency

π (π_f) = rate of inflation in the domestic (foreign) country

i (i_f) = nominal interest rate in the domestic (foreign) country

r (r_f) = real interest rate in the domestic (foreign) country

All variables are comparable in the sense that they are defined with respect to the same time unit. Expected values of variables are denoted by means of a superscripted asterisk (*). It is assumed that expectations are identical in the two countries. We begin with the definition of the real interest rate as the difference between the nominal interest rate and the expected rate of inflation. This identity, which Aliber (1978) calls the "Fisher Closed proposition," applies to both countries:

$$i \equiv r + \pi^*$$
$$i_f \equiv r_f + \pi_f^* \tag{5}$$

Next, one applies the "law of one price" to real interest rates:

$$r = r_f \tag{6}$$

International equality of real interest rates occurs because investors are concerned with the real, not nominal, return on their assets. In attempting to maximize the real return on their portfolios, they transfer capital from a country with a lower real interest rate to one with a higher real rate. This arbritrage process results in the equalization of real interest rates across countries. This "law of one interest rate" is an analogue to the "law of one price" formulation of the PPP theory.

For simplicity, in this and subsequent equations, a random error term and variables that might systematically affect the relationship are omitted. For the "law of one interest rate," such variables would include transactions costs, riskiness of returns, and taxation.

The Fisher Closed proposition (5) and the law of one interest rate (6) together imply that the nominal interest-rate differential between the two countries equals their difference in expected inflation:

$$i_f - i = \pi_f^* - \pi^* \tag{7}$$

Then one can assert what Aliber (1978) named the "Fisher Open proposition," called by Giddy (1976) the "interest-rate theory of exchange-rate expectations." If the domestic country's currency is expected to appreciate (depreciate) by a certain percentage, then assets denominated in that currency will experience a capital gain (loss) by that same amount. Unless the foreign nominal interest rate is greater (less) than the domestic rate by the same (absolute) percent, an arbitrage process involving international capital movements will take place to bring about this relationship. So we have

$$\frac{R^* - R}{R} = i_f - i \tag{8}$$

Substituting Equation (7) into (8), we obtain:

$$\frac{R^* - R}{R} = \pi_f^* - \pi^* \tag{9}$$

Equation (9) is a relative-PPP theory in which all variables take on their expectational value rather than current value. The expected appreciation (depreciation) of the domestic currency in the exchange market equals (apart from a random error term and systematic inhibiting influences) the difference between the expected inflation of the foreign and the domestic price levels.

If one is willing to assume universal rational expectations, then the actual percentage change in the exchange rate equals the foreign/domestic difference in the actual rate of inflation, apart from nonsystematic effects that may be embodied in a random error term.[14] The variables in Equation (9) are redefined as follows: R^* (R) is the current-period (base-period) exchange rate and π_f^* (π^*) the actual rate of foreign (domestic) inflation between the base and current periods.

What results is the conventional relative-PPP theory (expressed in rates of change of prices and the exchange rate),[15] and it has been obtained without reliance on the law of one price in commodity markets, indeed, without resort to commodity-market arbitrage at all. To recapitulate, the relative-PPP theory as developed here emanates from the Fisher Open and Closed propositions, the law of one interest rate, and rational expectations in the foreign-exchange market and commodity markets.

Equation (9) may also be obtained without reliance on the Fisher open proposition. Instead, one asserts the interest-rate parity theorem in its approximate form:

$$\frac{F - R}{R} = i_f - i \tag{10}$$

Substituting Equation (7) into Equation (10) yields:

$$\frac{F - R}{R} = \pi_f^* - \pi^* \tag{11}$$

Alternatively, Equation (11) may be derived by postulating that the absolute PPP theory holds both in the spot market (the usual formulation) and the forward market. In the latter market, absolute PPP is in terms of the forward exchange rate and *futures* prices (or rather, futures price levels). Equation (11) is then obtained as an approximate relationship.[16] Of course, the existence of futures markets for all commodities is an unrealistic assumption.[17] Pippenger (1972) derives Equation (11) using both approaches, but he does not take the further step of introducing exchange-rate expectations.

Suppose now that the forward rate equals the expected spot rate:

$$F = R^* \tag{12}$$

Equation (12), subject as always to a random error term, may be justified as a result of arbitrage between the spot and forward exchange markets. Substituting Equation (12) into Equation (11) yields Equation (9). Again, one can impose rational expectations and obtain a variant of the conventional relative-PPP theory.

There is an enormous body of literature on the non-PPP relationships discussed in this section, namely, the Fisher Open and Closed propositions, the interest-rate parity theory, the law of one (real) interest rate, and the theory that the forward rate is an unbiased measure of the expected spot rate.[18] So, with one exception, these relationships will not be discussed further in this volume.[19]

NOTES

1. The sole exception is the derivation of absolute price parity from a unit-factor-cost parity, discussed later in this chapter.
2. For example, Terborgh (1926, pp. 197–198).
3. For example, Yeager (1958, p. 516; 1976, p. 210).
4. For example, Humphrey (1979, pp. 3–4).
5. See Chapter IX.
6. For good discussions of the links that closely relate markets of different commodities and of similar commodities in different locations, see Yeager (1958, pp. 520, 522; 1976, p. 218) and the references cited there, as well as Batchelor (1977, p. 46).
7. For example, see Helliwell (1979, pp. 425–426).
8. Of course, some economists have a view of the world that involves this case as "normal" rather than "limiting." A good critical survey of the "rational-expectations" position that systematic macroeconomic policies can have no real effects on the economy is provided by Berkman (1980).
9. This property of the theorem is emphasized by Samuelson (1964, p. 146; 1971, p. 6, fn. 4; 1974, p. 602).
10. See Metzler (1947, p. 21), Ellsworth (1950, p. 596), Stern (1973, p. 147, fn. 31), and Harris (1936, pp. 39–40).
11. See Metzler (1947, p. 21), Samuelson (1964, p. 149), and Stern (1973, p. 147, fn. 31).
12. See Harris (1936, p. 40).
13. He provides numerical examples that "strongly suggest that absolute PPP is less useful for the analysis of disequilibrium than some proponents, including Houthakker (1962), had believed" (1978, p. 75).
14. This approach is consistent with the brief summary of Isard (1978, p. 4), actually a critic of the model.
15. For the redefined variables, Equation (9) may be readily derived as an approximate relationship from a usual form of the relative-PPP theory, say, the ratio of the current-period to base-period exchange rate equals the ratio of the foreign to the domestic price index. A step-by-step derivation is provided by Giddy (1976, pp. 884–885).
16. For the derivation of the corresponding exact relationship, see Pippenger (1972, pp. 377–378). Equation (11) may be obtained from the exact relationship by means of a procedure analogous to that found in Giddy (1976, pp. 884–885).

17. However, a justification for assuming the existence of futures prices for internationally traded goods is offered by Pippenger (1972, p. 377, fn. 4).

18. Solnik (1980) provides a careful theoretical discussion of some of these relationships under both the ideal circumstances that make them hold without error and deviations from these conditions.

19. The exception is the Fisher Open proposition, to be mentioned again in Chapter X.

Chapter IX

Criticisms of Purchasing Power Parity

"...the complete rejection of PPP is as mistaken as its complete acceptance." (Hendrik S. Houthakker, 1978, p. 71)

Limitations of the PPP theory can be divided into four groups: index-number problems of the price-parity concept; other weaknesses of price parity, absolute and relative forms separately; and difficulties with the cost-parity concept. Cassel himself recognized most of the objections to the PPP theory stated by opponents of the approach, except for those criticisms specific to cost parity.[1] In this chapter, reference to Cassel's views will be made principally for those limitations of PPP not specifically covered in Chapter VII.

I. INDEX-NUMBER PROBLEMS

The first set of limitations of PPP is statistical in nature, relating to the method of computing the parity itself. Of course, the individual prices used to construct the price level or price index for PPP must be presumed to reflect accurately the prices at which transactions occur in a free market. The existence of effective rationing and/or price controls in one or both countries would distort the measured PPP so it does not reflect true relative buying power in the countries. This point is mentioned by Yeager (1958, p. 530; 1976, p. 223), but had been made earlier by Cassel himself (1921, pp. 17–18; 1922, pp. 47–48).

Pigou (1922, pp. 67–68) noted that actual price indices are calculated from individual prices of only a sample of commodities rather than all

119

commodities in the economy. Therefore, any computed price parity is an imperfect representation of the true theoretical parity.

A related difficulty is present even if the entire population of commodities is used to construct the price measure in each country. The value of the parity will, in general, depend on the kind of price level (or price index) selected. In other words, the parity will vary with the weighting pattern of the price measures. The sole exception, as noted by Vanek (1962, p. 84), is when (1) the ratio of the price of a given commodity in one country to its price in the other country is the same for all commodities and (2) the identical weighting pattern is used for the computation of each country's price measure.

Even if the price measures refer to traded goods alone and there is costless international arbitrage of these goods (no trade restrictions or transport costs and no imperfection in the arbitrage process), different weighting schemes for the countries' price levels (or price indices) will, in general, lead to different parities, none of which can be expected to equal the "true" parity (namely, the current exchange rate, in this case), which equalizes all individual commodity prices internationally. Condition (1) is satisfied, but not condition (2). Samuelson (1964, p. 147) declares that this point is widely overlooked; but Keynes (1930, pp. 73-74) certainly had it in mind, and Viner (1937, pp. 383-84) stated it quite clearly.

Katseli-Papaefstratiou (1979, p. 5) believes that this aggregation problem is important "since countries' tastes, economic structures, and accounting practices vary widely." In a similar vein, Artus (1978, p. 286) sees the fact that "the various countries produce the various kinds of tradable goods in different proportions" as giving rise "to an unsolvable index number problem," because of changes in relative prices of the different kinds of tradable goods.

Keynes (1930, pp. 72-74) was the first to point out that a PPP calculated from traded-goods prices alone is close to a truism, drawing the implication that wholesale price indices (WPIs) are a poor basis for computing PPP. The reason is that such indices are heavily weighted with traded goods ("the staple commodities of international trade") and therefore relative price parities calculated from these indices come close to the actual exchange rate, resulting in a spurious verification of the theory. The bias in the test was overlooked, Keynes (1930, pp. 73-74) notes, just because the results could not be perfect:

> Since, however, these index-numbers generally include two or three commodities which do not enter freely into international trade, and since the systems of weighting and the grades and qualities of the selected articles are various, there has been

just that degree of discrepancy in the "verifications" to make the Theory seem *prima facie* interesting.

Keynes' observation led subsequent observers to recommend against calculating parities with price indices weighted entirely or heavily with internationally traded goods and, in particular, to reject export and import price indices and WPIs for this purpose.[2] A more sanguine view toward the WPI is taken by Thygesen (1978, p. 304), who argues that the WPI gives a heavy weight to "domestic cost elements, so that conformity to a parallel price trend in different countries cannot be interpreted mainly as a result of efficient commodity arbitrage." Thygesen's position is clearly outside the mainstream of the PPP literature.

In addition to the Keynesian negative case in favor of a broad price measure, one incorporating nontraded as well as traded commodities, several positive arguments for a price concept involving all commodities produced in the economy were offered in Chapters VII and VIII. Some recent authors suggest additional reasons. Genberg (1978, p. 263) declares that "purchasing power parity is a macroeconomic concept and as such should be measured by a relatively broadly based index." Frenkel (1976, pp. 201–203; 1978, pp. 172–174) takes the viewpoint that those who consider commodity arbitrage as the motivating force behind the PPP relationship must logically confine the price measure to traded-goods prices. In contrast, proponents of the asset-market approach to exchange-rate determination—for whom the exchange rate equilibrates financial markets by equalizing the purchasing power of currencies at home and abroad—advocate a general price measure for PPP, one incorporating both traded and nontraded commodities.

Surely the two approaches cited by Frenkel are complementary rather than competitive. In Chapter VIII we presented a case for a broad-based price measure based on commodity arbitrage and strong substitutability of commodities in production and consumption. One can just as well declare that the motivating force behind the PPP theory involves asset markets rather than commodity markets. If the purchasing power of money differs between countries, more of the higher-valued money will be demanded in place of the lower-valued money. The value of money, of course, is its purchasing power in terms of commodities, and therefore varies inversely with the price level in the country of issuance. So arbitrage involving the monies of the countries concerned leads to the usual PPP result.[3]

This international arbitrage in money is complementary to international arbitrage in commodities, and the former may be interpreted as an intermediate step to the latter. After all, the underlying motivation is the same in both cases: money is valued for its purchasing power, what it can buy in terms of goods and services.

It is within the spirit of both the PPP theory and the asset-market approach to the exchange rate, to extend the asset markets that must be equilibrated beyond domestic and foreign money to those for other financial instruments. The PPP result can then be viewed as one of the mechanisms that produces equilibrium in the various asset markets in the countries.[4]

With traded-goods price indices and WPIs unsuitable, evaluators of PPP generally suggest that parities be constructed with cost-of-living (COL) price measures.[5] For some observers, this recommendation carries with it the requirement that the weighting pattern be the same for each country's price level, that is, that an identical basket of goods be priced in each country. Thus Stern writes: "In principle, the calculation of PPP on the basis of the absolute interpretation requires taking a common basket of goods with a standard system of weighting for the individual countries" (1973, p. 143). Yeager takes the same position in stronger terms: "The 'absolute' or 'positive' approach to rate calculation ideally envisages the pricing in local currency in each of two countries of a standard assortment of goods and services, the same for the two countries and yet duly representative of economic life in each" (1958, p. 517). As this dual requirement is impossible (unless the countries happen to have identical consumption or production patterns), Yeager rejects absolute PPP as non-operational.

Insofar as price parity is founded on a factor-cost or unit-factor-cost (UFC) parity, however, Officer (1974, pp. 868–70) argues that each country's *own* pattern of production is the ideal source of weights to construct its price measure for the parity computation.[6] In effect, a PPP measure based on a gross-domestic-product (GDP) deflator or price level is advocated. This position is also taken implicitly by Houthakker (1962a, p. 296) and explicitly by Friedman and Schwartz (1963, pp. 62–63, fn. 66).

If the foundation of absolute price parity on UFC parity is to be rejected, the problem arises of selecting the common bundle of commodities. An obvious possibility is to take the consumption pattern in one of the countries and apply it to the prices of both. It is well known and now commonly pointed out in the literature that the two alternative weighting patterns entail divergent biases in the computed parity.[7] Consumption expenditure in each country will be concentrated on those commodities with lower relative prices. Consider the country the weighting pattern of which is used for the computation of both countries' price levels. The calculated parity will involve an exchange value for that country's currency greater than that given by the "true" parity. The usual practice is to apply Irving Fisher's ideal index-number formula, that is, to take the geometric mean of the parities calculated alternatively using the one and then the other country's expenditure weights.[8] The solution is reasonable because the biases are in opposite directions. As implied by Officer (1974, pp. 872–73), there is a case in which these biases do not exist; namely, if, at the current exchange rate, prices of all commodities are equalized in the two countries (the Vanek example noted above). In this event, all relative prices are the same in each country. Unless demand patterns happen to be identical in the two countries, the use of the consumption weights of one country or the other to construct both countries' price levels will, in general, still give rise to different computed parities; but there is now no reason to expect these parities to have divergent or even systematic biases with respect to an ideally constructed parity.

II. ABSOLUTE PRICE PARITY

Criticisms of absolute price parity fall neatly into two categories: (1) those that suggest a reduced accuracy with which the short-run equilibrium exchange rate approaches the PPP, without refuting the proposition that this tendency exists; and (2) those that deny the basic premise of PPP theory, namely, that a freely floating exchange rate tends to the PPP. The first group of criticisms can be incorporated within the existing framework of PPP theory, and indeed some are admitted modifications of the theory according to its proponents. The second group is incompatible with PPP as it stands; if these criticisms are correct, fundamental changes in the theory are needed to preserve its validity.

The existence of tariffs and transport costs may be expected to give rise to a deviation of the short-run equilibrium exchange rate from the PPP, the amount of this deviation varying directly with the severity of the imperfections.[9] In particular, when trade restrictions take the form of sufficiently high and comprehensive tariff walls, quotas, or exchange control, a freely floating (or any maintained) exchange rate may bear virtually no relationship to the PPP, because the price responsiveness of imports and exports is greatly reduced.[10] PPP becomes all the more inapplicable if controls are extended to the domestic sector in the form, for example, of price and wage controls, rationing of consumer goods, and industry allocation of raw materials and primary factors of production. Under these conditions, the buying power of the country's currency is but poorly reflected in market prices.[11] This issue was mentioned as an index-number problem in the previous section.

PPP theory emphasizes the role of prices in exchange-rate determination; yet incomes are also relevant. Yeager (1958, p. 518; 1976, p. 215) counters this criticism by arguing that deviations of the exchange rate from the PPP owing to income forces will bring about price-determined trade flows to reduce the deviations. Furthermore, he notes, movements in prices over the business cycle tend to correspond to movements in income, while long-run trends in real output are likely to affect import demand and export supply in the same direction. A point overlooked by Yeager is that PPP represents the *long-run* equilibrium exchange rate, which should not be responsive to cyclical variations in income. So the neglect of income considerations cannot be considered a fundamental weakness of the theory.

The existence of non-current-account items is a well-known limitation of PPP theory. Cassel himself assigned a role to both short-term speculation and long-run capital movements as determinants of the market exchange rate under a free float, that is, the short-run equilibrium exchange rate. Other authors; for example, Houthakker (1962a), Officer (1974), and Aliber (1978, p. 147, fn. 1); see long-term capital flows as influencing exchange-rate long-run equilibrium as well. In this context, unilateral transfers may be incorporated in long-term capital.

The impact of international capital movements on the PPP theory is a function of the magnitude and persistence of the flows involved. To have a long-run impact on the exchange rate, the flows must persist in significant magnitude net in one direction.[12] Furthermore, as Houthakker (1962a, p. 294; 1962b, p. 12) emphasizes, not all capital movements are autonomous variables in an extended PPP theory; some may be induced by the divergence of a pegged exchange rate from the PPP. Finally, Yeager (1958, p. 518; 1976, p. 215) notes again that a deviation of the actual exchange rate from the PPP, caused now by capital movements (or, in fact, by any nontrade flows), will give rise to the corrective force of price-induced trade flows.

A criticism of a different nature is that PPP views the exchange rate as the determined variable and price levels as causal variables, whereas there are also chains of causation running from exchange rates to prices. This is a long-standing criticism of PPP; so its advocates are numerous. Among them are Keynes (1923, pp. 95–96), Whittaker (1940, pp. 668–69), Machlup (1964, p. 27), Samuelson (1948, pp. 405–406), and Balassa (1964, pp. 591–92). Yeager (1958, pp. 520–22; 1976, pp. 223–26) presents the most creditable defense of the theory against this criticism. He declares that mutual causation of exchange rates and prices is compatible with PPP theory providing that the line of causation is stronger from price levels to the exchange rate, which he argues is true for a floating exchange rate under normal circumstances (these circumstances guaranteed by a responsible monetary policy). In other words, and more generally, one can resort to the traditional line of causation of PPP proponents: from the money supply to the price level to the exchange rate. This monetary influence on the exchange rate is so strong as to dominate any reverse causation of the exchange rate on domestic prices.

A further point in his favor overlooked by Yeager is that influences of the exchange rate on price levels are generally short run in nature, whereas the PPP theory asserts that price levels are *long-run* determinants of the equilibrium exchange rate. This reasoning suggests that proper timing in calculating the PPP is crucial to obtain a good representation of the long-run equilibrium exchange rate. In particular, the parity should not be computed while the exchange rate is affecting domestic prices, for example, while the effects of a devaluation on internal prices are working themselves out. It is also clear that the mutual-causation criticism would be less applicable to a cost than a price parity, for the reasons given in Chapter VIII.

Finally, one can always reinterpret the PPP theory in its weaker form, as the "law of one price" for general price levels. In this formulation, the direction of causation between prices and the exchange rate is irrelevant. Indeed, mutual causation enhances the validity of the theory, providing the stability of the exchange rate and prices (or inflation) is thereby increased, as a stable monetary policy would guarantee. Also, the PPP theory expressed as the law of one price can be considered as holding both for a fixed and a floating exchange rate.

Pigou (1922, pp 64–65) was the first to criticize absolute price parity on the grounds that, if one decomposes the general price level of each country into the price level of traded and that of nontraded commodities, there is no reason for the ratio of the former component price level to the latter (call it the tradable/nontradable price ratio) to be the same in each country. Pigou and later Ellsworth (1950, pp. 593–94), quoting Pigou approvingly, reject absolute PPP for this reason. If the criticism goes no further, however, then its implication concerns only the random error to which the PPP theory is subject. A *bias* in a parity computed from general price levels would require that a *systematic* divergence in the countries' tradable/nontradable price ratios exist, that is, a divergence explainable in terms of other variables.

One such variable can be the exchange rate itself. There is the argument that a currency depreciation causes an increase in the country's tradable/nontradable price ratio, that is, prices of exportables and importables increase in domestic currency relative to the price of non-traded commodities. This effect is part of the modern monetarist approach to the balance-of-payments adjustment mechanism. Clearly, the argument involves a systematic change in the tradable/nontradable price ratio induced by exchange-rate movements.

Yeager (1976, p. 214) reconciles this effect with the PPP-specified direction of causation by noting the assumption of high elasticities underlying the PPP theory. If demand and supply elasticities for exports and imports are high and if production and consumption of tradables with respect to nontradables are very sensitive to a small change in the tradable/nontradable price ratio, then changes in that ratio induced by exchange-rate changes will be small. Thus a basic assumption underlying the PPP theory—that of high trade elasticities and domestic substitution elasticities—implies that the monetarist reverse-causality argument is quantitatively unimportant.

Hagen (1957; 1960) offers the proposition that the nontradable/tradable price ratio is an increasing function of the per capita income of a country. His rationale is that in a low-income country, where labor is relatively cheap, nontraded commodities are labor intensive and exports are capital intensive or land intensive. Therefore, exports are higher priced relative to nontraded goods, compared with a high-income country. Also, the low-income country's imports are representative of prices in high-income countries. Therefore the country's relatively cheap labor is reflected only in the price level of its nontraded goods. Beckerman (1966, p. 25) points out that Hagen's argument is questionable; for the exports of many low-income countries are labor intensive, with textiles as an example.

It remained for Balassa (1961; 1964) to offer what many regard as the definitive reason why the nontradable/tradable price ratio increases with per capita income, both across countries at a given point in time (the relevant comparison to assess absolute parity) and for a given country over time. A high-income country is more productive technologically than a low-income country; but the efficiency advantage of the former country is not uniform over all industries. Rather, it is greater for traded goods (especially manufactured goods and agricultural products) than for nontraded goods (taken by Balassa to be consumer services—he does not mention the public sector).[13] Advances in productivity proceed in this asymmetric fashion for all countries.

Now, prices of traded goods are equalized across countries (abstracting from trade restrictions and transport costs); but this is not so for nontraded goods. With the wage rate higher in the more productive (higher-income) country and with wages equalized domestically across all industries, the nontradable/tradable price ratio must be higher in the higher-income country.

The prices of nontraded goods (relatively higher in the more productive country) are not directly relevant for balance-of-payments equilibrium. Therefore, a price parity calculated from general price levels yields an exchange value of the high-income country's currency that is lower than its true long-run equilibrium value, and this systematic bias increases with the overall productivity difference (represented by the per capita income difference) between the countries involved.

Officer (1976b) introduced the term "productivity-bias hypothesis" to designate the Balassa argument. Kravis and others (1978a; 1978b) call it the "productivity-differential model." Writers prior to Balassa had anticipated the productivity-bias hypothesis. Cassel himself (1932b, p. 660) noticed that services are relatively more expensive in a higher-income country. He writes: "If, for example, tourists observe that living in a rich country is much dearer than in another country, and from this form the hasty conclusion that the purchasing power of money in the former country is distinctly less than in the latter, this conclusion is based substantially on the fact that the traveling expenses of tourists are dependent to a great degree on the price of personal services, and must therefore be particularly high in a country with high wages."

Kravis and others (1978a; 1978b) credit Ricardo (1817–21; 1951, p. 142) as the first author to perceive that the nontradable/tradable price ratio ("the prices of home commodities") is higher in countries with greater per capita income ("those countries where manufactures flourish"). Other economists whom they see as having anticipated Balassa are Taussig, Ohlin, Viner, and Harrod (all writing in the interwar period), and Usher and Samuelson (writing at about the same time as Balassa).[14] Not mentioned is the work of Rothschild (1958), who provided as clear and complete a statement of the productivity-bias hypothesis as Balassa did six years later.

Balassa's productivity-bias hypothesis has been accepted by Maddison (1967, p. 297), Yeager (1968, pp. 77–80; 1976, pp. 216–17), Harry Johnson (1968, p. 92; 1973, p. 514), Kindleberger (1973, pp. 391–92), Samuelson (1974, pp. 604–605), and Katseli-Papaefstratiou (1979, pp. 6–7). At first sight, the hypothesis deals a severe blow to an absolute PPP theory applicable to countries at diverse levels of development. Officer (1974), however, has challenged Balassa's theoretical analysis on the grounds that it ignores quality differences in consumer services among countries. Admittedly, these differences are minimal for highly labor-intensive consumer services; but they would appear significant for professional services, such as education and medical care. The labor involved in such higher-level services embodies human capital and/or works with physical capital, including advanced technology. It is only logical to expect the more productive (higher-income) country to have an efficiency advantage in these services.

Balassa's response (1974a) is that, for Officer's criticism to hold, the asserted quality difference between a high-income and a low-income country would have to be large enough to offset the observed price differences over *all* consumer services (not just those services subject to an international quality difference). The validity of Balassa's argument thus reduces to an empirical question, the investigations of which are discussed in Chapter XI.

Even if Balassa's analysis is confirmed empirically, absolute price parity is not thereby destroyed as a workable theory. First, the theory would remain applicable as it stands for exchange-rate analyses among countries at approximately the same level of technological advancement. Second, to consider countries at diverse levels of development, the theory could be amended by including the effect of international productivity differences on the tradable/nontradable price ratio, thus correcting the bias of the simply computed parity.

III. RELATIVE PRICE PARITY

Relative price parity has one problem that absolute parity avoids: a base period is required for calculating relative parity. Ideally, the base-period exchange rate should be in long-run equilibrium; but unless the exchange rate was freely floating in the base period, there is no guarantee that it was even in short-run equilibrium. Furthermore, even if the exchange rate was freely floating, its value may have been influenced by temporary factors (for example, short-term capital flows) that pull it away from the long-run equilibrium.[15] Under these circumstances, the base-period exchange rate may have been in disequilibrium, and the relative price parity perpetuates this disequilibrium.

Traditionally, selection of the appropriate base period is one of the first problems mentioned by evaluators of relative parity.[16] The difficulty of finding a "normal" or equilibrium base period is sometimes viewed as so overwhelming that the theory becomes virtually unusable, a position taken by Bunting (1939, p. 285) and Bacha and Taylor (1971, p. 220).

Remaining criticisms of relative price parity center around the fact that economic conditions may have *changed* in some manner since the base period. The great advantage of relative over absolute PPP is that relative parity is not affected by the various limitations and biases of absolute parity, providing that these factors are invariant from the base to the current period.[17] Any change in these factors, however, will give rise to a deviation of the computed relative parity from the long-run equilibrium exchange rate.

Changes in economic conditions since the base period may be either structural or non-structural in nature. On the non-structural side, one condition that may have changed is the height of trade restrictions or the level of transport costs. Beginning with Pigou (1922, pp. 66–67), many have mentioned this deficiency of relative price parity.[18] The extent to which the theory is affected, of course, depends on the magnitude of the changes, and an assessment analogous to that of the impact of tariff and transport-cost *levels* on absolute parity is applicable.

Conditions determining international capital flows, unilateral transfers, and investment income may have changed since the base period. For example, capital flows may have become increasingly mobile over time—as stated by Kindleberger (1973, p. 391)—or a country may have lost overseas assets since the base period, owing, for example, to an intervening war—mentioned by Haberler (1945, pp. 312–13) and Hicks (1959, p. 131). To the extent that affected balance-of-payments flows have shifted in direction or magnitude since the base period, the long-run equilibrium exchange rate has changed in a way not captured by the relative-parity computation.

Changes in income would affect a country's short-run equilibrium exchange rate even without a change in price levels, a fact emphasized by Nurkse (1950, pp. 10–12) and Metzler (1947, pp. 19–20) and mentioned by many others.[19] Therefore the selection of base and current period at different phases of the business cycle would reduce the accuracy of the PPP theory. However, Scammell's statement (1961, p. 59, fn. 2) that relative PPP requires the assumption of constant national income is too strong, for the reasons mentioned in the preceding section.

Structural changes in the economies may produce a relative price parity that would diverge from the absolute parity for the current period and therefore from the long-run equilibrium exchange rate. Except under a neutrality condition [as noted by Bacha and Taylor (1971, p. 220)], these structural changes would be reflected in changes in relative prices domestically. A change in relative prices, by changing the volume and composition of international trade, will in general alter both the (long-run) equilibrium exchange rate and the level of a floating rate (the short-run equilibrium exchange rate, in the terminology of Chapter II). Cassel himself had mentioned that the pattern of relative prices at home and abroad are determinants of the equilibrium exchange rate (though secondary in importance to the PPP).

As Ellsworth states: "a general rise or fall of prices is always accompanied by a dispersion of prices, that is to say, by an unequal rate of movement . . . [This] would be almost certain to result in a different total demand for and supply of exchange in the foreign-exchange markets, with a different equilibrium rate of exchange as a consequence" (1950, p. 597). Furthermore, the change in relative prices within the economy might take place within a background of unchanged PPP. As Aliber (1978, p. 28) declares: "The statement that the equilibrium exchange rate must change if the price level relationship changes does not mean that the equilibrium exchange rate may not change when relative price levels remain unchanged. At issue is whether there can be meaningful deviations from the relative version of purchasing power parity . . . which might be attributed to structural factors. . . ."

Changes in tastes, technology, factor supplies (such as the discovery of petroleum deposits), and market form are the structural changes typically mentioned in the literature.[20] In terms of the pure theory of international trade, a structural change is one that affects the shape or position of the economy's reciprocal demand curve for foreign commodities with respect to their (real) price denominated in domestic commodities.

The implication for relative PPP is that the base period should be as close as possible to the current period in order to minimize the scope for structural changes, as first indicated by Bunting (1939, p. 285). The problem with this prescription is that it may conflict with the requirement of selecting a base period in which the exchange rate is in (or close to) long-run equilibrium. Thus the "'ancient-history' element in comparative-version parity calculations" (Yeager, 1958, p. 527) is perhaps the principal defect of the theory.

Yeager (1958, pp. 518–19; 1976, p. 216) comments that the problem of non-monetary (that is, non-PPP) influences on the exchange rate is mitigated by trade flows responding to price changes. However, Yeager does not point out that these flows are secondary effects, and so they may be expected to move the new long-run equilibrium only partway back to the relative parity. The type of structural change most damaging to PPP is one that involves a differential shift in the tradable/nontradable price ratio as between countries. Any systematic country differences in movements of this ratio give rise to a definite bias in relative PPP. The Balassa argument of a non-uniform productivity advantage (greater for traded than for nontraded goods) enjoyed by the technologically advanced country involves a bias in absolute PPP. An *increase* (*decrease*) *over time* in the advanced country's productivity advantage, as indicated by a higher (lower) rate of growth in per capita income compared with the less advanced country, imparts a similar bias to relative PPP.[21] Balassa

(1964) applied his analysis to relative PPP after making the case against absolute PPP, while an earlier study by Hicks (1959, pp. 66–84) anticipated the Balassa argument in a dynamic sense, hence as applicable to relative PPP alone. Since Balassa's contribution, the dynamic form of his argument has been accepted by Yeager (1968, p. 80; 1976, p. 217), Kindleberger (1973, pp. 391–92), Haberler (1975, p. 25), Fry (1976, pp. 222–23), and Dornbusch (1978, p. 91).

IV. COST PARITY

Criticisms of the cost-parity theory fall into two groups: those that point out the weaknesses of cost parity in comparison to the price-parity concept, and those that concentrate attention on the UFC parity. The earliest critic of the general idea of a cost parity is Harris (1936, p. 40). He points out that data problems abound. Differences in the work week, efficiency, classification of workers, payments in kind, and overtime make international comparison of labor costs difficult. For a relative-PPP concept of cost parity, Harris recognizes that these objections are less serious. However, a wage-rate parity concept fails to incorporate other components of cost, namely, social insurance, taxes, prices of raw materials, and, above all, capital costs. Measuring capital costs appropriately is so replete with problems that, in practice, users of cost parity to this day have computed PPP measures based solely on labor cost.

Another critic of the general idea of a cost parity is Haberler (1944b, p. 192; 1945, p. 312, fn. 4). He sees cost parity as having all the problems of price parity and the additional disadvantage of being vague and ambiguous, arguing that "cost level" or "level of cost of production" is a price level of a set of prices that is not clearly defined. Replacing cost parity by wage parity is no solution, he argues, because allowance would still have to be made for other factors of production. Also, a relative wage parity would require that changes in the productivity of labor be incorporated into the measure. In other words, a unit-labor-cost (ULC) concept is indicated.

Tamagna (1945, p. 68) points out that comparing wage rates in countries at different levels of development is meaningless, because the composition of output is so divergent (industry versus agricultural). Also, it is impossible to measure changes in productivity in different countries.

Objections of a more specific nature are offered by Metzler (1947, pp. 21–22) and repeated by Ellsworth (1950, pp. 596–97) and Stern (1973, p. 147, fn. 31). First, there is the need to select the firms whose costs are to be reflected in the economy's cost level or index. Costs vary among firms not only between industries but also within an industry; so the choice is not obvious. A related issue is that a firm's costs vary with its volume of output; therefore, there is also the need to determine the appropriate output level at which to measure cost. To complete the argument, one should add that either competition or oligopolistic price setting leads to uniform prices among the firms in an industry and also keeps prices stable over a single firm's output range. Thus, these problems are not apparent in the computation of price parity.

Finally, there is the problem of the availability of data. Information on factor prices and productivity is less comprehensive—if available at all—than is information on product prices. With the possible exception of wage data, this statement remains true today. Most recently, Artus (1978, p. 287) notes that: "Prices of intermediate inputs and capital services are practically always ignored." Also, using unit labor costs in manufacturing to measure long-run growth in productivity (the best approach, according to Artus) can lead to biased results because of long-run changes in the capital-labor input ratio.

The UFC or ULC parity as developed by Houthakker (1962a; 1962b; 1963) and later Officer (1974) has been subjected to direct criticism. Samuelson (1964, pp. 149–53) has two lines of attack against the concept. First, he has a series of objections that, in effect, coalesce into the observation that the trade-off between increases in ULC at home relative to abroad and depreciations of the domestic currency in the exchange market can be accepted while denying the rigid framework of the ULC parity. The latter theory locks the equilibrium exchange rate (price of foreign currency in terms of domestic currency) into equality with the ratio of ULC at home to ULC abroad. An explanation of this criticism is offered by Officer (1974, p. 869), who suggests that Samuelson views the cited trade-off as a short-run relationship, while the ULC parity represents the *long-run* equilibrium exchange rate.

Samuelson also attacks Houthakker's analysis for its dependence on a factor-price equalization model, which he rejects as unrealistic.[22] The use of a production function involving neutral productivity differences between countries and therefore allowing factor prices to differ internationally by this efficiency factor does not remove Samuelson's criticism, because he considers this model hardly more realistic than that of pure factor-price equalization.

Officer (1974, p. 870) responds to this criticism by noting, first, that Arrow and others (1961) provide econometric evidence that intercountry differences in production functions take the form of a neutral efficiency factor.[23] His second point is that the UFC model uses factor-price equalization only as a *long-run* phenomenon. He cites Hicks (1959, pp. 266–67) for an argument that factor-price equalization has validity as a long-run tendency when the many kinds and qualities of factors of production are aggregated into the two broad factors, labor and capital. Officer suggests that it is within the spirit of Hicks' analysis to aggregate commodities as well as factors, so that an aggregate production function may be considered for each country. However, it is not necessary to retain Hicks' condition of equal productivity throughout the world. The weaker assumption of neutral productivity differences between countries means that the "long run" need not be as long as that envisaged by Hicks; and the amended form of factor-price equalization—wage rates differing internationally by a relative-efficiency factor—is quite sufficient for the ULC theory.

Another critic of the UFC parity is Balassa (1974a), whose case against absolute price parity is directly applicable to absolute UFC parity, as both he and Officer (1974) note. For UFC parity to be an unbiased measure of the (long-run) equilibrium exchange rate, international efficiency differences must not vary systematically as between traded and nontraded industries. If one accepts the validity of Balassa's observation that the advanced country's productivity superiority is greater in the former than in the latter industries, then the absolute UFC parity understates the equilibrium exchange value of the advanced country's currency in the same way that absolute price parity does (although not necessarily by the same amount).

Correspondingly, if Balassa's argument is applicable to relative price parity, it would also be relevant for a relative version of UFC parity. Any limitations of Balassa's case against the price-parity theories are, of course, also applicable as a defense of the cost-parity theories.

V. RESIDUAL VALIDITY OF PURCHASING POWER PARITY

Most critics of PPP, after making their case against the theory, do not reject it outright. They recognize what may be termed the "residual validity" of PPP, the theory's range of applicability that remains even granted the criticisms that have been raised. Haberler sees three situations in which the PPP theory has applicability.[24] First, "under normal circumstances . . . the P.P.P. theory holds in an approximate fashion in the sense that it would hardly be possible to find under such circumstances a case where an equilibrium rate is, say, 15-20 percent off purchasing power par" (1961, p. 51). Second, when general price movements dominate changes in relative prices, relative PPP is a useful concept: "if cautiously used, along with other evidence, P.P.P. calculations have considerable diagnostic value, especially in periods of severe inflation" (1961, p. 50). Finally, when trade relations between countries have been interrupted (owing to war, for example) or have been reduced to a barter or government-to-government basis, PPP can provide an indication of the equilibrium exchange rate that would apply when normal trade relationships are resumed.

Metzler writes: "In my opinion, the criticism of the parity doctrine went too far, and the theory was rejected even for situations in which it was valid" (1948, p. 223, fn. 31). When large inflations have taken place in different countries, relative PPP provides an approximate measure of the new pattern of equilibrium exchange rates.[25]

Ellsworth notes that, in spite of the criticisms directed against it, PPP "continues to be widely used as a basis for estimating equilibrium exchange rates . . . for purchasing power par alone are data available which will permit the calculation of a concrete rate . . . Therefore purchasing power par has almost irresistible attractions, in spite of its pitfalls" (1950, p. 600). He agrees with Metzler that PPP is legitimately applicable to situations in which general price movements are dominant.

Other writers adopt a more restrictive scope for PPP, even while adopting the same line of argument. For example, Machlup accepts relative PPP as valid only when great changes in exchange rates are to be explained. He implies that the general movement of prices must be so large as to approach hyperinflation; for only then can one be certain that it dominates structural changes. "While changes in tastes, changes in productivity, changes in capital movements, etc., can change exchange rates somewhat (or even by substantial percentages), inflation in one of the countries can change the rates by huge multiples" (1964, p. 27). Stern also (1973, p. 147) would not apply PPP to periods of merely moderate inflation; for only under rapid inflation are changes in relative prices likely to be minimal. In the same vein, Lutz (1966, p. 23) notes that if "the purchasing-power-parity theory contains an important kernel of truth," the theory nevertheless applies only when disturbances in the balance of payments are due to monetary as distinct from real factors.

On the other hand, Kindleberger is in accord with Haberler in seeing a wider applicability of PPP, at least in its relative form. The computed parity provides an approximation to the new equilibrium exchange rate after an interruption of trade. More generally, "it helps suggest what changes are necessary in the exchange rate (or in price levels) when inflation is proceeding at different rates in different countries" (1973, p. 392). The implication is that even if rates of inflation are only moderate, nevertheless they provide scope for the theory to operate. Similarly, Harry Johnson (1968, pp. 92–93) observes that relative PPP "is a reasonable approximation for the analysis of short-run monetary disturbances of the type with which Cassel was concerned and provides a rough guide for policy makers obliged to decide the magnitude of exchange-rate changes. As a matter of fact, the exchange rates of the major countries do not depart very far (typically less than 20 per cent) from purchasing power parity."

Chacholiades (1978, p. 187) concedes "a grain of truth in the PPP theory," namely, that relative PPP correctly shows the "profound influence" of monetary factors on the exchange rate. Helliwell, after pointing out limitations of the PPP theory, writes: "Despite these qualifications, it is nevertheless clear that changes in the internal purchasing power of a country's currency are likely to be matched, more or less, and other things being equal, by changes in the foreign exchange value of that currency" (1979, p. 428).

McKinnon (1979, p. 122) states that "relative PPP calculations can prove insightful" given a base year in which the absolute PPP holds or a time span over which there is considerable relative inflation (or deflation) at home compared to abroad.

Meier (1980, p. 262) is more skeptical, arguing that: "At its best, the PPP theory applies to extremely large and general price changes over a long period of time (such as in periods of high inflation), not the short-run of a few years." Kohlhagen (1978, p. 43) also assesses PPP as seeming to hold in the long run but not the short run.

Other researchers, while acknowledging the same limitation, that PPP applies only to the long run, are kinder to the theory by interpreting the "long run" in periods of months or quarter-years rather than years or decades. Genberg (1978, p. 272) writes: "PPP is mainly a longer-run phenomenon in the sense that it should be expected to agree with data on price levels and exchange rates only as an average over several quarters." Frenkel (1978, p. 188) states that PPP provides "a guide as to the general trend of exchange rates rather than the day-to-day fluctuations."

The consensus even of critical members of the profession appears to be that PPP is a useful theory. Disagreement exists only on the range of circumstances for which the theory is applicable. In the next chapter we consider the real-world applications of the theory, the empirical uses of PPP that have actually been made.

NOTES

1. The reader may find it instructive to compare this chapter with the section on Cassel's "Recognized Limitations of PPP" in Chapter VII.

2. See, for example, Haberler (1945, pp. 311–12; 1961, pp. 48–49), Ellsworth (1950, pp. 594–95), and Stern (1973, pp. 144 and 147). However, Bresciani-Turroni (1934; 1937), a critic of PPP, stated the theory in terms of export prices.

136 / *Purchasing Power Parity and Exchange Rates*

3. An excellent discussion of this approach to PPP is presented by Humphrey (1979, p. 4).

4. The view that the asset-market approach and the PPP theory are complementary is also held by Batchelor (1977, pp. 45–47) and Artus (1978, pp. 279–84). A contrary, critical stance is taken by Katseli-Papaefstratiou (1979, pp. 13–16). She argues that under the asset approach: "the long-run equilibrium real exchange rate . . . will depend on all the determinants of the current account. There is no *a priori* reason to expect this to be the PPP value of unity" (1979, pp. 13–14).

5. See, for example, Haberler (1945, p. 312; 1961, p. 49) and Ellsworth (1950, p. 596).

6. See Chapter VIII.

7. See, for example, Houthakker (1962a, p. 297), Yeager (1968, pp. 77–78), Stern (1973, pp. 143–44), and Officer (1974, p. 873).

8. This procedure is followed in the computation of PPPs both for providing international comparisons of standard of living and GDP; for example, Kravis and others (1975; 1978a); and for indicating the long-run equilibrium exchange rate; for example, Houthakker (1962a) and Officer (1974).

9. Scammell (1961, p. 59) seems to argue that the very existence of imperfections involves a breakdown in the PPP theory. Others; for example, Ellsworth (1950, pp. 591–92) and Yeager (1958, p. 517; 1976, pp. 214–15); see moderate levels of tariffs and transport costs as reducing the accuracy of the theory but not destroying it outright.

10. See, for example, Haberler (1936, p. 38), Ellsworth (1950, p. 592), and Yeager (1958, p. 517; 1976, p. 214).

11. See Haberler (1945, pp. 313–15).

12. Also, their effect on the balance of payments must not be canceled through the associated cumulative reflow of interest and dividend payments.

13. The reasons for the higher productivity of the traded sector of the economy are not discussed by Balassa. Aukrust (1970, p. 53, fn. 3) suggests that the scope for technological progress afforded by the higher capital intensity of this sector is not the sole reason. Exposure to international competition itself may be a spur to increased efficiency.

14. For the precise references, see Kravis and others (1978a, p. 9, fn. 14; 1978b, p. 219).

15. One solution is to calculate the absolute price parity in the base period and let it play the role of the base-period exchange rate. This technique, adopted in Officer (1978), requires that sufficiently comprehensive data be available to compute an absolute price parity that is a good approximation to the long-run equilibrium exchange rate. Use of the actual base-period exchange rate, on the other hand, has the statistical advantage that the only product-price data required are the countries' own price indices.

16. See, for example, Haberler (1945, p. 311), Metzler (1947, p. 18), Yeager (1958, p. 517; 1976, p. 213), Kindleberger (1973, pp. 391, 392), and Stern (1973, p. 146).

17. It is assumed that the base-period exchange rate is correctly chosen.

18. For example, Haberler (1945, p. 312; 1947, p. 100), Scammell (1961, p. 59, fn. 2), Yeager (1958, pp. 517, 529; 1976, pp. 213–14), and Caves and Jones (1973, p. 337).

19. For example, Haberler (1947, p. 100), Vanek (1962, p. 84), Balassa (1964, p. 591), and Stern (1973, p. 146).

20. See, for example, Haberler (1945, p. 312; 1947, p. 100; 1961, pp. 49–50), Metzler (1947, p. 19; 1948, p. 223), Machlup (1964, p. 27), Yeager (1958, pp. 518–19; 1976, pp. 215–16), Vanek (1962, pp. 84–85), Kindleberger (1973, p. 391), Stern (1973, p. 146), Helliwell (1979, pp. 427–28), and Michaely (1980, p. 49).

21. Differential technological change in the various sectors of an economy can also have important *domestic* implications. A model with this viewpoint has been presented by

Baumol (1967). For comments and elaborations, see Birch and Cramer (1968), Robinson (1969), Keren (1972), and Baumol (1968; 1969; 1972).

22.   It is interesting to recall that Samuelson is one of the originators of the factor-price equalization model.

23.   This neutrality result is disputed by Gupta (1968) but defended by Minsol (1968).

24.   See Haberler (1936, pp. 37–38; 1945, pp. 313–15; 1961, pp. 50–51).

25.   See Metzler (1947, pp. 22–24; 1948, pp. 222–23).

Chapter X

Empirical Applications of PPP

"All in all it would be most unwise to ignore the unique insight which PPP calculations can afford." (Hendrik S. Houthakker, 1962a, pp. 296-297)

Unique among theories of the exchange rate, the PPP theory has regularly been put to empirical use by economic practitioners. Several reasons can be advanced for this phenomenon: the simplicity of the PPP approach, the ease in calculating at least relative PPP measures, and the intuitive appeal of PPP as a valid theory. A good number of empirical applications of PPP exist, each of which is discussed in a separate section.

I. DATA CONVERSION

Probably the most generally accepted use of PPP is as a conversion factor to transfer data from denomination in one national currency to another. The absolute rather than relative PPP measure is the appropriate concept for this purpose. There is one obvious alternative to (absolute) PPP as the factor enabling expression of data in a common currency: the current exchange rate. The exchange rate is an appropriate conversion factor to express countries' balance-of-payments flows and official reserves in a common currency.

However, international comparison of real output in different countries requires that the conversion rate reflect relative price levels. Now, an absolute PPP measure founded on a GNP or GDP price concept (depending on the definition of output) has precisely the property required of the conversion factor. It was argued in Chapters VII and VIII that a broadly-based PPP concept, say, one founded on the GDP price level, is optimal for PPP as a theory of exchange-rate determination. This concept is also ideal for conversion of GDP data of different countries into a common currency, thus enabling a valid comparison of the countries' real-output levels.[1]

Therefore the exchange rate is an inappropriate conversion factor unless it strictly reflects PPP, that is, unless the exchange rate equals PPP (a unitary H function) or differs from it by a factor of proportionality unvarying across country pairs and over time. Any of the criticisms outlined in Chapter IX that involve a divergence between the exchange rate and PPP now becomes an argument *in favor of* using PPP for data-conversion purposes (as far as national-accounts data are concerned). In particular, the productivity-bias hypothesis suggests that the use of exchange rates as conversion factors understates the output of lower-income countries (with income measured in per capita terms to represent productivity). Such countries have price levels lower than that suggested by exchange rates with respect to higher-income countries, as the higher nontradable/tradable price ratio in the latter countries reflects equalized prices for tradables and higher prices for nontradables (both converted to a common currency at current exchange rates).

The use of PPP for data-conversion purposes boasts a large body of theory (mainly index-number theory) and applications (predominantly to intercountry comparisons of GDP and its components).[2] As the present study is concerned rather with PPP as a theory of the exchange rate, the reader is referred to specialized works for further discussion of the data-conversion use of PPP.

A survey of those studies providing international comparisons of real output "based on extensive field work to make the essential price comparisons," that is, those that make true PPP comparisons of national or domestic product across countries, is offered by Kravis (1976, pp. 18–22). The survey is extended by Salazar-Carrillo (1977) to incorporate Latin American countries. The most recent landmark studies are those of the United Nations International Comparison Project, namely, Kravis and others (1975; 1978a).

The use of either PPP or the exchange rate as conversion factors is not the only method of performing international comparisons of real output. A third technique is to adjust the exchange rate for divergences from the PPP (based on observations for which the absolute PPP is known). In this connection, the most important, and often the only, correction is for deviations between PPP and the exchange rate due to the productivity-bias hypothesis. The adjusted exchange rate is then employed as the conversion factor. The most sophisticated use of this technique, to provide real GDP measures for a large number of countries, is by Kravis and others (1978b), and Summers, Kravis, and Heston (1980). Extension of the former study's results to countries of Eastern Europe is made by Pryor (1979).

A fourth method is to use physical indicators to extend PPP-based real-income results to those countries for which absolute PPP data do not exist. Barlow (1977) provides references to studies that employ this technique, and also compares results from using the four alternative strategies to express real income in comparable terms across countries.

II. SETTING A NEW EXCHANGE RATE

Three known cases exist of the apparent use of PPP by national governments in connection with the setting of a new exchange rate. All occurred in the period between the two World Wars. Two cases (the United Kingdom and Czechoslovakia) involved the use of PPP to calculate the amount of overvaluation of the currency that would remain at a predecided new exchange value of the country's currency, that is, to measure the amount of price-level adjustment at home or abroad that would be required to maintain the new exchange rate. The third situation (Belgium) involved the application of PPP actually to compute the new exchange rate.

The most famous of these experiences is the United Kingdom's return to the gold standard in 1925 at the prewar mint parity with the dollar. This event had followed an appreciation of the floating pound from 10 percent below parity to less than 2 percent below it, an appreciation of a temporary speculative nature, caused by the very anticipation of a return to parity. Immediately after the return to the gold standard, Keynes (1925; 1932, pp. 244–270) castigated the advisors of Winston Churchill (then Chancellor of the Exchequer) for using wholesale price indices (WPIs) to compute a relative PPP for the pound based on the prewar mint parity with the dollar.[3] (The computation was made at the time following the speculative appreciation of the pound.) As discussed in Chapter IX, the use of WPIs for this purpose tends to validate the existing exchange rate. Keynes correctly points out that the preponderance of traded goods in such indices makes them a poor choice for relative-parity calculations. Index numbers of domestic prices—for example, cost-of-living (COL) indices—or of wages would have been better measures, as they do not "adjust themselves hour by hour in accordance with the foreign exchanges" (1925; 1932, p. 249). Keynes declares that whereas a relative price parity computed from WPIs indicated an overvaluation of the pound of only 2 or 3 percent at its appreciated exchange value, the use of other indices would have revealed the true figure of 10 or 12 percent. So the required amount of downward adjustment of the U.K. price level to support the exchange rate was substantially underestimated. The outcome for the United Kingdom, as Keynes predicted, was deflation and unemployment.

Interestingly enough, an assessment similar to that of Keynes is made by Cassel (1925d; 1926, p. 1088), only he saw a lesser overvaluation of the pound, with prices having to be forced down by 4 or 5 percent. In fact, Keynes' analysis of the British experience became the standard account accepted in the literature.[4] This statement is justified by the comments of several scholars on the episode. Ellsworth (1950, p. 455) writes: "Restoration of the old parity is generally conceded to have overvalued the pound by at least ten per cent and to have subjected the island's economy for the next seven years to continuous deflationary pressure." Scammell notes: "It is generally agreed that during this period [1925–31] the pound was approximately 10 per cent overvalued. . . ." (1951, p. 56, fn. 1). Moggridge (1972, p. 100) declares: "Most observers since Keynes have accepted that in 1925 sterling was overvalued by at least 10 per cent of the pre-war parity of $4.86." The general acceptance of Keynes' assessment is also recognized by Yeager: ". . . the figure of 10 percent has become the traditional informed guess of how far the restored parity was above the pound's equilibrium value" (1976, p. 322).

A contemporary analysis contrary to, and critical of, that of Keynes is offered by Gregory (1926, pp. 39–96). Gregory criticizes Keynes' selection of the price (COL) index used in his PPP measure. That COL index, while regularly published in the *Federal Reserve Bulletin*, had its coverage confined to only one state (Massachusetts). Use of a COL measure with broader geographical scope, published (with less frequency) by the Bureau of Labor Statistics, indicated no exchange-rate deviation from PPP at the time of the revaluation.[5]

Sayers makes the most memorable, and anti-PPP, comment on the Keynes-Gregory controversy: "In short, Keynes used the wrong index numbers, and Gregory the right, yet Keynes got the right result and Gregory the wrong. So much for Purchasing Power Parity as an aid to policy!" (1960, p. 320, fn. 1). Yet Sayers is wrong; the traditional interpretation of the episode as according with the prediction of the PPP theory is correct. In a careful examination of all possible relative-PPP measures (those based on the WPI, COL index, export price index, and GNP deflator), with prewar base periods, Moggridge (1972, pp. 100–106) sees the evidence as conflicting. However, the PPP measure founded on the GNP deflator—recognized in the present study as an optimal price concept for PPP—registers an overvaluation of 11-12 percent in 1924-1925, a result quite consistent with Keynes' conclusion.[6]

Haberler notes that exactly the same mistake committed by Churchill was made by the Czechoslovakian authorities in 1934.[7] In this case the currency was recognized as overvalued; but with attention apparently paid to the movement of WPIs at home and abroad, the extent of the overvaluation was understated.[8] The currency was depreciated, but by an insufficient amount, and a further devaluation had to be carried out in the following year.

A case does exist in which policy-makers acted on the basis of a PPP calculated from COL price indices, thus avoiding some of the difficulties inherent in the WPI: the devaluation of the Belgian franc in 1935. The Belgian case is of interest because it is the mirror image of the British experience ten years earlier. As Triffin (1947, p. 76-77) points out, the overvalued Belgian franc in 1932-1935 was reflected not in a balance-of-payments deficit but rather "in a drastic decline in economic activity and incomes."

The same point is made by Dupriez: ". . . the heavy purchasing power disparities put such a strain on the Belgian economy that the country was on the verge of social upheavals. Nevertheless, no trouble could be registered in the relation of exports to imports, [and] central monetary reserves hardly diminished until 'the game was up'. . . ." (1946, pp. 306-307). Along the same lines, Garnsey writes: "It is obvious that in 1935 the Belgian authorities were primarily concerned with the problem of the large-scale unemployment of men and resources in their economy. Their interest in price disparities arose out of the relationship of prices and exchange rates to opportunities for profitable employment, not from a purely intellectual interest in an abstract problem" (1946, p. 627).

In the British case, revaluation to a level greater than true PPP (a level falsely judged appropriate using a misleading PPP calculation) resulted in deflation and unemployment. This experience is in clear contrast to the Belgian episode, in which a correct PPP computation indicated the amount of devaluation that was required to correct the price-level disparity at home relative to abroad, and the existing economic depression was thereby overcome.

The Belgian franc was devalued by 28 percent at the end of March 1935. Did the Belgian authorities truly decide on this amount by means of a PPP computation? The answer is affirmative. Triffin (1937) notes that the 28 percent figure is precisely (the depreciation that would correct) the amount of overvaluation of the franc with respect to the pound calculated for January 1935 by the Belgian central bank using a PPP computation, with the result later published by the bank. The base year is 1930, when both Belgium and the United Kingdom were on the gold standard; so the mint parity between the franc and the pound is the base-period exchange rate.[9]

It is unlikely that the bank's figure is coincidentally equivalent to the amount of devaluation or that it represents an attempt at *ex post* rationalization of the devaluation decision; for a reference to the use of relative PPP to indicate the degree of currency overvaluation was included in the official report to the legislature at the time of the devaluation decision. The central bank found an overvaluation correctable by a 28 percent devaluation, using COL price indices in the parity calculation, and by a 26 percent devaluation using wage indices. Triffin (1937, p. 47) writes that only the COL indices were used to determine the devaluation rate. This description clearly shows that the action of the Belgian government was indeed contingent upon the result of a PPP calculation.

A somewhat different account of the decision-making process of the Belgian authorities is provided by Garnsey (1945, pp. 117–124); but the reliance on PPP is confirmed. Originally, PPP calculations had been performed with base period 1928 rather than 1930; and the authorities used both base periods to arrive at their decision.[10] True, as Triffin noted, a 28 percent (Garnsey states 28–29 percent) devaluation was indicated by the PPP computation on the new, 1930, base period.

However, a PPP calculation was also made using the old, 1928, base period; and a 60 percent overvaluation of the franc was thereby shown. A correction factor of 20 percent was then applied to compensate for the undervaluation of the franc in 1928. In precise terms, an overvaluation of $160/120 - 100 = 33\frac{1}{3}$ percent was indicated. It could be corrected by a 25 percent depreciation (75% of 160 = 120). A safety margin of 3 percent was added to cover an anticipated rise in the Belgian COL index after devaluation due to higher prices of food imports. So the two PPP computations were deemed consistent with one another.

III. MEASURING THE DISEQUILIBRIUM OF A FIXED EXCHANGE RATE

Cassel (1925b; 1925d; 1926, p. 1088) put his relative PPP theory to work in assessing the equilibrium status of the Swedish krona and the British pound following these countries' postwar return to the gold standard, Sweden in April 1924 and the United Kingdom one year later. For Sweden, Cassel adopts two alternative base periods: October 1923 and March 1924. In each of these months, the krona (then floating) was 2 percent below its gold par. In December 1924, the krona was ½ of one percent *above* par, and yet in the interim Swedish prices and U.S. prices moved so as to imply a *reduction* in the purchasing power of the krona by 3.7 percent from the first base period and more than 6 percent from the second. He concludes that, as of December 1924, the krona was surely overvalued with respect to the U.S. dollar. The reason given is an inflow of capital to Sweden from the United States.

A similar analysis indicates a 4–5 percent overvaluation of the pound with respect to the dollar upon the return of the United Kingdom to the gold standard in April 1925. Cassel notes that this overvaluation was removed by June via a decline in British prices owing to two influences. First, the overvaluation of the pound involved a decrease in the prices of traded goods in England, which dampened the internal price level. Second, the Bank of England pursued a restrictive monetary policy.

Some years later, Cassel (1936, pp. 46–48) applied relative PPP (with base year apparently 1913 and a WPI price concept) to indicate that the return of France to the gold standard in 1928 involved an undervaluation of the franc of about 11 percent. This assessment is in line with that made by Keynes (1928; 1932, pp. 113–117) at the time of the return to the fixed rate. Keynes pointed out that relative PPP showed that the franc should be "nearer to one-quarter . . . than to one-fifth of the pre-war value" with respect to the pound. He excuses this divergence of the pegged exchange rate from the PPP for a variety of reasons, among which are the crudity of the French price data and avoidance of a capital loss in France's foreign-exchange reserves.

Metzler (1947) calculates WPI and consumer-price-index (CPI) parities in an attempt to indicate the extent to which the initial par values announced by the International Monetary Fund in 1946 made allowance for wartime inflation. The base period is October 1936–June 1937, and he justifies it on the grounds that it is close to World War II but free of the war's influences, and that it represents a period of relative stability in exchange markets following the devaluations earlier in the 1930s. The current period is November or December 1946 for most countries, and the U.S. dollar is the standard currency for the calculations.

The technique is to compare parity (PPP) with official rates (number of dollars per unit of domestic currency). About half the countries examined have par values substantially above parity, that is, are significantly overvalued in relation to the dollar. For non-member countries and member countries whose official rates had not yet been agreed upon, there is the same tendency for official rates to exceed parity rates, that is, for a general overvaluation of currencies against the dollar.

Kershaw (1948, p. 336, fn. 41) argues that Metzler's PPP calculation is about 29 percent too high for Brazil. The Brazilian COL index used by

Metzler is an underestimate of price inflation, because the index reflects official rent controls, which are ineffective. More generally, Samuelson (1948), in commenting on Metzler's results, sees the *neglect* of PPP considerations in the establishment of initial par values as a reasonable course to follow. World War II brought massive structural changes to the world economy, making relative PPP based on prewar exchange rates a dubious measure of new equilibrium exchange rates.

In memoranda submitted to the British Council on Prices, Productivity and Incomes in the late 1950s, Harrod and Hawtrey separately applied relative PPP with base year 1938 to reach the conclusion that the pound was substantially undervalued with respect to the dollar.[11] Harrod calculates that in 1955 there was an undervaluation of 30 or 36 percent based on a CPI or unit-labor-cost (ULC) parity, respectively. Hawtrey sees an undervaluation of 23 percent, applying a ULC parity. Their arguments are rejected by the Council, on the grounds that the base period was not a normal one and that various structural and nonstructural changes had affected the U.S. and U.K. balances of payments since that time. Haberler (1976, p. 166) supports the position of the Council, the most influential member of which was Sir Dennis Robertson.

Several years later, absolute PPP was applied by Houthakker (1962a) to show the changed equilibrium status of the dollar, now overvalued with respect to the mark. Cost-of-living (that is, household-consumption-weighted) price parities published by the Statistical Office of the Federal Republic of Germany are the source of Houthakker's computations. These parities (for various countries) are based, alternatively, on the weighting pattern of the Federal Republic of Germany and the domestic weighting pattern. Houthakker takes the geometric mean (Fisher ideal index) of each pair of parities and compares it with the official deutsche-mark/domestic-currency exchange rate in March 1962. Among other results, he notes that the U.S. dollar is overvalued by 22 percent with respect to the deutsche mark.

Houthakker also makes a dollar/pound comparison, using results of a PPP study of the data-conversion genre. Paige and Bombach (1959) computed an absolute gross national product (GNP) price parity for the pound in terms of the dollar. Their calculated parity for 1957 was 3.9, taking the geometric mean of the U.S.-weighted and U.K.-weighted parities. Houthakker (1962a) compares this result with the official exchange rate of 2.8 to reach the conclusion that the dollar was overvalued by 28 percent against the pound in 1957.[12] Taking a relative-PPP approach with 1937 as the base year, Houthakker obtains a PPP of $4.04

in 1957, which he sees as "not very different" from the Paige-Bombach absolute PPP of $3.90.

McLeod (1965, pp. 56–62) provides a number of relative-PPP calculations for the Canadian dollar with respect to the U.S. dollar in 1964. In a return to the par-value system following a floating-rate experience that lasted a decade, the Canadian dollar had been pegged at $.925 U.S. two years earlier. McLeod's preferred base period is either 1949 (second quarter) or 1951, and his preferred price concept underlying PPP is the CPI. The computations then suggest a PPP between $.95 and $1.00 U.S. in 1964 (fourth quarter), thus an undervalued Canadian dollar. In contrast, use of the GNP deflator shows a PPP as low as $.90 U.S., that is, a slight overvaluation of the Canadian currency at its pegged value.

IV. MEASURING THE DISEQUILIBRIUM OF A FLOATING EXCHANGE RATE

The use of PPP to measure the amount of disequilibrium of a floating exchange rate implies that some force is keeping the floating rate from its long-term equilibrium (assumed to be the PPP). In the literature with this theme, speculation is always cited as the explanation of disequilibrium. However, the concept of speculation has different meanings to the various authors.

Cassel (1925d) examined the floating currencies of Denmark and Norway. Taking Sweden (on the gold standard since April 1924) as the standard country, he computes PPPs and compares them with exchange rates (number of units of Swedish currency per unit of domestic currency). For each country, the percentage increase in the exchange rate during 1925 is greater than that in the PPP: the external value of the currency increased more than the internal value. Cassel's explanation: "a very intense and widespread speculation, on the part of those who believed in the restoration of the gold parity, had forced up the external value of the currency" (1925d, p. 57). The reason for this speculation was the announced goal, on the part of the Danish and Norwegian authorities, of a return (appreciation) of their currencies to their former gold parities.

In 1931, the United Kingdom and Sweden, followed by other countries, abandoned the gold standard and let their currencies float. Letting the U.S. dollar be the standard currency, 1926–1928 the base period, and January 1932 the current period, Cassel (1932a, pp. 85–87) computed PPPs for the pound and the krona and compared them with the exchange rate (number of dollars per unit of domestic currency). In each case the PPP is far above the exchange rate, that is, the currency is substantially undervalued on the exchange market. The explanation, according to Cassel, is an "exaggerated distrust" of paper standards (that is, floating currencies) in relation to currencies still on the gold standard (represented by the dollar).

Tsiang (1959) suggests that the deviation of a floating exchange rate from the PPP can be taken as a measure of the amount of speculative activity in the foreign-exchange market. Without accepting the theory that the long-run equilibrium exchange rate is the PPP, one can infer that a widening divergence of the actual exchange rate from the PPP within a short time period is due to speculation, unless changes in "nonspeculative factors" (such as supply and demand conditions for traded goods and non-speculative capital movements) are present. Tsiang uses WPIs to compute the PPP, with the base year 1913 and the dollar as the standard currency. The subjects of the analysis are the post-World War I floating exchange rates of the United Kingdom, Norway, and France.

Tsiang's results are not discussed here—only his approach is of interest—for he is not prepared to use PPP/exchange-rate comparisons to form a judgment about the overvaluation or undervaluation of a currency. The selection of WPIs to construct the PPPs may have resulted in smaller deviations of the actual exchange rates from the PPPs and therefore, in Tsiang's framework, less speculation than if a price index less weighted with traded goods had been used. Indeed, a related study by Aliber (1962), who uses retail as well as wholesale price indices to construct PPPs, finds greater evidence of speculation for the same time period. Countries examined are the United Kingdom, France, Belgium, the Netherlands, and Switzerland; and both PPP/exchange-rate disparities and divergences from interest-rate parity are used to investigate the nature and extent of speculation in the foreign-exchange market.[13] Most interestingly, Aliber concludes that speculation was destabilizing in the French floating-rate experience after World War I, a result further discussed in Aliber (1970; 1973), Pippenger (1973), and Thomas (1973a).[14]

V. CALCULATING REAL EXCHANGE RATES

Purchasing power parity can have analytical value simply as a computational device. De Vries (1968) uses relative price parity to calculate depreciation or appreciation "in real terms" for the currencies of 64 countries compared with the dollar. Alternative base years are 1948 and 1955. The author stresses that PPPs are *not* equilibrium exchange rates and do not provide a guide for measuring the degree of overvaluation or undervaluation of a currency. Thus, it is not necessary that the base years be periods of equilibrium. The PPPs (calculated from COL price indices) enable a comparison of external exchange depreciation with the internal depreciation of the currency, both in relation to the dollar.

For each country, de Vries calculates the ratio of PPP to the exchange rate (number of units of domestic currency per dollar) in 1967. Although the term is not used by de Vries, this ratio is the real exchange rate, that is, the real exchange value of the domestic currency. If the ratio is less than unity, then the external depreciation has exceeded the internal depreciation for the currency in question; depreciation in real terms has in fact occurred (the real exchange value of the currency has fallen). Countries are grouped according to level of development and degree of inflation over the periods considered. The general conclusion is that less developed countries as a group had greater real depreciation of their currencies than did developed countries, especially with the 1948 base.

A similar analysis is applied by Paul Johnson (1970) to devaluations of the Colombian currency over the period 1958–1965. He notes that Colombian price indices (WPI and COL) doubled over this period, while U.S. price indices were almost stable. "Naive purchasing power parity considerations would call for a doubling of the Colombian exchange rate. Comparing 1958 and 1965 . . . this is almost exactly what happened" (1970, p. 169). However, the 1965 exchange rate cannot be considered to be at the appropriate level, because the exchange market was not in equilibrium in 1958.

Using a WPI PPP concept, Tyler (1973) computes monthly real exchange rates for the Brazilian cruzeiro with respect to the dollar for the time period 1963–1971. Since mid-1968, with the institution of Brazil's "mini-devaluation" policy, there were frequent depreciations of the cruzeiro, that is, frequent policy-imposed decreases in its nominal exchange value. The average monthly variation in the *real* exchange rate was 7 percent until the onset of the mini-devaluation policy and only 1.5 percent afterwards. The author argues that the stable real exchange rate in the 1968–1971 period fostered Brazilian exports by reducing uncertainty and exchange-rate risk.

Porzecanski (1978) computes the real exchange rate for Argentina, Brazil, Chile, and Uruguay over the time period 1957–72. Using the WPI, he finds that while all four countries exhibited high inflation, the fluctuation of the Uruguayan real exchange rate was much greater than that of the other countries. This result suggests, for the author, that "the Uruguayan authorities placed relatively little importance on the maintenance of a realistic exchange rate" (1978, p. 137).

Finally, Vaubel (1976; 1978) applies the real-exchange-rate concept to the countries of the European Community (EC). He computes the variation of real and nominal exchange rates using a CPI concept and a number of time spans over 1959–1976. For comparative purposes, a similar analysis is applied to regions of Germany, Italy, and the United States (for which, of course, nominal exchange rates are invariant). The intra-Community variance in the real exchange rate is significantly greater than that within each of the three countries, leading Vaubel to conclude that the EC is not as desirable a currency area as the three countries, because the EC requires greater real exchange-rate adjustment.

However, Vaubel emphasizes that this result does not imply that lack of progress toward monetary unification in the EC is due to divergences in economic conditions in the member countries. He presents two reasons justifying the position. First, nominal exchange-rate changes between the countries substantially exceeded real exchange-rate changes. This implies that the nominal exchange-rate changes were primarily due to divergent inflation rates within the Community and therefore, ultimately, to lack of monetary-policy harmonization. Second, an intertemporal analysis shows that real exchange-rate changes increased interregionally (within the three reference countries) more than among the EC members. This finding suggests that the need for real exchange-rate changes within the Community has decreased over time.

Vaubel's conclusion is that the absence of progress toward European monetary unification at the time was due to lack of the political will to harmonize monetary policies (and thereby correct divergent inflation rates). The subsequent establishment of the European Monetary System, in 1979, indicates that Vaubel's conclusion was correct.

VI. ASSESSING THE RATIONALITY OF EXCHANGE-RATE POLICIES OF STATE-TRADING ECONOMIES

The conventional wisdom is that the exchange-rate systems of state-trading economies (STEs) are of little economic significance and indeed are irrational and artificial.[15] Amacher and Hodgson (1974) seek to test this view by taking the PPP as the norm and comparing the actual exchange rate with it. The idea is that the purchasing power of a currency in relation to that abroad represents fundamental factors that a rational exchange-rate policy would take into account. The authors take Yugoslavia as the country of interest (for it is an STE that has become increasingly market oriented over time) and its major trading partners, namely,

Italy and the Federal Republic of Germany, as the countries of comparison. The model employed is one of the relative price parity and is as follows. The epitome of a rational exchange-rate policy over time requires that:

$$R = P \cdot R_0$$

where R and P are the exchange rate (price of foreign currency in terms of domestic currency) and PPP (ratio of the domestic to the foreign price index), respectively, and R_0 is the base-period exchange rate.

Given a base period, R_0 is a constant. Therefore, taking logarithms, one obtains the estimating equation:[16]

$$\log R = \alpha + \beta \log P$$

R and P are denominated in the number of dinars per lira or per deutsche mark. A successful testing of the hypothesis requires that β be positive and significant, and that the equation have a high explanatory power. The model consists of two such equations, one for the dinar/lira, the other the dinar/deutsche-mark comparison.

To construct the variable P, an index of "producer's prices, industrial goods" is used for Yugoslavia, WPIs for Italy and the Federal Republic of Germany. The base period is 1952 and the time period of the regressions is 1952–1971 (annual data). The dinar/lira and dinar/deutsche-mark exchange rates are not available directly; they are obtained through cross rates with the dollar. One might question the assumption of consistent cross rates as less valid for Yugoslavia than for a market economy.

It turns out that movements in price levels explain 40–45 percent of the variation in exchange rates. The authors see the relationship as weakened by the fact that the base-period exchange rate is probably not in equilibrium. They conclude that the devaluations of the dinar in the 1950s and 1960s are in accordance with PPP theory.[17] It is questionable, however, whether the result of a rational or partly rational exchange-rate system can be projected to other STEs, which are further away from a market economy than is Yugoslavia.

This last comment of the present author is contrary to the position of Wiles (1969), who, in his treatise on the international economics of STEs, argues that the PPP theory (as an indicator of currency overvaluation or undervaluation) is *more* appropriate for the STEs than it is for market economies. The reason is that limitations of PPP based on macroeconomic considerations do not apply to an STE.[18]

Holzman (1968a) adopts an absolute-PPP approach to evaluate historically the exchange-rate policy of the Soviet Union. He compares Soviet domestic (internal) prices with export and import (external) unit values for the same commodities. On the assumption that the Soviet Union is a price-taker in world markets, the divergence between internal and external price levels (compared as a weighted average of internal to external prices of various commodities) provides a measure of the overvaluation or undervaluation of the ruble. In three out of four sample years, internal prices were substantially above external prices, suggesting a greatly overvalued ruble in the foreign-exchange market. Other evidence assembled by Holzman supports this conclusion.

It should be noted that Holzman's price comparison is restricted to tradables alone. The neglect of nontradable prices is legitimate for a non-market, controlled economy, one in which there is rigid control of all prices. Links between the tradable and nontradable sectors are thereby broken (except as decided by the economic planners). Also, the divergence between the internal and external prices of tradables is not due merely to imperfections in the arbitrage process (as would be the case for a market economy), but can correctly be viewed as the result of a deliberate policy on the part of the planners.

VII. FORECASTING EXCHANGE RATES

The PPP theory, in relative form, may be used to forecast floating exchange rates. One requires only projections of price indices for this purpose, and one way in which these may be obtained is as forecasts from existing econometric models. Furthermore, in a distributed-lag formulation of PPP, much of the required price information may be available without forecasting. This section is concerned with forecasting the movements of a floating exchange rate rather than a change in the par value of an adjustably pegged rate. Of course, PPP can also play a role in forecasting par-value changes, because it provides a measure of the amount of overvaluation or undervaluation of a currency (as discussed earlier in this chapter).[19]

Under the current system of floating rates, a good number of firms offer exchange-rate forecasts as a service available for purchase. Goodman (1979) states that at least 23 commercial services throughout the world provide exchange-rate forecasts. Only six of the services rely principally on formal economic models to produce their forecasts. Relative inflation rates are mentioned by Goodman as only one of a number of variables in these models; apparently the models do not adhere to the PPP approach as such. Goodman tests the forecasting performance both of the six economic-oriented services and of four other services that rely on technical decision rules.[20] He obtains the (perhaps surprising) result that the latter firms provide exchange-rate forecasts that generally out-perform the former.[21]

Jacque (1978, ch. 3) distinguishes four forecasting services that provide econometric forecasts of exchange rates. Again, from his description of the forecasting techniques, none of these firms use the PPP theory as such in their forecasts. It appears, then, that no commercial service forecasts exchange rates on the basis of the PPP theory. However, a PPP approach to forecasting is advocated by Kern (1976).

Jacque himself explicitly considers the PPP theory as a forecasting tool. He concludes: "...the Purchasing Power Parity hypothesis was found to be of most helpful forecasting value in the context of medium- and long-range forecasts as well as in the case of a pair of countries suffering from widely discrepant rates of inflation" (1978, p. 90). It should be noted that, for Jacque (and indeed for the entirety of this discussion in this section), the PPP theory is interpreted in the strict sense as having relative inflation rates as the sole explanatory variable.

One can readily agree with Jacque that if the PPP theory is to be used to forecast a floating exchange rate, the time horizon should be longer than the short term. Month-to-month and even quarter-to-quarter movements in an exchange rate can be considerably influenced by private speculation, official market intervention, and other factors that have a volatile effect on the rate. Normally, inflation rates, which represent fundamental influences on the exchange rate, are not flexible enough to predict short-term variations in the exchange rate.

For best results, Jacque advocates that the PPP theory be expressed in multilateral form so that the foreign inflation rate is a weighted average of inflation rates of the country's major trading partners. Essentially, he is advocating that the effective-exchange-rate concept be applied to PPP in its role as a forecasting tool.[22] Earlier, as mentioned in Chapter II, I had made the general suggestion that the effective-exchange-rate approach be used in analytical and empirical work on PPP.

Jacque apparently sees the PPP method of exchange-rate forecasting as inferior to a more sophisticated econometric approach; and the latter, he notes, is followed by the four econometric forecasting services. He writes: "By enlarging considerably the set of exogenous variables, the econometric modeling approach to exchange rates forecasting constitutes a more systematic and sophisticated attempt at accounting for the behavior of exchange rates than the Purchasing Power Parity theory" (1978, pp. 90–91). However, he provides no test of the comparative forecasting performance of the PPP approach and the established econometric procedures of the forecasting services. In fact, in the professional literature, the forecasting ability of PPP has yet to be compared with other approaches, both more and less sophisticated. It is true that comparisons of the ex post explanatory power of PPP and other models have appeared (though rarely) in the literature; but the ex ante forecasting record of PPP as against alternative approaches remains to be explored.

Duffy and Giddy (1975) argue that the PPP theory can be used for predictive purposes only under fixed exchange rates. The reason is that under that system—but *not* under floating rates—there exists a time lag delaying the adjustment of exchange rates to the PPP. They write: "...otherwise, the purchasing power theorem remains simply an ex post statistical phenomenon that says little about the direction of causation between price levels and exchange rates" (1975, p. 33). Duffy and Giddy are taking a firm stance that the structural and forecasting abilities of economic models are complementary. Another legitimate position is that a good forecasting approach can prevail even if the underlying structure is sub-optimal. Suppose that the relationship between the exchange rate and price levels is strictly contemporaneous, so that a direction of causation cannot be established as a lead-lag phenomenon. Then the PPP theory is valid only in weak form as the law of one price. Even so, if inflation rates can be projected with relative ease and accuracy, the PPP relationship may be of use in forecasting exchange rates.

VIII.   FIRMS' ACCOUNTING PRACTICES

Aliber and Stickney (1975) point out that the accounting practice of firms with assets or liabilities abroad can reflect an implicit acceptance of the PPP theory. They note that foreign-currency-denominated *real* assets or liabilities are typically expressed in domestic currency at the historical exchange rate (that at which the asset or liability was originally obtained or incurred), and not at the current exchange rate. This accounting convention involves the assumption that the exchange rate and relative inflation rates at home and abroad move so as to compensate for one another, with no change in the real exchange rate. Therefore, the firms' real assets and liabilities abroad are deemed not to be exposed to exchange-rate risk. As Aliber and Stickney (1975, pp. 45–46) write: "If the PPP theory holds perfectly for all commodities, exchange losses and changes in local prices of nonmonetary assets are offsetting and thereby not exposed."

In   contrast,   foreign-currency-denominated   *monetary*   assets   or liabilities in a firm's balance sheet are converted to domestic currency at the current exchange rate. This practice means that monetary assets and liabilities in foreign currency are considered fully exposed to exchange-rate risk. The Fisher Open proposition, that the domestic/foreign interest-rate differential compensates for expected exchange-rate changes, is implicitly rejected. Again, as described by Aliber and Stickney (1975, p. 46); "If the Fisher Effect holds, cumulative interest revenue (expense) over the maturity of the financial asset includes an amount equal to the exchange loss (gain) from changes in the exchange rate . . . monetary items are not exposed to losses from exchange rate changes."

Aliber and Stickney conclude that the conventional accounting practice is founded wrongly on the dichotomy between real and monetary assets and liabilities. The reason is that empirical testing shows that both the PPP and Fisher Open theories exhibit increasing validity over time. So, as the firm's planning horizon lengthens, *all* its assets and liabilities tend not to be exposed to exchange-rate risk.

IX. GUIDE TO INTERVENTION POLICY

A policy application of the PPP theory under the present system of managed exchange rates is proposed in a report by a group of economists established by the Commission of European Communities (1977, pp. 79–96). A good summary of its so-called OPTICA (for "OPTImum Currency Area") report is provided elsewhere by Thygesen (1978), a member of the group.

Basically, the proposal envisages each country in the EC as establishing a reference rate for its currency, using the effective-exchange-rate concept. A corresponding "effective PPP index" is calculated by dividing the domestic country's WPI by a weighted average of the WPIs of its competitors. The reference rate is to be changed periodically (at least quarterly) in proportion to a moving average of its PPP index.

A band is to be established around the reference rate. At the beginning of every period (month or quarter), it is ascertained whether the country's exchange rate has depreciated or appreciated with respect to the moving average of its PPP index over the past year. For a depreciated (appreciated) currency, the monetary authorities must buy (sell) their currency on the foreign-exchange market to prevent the exchange value of their currency from falling below (rising above) its lowest (highest) permissible value within the band.

These rules establish that, apart from the permissible movement within the band, a country's currency cannot depreciate (appreciate) beyond its relative inflation (deflation) with respect to the rate of change of the foreign price level. Thus, relative PPP provides a crawling-peg or sliding-parity reference rate from which the market exchange rate can deviate only within a margin on either side, and the limits are respected by means of official market intervention.

What are the advantages and disadvantages of the OPTICA rule for official management of exchange rates? The principal advantage is that, if strictly followed, the rule would help stabilize the macro-economy in the face of exchange-rate changes. Following a careful analytical examination of the workings of the rule, Basevi and De Grauwe (1977, p. 300) conclude: "the OPTICA proposal for managing exchange rates has been shown to constitute a powerful built-in stabilizer both for avoiding excessive inflation and depreciation in 'vicious' countries, and for preventing monetary authorities from causing unnecessary unemployment on the basis of their rigidly set monetary targets."

One disadvantage of the rule is that, if rigidly followed, it can prevent a change in the real exchange rate required by a structural or nonstructural real change in the economy.[23] So some flexibility in the rule would be required, perhaps in the form of changing the base period for calculation of the relative PPP that constitutes the crawling reference rate.

Another aspect of the rule can be deemed either an advantage or a disadvantage. As Thygesen (1978) points out, in permitting nominal exchange rates to compensate for divergent inflation rates, the intervention rule is too permissive; for the EC objective of becoming a common currency area does not receive support in the form of pressure on the member countries to harmonize monetary policy, thus correcting divergent rates of inflation. However, if fixed exchange rates among EC members are chosen as a path to a common currency area, then divergent inflation rates give rise to pressure for exchange-rate adjustments. As the OPTICA report, Commission of the European Communities (1977, p. 92), states: "... contrary to the snake arrangement—this scheme cannot be endangered by a persistent divergence between countries' monetary and income polices."

It is noteworthy that the European Monetary System, established in 1979, involves the second route to adjustment—pegged exchange rates within bands, with provision for changes in these rates. The OPTICA rule for a PPP-based crawling peg for EC members was not adopted.

A definite weakness of the OPTICA proposal is the selection of the price concept underlying PPP. Because it is heavily weighted with internationally traded goods, the WPI tends to justify the current exchange rate—whatever its level—as corresponding closely to an equilibrium rate in terms of PPP. So, divergences of the actual rate from the true equilibrium exchange rate (defined by an optimal PPP measure) are likely to be underestimated. Therefore, the magnitude of exchange-rate adjustment necessary to keep the actual rate in line with the true equilibrium rate will also tend to be underestimated. It is noteworthy that the OPTICA group considered the GDP deflator as the price concept for PPP, but rejected it because of data unavailability: most EC countries do not publish national accounts on a quarterly basis.[24]

It should be emphasized that the PPP-based market-intervention rule was proposed for the EC countries alone. As these countries have the goal of establishing a common currency area, the achievement of rigidly fixed exchange rates among their currencies is part of this ultimate objective. If the intervention rule is to be considered for countries outside the EC, one must assess it on other grounds. If the PPP theory is essentially correct as an explanation of the movements of a floating exchange rate, then it is arguable that the better route of conformity with exchange-market equilibrium is to cease all market intervention and have freely floating exchange rates.

It can be objected that while PPP is a good indicator of the long-run tendency of a floating rate, forces such as private speculation cause divergences from the path to long-run equilibrium. Then the issue becomes, whether speculation is stabilizing or destabilizing, and whether attempted "counter-speculation" by the monetary authorities is itself a source of stability or instability. The literature on this subject is too vast to be explored here. My own position on the matter is one of skepticism as to the stabilizing force that official market intervention can provide. In a review of McKinnon's *Money in International Exchange*, I commented as follows:

> McKinnon does not pay much attention to official intervention in the exchange market. He views such transactions as having a *stabilizing* effect on the exchange rate because central bankers lack a capital constraint and have maximum knowledge of the future course of monetary policy. Other observers might object that central banks do not consistently behave "rationally" and that private market participants can be so affected by official intervention that stabilizing speculation becomes destabilizing speculation. The Canadian case of 1961–62 comes to mind: the minimal variations in the Canadian dollar under the previous, essentially free, float gave way to destabilizing speculation and a destabilized rate consequent upon government intervention. It can be reasonably argued that the large variations in the floating exchange rates of the 1970s are, in large part, a *result* of official intervention (Officer, 1980b, p. 564).

NOTES

1. Of course, for comparison of components of GDP or categories of national expenditure rather than overall GDP, the price concept underlying PPP must be suitably restricted in coverage. The PPP technique has been used for the currency conversion of

national-accounts data at finely disaggregative levels of expenditure. See Kravis and others (1975; 1978a).

2. It should be noted that the comparison technique need not directly involve multiplication of a country's output by its PPP (with respect to a standard country). Rather, the procedure can involve evaluating components of GDP for a set of countries in terms of a common set of prices. Selection of the precise vector of prices to be used involves an index-number problem analogous to that discussed in Chapter IX. In applying this method, a measure of absolute PPP is naturally computed for each country.

3. Appropriately enough, the discussion is entitled "The Misleading of Mr. Churchill." (See Keynes, 1925; 1932, pp. 244-253.)

4. Examples of authors who state the Keynesian viewpoint are Nurkse (1944, pp. 125-126), Gudin and Kingston (1951, pp. 61-62), and Balassa (1964, p. 592). Some other writers with this position are cited by Moggridge (1972, p. 100, fn. 1).

5. References to those authors that support Gregory's minority position are provided by Moggridge (1972, p. 101, fn. 1). For references to authors with other challenges to the Keynesian view that the pound was overvalued, see Yeager (1976, p. 323, fn. 32).

6. Moggridge (1972, ch. 4) and Yeager (1976, pp. 321-334) offer recent assessments of the U.K. return to the gold standard. Moggridge (1972, ch. 3) also provides a comprehensive account of the elements in Churchill's decision.

7. See Haberler (1945, p. 312; 1961, p. 49, fn. 37). A different criticism is made by Nurkse (1944, p. 128), who points out that the precise application of PPP left no margin in the new rate for balance-of-payments pressure arising from expansion of output.

8. An analysis of the Czechoslovakian experience by the League of Nations (1936) implies that WPIs were so used: "the sole purpose of devaluation was to adjust Czechoslovak prices to world levels" (1936, p. 50). This statement is followed by a reference to the necessity of preventing "any considerable internal rise of prices lest the competitive capacity of Czech exporters be again impaired," and then a discussion of *rising wholesale prices* in connection with the Belgian devaluation in the following year.

9. One might comment that this had not necessarily been an equilibrium parity at the time (1930). It is also true that by taking into account only the pound, the Belgian authorities could not obtain optimal results. However, Britain was the country with which Belgium's trade links were strongest. As Triffin (1937, p. 45) writes: "it appears in every way to be the country that best characterizes the international influences to which our prices are exposed."

10. The PPP measures also differed in that the 1930-based concept involved expression of the Belgian and British COL indices in gold prices.

11. See Council on Prices, Productivity and Incomes (1958, p. 70).

12. Casual observation would suggest that this estimate is too high, whereas the dollar/deutsche-mark result would appear more reasonable.

13. A summary of the Tsiang and Aliber studies is provided by Stern (1973, pp. 95-101).

14. A good critical survey of the entire literature on attempts to identify destabilizing speculation is made by Kohlhagen (1978, pp. 36-42).

15. See, for example, Holzman (1968b) and Wiles (1969).

16. The error term is omitted here and in subsequent equations.

17. This is the assessment also of Neuberger (1968, p. 362).

18. See, in particular, Wiles (1969, pp. 130, 154-155, 190, 424-427).

19. For discussions of exchange-rate forecasting under the par-value system, see Jacque (1978, ch. 4) and the references cited there.

20. For example, turning points may be forecasted based on the percent deviation of an exchange rate from its previous high or low.

21. A rigorous treatment of the methodology of forecasting exchange rates and an assessment of some forecasting techniques (though not including PPP) are provided by Levich (1979).

22. For a useful survey of the effective-exchange-rate concept, see Rhomberg (1976).

23. However, not all real exchange-rate changes are thwarted. The asymmetrical nature of the intervention rule allows some such changes to take place. For a rigorous treatment of this issue, see Basevi and De Grauwe (1977).

24. See Thygesen (1978, pp. 303–304). He comments that some observers regard the GDP deflator as "the most suitable in measuring PPP, because it is the most broadly based."

Chapter XI

Tests of the Validity of the Absolute PPP Theory

"The empirical results provide evidence for the validity of my proposition regarding the relationship between purchasing-power parities, exchange rates, and per capita income levels." (Bela Balassa, 1964, p. 589)

Empirical testing of the absolute PPP theory, the subject of the present chapter, is limited by the available data on absolute PPP. It is, of course, much easier to compute measures of relative PPP; so tests of the relative form of the PPP theory—to be surveyed in Chapter XII—are much more numerous and varied. On the absolute-PPP side, the productivity-bias hypothesis is generally viewed as the most serious criticism of the theory. Therefore, it is not surprising that most empirical testing of absolute PPP has involved investigating the productivity-bias hypothesis. Other approaches to testing the absolute-PPP theory are also reviewed in this chapter.

I. REPRESENTATION OF THE NONTRADABLE/TRADABLE PRICE RATIO

A fundamental criticism of the absolute-PPP theory is that the ratio of the price level of nontraded commodities to that of traded commodities may differ systematically between countries.[1] Now, in empirical testing of this aspect of PPP theory, the ratio of a domestic country's nontradable/tradable price ratio to that of a standard country (say, the United States) is typically proxied by the ratio of absolute PPP to the actual exchange rate (number of units of domestic currency per dollar). Is this a justifiable procedure? Consider the following notation:

PL^i = general price level in country i

PT^i = price level of traded commodities in country i, with a weight of α^i in the general price level

PN^i = price level of nontraded commodities in country i, with a weight of β^i in the general price level

R = actual exchange rate, price of the dollar in terms of domestic currency

PPP = absolute purchasing power parity, ratio of the domestic to the foreign general price level

where $\alpha^i + \beta^i = 1$, and the superscript "US" will be used to refer to the United States.

Then the issue concerns the legitimacy of the approximation

$$\frac{PPP}{R} \approx \frac{PN^i/PT^i}{PN^{US}/PT^{US}} \tag{1}$$

It is expected that

$$R \approx PT^i/PT^{US} \tag{2}$$

The exchange rate is only approximately equal to the ratio of the price levels of traded goods for two reasons. First, trade restrictions and transport costs prevent an exact equalization of prices of traded goods. Second, the weighting pattern *within* the traded-goods price level may differ in the two countries.[2] If relationship (2) is accepted, then

$$\frac{PPP}{R} \equiv \frac{PL^i/PL^{US}}{R} \approx \frac{PL^i/PL^{US}}{PT^i/PT^{US}} = \frac{PL^i/PT^i}{PL^{US}/PT^{US}}$$

$$= \frac{\dfrac{\alpha^i PT^i + \beta^i PN^i}{PT^i}}{\dfrac{\alpha^{US} PT^{US} + \beta^{US} PN^{US}}{PT^{US}}} = \frac{\alpha^i + \beta^i \dfrac{PN^i}{PT^i}}{\alpha^{US} + \beta^{US} \dfrac{PN^{US}}{PT^{US}}}$$

Therefore, a deviation between a country's (actual) exchange rate and its PPP involves (a) a divergence between the country's nontradable/tradable price ratio and that of the standard country (PN/PT) and/or (b) a divergence between the relative weights of traded and nontraded commodities (α/β) in the two countries' price levels. Considering a multicountry comparison, a systematic deviation between exchange rates and PPPs among countries entails a systematic divergence either in their nontradable/tradable price ratios and/or in the relative importance of traded and nontraded goods in the countries' economies. The latter difference in economic structure among countries is thus ignored by those who use *PPP/R* to represent the ratio of the nontradable/tradable price ratios at home and abroad. It is not obvious that a systematic difference in *PPP/R* among countries implies a corresponding difference in their nontradable/tradable price ratios, and hence a case against the validity of the PPP theory. To the extent that there is a systematic variation in the relative importance of traded and nontraded goods in the countries' economies, the *PPP/R* differences may be a reflection of this fact.

II. THE PRODUCTIVITY-BIAS HYPOTHESIS

Empirical testing of the productivity-bias hypothesis did not begin with the standard work of Balassa (1964), although references to earlier studies of this nature are rarely made. Among the several antecedents to Balassa's well-known study is one by Balassa himself three years earlier. With one exception, Rothschild (1958), the earlier empirical investigations, while using per capita income, do not interpret it as a proxy for an international productivity differential. In this respect, the early tests (excepting that of Rothschild) are comparable to that of Balassa (1964) only in form, not in underlying rationale.

In 1957, Hagen tested the hypothesis "that the greater the difference between the two countries in per capita income, the greater the error caused by use of the exchange rate to compare their price levels" (1957, p. 383).[3] He finds that, using data for the year 1950 developed by Gilbert and Kravis (1954), the hypothesis holds true among France, the Federal Republic of Germany, and Italy (with the United States as the standard country). However, the data point for the United Kingdom (the final country in the Gilbert-Kravis study) would fit the hypothesis only prior to the 1949 devaluation of the pound.

Balassa (1961) offers a hypothesis equivalent to that of Hagen and tests it using results of Gilbert and associates (1958). The variables *PPP/R* and per capita income have closely corresponding rankings for eight European countries in 1955.

Taking absolute PPP data from a variety of sources, Delahaut and Kirschen (1961) correlate *R/PPP* with per capita national income (converted into dollars at the actual exchange rate). The result, for the year 1957 with 18 countries providing data points, is a correlation coefficient of -0.86 (the correct sign, since the dependent variable is inverted). However, there is no discussion of a theory underlying this relationship.

Rothschild (1958) was the first author both to develop analytically and to test the productivity-bias hypothesis as such. He states the hypothesis as follows:

> ... purchasing-power equivalents (implied exchange rates) ... will normally yield exchange rates which are less favorable to the richer country than the official or 'equilibrium' rate. And the greater the differences in efficiency in manufacturing and, therefore, in manufacturing *wages* are, the more will the *price* of tertiary output in the wealthier country surpass the poorer country's prices and the more will the implied exchange rate diverge from the 'equilibrium' rate (1958, p. 232).

"Tertiary output," of course, refers principally to the services sector, composed primarily of nontradables. Also noted by Rothschild is the tendency for wages to be equalized in all producing sectors of a given country, in particular, in manufacturing and services.

Making use of cross-sectional absolute-PPP and exchange-rate data both with the United States as the standard country, these data taken from Gilbert and associates (1958), and with the Federal Republic of Germany in that role, taken from the German Statistical Office, Rothschild performs a number of tests that confirm the productivity-bias hypothesis. The former data base PPP on a GNP price concept, while the latter involve household-consumption weights for price levels (a COL price concept). Also, in the first data set, the United States is the standard country; while in the second, Germany plays that role. Further, the year is 1950 in the first case, 1955 in the second. No matter; in both cases the *PPP/R* ratio is positively related to per capita GNP (though a formal correlation analysis is not used). Rothschild also shows, using the Gilbert and associates data for components of GNP, that the divergence between *PPP* (specific to the GNP component) and the exchange rate (*R*) is much greater for manufactured goods than for services—again a result consistent with the productivity-bias hypothesis.

So Balassa (1964) was the second author to state explicitly, and to test empirically, the hypothesis of a systematic bias in (absolute) PPP as a measure of the equilibrium exchange rate, this bias arising from productivity differntials: "the higher level of service prices at higher income levels leads to systematic differences between purchasing-power parities and equilibrium exchange rates" (1964, p. 589). He provides two kinds of evidence for this hypothesis. First, he uses sectoral PPP computations for the year 1950[4] to show that "services [i.e., nontraded goods] are by and large cheaper in countries with relatively low incomes" (1964, p. 588). Second, he regresses *PPP/R* on per capita GNP (converted into dollars using *R*) for 12 member countries of the Organization for Economic Cooperation and Development (OECD) for the year 1960.[5] The correlation coefficient is 0.92.

Later, a non-structural form of this relationship was "rediscovered" by David (1972; 1973); and in commenting on David's analysis, Balassa (1973)[6] re-expresses his equation so that the independent variable is the ratio of domestic to U.S. per capita GNP and re-estimates the equation using revised data for the independent variable. He converts domestic currency GNP to dollars by means of, alternatively, the actual exchange rate and the PPP. Results are consistent with those of the original regression. In fact, Clague and Tanzi (1972) had earlier re-estimated Balassa's original regression using the exchange rate and PPP as alternative conversion factors for output, and found little difference in the results.

To counter Officer's criticism (1974) that his first set of evidence assumes equal quality of services across countries,[7] Balassa (1974a) calculates that the quality of education and medical care in the United States would have to exceed that in Europe by a factor ranging from 2.5 to 5 (depending on the country) for the criticism to be validated empirically. The data refer to the year 1950 and the computations assume that there are no international quality differences in other kinds of services.

Officer (1974) also questioned Balassa's econometric test of PPP. One criticism concerns the choice of independent variable. The ratio of GDP to employment would appear to be a better measure of a country's level of productivity than GNP divided by total population.

Another problem with Balassa's test is common to the tests and empirical commentaries of Balassa's predecessors. The hypothesis of a systematic bias in PPP can be tested, strictly speaking, only by comparing PPP with the long-run equilibrium value of the exchange rate.[8] Balassa and his predecessors substitute the actual (that is, official) exchange rate (generally the par value) for the equilibrium rate. The validity of the test then hinges on the assumption that, across countries at a given point in time, the actual exchange rate is proportional to the long-run equilibrium rate. The test would be less powerful (but retain some validity) if the correlation between the actual and equilibrium exchange rate exceeded the correlation between the PPP and the equilibrium rate. Therefore, a judicious choice of the year to which the test is applied could assure a high correlation between the former set of variables and thus validate the test. Balassa suggests an alternative criterion to judge the applicability of his test. The test would be invalid only if "the ratio of the equilibrium to the actual exchange rate . . . [were] positively related to productivity in the same way as in the ratio of purchasing power parity to the actual exchange rate" (1974a, p. 882, fn.3).

A few authors have tested whether Balassa's result is also applicable to less developed countries (LDCs). Grunwald and Salazar-Carrillo (1972) present PPPs for 11 Latin American countries in 1968, based on specially collected data. Letting Venezuela replace the United States as the standard country, they find that the rank correlation between *PPP/R* and per capita GDP has the wrong sign, irrespective of whether official exchange rates or free rates are used. The authors conclude that the Balassa hypothesis is not applicable to Latin America.

Clague and Tanzi (1972) perform Balassa's regression (*PPP/R* on per capita output) for a sample of 19 Latin American countries, with the United States as the standard country, for the year 1960. The explanatory variable, per capita GDP, is converted from domestic currency to dollars using, alternatively, *R* and *PPP*. The PPP measures are absolute parities with a GDP price concept.[9] The authors report $\bar{R}^2$ to be .24 in the first case and −.05 in the second. Again, these results are unfavorable to the productivity-bias hypothesis.

These challenges to the hypothesis are confined to samples of LDCs. In an examination of the data underlying Balassa's (1964) own regression equation and a reconsideration of the methodology of his testing procedure (and that of others who tested the hypothesis), Officer (1976b) concludes that some of Balassa's data points are illegitimate and should be dropped.[10] Then estimation of Balassa-type regressions (*PPP/R* on per capita GDP or GDP per worker) results in an elimination of the statistical significance of the slope coefficient.

Drawing on data from a variety of sources, Officer assembles four sets of *PPP/R* data: two sets with the Federal Republic of Germany as the standard country and a COL price concept for PPP, and two with the United States as the standard country and a GNP or GDP price concept. Three alternative explanatory variables are used. The first such variable is per capita GDP, the usual independent variable (which can also be GNP per capita) in regressions testing the productivity-bias hypothesis. The second variable is GDP per employed worker, a finer measure of productivity. A productivity variable with even greater precision is the third alternative: the ratio of productivity in the tradable sector of the economy to productivity in the nontradable sector.[11] All three variables are constructed as ratios of the domestic to the standard country's productivity measure.

Over 150 regressions are estimated, and only two exhibit a productivity variable the coefficient of which is significant at even the 5-percent level. The conclusion is that a careful examination of the empirical evidence does not justify acceptance of the productivity-bias hypothesis. It should be noted that the data consist entirely of developed countries. The negative results for country groups that exclude LDCs are unique in the literature.[12]

In several pathbreaking studies of international comparisons of output and purchasing power, Kravis and his associates investigate the productivity-bias hypothesis. As the dependent variable they use the ratio of the domestic country's GDP obtained on a PPP basis relative to the United States to GDP relative to the United States when data conversion is made using the exchange rate,[13] and they call it the "exchange-rate deviation index." Redefining *PPP* and *R* (the exchange rate) so that they are the ratio of the foreign to the domestic price level and the price of domestic currency in terms of foreign currency, respectively (that is, so that their common dimension is units of foreign currency per unit of domestic currency), the exchange-rate deviation index is essentially *PPP/R*. The measures differ slightly, because internationally comparable GDP is obtained directly by weighting component outputs by prices (actually a Fisher index is used).[14] The exchange-rate deviation index is a good representation of a *PPP/R* measure in which a GDP price concept underlies PPP and a Fisher ideal index of the parities based upon the U.S. and domestic weighting patterns is used. It should be noted that this *PPP/R* measure is the inverse of that defined earlier in the chapter, and is therefore expected to be negatively related to the productivity variable.

Certainly among the most reliable absolute-PPP, and associated GDP, data computed to date are those assembled by Kravis and others (1975, especially ch. 13). A variety of countries are considered: three LDCs, five market developed countries (DCs), and one state-trading economy (STE), with the United States as the standard country. They consider the year 1970 and plot the exchange-rate deviation index against PPP-based per capita GDP. The exchange-rate deviation index is greater than unity for all countries, because the United States, the richest country, is the standard country. The correlation of the index with per capita GDP is negative, as predicted by the productivity-bias hypothesis, but not strong.

Also, the authors plot the exchange-rate deviation index against the ratio of the PPP for traded goods to the PPP for nontraded goods,[15] that is, the reciprocal of the nontradable/tradable price ratio in the domestic country to that in the United States. This is an extremely important relationship to consider; for, in effect (taking reciprocals of the variables), the relationship tests the fundamental assumption that *PPP/R* (with its former dimension: units of domestic currency per dollar) is a satisfactory proxy for the ratio of the nontradable/tradable price ratio at home to that in the United States; that is, it tests "Equation" (1). It turns out that the observed relationship is positive and quite strong. Certainly, a scanning of the two graphs indicates that the exchange-rate deviation index versus per capita GDP relationship is weaker in comparison.

Using a variety of sources, Kravis (1976) assembles per capita output converted to dollars by the exchange rate and on a PPP basis for some 40 countries. He notes that "there is a strong tendency for conversions via the exchange rate to show a bigger understatement for low-income countries than for higher income countries" (1976, p. 21). This result is consistent with the productivity-bias hypothesis.

Kravis and Lipsey (1978) perform a double-logarithmic regression of the GDP price level on PPP-based GDP (both relative to the United States) for a cross-section of 10 countries, with the data taken from Kravis and others (1975). The positive relationship predicted by the productivity-bias hypothesis is obtained. Substituting the price level of nontradables for the GDP price level, again a positive slope coefficient is obtained. This result, too, supports the productivity-bias hypothesis. Using the tradables price level as the dependent variable, no systematic relationship is expected to obtain. In fact, there is again a positive slope coefficient with an equal statistical significance to that for the nontradables variable, though only one-quarter the magnitude. This last result, which shows "that even tradables tend to be more expensive in higher income countries" (1978, p. 223), suggests that the productivity-bias hypothesis does not provide a full explanation of the variation in *PPP/R* among countries. It also, of course, casts some doubt on the law of one price for tradables.[16]

In a second important contribution to data on absolute PPP and internationally comparable GDP, Kravis and others (1978a) provide such information for 16 countries, the ten in the 1975 study plus 4 more LDCs and two additional DCs. They show that, as a cross-sectional relationship over the 16 countries, the relative price of services, or of services and construction (representing the nontradable sector), increases with per capita income.[17] This result is again favorable to the productivity-bias hypothesis.

III. EXTENSIONS OF THE PRODUCTIVITY-BIAS HYPOTHESIS

Clague and Tanzi (1972) extend the productivity-bias hypothesis by including, in addition to per capita income, two variables measuring the severity of trade restrictions: import (export) duties as a percentage of imports (exports). Import (export) restrictions increase (reduce) the general price level at fixed exchange rates; therefore, the country's *PPP/R* ratio—with numerator and denominator having dimension number of units of domestic currency per unit of foreign currency—is positively (negatively) related to the import-restriction (export-restriction) variable. Clague and Tanzi fit the expanded productivity-bias regression to their sample of 19 Latin American countries, with per capita income obtained alternatively using R and PPP. They find that the new variables have the theoretically correct signs and improve the explanatory power of the regression.

Kravis and others (1975, pp. 187–88) assert that variables other than income are required to explain country differences in the exchange-rate deviation index. They suggest that one such variable is the importance of a country's international trading relationships. A country with a higher ratio of trade (exports plus imports) to GDP is expected to have the index closer to unity, because its economy is more influenced by world prices. The authors find firm support for this hypothesis among the LDCs but only mixed support among the market DCs.

Using the data for 16 countries developed in Kravis and others (1978a), these same authors (1978b) estimate an extended productivity-bias model in which PPP-based GDP per capita is a uniformly-logarithmic function of (i) exchange-rate converted GDP per capita, (ii) the square of the former variable, (iii) the mean squared difference for the years 1963–1970 between the domestic country's GDP deflator and a world GDP deflator, and (iv) the ratio of exports plus imports to GNP. All variables are defined relative to the United States, and regressions are estimated for both 1970 and 1973. The explanatory power of the regressions is very high, with the coefficient of variable (i), representing the elemental productivity-bias effect, the most significant of all the effects.

It should be noted that the purpose of the equation is to estimate PPP-based GDP for countries outside the sample, hence the specification of variable (i) as an independent, rather than part of the dependent, variable; hence also the inclusion of variable (ii). Variables (iii) and (iv) are included as measures of the susceptibility of the domestic country's price level to international influences. This modification of the productivity-bias hypothesis had been suggested in Kravis and others (1975), as noted above. One would expect a negative effect of variable (iii) and, correspondingly, a positive influence of variable (iv); though effects working in the opposite direction could exist.[18] It turns out that the expected directional effects are obtained.

IV. ALTERNATIVES TO THE PRODUCTIVITY-BIAS HYPOTHESIS

Clague and Tanzi (1972) extend Balassa's analysis from a model in which labor is the only limiting factor of production to a three-factor model involving unskilled labor, human capital, and natural resources. Their theory results in an equation with the nontradable/tradable price ratio (represented by *PPP/R*) as the dependent variable, and human capital per worker and the ratio of natural resources to other factors of production as principal explanatory variables. The independent variables are not available directly; so, to proxy them the authors engage in data selection and construction of a rather rarefied kind. Human capital per worker is measured by an index of enrollment rates beyond primary school. Natural resource abundance is proxied by deviations from a regression of per capita income on the human-capital variable. The trade-restriction variables are also included in the regression.

The authors then test their model against that of Balassa, applying the models to Balassa's sample of 12 OECD countries and to their sample of 19 Latin American countries, each pertaining to the year 1960. For the Balassa model, per capita income (presumably GNP for the OECD countries, GDP for the Latin American countries) is expressed in U.S. dollars with *R* and *PPP* as alternative conversion factors.

The findings are that the Balassa hypothesis performs better for the OECD countries, but the Clague-Tanzi equation is far superior for the Latin American countries. In fairness to Balassa, he does not consider his equation to be applicable to LDCs, and indeed warns against such an extrapolation of his results. He mentions as reasons the differences between DCs and LDCs in the importance of nontraded goods, endowment of natural resources, height of tariffs, and amount of capital inflow. He criticizes the Clague-Tanzi selection of variables as inadequate attempts to take account of these differences.[19]

Isenman (1979) combines elements of both the Kravis and others (1978b) and Clague-Tanzi (1972) models. Using the former authors' data, Isenman regresses the logarithm of the exchange-rate deviation index on the four explanatory variables of these authors' equation (variables (i) to (iv) above, again expressed in logarithmic form) and also on (v) the ratio of teacher salaries, converted to dollars at the official exchange rate, to exchange-rate-converted GDP per capita relative to U.S. GDP per capita, and (vi) the logarithm of the secondary-school enrollment rate. Variable (v) represents wages in service industries. It is expected to have a negative effect on the dependent variable, because higher wages in the nontradable sector mean a higher price level and therefore a lower PPP-converted income. Variable (vi) has the opposite effect, because it represents the supply of skilled workers, which is negatively related to the price of services, and therefore positively related to PPP-converted income.

Results are not as strong as those of Kravis and others (1978b), but Isenman makes a good case that their specification is inferior. He especially criticizes the form of their dependent variable.

V. ALTERNATIVE COMPUTATIONS OF EXCHANGE-RATE DISEQUILIBRIUM

If a comparison of PPP with the official exchange rate is used to measure the amount of currency overvaluation or undervaluation, the result may be checked by computing the disequilibrium using another method. Houthakker (1962a) had applied absolute PPP to reach the conclusion that the U.S. dollar was overvalued by about 20 percent in 1962. Floyd (1965) questions this result as too high. He develops a model in which the disequilibrium of a country's currency (that is, the depreciation or appreciation percentage that would restore exchange-rate equilibrium) is a specified function of various variables and parameters. He selects alternative sets of values of the parameters to show that the dollar was overvalued by only about 7 percent. Obviously, however, one cannot judge between the Houthakker and Floyd results on the basis of divergent estimates alone.

VI. COST PARITY

There is no literature involving direct testing of the cost-parity version of absolute-PPP theory, but there is a related empirical study. If the unit-labor-cost parity is to yield the same value as a price parity, then the following relationship must hold.[20]

$$\frac{W^B}{W^A} = \frac{PR^B}{PR^A} \cdot \frac{P^B}{P^A} \tag{3}$$

Officer (1974) collected annual data for 10 DCs over the years 1952–1970, with the Federal Republic of Germany (B) as the base country. The ratio of the price level of the Federal Republic of Germany to the domestic price level is measured as the geometric mean (Fisher ideal index) of the German-weighted and domestic-weighted COL PPPs computed by the Statistical Office of the Federal Republic of Germany. Wage rates are represented by hourly earnings in manufacturing and productivity by the ratio of GDP to employment, where GDP is converted into deutsche mark using the computed PPP (Fisher index). The equation

$$\log \left(\frac{W^B}{W^A} \right) = \alpha + \beta \log \left(\frac{PR^B}{PR^A} \cdot \frac{P^B}{P^A} \right)$$

is fitted to the pooled cross-sectional and time-series data, with the result that the hypothesis "$\alpha = 0$ and $\beta = 1$" cannot be rejected even at a high level of significance. Therefore, there are some grounds for using a price-parity measure as a proxy for a cost parity—a useful result, given the less favorable data situation regarding factor costs and productivity compared with product prices.

NOTES

1. See Chapter IX.
2. Again, for an elaboration of these points, see Chapter IX.
3. For an even earlier discussion of this hypothesis, accompanied by empirical computations (involving the Netherlands Indies guilder in relationship to the U.S. dollar), see Polak (1943, ch. 17).
4. The data source is the same used by Rothschild: Gilbert and associates (1958).
5. The PPP concept used is that of an absolute GNP price parity, A geometric mean (Fisher ideal index) of U.S. and domestic quantity-weighted PPPs is used for most countries. The basic data come from a variety of sources and, where necessary, are extrapolated to bring them up to date.
6. David's relationship is further discussed by Balassa (1974b) and Hulsman-Vejsová (1975).
7. See Chapter IX. Officer (1974) is reprinted as Chapter XIII of this volume.
8. Equivalently, nontradable/tradable price ratios should be compared between countries only when exchange rates are in long-run equilibrium.
9. The data source is Economic Commission for Latin American (1967). Presumably, the PPPs are the geometric means of the parities based on the average Latin American and on the U.S. weighting pattern. (The data source uses average Latin American expenditure patterns rather than those for individual countries.)
10. Officer (1976b) appears as Chapter XIV in the present volume.
11. For details on construction of this variable and its relationship to the other productivity measures, see Chapter XIV, Goldstein and Officer (1979), and Goldstein, Khan, and Officer (1980, pp. 192-94).
12. The unusual findings of Officer's study have been noticed by the OPTICA report, that is, Commission of the European Communities (1977, p. 8), Isard (1978, p. 5, fn. 2), Genberg (1978, pp. 264, 267), and Kravis and Lipsey (1978, p. 224).
13. The formal definition of Kravis and his associates involves *per capita* GDP. Obviously, the definition is invariant to expressing GDP in absolute-level or per capita terms.
14. See footnote 2 of Chapter X.
15. Both PPPs are Fisher indices of the respective U.S.-weighted and domestic-currency-weighted parities.
16. Kravis and Lipsey (1978, p. 223) also explore some other possible explanations of the result.
17. See Kravis and others (1978a, pp. 123-28).
18. See Kravis and others (1978a, p. 223).
19. See Balassa (1973; 1974b).
20. Equation (3) is simply a rearrangement of Equation (4) in Chapter VIII.

Chapter XII

Tests of the Validity of the
Relative PPP Theory

"Each analyst will have to decide in the light of his own purposes whether the PPP relationships fall close enough to 1.00 to satisfy the theories." (Kravis and Lipsey, 1978, p. 214)

Principally because of the ease of calculating relative-parity measures, there exist a large number of empirical tests of the relative PPP hypothesis. To make a review of this literature manageable, a number of areas of empirical investigations that bear on the validity of relative PPP are nevertheless excluded from this discussion. These omitted topics include tests of the following issues: the uniformity or convergence of countries' inflation rates under fixed exchange rates, the international transmission of inflation, the law of one price at disaggregative levels,[1] "Scandinavian-type" models of the economy (models focusing on the distinction between the tradable and nontradable sectors), and "ratchet" theories (such as the so-called Mundell-Laffer hypothesis) involving asymmetrical relationships between exchange rates and prices. Generally, the authors of studies in these areas do not explicitly relate their work to the PPP theory.

A final exclusion, however, is of certain studies ostensibly in the PPP domain, namely, those in which a price concept clearly unsuited for PPP is used. Examples of such price measures are those restricted to traded goods—the export price index (EPI) or import price index—and any wholesale price index (WPI) at a disaggregative level (typically this would be the WPI for manufactures).[2] A case can be made that even a *general* WPI is illegitimate for testing the PPP theory;[3] but a large number of studies would thereby be excluded from consideration.

Even with these exclusions, a large body of literature remains to be surveyed. It is convenient to consider this literature within the framework of six different types of empirical tests of the relative PPP theory. First, there are time-series comparisons of PPP with a floating exchange rate in which a contemporaneous relationship is postulated. Second, the same comparison may be made with lagged relationships, and formal tests for causality may be employed. Third, comparative-static comparisons of PPP and the exchange rate may apply both to fixed and floating exchange-rate systems and extend over time periods of any length. Fourth, the PPP theory may be restated in "augmented" form to incorporate variables in addition to the PPP, for better determination of a floating exchange rate. Fifth, the PPP theory may be tested in the form of the real exchange rate. Sixth, and finally, movements in the nontradable/tradable price ratio may be investigated.

I. TIME-SERIES COMPARISONS OF PPP WITH A FLOATING EXCHANGE RATE: CONTEMPORANEOUS RELATIONSHIP

An obvious test of PPP theory is the following: calculate a time series of relative PPP during a period when the exchange rate is floating and compare it with the corresponding time series of the floating rate. PPP theory asserts that there is a tendency for the short-run equilibrium exchange rate, that is, a freely floating rate, to equal the PPP.[4] Noticeable divergences between the actual rate and PPP are then explained in terms of other influences on the rate.

In those studies that deal with the period during or after World War I, the base-period rate is always the prewar (generally 1913) mint parity of the two currencies involved. The early writers do not always specify the nature of the price series used to construct the PPP or cite the data sources; in these cases it is reasonable to assume that WPIs are used, as these were the first general price indices available. Some authors adopt the consumer price index (CPI) or an early variant of this measure. Often, the standard currency is taken to be the dollar, which remained on the gold standard while most European currencies floated after World War I. The next most commonly used standard currency is the British pound. In later work also, the dollar is the usual standard currency. The German mark is also used for that purpose, and recent work sometimes adopts an effective-exchange-rate framework. This discussion of the standard currency applies not just to the present section but to the entire chapter.

The earliest time-series study is performed by Gustav Cassel himself

1916a). Taking a prewar period as the base, he computes a PPP between the pound and the floating Swedish krona monthly for the year 1915. Cassel concludes: "The unmistakable conformity of the curves for the theoretical and actual rates may be regarded as a remarkably good proof of the theory here set forth" (1916a, p. 64). Because of acknowledged data limitations,[5] this was regarded as only a preliminary test of the PPP theory. For Cassel, the definitive test was a comparison of the pound/dollar PPP and exchange rate during the floating-pound period that followed World War I.[6] Cassel (1925c) computes R/PPP (both numerator and denominator expressed in number of pounds per dollar)[7] monthly for the period 1919–1924. He notes that the dollar is overvalued or undervalued with respect to the pound according as R/PPP is greater or less than unity. The average overvaluation is only 0.3 percent, and Cassel's explanation of the subperiods of overvaluation or undervaluation of the dollar centers on international capital movements. For example, he points out that dollar undervaluation occurs in periods of substantial capital outflow from the United States. Cassel is emphatic that the results imply rejection of the conventional explanation of exchange-rate movements in terms of variations in the balance of trade; for the R/PPP series does not exhibit regular seasonal fluctuations.[8]

This last conclusion is disputed by Crump (1925), who plots three R/PPP series monthly for the period 1920–1924, one of which is Cassel's series, the other two computed from alternative price indices for the United States and the United Kingdom. Crump notes that all three series rise in the autumn and decline in the spring, following the known balance-of-trade pattern.

Keynes (1919; 1923) twice provided empirical evidence to support Cassel's PPP theory. As editor of the *Economic Journal*, he called attention to data for a number of countries over 1913–1919, showing that the expansion of currency corresponds closely both to the increase in domestic prices and to the exchange rate (with Britain as the standard currency). Later, Keynes (1923, pp. 99–106) computed PPPs for the British, French, and Italian currencies versus the dollar monthly for the period 1919–1923. The dollar/pound comparison provides "a remarkable illustration of the tendency to concordance between the purchasing power parity and the rate of exchange," and the results for France and Italy show that "the Purchasing Power Parity Theory, even in its crude form, has worked passably well" (1923, pp. 100–106).

Furniss (1922, pp. 56-60) makes a number of comparisons, exhibited in tabular and graphical form with time span 1913 to 1920–1921, to show "the tendency of the exchange rates to conform to the purchasing power parities of the different national moneys" (1922, p. 58). Similar evidence, but with the United Kingdom rather than the United States as the standard country, is offered by Gregory (1925, pp. 86-90) in support of the PPP theory. Gregory notices that countries with the greatest inflation exhibit the largest deviations of the exchange rate from PPP. This leads him to explain divergences of exchange rates from PPP largely in terms of anticipated inflation.

The United States Tariff Commission (1922) computed monthly series of the real exchange rate (WPI concept) for several countries over 1919-1921, with the United States as the standard country. Major divergences of the rate from unity are noted. It seems that the authors see the empirical evidence as indicating either lags or inhibiting factors (such as trade restrictions) in the adjustment process.

An impressive collection of studies dealing with the post-World War I exchange-rate experience of the United States and a large number of European countries was assembled by Young (1925). Government officials or academic persons were invited to submit reports dealing with their own country. Many adopt a PPP approach to the exchange rate, and in effect the theory is subjected to empirical testing. The evidence is generally favorable to PPP, with various explanations (consistent with those proposed by Cassel) offered to explain deviations from the strict form of the theory.

Angell (1926, pp. 424-40) presents time series of the PPP and exchange rate for the floating pound and French franc versus the dollar for the period 1919-1924. He sees the variation of both series as being due to a third force: the degree of confidence in a country's currency, itself determined by the amount of government inflationary finance and by the past depreciation of the currency.

The floating Swedish krona during World War I is the vehicle for Heckscher's time-series test of the PPP theory (1930, pp. 147-69, 212-14). He finds that the krona depreciated generally less than half as much with respect to the pound on the foreign-exchange market as in its relative internal purchasing power, and he rejects the PPP theory.

Results that confirm the PPP theory are reported by Graham (1930, pp. 117-26). He calculates WPI parities for 12 floating European currencies and computes the real exchange rate, *PPP/R* (both numerator and denominator expressed in number of dollars per unit of domestic currency), monthly over the period 1919-1923. His result: "If we exclude Germany, the clustering around the 100% figure is marked and aberrations were apparently self corrective" (1930, p. 121). For Germany, where hyperinflation occurred, *PPP/R* is well over 100 percent, that is, the exchange value of the deutsche mark was very low compared with its purchasing power.[9] To the extent that deviations of *R* from *PPP* do occur in countries other than Germany, Graham explains them as being due largely to capital flows, expectations of exchange-rate changes, and trade restrictions. He sees the determining factors in the German case as recurring fixed international liabilities and panic demand for foreign exchange in the face of a decline in the exchange value and purchasing power of the domestic currency.

The German hyperinflation is also the subject of a PPP investigation by Haberler (1936, pp. 61–62). The acute undervaluation of the mark with respect to the dollar is confirmed for the period of hyperinflation. For 1924–1925, while there is a close conformity with PPP, the mark remains slightly undervalued. The latter result, as Haberler notes, in effect indicates that not only monetary, but also real economic changes that influence the exchange rate occurred during the hyperinflation. A more systematic quantitative study of the relationship between Germany's exchange rate and PPP during the time of hyperinflation is offered by Bresciani-Turroni (1937, pp. 120–254). He ascribes divergences from the PPP hypothesis to the long-run nature of the theory.

In a study of the French inflation following World War I, Wasserman (1936) shows that the PPP theory is not corroborated. His explanation hinges on the workings of price-setting in French commodity and factor markets.

Young (1938, pp. 159–160) plots the U.S./U.K. exchange rate and PPP (based on the WPI) over the period 1912–1937. It is noted that this quarter-century spans periods of both fixed and floating rates. Deviations between the series are substantial during the war, as a result of exchange-rate management, and in the 1930s, explained as due to trade restrictions, capital flows, the balance of trade, and drastic price-level changes. One might comment that the 1930s were a period of severe world-wide deflation and depression rather than a "normal" period or one of substantial inflation, and it is the latter situations to which the PPP theory has been viewed as applicable.[10] The failure of PPP theory to predict exchange-rate movements in the 1930s is reflected in another study spanning the 1920s and 1930s.

This longer-run test of PPP is presented by Katano (1957), who computes a Japanese/U.S. WPI parity annually for the period 1921–1936. The yen was floating throughout that period except in 1930–1931; so the base year selected is 1930, with the mint parity between the yen and dollar taken as the base-period exchange rate. Katano computes the correlation coefficient between the exchange rate and PPP for the entire period 1921–1936 and for the subperiod 1925–1929. The coefficient is −0.06 for the overall period and 0.93 for the subperiod.[11]

Katano shows that these divergent correlations can be explained by the close approximation to pure price inflation in each country during the subperiod 1925-1929. He takes six commodities for Japan and six commodity groups for the United States, all of which weigh heavily in the respective country's WPI. For each commodity or commodity group, he computes the ratio of its price index to the WPI in the current year and compares it with the same ratio in the base year. There is no large divergence in these relative prices in the years 1926-1929 but a substantial change in relative prices in the years 1932-1936, during which time there is a large deviation of the exchange rate from PPP.

Yeager (1958) tests how well movements of the floating Canadian dollar (with respect to the U.S. dollar) were explainable in terms of PPP during the period 1950-1957. He finds a good correspondence of the exchange rate with a WPI parity but a low correlation with a CPI parity. The greater weight of traded goods in the WPI is not mentioned by Yeager as a possible cause of the differential result. Rather, he suggests as explanatory factors a slower response of retail than wholesale prices to monetary conditions and the narrow range of fluctuation of the U.S.-Canadian CPI ratio.

In a later study, Yeager (1969) looks back at the 19th century and correlates a WPI parity with the exchange rate of the floating Austrian gulden with respect to the pound. The correlation coefficient varies between 0.52 and 0.79, depending on the time period of the analysis and whether levels of the series or percentage changes are considered.

The model employed by Amacher and Hodgson (1974) to examine the exchange-rate policy of Yugoslavia[12] was used in an earlier study, pertaining once more to the floating currencies after World War I.

Letting R denote the exchange rate (number of dollars per unit of domestic currency) and P the ratio of the domestic to the U.S. WPI, Thomas (1973b) regresses $\log R$ on $\log P$ separately for 12 countries (10 European countries *plus* Canada and Japan) for which monthly data are available over the period 1920-1924.[13] He interprets the PPP theory in terms of percentage changes, that is, it predicts a unitary elasticity of the exchange rate (R) with respect to the purchasing power parity (P). Given his definition of the variables, the elasticity (β, the slope coefficient) is expected to be *minus* one.[14] Certainly, β must be significantly negative for the PPP theory to receive some confirmation. It turns out that while β is significantly negative for all countries, for all but one country (France) the value of β is also significantly below unity in absolute value. Thus, there is a systematic divergence between (percentage changes in) the exchange rate and PPP, which Thomas attributes to speculation.[15]

The same model is applied by Hodgson and Phelps (1975) to 14 countries with floating currencies in the period 1919–1925. WPIs are used to construct the P variable for all countries except Austria, for which a retail price index is employed.[16] The PPP variable (P) is significant with the correct sign in 9 of 14 cases. Hodgson and Phelps see this model as involving a severe test of PPP; for it requires a simultaneous movement of monthly exchange rates and prices, in contrast to a distributed-lag effect of PPP on the exchange rate.[17]

Where a pegged exchange rate is coupled with exchange control, a black-market exchange rate may play the role of a floating rate. Culbertson (1975) uses a CPI parity along with other variables (the official exchange rate and the amount of exchange-market intervention) to explain the black-market dollar exchange rates of India, the Philippines, and Turkey annually for the years 1952–1971. Fitting his equations in logarithmic form, Culbertson finds that in all cases the PPP not only provides the largest elasticity but also is the most significant explanatory variable.

Aliber and Stickney (1975) present average annual percentage deviations of a CPI-based PPP from the exchange rate for 48 countries over the period 1960–1971, as well as the maximum annual deviation for each country. Taking averages in algebraic terms, they show that the PPP theory exhibits increasing validity over time. While not purporting to test the validity of PPP, their "matrix suggests the PPP theory as a central tendency" (1975, p. 48).

In the latter half of the 1970s, there was a veritable explosion of empirical work on PPP, including use of the contemporaneous time-series approach. Myhrman (1976) selects a variety of historical episodes, and plots annual time series of the exchange rate against PPP (or simply the domestic price index, where foreign data are presumably lacking). In most cases, there is a good correspondence between the exchange rate and PPP (and also the money supply).

Frenkel (1976) re-examines the German hyperinflation. He finds a high correlation between the exchange rate and both the domestic WPI and wage-rate index. In contrast, Dornbusch (1979, pp. 98–99) finds that the ratio of the CPI to the exchange rate varies considerably, a result unfavorable for the PPP theory.

Examining floating exchange rates after World War I, Frenkel (1978) regresses a country's exchange rate on its own WPI and the foreign WPI.[18] Variables are expressed alternatively as logarithms and changes in logarithms. Generally, the PPP theory cannot be rejected. Later, plotting the U.S./German exchange rate and COL-based PPP for the 1970s, Frenkel and Mussa (1980) see the data as exhibiting both short-run deviations and large cumulative divergences from the strict PPP relationship. Their explanation is that price levels are much more serially correlated (sticky) than are exchange rates.

Aliber (1976a) regresses the percentage change in the exchange rate on the percentage change in PPP, for a group of countries for 1964–1971 (monthly observations) and 1957–1971 (quarterly observations). Results are not favorable to PPP. Aliber notes that the results are affected by periods of fixed exchange rates. In another study, Aliber (1976b) computes the percentage deviation from PPP with the United States, for several countries in 1969–1973. Both the WPI and CPI are used, and deviations are greater in the floating-rate than fixed-rate sub-periods. In a still later study along these lines, Aliber (1978) considers almost 50 countries and a time period ranging from 1950 to 1970. Cumulative average annual deviations from PPP decrease as the time interval lengthens, and are small for periods of five years or longer. For short time periods (one or two years), deviations can be large.

Kern (1976) regresses the average annual percentage change in the exchange rate against that of PPP for 12 countries over a 20-year period, using the WPI and the United States as standard country. Results are favorable to the PPP theory. In a similar analysis, Kemp (1976) performs cross-section correlations of the exchange rate with PPP, both defined in terms of percentage changes over a given time period. The CPI and WPI are both used, and calculations are made for various time periods in the 1970s. Results again support the PPP theory.

In an ambitious study of a number of countries over most of the 20th century to 1972, Lee (1976) shows that the mean deviation of the exchange rate from PPP (both expressed as annual rates of change) is statistically nonsignificant in all cases. The WPI and CPI are used as alternative price concepts, with the United States as the standard country. Lee interprets these findings as confirming the long-run validity of the PPP theory.

Pooling observations across 19 countries and over time, King (1977) regresses the percentage change in the exchange rate on the percentage change in PPP, with the United States as the standard country. The time period is the early 1970s, and a number of regressions are calculated by varying the unit of observation (quarterly, semiannual, annual, biennial) and the price concept (WPI, CPI, wage rate). He finds that the PPP relationship is a good predictor of the *direction* of exchange-rate change in the short run and of not only the direction but also the *magnitude* of exchange-rate change as the observation period lengthens. In contrast, Quirk (1977) obtains very poor results when he regresses the Japanese/

U.S. exchange rate on a WPI-based PPP (and time trend) using monthly data over 1973–1976.

The authors of the OPTICA Report undertook a comprehensive econometric examination of the PPP relationship for EC countries, as evidence for their policy recommendation.[19] They tested both the usual (bilateral) relationship, with Germany as the standard country, and a multilateral relationship embodied in the effective-exchange-rate (and effective-PPP) concept. Alternative base periods are 1961 and 1971, and the current (terminal) period is 1975 (sometimes 1976). Alternative price concepts for PPP are the CPI, WPI, EPI, and unit labor cost (ULC). Techniques used are regression analysis and computation of the "root mean square error" of the exchange rate from the PPP. Results are favorable to the PPP theory when the EPI or WPI are used, but unfavorable for the CPI or ULC. Divergences from PPP, that is, changes in the real exchange rate, are explained by exchange-rate rigidity (under the par-value system or European joint float), large fluctuations in floating exchange rates, destabilizing speculation, and the arbitrary choice of the terminal period of the analysis.

Krugman (1978) argues that, unless monetary disturbances are dominant, the PPP hypothesis can be legitimately tested only by accounting for the simultaneous determination of exchange rates and prices. An instrumental-variables method of estimation rather than ordinary least-squares (the usual technique) is indicated. Correcting also for serial correlation, he estimates monthly double-logarithmic regressions of R on PPP for a number of country episodes in the 1920s and 1970s. He also examines statistical properties of the real exchange rate, which the PPP theory predicts to be relatively constant. Results show that "deviations of exchange rates from PPP are large, fairly persistent, and seem to be larger in countries with unstable monetary policies" (1978, p. 407).

Kravis and Lipsey (1978, pp. 215–217) present mean coefficients of correlation between annual percentage changes in countries' real exchange rates over 1950–1973. Alternative price concepts are the GDP deflator, WPI and CPI. The authors interpret the results as nonsupportive of a quickly adjusting, tightly integrated international price structure.

Genberg (1978) considers the logarithm of the real exchange rate based on the effective exchange-rate and PPP concepts and also of the bilateral real rate against the United States. Quarterly data over 1957–1976 show that deviations from PPP are greater for the post-1972, floating-rate period than the earlier, fixed-rate or adjustable-peg periods. Wihlborg (1978; 1979) obtains a similar result when he plots annual percentage rates of change of deviations from WPI-based PPP for the United States, United Kingdom, and Germany. He also finds that changes in the deviations are much greater over quarters than over years. Using a CPI concept of PPP, Mudd (1978) plots quarterly data for 9 countries with respect to the United States. showing that "exchange rate movements since the beginning of 1975 generally have been in the appropriate direction to offset changes in relative inflation rates" (1978, p. 5).

Bilson (1978a) regresses the German/U.K. exchange rate on the PPP (CPI concept), using monthly data over 1972-1976. The PPP formulation fits the data worse than alternative models. Connolly and da Silveira (1979) plot the rate of depreciation of the Brazilian cruzeiro and the rate of change of the PPP (WPI concept) against the United States over 1955-1975. The correspondence is very close except for 1955-1961, when Brazil had stringent exchange control.

Mixed evidence regarding the validity of the PPP theory is provided in two further papers by Frenkel (1980; 1981). Taking France, Germany, the United States, and the United Kingdom as the countries of interest, he regresses the exchange rate on PPP (using logarithmic transformations) for several country pairs and two floating-rate periods, the 1920s and the 1970s. Results are supportive of the PPP theory in the early period, and in the later period when Germany is used as the standard country. However, results are poor for the 1970s with the United States as the standard country. Re-expressing the PPP equation as relating the domestic price index to the exchange-rate-corrected price index yields findings generally favorable to the theory.

II. TIME-SERIES COMPARISONS OF PPP WITH A FLOATING EXCHANGE RATE: LAGGED RELATIONSHIP

If PPP determines the exchange rate, there is no necessity for the relationship to be simultaneous. Allowance of a lagged influence not only is consistent with the theory but also may improve its explanatory power, especially if the lag is distributed through time. Also, investigations of lead-lag relationships are used to test the PPP-postulated direction of causality: from price levels to the exchange rate.

All the early studies of this nature are unfavorable to PPP. Flux (1924, pp. 92-96) plots the exchange rate and PPP (WPI concept) for a number of countries in the 1920s. He notes that PPPs lag behind large exchange-rate movements, but does not point out that this behavior is contrary to the PPP theory. Rogers (1929) examines the French/U.S. and

German/U.S. exchange rates after World War I in relation to a WPI-based PPP (simply the WPI, for Germany). He, too, notices a lag of prices behind the exchange rate. White (1935) examines the floating exchange rates of the United Kingdom, Sweden, and Argentina over the period 1930–1933. Using monthly data, he finds that again the exchange rate frequently led the WPI, in contradiction to the PPP theory.

Bunting (1939) examines the French-franc/dollar and pound/dollar exchange rates for the period 1919–1936.[20] Regarding the base period, Bunting selects the year 1926 rather than 1913, which he argues is too far in the past. He graphs WPI parities together with the exchange rate (a) unled, (b) led one month, (c) led two months, and (d) led three months. Bunting criticizes previous studies of PPP for considering only an unlagged relationship. "Not to allow a lag is to suppose that changes in domestic price levels will be immediately acted upon by foreign buyers" (1939, p. 293). For both the franc and the pound, Bunting finds substantial deviations of the exchange rate from the PPP even using lags. He concludes: "This is damaging statistical evidence against the purchasing power parity theory. . . . Professor Cassel's theory finds meager support from a statistical analysis designed to show it in the most favorable light possible" (1939, p. 299).

Ingram (1960) correlates the change in the Canada/U.S. exchange rate with the change in the PPP (both WPI and CPI concept), trying lead and lag, as well as simultaneous, specifications. The only statistically significant correlation is that between the exchange rate and contemporaneous WPI-based PPP.

Thomas (1973a; 1973b) suggests an adaptive-expectations model relating expected to actual PPP. Retaining the previous notation, and letting P^E denote the expected PPP (ratio of WPIs) and the subscript "−1" a one-month lag, he presents the following model:

$$R = \alpha P + \gamma P^E$$
$$P^E - P^E_{-1} = \beta(P - P^E_{-1})$$

The first equation expresses the theory that the current PPP determines the trade balance while the expected PPP determines speculative capital flows (because the optimal method of forecasting the exchange rate is to consider the future PPP). Thomas derives two alternative estimable equations from this model and fits the equations for 11 countries with floating currencies, using monthly data for the period 1920–1924. It turns out that the estimated value of β is generally close to zero, implying a low elasticity of expectations. This result is favorable to the PPP theory; for a β substantially above zero would involve an increase in "measured" PPP, leading to an increase in expected PPP, and thence to an increase in speculative capital flows.

Hodgson and Phelps (1975) extend the model in another way. They consider two alternative lag distributions of the PPP as follows:

$$\log R = \alpha_0 + \alpha_1 \log P + \beta_1 \log R_{-1}$$

$$\log R = \alpha_0 + \alpha_1 \log P + \beta_1 \log R_{-1} + \beta_2 \log R_{-2}$$

The first equation involves the lag weights declining geometrically from the current month; the second allows the peak of the lag distribution to occur after the current month.

Both models are fitted to 14 floating currencies in the period 1919–1925. The authors find that, in both models, movements in PPP explain more than 90 percent of the variation in the exchange rate for 11 countries, and that the average lag is less than six months for the preponderance of the countries. They conclude: "with the passage of a relatively short period of time, currency purchasing powers begin to exert a dominant influence on exchange rates and explain a remarkably high percentage of their variation" (1975, p. 63).

Lee (1976) extends his analysis by specifying and estimating regression models in which the exchange rate, U.S. price index, and domestic price index are related via distributed-lag functions. The PPP theory (in the form of the law of one price) is confirmed, with relatively short periods of adjustment.

Genberg (1978, p. 261) reports on estimating a model in which the real exchange rate is a function of its normal value and a proportion of last period's deviation from the normal value. The normal value is specified to be either a constant or a function of a time trend. A mean time lag ranging up to several years casts doubt on the PPP theory. The mean lag is longer during the floating-rate period than earlier, corresponding to his results discussed above. Genberg concludes that PPP is mainly a longer-run phenomenon. A similar approach is taken by Bilson (1978b), who specifies deviations of the exchange rate from the PPP (CPI concept) as dependent on the interest-rate differential and the difference between last period's exchange rate and the current PPP. The model provides good results for the deutsche-mark/pound exchange rate in 1970–1977.

Formal statistical tests of causality between the exchange rate and PPP are conducted by several authors.[21] Using monthly exchange-rate and WPI data for 6 countries in the 1920s and Canada during 1953–1957, Rogalski and Vinso (1977) find no significant lagged relationship. So the PPP-posited direction of causality is not contradicted. In contrast, applying such a causality test to his data, Frenkel (1978) finds that the results support the reverse direction of causality, that from exchange rates to prices. He proceeds to estimate regressions in which the change in PPP is the dependent variable, and both the actual, and a measure of unanticipated, exchange-rate change are dependent variables. Kawai (1980) uses monthly data in 1975–1978 for ten countries and the effective-exchange-rate and effective-PPP concepts (based on both the CPI and WPI). He finds that causal relationships between unanticipated movements in the exchange rate and PPP are definitely present, but their pattern varies.

A somewhat different approach to causality, based on an efficient-market framework, is taken by Roll (1979). Using monthly data over 1957–1976, 23 countries, and a CPI concept of PPP, he finds, in effect, that causation runs from the exchange rate to the PPP (or rather, the inflation-rate differential adjusted for the exchange rate).

III. COMPARATIVE-STATIC COMPARISONS OF PPP AND THE EXCHANGE RATE

A time-series comparison of the exchange rate and PPP may be distinguished from a comparative-static comparison of the variables at two points in time. Under the comparative-static framework, the earlier time point has the usual interpretation of the base period. The later time point may be an arbitrary "current period" if the exchange rate is floating, in which case the approach is a special case of the time-series analysis. However, if the exchange rate is fixed in the later period, then this period should have the same properties as the base period; that is, it should be one in which the exchange rate ideally is in long-run equilibrium, or, at the least, it should be a "normal" period. This symmetric property of the two time periods offers a balanced framework with which to test the PPP theory. A more difficult test to pass would result from choosing the later period quite arbitrarily. Such a test has some foundation; for if PPP does represent the long-run equilibrium exchange rate, then gold points or market intervention points must envelop the PPP for the country to avoid sustained gains or losses of international reserves.[22]

As with the time-series approach, Cassel (1916a) was the first to test the PPP theory in a comparative-static way. In all cases, he uses a prewar base period. His first test involved a comparison of the PPP and the actual exchange rate of December 1915 for each of three countries with floating rates (France, Germany, and Russia), with Sweden (also under a floating rate) as the standard country. "The divergencies between the theoretical and actual rates are very small, and all lie within the limits of the errors unavoidable in such a calculation as this and the occasional fluctuations of the rates of exchange" (1916a, p. 64). The floating Swedish currency was the object of a similar test of PPP in the autumn of 1918. Cassel (1918) shows that the Swedish currency is overvalued with respect to the pound. His explanation is the much greater restrictions on Sweden's imports than on its exports.

Finally, Cassel (1919) examines the extent of depreciation of the floating deutsche mark at the end of 1919. He describes his findings: "Thus, with all allowance for the uncertainty of our estimation of the purchasing power parity, an enormous undervaluation of the mark as compared with the Swedish crown must be taken as established" (1919, p. 493). Cassel offers two reasons for this result. First, with international credit unavailable, the German government was able to obtain foreign exchange only from speculators abroad and at very disadvantageous exchange rates. Second, there was a flight of capital from Germany.

Robertson (1922, pp. 139–141) computes the exchange-rate index and PPP (WPI concept) for 9 countries with respect to the United States, taking 1913 as the base and 1920 the current period. The figures both "illustrate the general normal relation between price-levels and exchanges" and indicate "abnormal cases," such as Germany. Lester (1939) reports that the PPP theory held during the U.S. Civil War, in which the North was on a paper (greenback) standard while the Far West remained on the gold standard. Prices approximately doubled in the North, as did the greenback price of gold; whereas prices in the West rose only about 10 percent.

Some later studies apply the comparative-static test to currencies that are pegged rather than floating. Yeager (1958) computes PPPs for 35 countries[23] as of July 1957, taking a pre-World War II year as the base period and the United States as the standard country. He discusses his selection of the price measures used to compute PPP. The average of the CPI and WPI is used, except when only one index is available. Given various WPIs for a country, the one weighted most heavily with non-traded goods is chosen. The ratio of the actual exchange rate to the PPP is within the range 75–125 percent for three fourths of the countries considered. Yeager concludes: "These results and those mentioned earlier [other studies] hardly leave room to doubt a broad correspondence between actual and purchasing-power-parity exchange rates, especially in comparison with the huge discrepancies to be expected if Cassel's doctrine were quite wrong" (1958, p. 527).

While Caves and Jones (1973, p. 338) agree with Yeager that the PPP theory performs well in this test, Balassa (1964, p. 591) emphatically disagrees. His argument is threefold. (1) There is no statistical significance attached to the selected range. (2) The results depend on which country is selected as the standard. (Balassa sees no a priori reason for the United States to play this role.) (3) The cause-effect relationship between the exchange rate and PPP is not involved in the test.

A long-term comparative-static test of PPP is applied by Gailliot (1970) to seven industrial countries, with the United States as the standard country and the WPI as the price measure. The two periods selected are 1900–1904 and 1963–1967, each of which involved pegged rather than floating exchange rates for the countries considered. However, the periods are carefully chosen to be "normal." Gailliot points out that each period had relatively free international trade and capital flows and convertible currencies. Also, both were preceded by a long interval of relative peace and prosperity for the industrial countries.

The ratio of the exchange rate to the PPP is close enough to unity for all countries (except Japan) to enable Gailliot to conclude: "The results are exceptionally good when one considers the myriad social and economic upheavals that have occurred during the twentieth century and the difficulty of acquiring reasonably accurate estimates of wholesale prices, especially for the earlier periods.... It appears that Cassel's theory receives significant support from the empirical evidence" (1970, pp. 351–52).

Gailliot computes the ratio of the exchange rate to the PPP on a decade-by-decade basis (again in the form of five-year averages). There are greater deviations from unity (as expected, because the periods are not chosen on the basis of "normality"), but a tendency to return to unity in the next period (with the exception of Japan). "Again, these figures offer significant support to Cassel's thesis... " (1970, p. 353).

Kravis and Lipsey (1978) compute the ratio of *absolute* PPP to the exchange rate (that is, the inverted real exchange rate) for 1950 and 1970 for 6 countries in relation to the United States. They take the ratio of the 1970 to the 1950 inverted real exchange rate. According to the strict PPP theory, this ratio should be unity. For half the countries, they are close to that level. They repeat the analysis for relative PPP, using the GDP deflator and various time spans. They find that PPP holds for short time spans, but deviations from the relationship become greater as the time period increases. The relative-PPP analysis is repeated using the WPI and CPI. A similar set of computations is made by Isard (1978, pp. 5–8), with results viewed as unfavorable for PPP as a predictor of short-run movements in exchange rates.

Finally, two studies by Officer (1978; 1980a) adopt the comparative-static approach.[24] The first involves a technique similar to the Kravis-Lipsey absolute-PPP analysis; the second is related to the Gailliot study.

IV. AUGMENTED PPP THEORY

The PPP theory need not explain movements of a floating exchange rate by relative prices (the PPP itself) alone; various authors have augmented the theory by introducing other explanatory variables. A time-series approach is always used, generally taking the form of regression analysis. We consider the model to be in the domain of the PPP theory providing the PPP remains the most important explanatory variable.[25]

Although his study is neither mathematical nor econometric, Stolper (1948) can be credited with the earliest testing of an augmented PPP theory.[26] The subject of his analysis is the exchange value of the floating pound during the years 1919–1925, with monthly observations of the exchange rate (number of dollars per pound) taken as percentages of the prewar mint parity. The exchange-rate series is charted with, in turn, (a) three alternative PPP series (based on general WPIs, raw-material WPIs, and COL indices), (b) three trade-balance series (bilateral U.S.-U.K. balance, overall U.S. balance, and overall U.K. balance), (c) U.S. employment and U.K. unemployment (used in the absence of national-accounts data), and (d) short-term interest rates in the two countries. There are noticeable deviations of the exchange rate from each PPP, and comparison of the exchange rate with the employment variables leads Stolper to the conclusion that differences in timing of the business cycle in the two countries are the principal explanation of these deviations. Indeed, he argues that for much of the period relative income in the two countries has higher explanatory power for the exchange rate than do relative prices.

Ingram (1960) regresses the Canadian floating exchange rate in 1950–1957 on the Canada/U.S. WPI and GNP, as well as the export/import ratio and short-term capital movements. Except for the last, all variables are expressed as quarter-to-quarter index numbers. Only the PPP and trade variables have significant coefficients. Poole (1967) explains the narrow range of the Canadian floating rate in 1951–1961 by the fact that U.S. and Canadian WPIs, industrial production indices, and interest rates were so highly correlated.

Farag and Ott (1964) suggest a model in which the exchange rate is a function of the domestic/foreign price level (measured by WPIs), industrial production, and interest rate, plus the change in official reserves and a proxy for speculative capital movements. They apply the model to various floating-rate episodes, with the price effect always significant. One of the periods examined is the U.S. greenback experience of 1862–1878, for which the income variable is omitted due to data unavailability. This period is also the subject of Thompson's (1972) PPP investigation, which is distinctive for an attempt to use a price measure superior to the WPI. His solution is to try price indices for "domestic" commodities developed by Graham (1922); but these series are merely components of the overall WPIs (for the United States and Britain). Augmenting the PPP theory to include capital movements, Thompson finds that the additional variable has nonsignificant effect for equations in which Britain is the foreign country (the only reasonable choice).

The floating pound after World War I is examined by Hodgson (1972), who explains the monthly dollar/pound exchange rate in the context of an explicit econometric model. He derives the reduced-form equation for the exchange rate as a function of U.S. and U.K. price levels (entered as separate variables), U.S. and U.K. real income, the short-term interest-rate differential, money supplies in the two countries, gold flows, a trend term, and dichotomous variables to represent the seasons and special events. The price measures are not identified in the article; income is proxied by employment in the United States, unemployment in the United Kingdom (Stolper's variables).

Hodgson's purpose is to test the role of "fundamental determinants" of the exchange rate as against that of special events. In the final equation, the income variables are dropped (because they are imperfect measures and are collinear with the price variables) and the money variables and interest-rate differential are lagged one month. The results are (1) "the exchange rate closely followed a path predicted by the 'fundamental' determinants;" (2) "price levels were the most significant of the 'fundamental' determinants" (Hodgson, 1972, p. 250). Because the price-level variables enter the equation independently rather than in ratio form, this is not a precise test of the PPP theory. Nevertheless, the findings are implicitly supportive of PPP.[27]

The Hodgson model is adopted by Thomas (1972; 1973a; 1973b), who drops the money-supply variables and (to reduce multicollinearity and to increase degrees of freedom) expresses price levels, income, and interest rates in ratio form. Monthly data are used to examine the exchange rates of six floating currencies with respect to the dollar in the period 1920–1924. WPIs are used as the price measure, and various variables proxy income in the absence of national-accounts data. The price variable (PPP) is highly significant in all cases.

Goldstein (1979) postulates a model with the novel features of using the effective-exchange-rate concept and incorporating a measure of relative real (rather than nominal) interest rates, and applies the model to floating exchange rates of the 1970s. Unfortunately, his analysis is marred by selection of the WPI for manufactures as the price variable.

A unique model to test the PPP theory under special circumstances is presented by Holmes (1967a). The approach requires that one country (*A*) be small in comparison to the other (*B*). Then, under the PPP theory, the external value of country B's currency is adjusted to its internal value through changes in either the exchange rate (under a floating rate) or country A's price level (under a fixed rate). Hence, whether the exchange rate is floating or fixed, the PPP theory takes the form of a relationship in which RP^A is the dependent variable and P^B the independent variable, where P^i is the price level in country i.

More generally, RP^A is a current-endogenous variable and P^B an exogenous variable in an aggregate model from which Holmes derives an estimable equation with RP^A as the dependent variable and two groups of explanatory variables in addition to P^B. The first group consists of variables that are recognized by Cassel as nonmonetary influences on the exchange rate: tariffs in each country, capital flows and unilateral transfers (into the small country), and a variable representing government intervention in the foreign-exchange market (this variable is the official rate when applicable, the market rate otherwise). The second group includes variables that are influences on demand for commodities, but not mentioned by Cassel: real income and population in each country. For the test to be passed by the PPP theory: (1) P^B should be the most significant explanatory variable; and (2) as regards other explanatory variables, the first group (those mentioned by Cassel) should be more significant than the second group.

Holmes takes Canada as the small country, the United States as the large country, and fits the equation to annual data for the period 1870–1960. It turns out that the U.S. price level (measured by the CPI) is the most significant explanatory variable, followed by the market-intervention variable, the Canadian tariff, and capital inflow into Canada. Holmes concludes: "The Purchasing Power Parity Theory of Gustav Cassel as formulated by our model is confirmed by the evidence in this study" (1967a, p. 52).

Given the dependence of the Canadian upon the U.S. economy, a high correlation between the Canadian price level in U.S. dollars (RP^A) and the U.S. price level (P^B) is to be expected irrespective of the validity of PPP theory. Therefore, a weaker conclusion is indicated. Holmes' test shows, rather, that the PPP theory cannot be rejected on the basis of the model and the data used. The Holmes model is extended and reestimated for a longer period by Dino (1976).

The augmented PPP approach, like the ordinary PPP theory, is not without its critics. Rhomberg (1960) argues that a simultaneous-equation model is a preferred specification. Kohlhagen (1978) also notes the presence of simultaneity bias. Willett (1979) points out that the augmented PPP model is a reduced form, in which the income and interest-rate effects can be either negative or positive. Also, exchange-rate expectations should not be ignored.

V. INVESTIGATIONS OF THE REAL EXCHANGE RATE

Some studies that involve direct computation of the real exchange rate have been reviewed above. The rest are described in this section.

Friedman and Schwartz (1963, pp. 58–78) compute a WPI parity between the dollar and the pound annually for the greenback period (1861–1879) and compare it (as do all studies of this period) with the greenback price of gold, representing the dollar/pound exchange rate (since the United Kingdom remained on the gold standard). Alternatively, the PPP (number of dollars per pound) may be considered the hypothetical price of gold. Friedman and Schwartz note that the actual price of gold (the exchange rate) varies over a range of more than 2 to 1, whereas the ratio of the actual to the hypothetical price (the ratio of the exchange rate to the PPP, that is, the real exchange rate) varies over a range of only 1.3 to 1. They explain the residual movement in this ratio in terms of (1) the cutoff of trade during the U.S. Civil War and (2) international capital flows that occurred after the war.

Earlier, Kindahl (1961) had computed an inverted real-exchange-rate series for the greenback period, explaining deviations from unity in terms of international capital movements. Aldrich (1975, pp. 401–405) modifies Kindahl's analysis by noting that structural changes favored U.S. comparative advantage in new goods after the Civil War and helped explain the higher real exchange value of the greenback. This point is also made by Friedman and Schwartz (1963, p. 78).

The Economics Department of the First National City Bank (1973) plotted inverted real exchange rates of various countries with respect to the United States. Overvalued currencies are explained by official market intervention, short-term speculation against the dollar, and longer-term portfolio shifts away from the dollar. In an impressive study, Brillembourg (1977) adopts a multilateral approach to the real exchange rate (based alternatively on the CPI and WPI), and uses the real rate, along with a relative business-cycle index, to determine international payments (or trade) imbalances for 14 countries in 1963–1976. Results suggest a highly complex relationship between the real exchange rate and the balance of payments. Batchelor (1977) explains both bilateral and multilateral real exchange values of the pound in the 1970s, using the CPI and EPI as price series. Explanatory variables include measures of official reserves, portfolio size, interest rates, and the trade balance. The author views his approach as an extension of the PPP model.

Dornbusch (1978, pp. 106–108) examines the U.S./German real exchange rate (CPI concept) over 1974–1978. It varies systematically with the nominal exchange rate, a point against the PPP theory. Also, the deviation from PPP is closely related to its lagged value, indicating a strong persistence effect. Genberg (1978) computes average annual deviations from PPP over 1957–1976, with deviations defined as residuals from a regression of the real exchange rate (effective, CPI concept) on a time trend. Deviations are greater for the floating-rate period. Genberg shows that in this period short-run variations in the real exchange rate emanate overwhelmingly from the nominal exchange rate rather than relative price levels. Krugman (1978) provides statistics indicating that the real exchange rate is much more stable than the nominal rate (a result favorable to the PPP theory); but variations in the real rate seem substantial and deviations of the real rate from its mean are serially correlated (results unfavorable to the theory).

Stockman (1979) estimates a third-order autoregressive equation for the (inverted) real exchange rate (GDP-deflator concept) for 8 countries in 1957–1976, with the United States as the standard country. Results suggest that a disturbance is followed by only a slow reversion to a mean value of the real rate. Adopting an augmented PPP approach, Sakakibara (1979) regresses the Japan/U.S. real-exchange rate on variables based on industrial production in the two countries and Japan's trade surplus. McKinnon (1979, pp. 123–133) computes the real exchange rate for various countries over 1955–1977, both multilaterally and bilaterally (with respect to the United States). Three alternative price concepts (the CPI, WPI, and EPI) are used. For the multilateral computations, results are generally favorable to the PPP theory, especially for the long run.

Dornbusch (1980, pp. 146–149) compares average annual CPI inflation rates with exchange rates for five industrial countries against the United States (both bilaterally and multilaterally) over 1973–1979. He finds a real depreciation of the dollar averaging more than two percent annually. Broader multilateral data taken from the international Monetary Fund support his observation. He concludes: "The key link between the exchange rate and PPP fails to hold . . . " (1980, p. 151).

VI. INVESTIGATIONS OF MOVEMENTS OF THE NONTRADABLE/TRADABLE PRICE RATIO

If the difference between countries' nontradable/tradable price ratios changes over time, a case is thereby made against the relative PPP theory. One reason for such an event is emphasized by Balassa: productivity increases occurring in a non-uniform fashion among countries. Balassa (1964) himself tests this hypothesis for seven industrial countries. For each country, he computes the ratio of the GNP price deflator (representing the general price index) to the WPI of manufactured goods (representing the price index of traded goods) for the year 1961, taking 1953 as the base year. The nontradable/tradable price ratio is thus proxied by the ratio of a price index of the nontraded *plus* traded sectors of the economy to a price index of the traded sector. The resulting variable is regressed on the increase in manufacturing output per man-hour—representing productivity change in the traded sector—over the same period. The correlation coefficient is 0.91, implying that disparate productivity advances among countries do in fact lead to the predicted divergent movements in their nontradable/tradable price ratios.

A similar test is performed by McKinnon (1971, pp. 21–23) and is cited approvingly by Haberler.[28] Again taking 1953 as the base year, the CPI (a general price index), WPI, EPI, and an index of output per man-hour are calculated for the first quarter of 1970 for six industrial countries. The countries with high growth in productivity have substantially higher CPI/WPI and CPI/EPI ratios than do the countries with low growth in productivity.[29] The divergence between the rapidly and the slowly growing economies is greater for the CPI/EPI ratio—an expected result, for the WPI incorporates some nontraded goods. The implication once more is that Balassa's hypothesis is applicable to relative PPP.

Dornbusch (1978, p. 108) calculates annual average rates of inflation for Germany and Japan over 1958–1977, using the CPI, EPI, import price index, and GNP deflator. The greater inflation in the CPI and GNP deflator supports the productivity-bias hypothesis. In another study, Dornbusch (1979, pp. 101–102) graphs productivity growth against the percentage change in the ratio of the GNP deflator to the WPI for manufactures, both variables expressed as average annual percentage changes over 1960–1977. With nine observations (countries), the relationship is strongly positive, lending further support to the productivity-bias hypothesis.

As part of a study showing the effect of structural change on deviations from PPP, Hekman (1977) postulates that a country's nontradable/tradable price ratio (proxied by CPI/WPI) is a function of real GNP, labor productivity, and the labor force and capital stock. Regression equations with this specification are estimated for Japan and the United States over various time periods.

Officer (1976b) performs cross-section regressions of the nontradable/tradable price ratio on productivity, using a variety of measures for each variable.[30] Results are mixed, contrary to the usual findings supportive of the productivity-bias hypothesis (for relative PPP).

NOTES

1. A similar omission of tests pertaining to *absolute* PPP at disaggregative levels was made in Chapter XI.

2. The assertion is *not* that studies employing such price indices are invalid, only that they do not provide legitimate testing of the PPP theory. See Chapter IX.

3. Again, see Chapter IX.

4. This statement applies to the second concept of relative PPP, defined in Chapter II. If the first PPP concept is used, then the statement refers to the exchange-rate index (using the same base period as for PPP).

5. See, for example, Cassel (1922, pp. 181–182).

6. For Cassel's view in his subsequent writing that this test provided definitive proof of the PPP theory, see Cassel (1925a, pp. 151–152; 1932b, pp. 678–79).

7. Of course, Cassel is here computing the real exchange rate but he does not use the term.

8. Earlier, an anonymous author (1921) writing in the Skandinaviska Kreditaktie-bolaget *Quarterly Report* showed that the exchange rate between the pound and the krona closely corresponded to a PPP based on export price indices, whereas use of a more general price measure (presumably the WPI) indicated an overvalued krona. The author concludes that export prices are the preferred basis for PPP, a viewpoint quite contrary to that of Cassel (who, ironically, was to become a frequent contributor to the journal over the time period 1923–1925).

9. Angell did not calculate a PPP series for Germany, apparently because "the grotesque size of the figures makes it almost impossible to handle them" (1926, p. 440).

10. See the final section of Chapter IX. Of course, a deflation predominantly in price rather than in output would be as applicable for PPP as is inflation. An example is the U.S. greenback experience during and after the Civil War (see below).

11. See also Katano (1956, pp. 23–25).

12. See Chapter X.

13. See also Thomas (1972; 1973a).

14. It is unusual to express the exchange rate and PPP in units inverse to one another.

15. For an outline of his subsequent analysis, see below.

16. As in many empirical studies of PPP, there is no discussion of the selection of the price index.

17. Their distributed-lag model is discussed below.

18. Some narrower price indices are also used, in alternative regressions.

19. See Chapter X. Their econometric work is described in Commission of the European Communities (1977, pp. 43–73) and Thygesen (1978, pp. 303–307).

20. He makes no comment about the fact that the period spans intervals of both floating rates and the gold standard.

21. Techniques used here are those developed by Sims (1972), Haugh (1976), and Hsiao (1978a; 1978b).

22. This point was clearly stated by Cassel, who viewed PPP as the principal determinant of the exchange rate under both floating rates and the gold standard. See Chapter VII and Cassel (1922, pp. 185–186; 1925a, pp. 149–150; 1928a, pp. 31–32; 1932b, pp. 519–524). For the same interpretation of PPP theory, see Yeager (1958, p. 526).

23. Of the countries considered, only Canada and Thailand had floating rates.

24. These studies appear as Chapters XV and XVI, respectively, in the present volume.

25. See Chapter II.

26. An even earlier work is that of Graham (1922), who examines the U.S. floating exchange rate in 1862–1878. In addition to comparing the greenback price of gold to the domestic (though not the foreign) price (dollar) level, Graham considers the influence of international capital flows.

27. Other authors have applied variants of the Hodgson model. Bond and Haroz

(1976) consider the floating Canadian dollar of 1970-1973. They extend the model (though not explicitly) by incorporating bilateral-trade-balance and relative-reserves explanatory variables. Whitaker and Hudgins (1977) apply a sophisticated version of the Hodgson model to the floating pound of the 1930s. Both studies use the WPI as the price measure.

28.   See Haberler (1973, pp. 91-92; 1975, pp. 16 and 24-25). See also McKinnon (1973, pp. 96-97; 1979, pp. 233-235).

29.   The country with the highest ratios is Japan. Specific studies of the divergence between the CPI and WPI in the Japanese case are provided by Kato (1967) and Komiya and Suzuki (1977, pp. 306-313).

30.   Officer (1976b) appears as Chapter XIV of the present volume. Novel variables used in the regressions are described also in Goldstein and Officer (1979) and Goldstein, Khan, and Officer (1980, pp. 192-194).

Part IV

SELECTED PPP STUDIES

Chapter XIII

Purchasing Power Parity and Factor Price Equalization[1]

A decade ago H.S. Houthakker (1962a) presented an analysis of exchange-rate equilibrium that merged two hitherto disjoint theories in economics: purchasing power parity and factor price equalization. This work is one of the few integrations of the monetary and pure theories of international trade, and one would have expected it to have generated further analysis along this line. In fact, Houthakker's contribution was examined by Samuelson (1964), who contended that the analysis was wrong theoretically, and by Balassa (1964), who asserted that Houthakker's model must be rejected on the basis of econometric evidence. These findings apparently have been accepted by the profession at large, as evidenced by the subsequent neglect of Houthakker's approach.

I contend, however, that Houthakker's theory is not wrong but rather undeveloped, because it has never been presented systematically. Both Houthakker and his critics confine themselves to verbal expositions, avoiding the use of symbols or mathematical shorthand. Furthermore, Houthakker makes no explicit reference to factor price equalization, although a form of that theorem is an integral part of the theory. Finally, and perhaps in explanation, Houthakker offered his analysis in Congressional testimony; so he had a policy rather than theoretical purpose in mind: to exhibit the overvaluation of the dollar.

In this paper I present a model of exchange-rate equilibrium that incorporates the purchasing-power-parity and factor-price-equalization theories along the lines suggested by Houthakker's earlier work. I also provide a test of how well this model predicts real-world behavior. The model is outlined in Section I and its implications for computing purchasing power parity examined in Section II. Then in Section III Balas-

199

sa's econometric test of the model is shown to be inapplicable, and an alternative test is presented in Section IV. Some concluding remarks in support of the theory are offered in Section V.

I. A MODEL OF FACTOR PRICE EQUALIZATION AND THE EQUILIBRIUM EXCHANGE RATE

Consider the following definition of the equilibrium exchange rate. It must be at that level which yields international equalization of unit factor costs. Abstracting from other factors of production, the equilibrium exchange rate equalizes unit labor costs internationally. Given two countries, A and B, let

R = equilibrium exchange rate, number of units of A-currency per unit of B-currency
W^i = wage rate in country i
P^i = price level in country i
PR^i = productivity in country i
MPL^i = marginal product of labor in country i
ULC^i = unit labor cost in country i

Then what one might call the unit-factor-cost theory asserts that

$$R = \frac{ULC^A}{ULC^B} = \frac{W^A/PR^A}{W^B/PR^B} = \frac{W^A}{W^B} \cdot \frac{PR^B}{PR^A} \tag{1}$$

where Equation (1) is a definition of the equilibrium exchange rate.

This theory carries to its logical extreme the generally accepted idea that, given initial balance-of-payments equilibrium, a rising wage rate at home relative to abroad may be compensated by a depreciation of the exchange rate. Samuelson (1964, pp. 150–53) has argued, however, that this trade-off relationship does not necessarily imply the unit-factor-cost-theory. He is correct in that at any point in time the true equilibrium exchange rate may differ from that given by (1) and yet the trade-off exist. The unit-factor-cost theory yields the *long-run* equilibrium exchange rate, a proviso consistent with both Samuelson's comment and Houthakker's original presentation of the theory (1962a, p. 293). Even in the long run, the role of factors of production other than labor and the existence of balance-of-payments flows other than goods and services might require that Equation (1) be altered.[2]

The next step is to apply the marginal-productivity theory of wages, again a long-run theory:

$$W^A = P^A \cdot MPL^A \left. \right\}$$
$$W^B = P^B \cdot MPL^B \left. \right\} \tag{2}$$

and the unit-factor-cost theory becomes

$$R = \frac{P^A \cdot MPL^A}{P^B \cdot MPL^B} \cdot \frac{PR^B}{PR^A} \tag{3}$$

If one assumes that

$$MPL^A \cdot PR^B = MPL^B \cdot PR^A \tag{4}$$

then (3) reduces to

$$R = \frac{P^A}{P^B} \tag{5}$$

How can Equation (4) be justified? One must accept the occurrence of factor price equalization, but of a special nature in two respects. First, the factor-price-equalization theorem is being applied on a macroeconomic level to aggregate production functions rather than on a microeconomic level to individual-industry production functions. Thus one might designate this theory as *macro factor price equalization* as distinct from *micro factor price equalization,* the conventional theorem. Second, following Houthakker, I am allowing for a productivity difference between the countries so that their aggregate production functions differ proportionately by a neutral efficiency factor, PR^B/PR^A, that carries over into the relationship of factor prices.[3] Therefore macro factor price equalization implies

$$MPL^B = \frac{PR^B}{PR^A} \cdot MPL^A \tag{6}$$

which substituted into (3) yields (5).

The unrealistic assumptions of factor price equalization have discredited the theorem to such an extent that it now appears to be the province exclusively of esoteric theorists. However, an altered factor-price-equalization theory that fits an aggregate context cannot be dismissed out of hand. Hicks (1959, pp. 266–67) has argued convincingly that when the many kinds and qualities of factors of production are *aggregated* into the two broad factors, labor and capital, factor price equalization has validity as a long-run tendency. It is within the spirit of Hicks' approach to aggregate commodities as well as factors, so that one considers an aggregate production function for each country. Finally, permitting international productivity differences to exist implies that the required "long run" need not be as long as Hicks perceived.

Equation (5) asserts that the equilibrium exchange rate is equal to the ratio of the countries' price levels, where each country's price level is a production-weighted average of individual commodity prices, these weights specific to its own economy. This is the purchasing-power-parity theory, a degree of freedom in which has always been the weighting scheme.[4] The price levels in (5) are production-weighted because the theoretical ingredients of this equation, namely, the unit-factor-cost theory (1), the marginal-productivity theory of wages (2), and the macro factor-price-equalization theorem (6) all refer to *production* in the respective countries.

I have demonstrated that the unit-factor-cost theory of the exchange rate and the macro factor-price-equalization theorem together imply the purchasing-power-parity theory (with production weights and in its absolute rather than relative form). True, the marginal-productivity theory of wages was also applied, but pure competition in factor markets is a necessary condition for factor price equalization. Thus the factor-price-equalization theorem is a sufficient condition for the marginal-productivity theory of income distribution.

Application of the macro factor-price-equalization theorem to the unit-factor-cost theory, a particular theory of the equilibrium exchange rate, yields purchasing power parity, an alternative theory of the equilibrium exchange rate. Can macro factor price equalization also do the reverse? Can it transform purchasing power parity into the unit-factor-cost theory?

Assume that macro factor price equalization holds, allowing as before for a neutral productivity difference between the two countries. Thus Equation (6) is satisfied. The marginal-productivity theory of wages (2) applied to (6) yields

$$\frac{W^B}{P^B} = \frac{PR^B}{PR^A} \cdot \frac{W^A}{P^A} \tag{7}$$

which can be rewritten as

$$\frac{P^A}{P^B} = \frac{W^A}{W^B} \cdot \frac{PR^B}{PR^A} \tag{8}$$

Now assume the purchasing-power-parity theory (5). Substituting (5) into (8) yields (1), which is the unit-factor-cost theory. Thus macro factor price equalization and purchasing power parity together imply the unit-factor-cost theory of the equilibrium exchange rate.

It has been shown that macro factor price equalization and either theory of the equilibrium exchange rate together imply the other exchange-rate theory. To complete the analysis, one should ask if the two exchange-rate theories together yield macro factor price equalization. The answer is affirmative; for Equations (1) and (5) satisfied simultaneously yield (7), which is a statement of the equality of real wages in the two countries, allowing for a productivity factor, and therefore is the macro factor-price-equalization theorem. I have chosen to express the theorem alternatively as the equating of marginal productivities of labor (6), an equivalent form given the marginal-productivity theory of wages.

To summarize, consider the unit-factor-cost and purchasing-power-parity theories of the exchange rate and the macro factor-price-equalization theorem. I have shown that any two of these theories together imply the third. Therefore any one of these theories need not stand on its own feet; if the other two apply, this first theory necessarily must hold.

II. THE WEIGHTING PROBLEM

The above model requires that the price levels in the purchasing power parity be production-weighted. The question arises as to whether the theory is applicable also to purchasing power parities based on consumption weights. Houthakker (1962a, p. 296) argues that consumption weights can be substituted for production weights in the calculation of the countries' price levels without altering the computed purchasing power parity (5). He asserts that while the marginal-productivity theory is stated in terms of produced commodities, it can be restated in terms of consumed commodities because competition equalizes prices of domestically produced goods and imports. This argument is misleading; for suppose we abstract from trade restrictions and transportation costs. Then international arbitrage alone guarantees the price equalization of *traded* commodities, where prices in one country are converted into the other country's currency using the actual (not necessarily the equilibrium) exchange rate as the conversion factor. Pure competition domestically in product and factor markets would not be needed for this equalization. However, what ensures the price equalization of *nontraded* commodities in the model?

The answer is: the unit-factor-cost theory together with pure competition in product markets. The first element implies that at the equilibrium exchange rate unit factor costs are equalized internationally; the second ensures that prices are equal to unit factor costs. Actually, pure competition is not required; "equal degrees of monopoly" in the two countries would suffice for price equalization, as the same percentage divergence between prices and unit factor costs in each country would result. However, pure competition in both product and factor markets is a necessary condition for macro factor price equalization and hence for the purchasing-power-parity theory to apply. Thus Houthakker's assertion of equalized prices is validated.

However, equalization of prices is not sufficient for a purchasing power parity invariant with respect to a production or consumption weighting scheme, with each country's price level calculated using its own specific weighting pattern. Houthakker's position would be correct if the countries' production patterns were identical and equal to their consumption patterns, which then would also be identical. Otherwise, only extremely improbable configurations of weighting patterns could lead to an invariant purchasing power parity. However, the case of identical weighting patterns is itself very improbable. A specific reason is that a commodity might be imported, and therefore consumed, by one of the countries without being produced at home. Similarly, a commodity might be produced for export alone, not for domestic consumption. More generally, even if prices are equalized internationally, consumption patterns will differ unless demand conditions are the same in the two countries. Nevertheless, while Houthakker's switching of the weighting patterns is technically incorrect, equalization of individual commodity prices does suggest that the production-weighted and consumption-weighted purchasing power parities will be closer to equality than otherwise and that there will be a high correlation of their movements over time. One could subsume the switching of the weights under the heading of index-number problems.

The use of actual purchasing-power-parity data involves additional index-number problems. Houthakker employed the series comparing the German mark and other currencies which are published by the German Statistical Office, and these are based on consumption weights. Indeed, the German Statistical Office refers to its computations not as purchasing power parities but rather as "consumer monetary parities" (*Verbrauchergeldparitäten*). These series do not conform to the purchasing-power-parity concept in our model, first, because they are consumption-weighted and, second, because they impose the same weighting pattern in computing each country's price level. In contrast, the model requires that the purchasing power parity be production-weighted and that each country's price level be calculated using its own specific weighting pattern. The German Statistical Office provides two purchasing-power-parity computations for each country, one using the German, the other the domestic country's weights. Only if the weighting patterns for the two countries were identical and if all prices were equalized internationally would the two computations be guaranteed to give the same result.

As argued above, however, the existence of different demand conditions in the countries itself implies distinct weighting patterns even under full price equalization. Furthermore, in general, the actual exchange rate (that currently in effect) will differ from the equilibrium exchange rate defined by the unit-factor-cost theory. Under this circumstance, prices of nontraded goods and services will not be equalized internationally. In addition, prices of traded commodities are not equalized in the real world because of the existence of tariffs, quantitative restrictions, and transportation costs. The non-equalization of prices produces divergent biases in the two purchasing-power-parity computations of the German Statistical Office. Application of the German consumption pattern involves greater weight for commodities that are cheap in Germany. The mark then appears to have greater buying power than it actually has and therefore appears to be relatively more expensive in equilibrium compared to the other currency; vice versa for the weighting pattern of the other country. Houthakker (1962a, p. 297) applies Irving Fisher's ideal price index to correct (or average) the divergent biases.

III. BALASSA'S TEST OF THE MODEL

Balassa (1964) has questioned the validity of purchasing power parity (and, implicitly, unit factor costs) as a theory of the equilibrium exchange rate. He argues that while one country might be generally more productive than another country, its efficiency advantage would be less in nontraded commodities (considered to be consumer services) than in traded commodities. With prices of traded goods equalized internationally and the same wage rate faced by all industries in a given country, the prices of services will be relatively higher in the technologically advanced country. Services are not traded, so can have no direct effect on the balance of payments. Therefore a purchasing power parity calculated from price levels inclusive of consumer services would understate the true equilibrium value of the currency of the technologically advanced country.

The logic of Balassa's argument is irrefutable. I take issue with his basic assumption, namely, that international productivity differences are greater in traded goods than in services. I concede that this statement is true for personal services narrowly defined, those consumer services that are highly labor intensive. As Samuelson (1964, p. 148) remarks, "Professors, particularly cultured ones, are particularly prone to infer an overvaluation of the dollar by the cheapness abroad of personal services (maids, tenors, and Doctors of Philosophy). By this reasoning, every prosperous region has a chronically overvalued currency." However, in the cases of professional services for which the labor embodies large amounts of human capital and/or requires substantial co-operating input of physical capital—such as education and medical care—the efficiency advantage of the technologically advanced country would be greater than its advantage in traded commodities.

I do not dispute Balassa's contention (1964, pp. 587–89) that inter-country comparisons of the price statistics of consumer services justify his thesis across the board, i.e., including professional services of all kinds. My objection is that such a straightforward use of these price data neglects a tremendous problem of achieving international comparability in measurement of output. In a technologically inferior country, education and medical care might be superficially cheaper than in an advanced country, but actually would be more expensive when proper account is taken of the difference in the qualities of the services. Indeed, travel statistics would show that the international flow of human traffic for the use of these services is predominantly from the technologically inferior to the technologically advanced country, and becomes overwhelmingly one-sided for great productivity differences in the countries involved.

So there is some justification for an assertion opposite to Balassa's thesis, that purchasing power parity *overstates* the equilibrium value of the currency of the technologically advanced country. However, a balanced view would be that neither Balassa's casual empiricism nor my own suffices to establish a presumption that the technologically advanced country's productive advantage in traded commodities differs in either direction from its advantage in nontraded commodities.

To Balassa's credit, he is not content with casual empiricism but attempts to test his thesis econometrically. He takes per capita GNP as a proxy for a country's productivity level; so his hypothesis becomes that the ratio of a country's purchasing power parity (*PPP*) to its equilibrium exchange rate R (number of units of domestic currency per U.S. dollar) is positively correlated with per capita GNP. Balassa takes the ratio of PPP to the official exchange rate r and correlates it with per capita GNP (in U.S. dollars) for 12 countries in the year 1960. He finds that the correlation coefficient is 0.92 and asserts: "The empirical results provide evidence for the validity of my proposition regarding the relationship between purchasing-power parities, exchange rates, and per capita income levels" (1964, p. 589).

However, Balassa's findings are subject to some question for the following reasons. First, the correct income concept to use is GDP rather than GNP, as Balassa's thesis concerns prices and production within the boundaries of a country. I grant that this is a minor flaw and would not affect the results at all significantly. More serious is Balassa's selection of per capita GNP as the proxy for a country's productivity level. A better measure of productivity would be the ratio of GNP to employment rather than total population.

The fundamental weakness of Balassa's test is that (without explanation) he substitutes the current official exchange rate r for the equilibrium rate R. The correlation is thus between PPP/r and per capita GNP. The result therefore indicates that the higher is the country's per capita GNP, the more is its purchasing power parity undervalued compared to the *actual* (not the equilibrium) exchange rate. This result in itself implies nothing about the validity of equating the purchasing power parity to the equilibrium exchange rate; *it does not test the Balassa hypothesis.*

Of course, if one were to make the assumption that, across countries at a given point in time, the actual exchange rate is proportional to the equilibrium exchange rate, then the correlation would be a legitimate test of Balassa's thesis. However, it would be no less reasonable to make the alternative assumption that the purchasing power parity is proportional to the equilibrium exchange rate, in which case the correlation would not provide such a test. Balassa offers no reason why the former assumption is valid or even, more weakly, why the correlation of R with r should be greater than the correlation of R with PPP. Therefore his econometric result, while perhaps interesting in itself, provides no test of the purchasing-power-parity and unit-factor-cost theories.

IV. AN ALTERNATIVE TEST OF THE MODEL

Central to my model is the satisfaction of the equation

$$\frac{W^A}{W^B} = \frac{PR^A}{PR^B} \cdot \frac{P^A}{P^B} \tag{9}$$

which states that macro factor price equalization is fulfilled. As shown in Section I, this relationship is also the statement that the unit-factor-cost and purchasing-power-parity theories define the same equilibrium exchange rate. How then can Equation (9) be tested?

Can one obtain guidance by consulting the literature on empirical investigation of the *micro* factor-price-equalization theorem? This theorem has been tested in only one way—by checking if the *conditions* for factor price equalization exist in the real world. The landmark study is that of Minhas (1963), who demonstrated that the application of CES production functions to real-world data leads to factor-intensity reversals, thus eliminating a necessary condition for factor price equalization.[5] Pearce (1970, pp. 514-20) argues that the ideal test would investigate the basic roots of the theorem. He suggests a step-by-step procedure to test whether the condition for the existence of an inverse to the cost function is not satisfied, in which case factor price equalization is not fulfilled.

I suggest that an appropriate test for factor price equalization would be an empirical investigation of its results rather than its assumptions. Let us examine directly how close Equation (9) comes to fulfillment in the real world. This approach tests the robustness of the macro factor-price-equalization theorem. Even granted that its assumptions may not be satisfied, how well does the theorem perform as a predictor of factor prices in the real world?

Letting Germany (A) be the base country, I collected data also for ten other countries[6] for the years 1952-1970 (data permitting), resulting in 166 observations on the variables entering Equation (9). The ratio of the German to the domestic price level (P^A/P^B) is calculated as the geometric mean of the German-weighted and domestic-weighted purchasing power parities (number of marks per unit of domestic currency) published by the German Statistical Office, the computation also employed by Houthakker. Wage rates $(W^A$ and $W^B)$ are measured by earnings per hour in manufacturing, obtained from ILO publications.[7] This series provides factor prices for a homogeneous kind of labor compatible across countries. Productivity (PR) is measured by the ratio of GDP to employment in the total economy. Sources of the GDP and employment series are UN and ILO publications, respectively. GDP is converted from domestic currency to marks by using the purchasing power parity (described above) as the conversion factor.

Letting $W = W^A/W^B$ and $P = (PR^A/PR^B)\cdot(P^A/P^B)$, the strategy I followed was to fit the equation

$$\log W = \alpha + \beta \log P + u$$

and to test jointly that $\alpha = \beta - 1 = 0$. The variables are transformed into logarithms because in original form they are not invariant to a change in the exchange-rate unit.[8]

Letting a, b, and s^2 be the least-squares estimates of α, β, and the variance of u, respectively, I computed the test statistic

$$F = \frac{166\ a^2 + (b - 1)\ [332(\overline{\log P})\ a + \Sigma(\log P)^2\ (b - 1)]}{2s^2}$$

which has an F distribution with (2, 164) degrees of freedom.[9]

The fitted equation, with t-values in parentheses, was:

$$\log W = -0.0007 + 0.9672 \log P \quad \bar{R}^2 = 0.9864$$
$$(0.04) \quad (109.30)$$

and $F = 6.90$, a value which involves rejection of the hypothesis $\alpha = \beta - 1 = 0$ even at the 1-percent level of significance.

It turns out that a data peculiarity is responsible for the negative result. One expects that inclusion of the productivity term (PR^A/PR^B) would narrow the divergence between the relative wage rate (W^A/W^B) and relative price level (P^A/P^B). Indeed, this is the reason for permitting production functions to differ in efficiency internationally. However, for two countries (France and Netherlands) inclusion of the productivity term actually widened the divergence. Therefore I imposed identical productive efficiency $(PR^A/PR^B = 1)$ for Germany, France, and Netherlands, then reestimated the equation with the following results:

$$\log W = -0.0493 + 0.9703 \log P \quad \bar{R}^2 = 0.9941$$
$$(4.71) \quad (166.88)$$

with $F = 1.45$, a value which disallows rejection of the hypothesis $\alpha = \beta - 1 = 0$ even at the 20 percent level of significance.[10]

V. CONCLUDING COMMENTS

I have shown that the predictive power of the model developed in this paper is remarkably high. In particular, the macro factor-price-equalization theorem comes close to fulfillment in the real world, which implies that the equilibrium exchange rates defined by the unit-factor-cost and purchasing-power-parity theories are close to identical.

Yet many observers deny the applicability of factor price equalization to the real world. For example, Pearce (1970, p. 512) writes:

> We believe in the existence of a competitive mechanism common to all countries which, up to a reasonable degree of approximation, determines factor rewards wherever in the world the factor is located. It is taken for granted also that the laws of physics are everywhere the same. We have to explain why, despite these two apparent facts, factor prices differ quite remarkably according to location.

Pearce submits as explanations either that the competitive process does not work or that inverse cost functions do not exist. A better explanation, unfortunately, is that there has been little attempt to examine real-world data to see how closely factor price equalization is approached. Furthermore, Pearce's assumption of identical production functions is not always valid. If correction is made for international productivity differences, then the factor-price-equalization theorem is a good predictor of real-world behavior.

Also relevant is a theoretical implication. The model presented in this paper is an extension of Houthakker's approach to purchasing power parity. I suggest that the empirical results provide further justification for absolute purchasing power parity based on factor price equalization rather than on a self-contradictory arbitrage involving nontraded commodities.

NOTES

1. This chapter appears in the bibliography as Officer (1974). It is reprinted by permission of *Kyklos*.
2. Houthakker (1962a, pp. 293–94) discusses the modification to the theory required by the existence of unilateral transfers and capital flows.
3. Again, Samuelson (1964, p. 152) has objected that factor price equalization involves a form of production function that "would not seem realistic enough for empirical calculations." However, his contention is countered by the Arrow, Chenery, Minhas, Solow (1961) study. These authors provide econometric evidence that intercountry differences in production functions take the form of a neutral efficiency factor.
4. In fact, there are two degrees of freedom, as the weighting structure for country A might differ from that for country B, which indeed is the case in (5). Thus, from the standpoint of the present model, Yeager (1958, p. 517) is wrong in his assertion that "The 'absolute' or 'positive' approach to rate calculation ideally envisages the pricing in local currency in each of two countries of a standard assortment of goods and services, the same for the two countries and yet duly representative of economic life in each."
5. The Minhas study has been subjected to many criticisms. A summary of the subsequent literature is provided by Bhagwati (1969, pp. 100–107).
6. France, Italy, Netherlands, Finland, Norway, Sweden, Canada, United States, United Kingdom, and New Zealand.
7. These data measure wages received by the employee before deducting income taxes and his own social-security contributions. They do not include fringes such as family allowances or social-security contributions paid by the employer.
8. The transformation would be unnecessary, of course, if the observations referred to only one country (B).
9. See Johnston (1972, pp. 28–29).
10. Critical values for the F distribution at the 20 percent significance level are not published in an accessible source. However, the critical value at this level for $F(2, \infty)$ is readily obtained as 1.61; for this degrees-of-freedom configuration reduces the F to a chi-square distribution with 2 degrees of freedom. The corresponding critical value for $F(2, 164)$ is necessarily greater than 1.61.

Chapter XIV

The Productivity Bias in Purchasing Power Parity: An Econometric Investigation[1]

A recent paper by the author (Officer, 1976a) reviewed the various biases and limitations of the purchasing-power-parity (PPP) theory of exchange rates. It was shown that the imperfections of PPP theory fall into three categories: (1) those that reflect the fact that the PPP theory is subject to random error in its predictions; (2) those that emphasize the role of variables other than price levels in exchange-rate determination; and (3) those that involve the hypothesis of a systematic bias in PPP as a measure of the equilibrium exchange rate.[2] While the first type of weakness—random error—is common to all theories and the second type—other explanatory variables—can generally be corrected by a simple alteration or extension of the PPP theory, the third type—systematic bias—might require fundamental alterations in the theory to preserve its validity. Although the bias could be allowed for in empirical applications, the result might involve a theory of the exchange rate that was no longer recognized as being in the PPP tradition.

The most important reason for a systematic divergence between PPP and the equilibrium exchange rate is the existence of productivity differences between countries. Although others had perceived the existence of such a "productivity bias,"[3] Balassa (1964) provided the most persuasive analytical argument for this bias. Elsewhere his reasoning is summarized as follows (Officer, 1976a, pp. 18–19):

211

... A high-income country is more productive technologically than a low-income country; but the efficiency advantage of the former country is not uniform over all industries. Rather, it is greater for traded goods (especially manufactured goods and agricultural products) than for nontraded goods (taken by Balassa to be consumer services—he does not mention the public sector). Advances in productivity proceed in this asymmetric fashion for all countries.

Now, prices of traded goods are equalized across countries (abstracting from trade restrictions and transport costs); but this is not so for nontraded goods. With the wage rate higher in the more productive (higher-income) country and with wages equalized domestically across all industries, the internal price ratio [ratio of the price level of nontraded commodities to the price level of traded commodities] must be higher in the higher-income country.

The prices of nontraded goods (relatively higher in the more productive country) are not directly relevant for balance of payments equilibrium. Therefore, a price parity calculated from general price levels yields an exchange value of the high-income country's currency that is lower than its true long-run equilibrium value, and this systematic bias increases with the overall productivity difference (represented by the per capita income difference) between the countries involved.

As Balassa (1964, pp. 586, 589) writes:

> In other words, assuming that international productivity differences are greater in the production of traded goods than in the production of non-traded goods, the currency of the country with the higher productivity levels will appear to be overvalued in terms of purchasing-power parity. If per capita incomes are taken as representative of levels of productivity, the ratio of purchasing-power parity to the exchange rate [number of units of domestic currency per unit of the standard currency] will thus be an increasing function of income levels . . . the higher level of service prices at higher income levels leads to systematic differences between purchasing power parities and equilibrium exchange rates.

The productivity bias and Balassa's justification of it seem to have won general acceptance in the profession. Among those who have been persuaded of the existence and importance of the productivity bias are Gottfried Haberler, Harry G. Johnson, Charles P. Kindleberger, Angus Maddison, and Leland B. Yeager.[4] The only challenge to Balassa's theoretical argument was provided by Officer (1974) and rejected by Balassa (1974a).[5]

The present study is not concerned with the analytical argument for the productivity bias but focuses on econometric testing of the existence and magnitude of the bias. Like any hypothesis, the productivity bias may be tested in two ways—through its operational impact and in terms of its assumptions. In this case, the first test investigates whether productivity is a variable that interposes itself in the relationship between PPP and the equilibrium exchange rate. The second test explores the theoretical underpinning of the bias, determining whether disparate productivity advances among countries do lead to divergent movements in their internal price ratios, where the internal price ratio is defined as the ratio of the price level of nontraded commodities to that of traded commodities. According to the productivity-bias hypothesis, the expected relationship is that the change in a country's internal price ratio is positively related to the change in the country's productivity.

Section I of the study is concerned with the first type of test of the productivity bias—its operational impact, and Section II with the second type—its theoretical underpinning. In each case the evidence from the existing econometric literature is outlined and evaluated, and the results of new investigations are presented. Section III provides a summary of the study's findings and their implications for the validity of PPP theory. An Appendix describes the data sources and the construction of the variables used in the study.

I. TESTING THE OPERATIONAL IMPACT OF THE PRODUCTIVITY BIAS

Consider the following notation:

PPP_i = purchasing power parity of country i, number of units of domestic currency per unit of standard currency

R_i = exchange rate of country i, number of units of domestic currency per unit of standard currency

$PROD_i$ = ratio of productivity in country i to productivity in the standard country

Then a method of testing the operational impact of the productivity bias is to fit the following regression equation by ordinary least-squares estimation.

$$PPP_i/R_i = \alpha + \beta PROD_i + \epsilon_i \qquad (1)$$

for a sample of N countries, $i = 1, \ldots, N$, where α and β are parameters and the error term ϵ_i is assumed to be normally, identically, and independently distributed for all i. The productivity-bias hypothesis is accepted if the estimate of β is significantly different from zero.[6] The hypothesis also predicts a positive value for this coefficient.

A. Previous Tests of the Operational Impact of the Bias

The above approach was followed by Balassa in testing the productivity-bias hypothesis. He took the United States as the standard country and per capita gross national product (GNP) at current prices as the measure of productivity. In his initial regression, Balassa (1964) converts GNP from domestic currency to U.S. dollars by means of the exchange rate (R). In a later study that makes use of revised data on the explanatory variable, Balassa (1973) presents results for GNP converted alternatively by means of R and *PPP*. The variables refer to the year 1960, and the absolute version of *PPP* is used.[7] The sample consists of 12 industrial countries; it includes the standard country (the United States), which is inappropriate, as is pointed out in the next section. Consider the following additional notation:

GNP/POP_i =   ratio of per capita GNP (at current prices) in country i to per capita GNP (at current prices) in the standard country, where the numerator is converted from domestic currency to the standard currency by means of the PPP between the two countries, except where otherwise stated

$\bar{R}^2$ =   adjusted coefficient of determination

df =   degrees of freedom

Balassa's regressions are presented in Table 1. In this and subsequent tables, the estimated coefficient and t-value (in parentheses) of α and of β are presented in the columns headed by "Constant" and the productivity variable (in this case "GNP/POP"), respectively. A double star following the t-value of the estimate of β denotes that the estimate is significantly different from zero at the 1 percent level; a single star indicates significance[8] at the 5 percent level. One notes that in all three of Balassa's regressions the estimate of β is significant at the 1 percent level, lending strong support to the productivity-bias hypothesis.

Attempts to reproduce Balassa's findings using other data have not led to positive results regarding the existence of the productivity bias. De Vries (1968) reports on fitting Equation (1) to a sample of 62 countries, including both developed countries (DCs) and less developed countries (LDCs), with the United States as the standard country. The explanatory variable is per capita gross domestic product (GDP) at current prices for the year 1958, with the exchange rate for that year used to convert GDP from domestic currency to dollars.[9] The dependent variable involves a relative PPP measure, with the base period being 1955 and the current period being mid-1966. De Vries reports a t-value of 1.716 for the estimate of β; thus the coefficient is not quite significant at the 5 percent level.

Clague and Tanzi (1972) estimate Equation (1) for a sample of 19

Table 1. Regressions of *PPP/R* on *GNP/POP*, with the United States
as the Standard Country, 1960[1]

Equation	Constant		GNP/POP[2]		$\bar{R}^2$	Degrees of Freedom
A	0.49	[3]	0.51**	(8.33)	[4]	10
B	0.57	(26.05)	0.46**	(10.72)	0.92	10
C	0.49	(12.94)	0.51**	(8.41)	0.86	10

Notes:
**The coefficient is significantly different from zero at the 1 percent level.
[1]Equation A is from Balassa (1964), and equations B and C are from Balassa (1973). Balassa provides standard errors of the coefficients, which are converted here into *t*-values.
[2]In equations A and B, *R* rather than *PPP* is used to convert GNP from domestic currency to U.S. dollars.
   In equation A, Balassa shows the coefficient for absolute per capita GNP as the explanatory variable. The coefficient is altered here to reflect the explanatory variable as defined in relation to per capita GNP for the United States.
[3]The *t*-value is not provided.
[4]$\bar{R}^2$ is not provided; the correlation coefficient = 0.92.

Latin American countries, again with the United States as the standard country, for the year 1960. The absolute PPP concept is used, and, as the explanatory variable, per capita GDP (at current prices) is converted from domestic currency to dollars using, alternatively, *R* and *PPP*. Clague and Tanzi report $\bar{R}^2$ to be 0.24 in the first case and −0.05 in the second case. Thus, using *PPP* as the conversion factor results in a negative $\bar{R}^2$, that is, in a *t*-value below unity for the estimate of β.

A weaker test of the productivity bias than that provided by the fitting of Equation (1) is offered by Grunwald and Salazar-Carrillo (1972). For ten member countries of the Latin American Free Trade Association, they perform a rank correlation of *PPP/R* and per capita *GDP*. For the former variable, the standard country is Venezuela and the time period is May 1968. On the other hand, GDP refers to the year 1963 and is converted to dollars using the exchange rate for that year.[10] The rank correlation coefficient between the two variables is reported as −0.27 when *R* is the official exchange rate and −0.30 when it is the free exchange rate (which differs from the official rate for five of the countries). Thus, the rank correlation of *PPP/R* and per capita *GDP* is not only low in magnitude but has a sign opposite to that predicted by the productivity-bias hypothesis.

It should be a source of some amazement that the studies cited are apparently all the published econometric work on the operational impact of the productivity bias. It would be even more amazing that the conflicting findings regarding the bias—affirmative on the part of Balassa, not so on the part of the other authors—have not disturbed the profession's general acceptance of the validity of the bias, except that Balassa (1973) has argued that Equation (1) is not applicable to LDCs.[11]

At this stage it would appear a good procedure (a) to specify an optimum experimental design in using Equation (1) to test the productivity-bias hypothesis, (b) to assess to what extent the previous studies have followed this experimental design, and (c) to provide a new test of the hypothesis following the specified experimental design as closely as possible.

B. The Experimental Design

1. In order to obtain a clear test of the productivity-bias hypothesis, the sample should be restricted to developed countries. As described earlier, the studies of Clague and Tanzi (1972) and Grunwald and Salazar-Carrillo (1972) show that a sample composed entirely of LDCs provides no evidence of a productivity bias, and in the work of de Vries (1968) a mixed sample of DCs and LDCs also failed to produce positive implications for the existence of such a bias. These results indicate that inclusion of LDCs in the sample would orient the test toward rejecting the productivity-bias hypothesis. However, it would be wrong to conclude that *PPP* is an unbiased measure of the equilibrium exchange rate for LDCs. On the contrary, Clague and Tanzi (1972) and Balassa (1973) provide analytical arguments that there exist systematic biases in representing the equilibrium exchange rate by the *PPP* in the case of LDCs, but that these biases are of a different nature from the productivity bias. Clague and Tanzi also offer econometric results suggesting the existence of such biases.

Of the authors considered, only Balassa observes the rule of using a sample composed exclusively of developed countries.

2. Both the dependent and independent variable should refer to the same time period, because the effect of productivity on *PPP/R* is a contemporaneous one.[12] An implication of this precept is that absolute rather than relative *PPP* is the appropriate version to use in testing the productivity-bias hypothesis.

This rule is followed by Balassa and Clague and Tanzi but not by de Vries or Grunwald and Salazar-Carrillo.

3. All observations on the variables should be comparable in concept. In particular, the *PPP* should be computed in the same manner and using data of the same nature for all countries.

In contrast to the other authors, Balassa does not follow this rule, as his *PPP* measure emanates from a variety of sources and methods of computation, depending on the country. Although this procedure enabled Balassa to increase the size of his sample, it led to misleading regression results, as will be shown later.

4. Given that the absolute *PPP* concept is used, the *PPP* measure should be computed from individual prices in the domestic country and the standard country using a formula that incorporates the weighting patterns of both countries. If only one country's weights are used, the computed *PPP* will be biased in the direction of an overvalued *PPP* for that country.[13] A typical formula is Irving Fisher's ideal index number—that is, the geometric mean of the parities calculated alternatively using the weighting pattern of the domestic country and that of the standard country.

This precept is followed by Grunwald and Salazar-Carrillo and by Clague and Tanzi, although their PPP measures are based on the average Latin American (rather than the individual country) weighting pattern and the U.S. weighting pattern. Balassa's PPP measure is based on Fisher's ideal index for 9 of the 12 countries in his sample; the rule stated here is not observed for the remaining 3 countries.

5. The optimum price-level concept of the *PPP* measure is the GDP price level, because the GDP price level is the appropriate concept to use in computing the *PPP* as a representation of the equilibrium exchange rate (Officer, 1976a, pp. 11–12).

The GDP-price-level concept is used by Clague and Tanzi, and a cost-of-living (COL) price level is used by Grunwald an Salazar-Carrillo. The concept employed by de Vries is a COL level, as COL indices are used to construct her relative PPP measure. As for Balassa, with 11 countries plus the standard country in his sample, a GNP-price-level concept underlies the PPP measure for 8 of the countries. The remaining 3 countries represent a mixture of concepts: a COL price level for Canada, an imprecise price level for Japan, and an unknown price level for Sweden.[14]

Obviously, the difference between a PPP founded on a GNP price level and one founded on a GDP price level would be minimal, although a purist would prefer the latter concept. A PPP based on a COL price level, however, can differ noticeably from one based on a GDP price level (Officer, 1976a, pp. 12–13).

6. The standard country should not be included as an observation in the regression. With both the dependent and independent variable having a value identically equal to unity for this country, the degree of

freedom gained is illusory, as the information concerning the standard country has already been used in constructing the variables for the other countries.[15]

This precept is observed by all authors except Balassa.

7. The income measure for an individual country (for use in the productivity variable) should be converted from domestic currency to the standard currency by using *PPP* rather than *R*. It is well known that the use of exchange rates rather than PPPs to convert national-income data from one national currency to another misrepresents the relative positions of different countries' real incomes. A substantial literature now exists on the application of PPP to intercountry comparisons of national-income variables.[16]

De Vries and Grunwald and Salazar-Carrillo employ exchange rates for the conversion purpose,[17] while Balassa and Clague and Tanzi show results for R and PPP used alternatively.

8. The appropriate income concept for the productivity variable is GDP rather than GNP. The reason is that the productivity-bias hypothesis concerns prices and production within the boundaries of a country. This point has been made elsewhere by Officer (1974, p. 874), with acknowledgment that its quantitative significance is small.

Of the authors considered, only Balassa does not use the GDP concept. However, as with point 5, the use of a GNP rather than a GDP concept would lead to only minor differences in the variable.

9. While per capita GDP is an acceptable concept of productivity, a better measure would be the ratio of GDP to total employment in the economy rather than to total population of the country—a point also made by Officer (1974, p. 874). A reasonable approach is to adopt both measures of productivity—per capita GDP and GDP per employed worker—alternatively, for the specification of the explanatory variable. None of the authors uses employment in place of population to construct an alternative productivity variable.

10. A still better measure of productivity can be employed to construct the explanatory variable. This measure is the ratio of productivity in the traded sector of the economy to productivity in the nontraded sector, where productivity in each sector is defined as the ratio of GDP (at constant prices) originating in the sector to total employment in the sector. Such a measure of productivity is closest to the productivity concept involved in the theoretical argument for the productivity bias.[18] This third measure of productivity, which is not used by any of the authors, would provide another explanatory variable to be used alternatively in Equation (1).[19]

11. Strictly speaking, the exchange rate (*R*) used in the dependent

variable should be the equilibrium value of the exchange rate, as the productivity bias refers to the relationship between PPP and the *equilibrium* exchange rate (Officer, 1974, pp. 874-75; 1976a, p. 36). Given that the actual exchange rate is to be employed as a proxy for the equilibrium exchange rate, Equation (1) should be estimated for a number of years, preferably consecutive, so that periods in which exchange rates are close to equilibrium will be considered. Furthermore, the variables used should be comparable in concept and construction from year to year, so that year-to-year comparisons of results may be made. In other words, a moving cross-sectional regression, fitted independently over a number of years (and *not* pooling data of different years), is indicated.

All the previous authors estimated Equation (1) for only one year.

C. Tests Using the Experimental Design

Consider the following notation:

GDP/POP_i = ratio of per capita GDP (at current prices) in country *i* to per capita GDP (at current prices) in the standard country, where the numerator is converted from domestic currency to the standard currency by means of the *PPP* between the two countries

GDP/EMP_i = ratio of GDP (at current prices) per employed worker in country *i* to GDP (at current prices) per employed worker in the standard country, where the numerator is converted from domestic currency to the standard currency by means of the *PPP* between the two countries

$PRODT/PRODNT_i$ = ratio of "ratio of productivity in the traded sector of the economy of country *i* to productivity in the nontraded sector" to "ratio of productivity in the traded sector of the economy of the standard country to productivity in the nontraded sector," where "productivity" is defined as GDP (at constant prices) originating in the sector per employed worker in the sector

The traded sector consists of (1) agriculture, hunting, forestry, and fishing, (2) mining and quarrying, and (3) manufacturing. The nontraded sector encompasses all other industries (including government) in which GDP originates.[20]

The GDP measures in the *PRODT/PRODNT* variable are at constant prices in order to remove the effect of inflation on the productivity measures, thus facilitating year-to-year comparisons of results of the moving cross-sectional regression specified in point 11 above. In contrast, the GDP measures in the *GDP/POP* and *GDP/EMP* variables are correctly expressed in current prices, because the GDP of the domestic country is converted from domestic currency to the currency of the standard country by using the price levels of the two countries (i.e., the PPP) in the period (year) to which the GDP measures pertain.

The experimental design described earlier was applied to four sets of *PPP/R* data, two sets involving the Federal Republic of Germany as the standard country and two involving the United States in that role.

Table 2. Regressions of Unadjusted *PPP/R* on *GDP/POP*, with the Federal Republic of Germany as the Standard Country, 1950–1973

Year	Constant		GDP/POP		$\bar{R}^2$	Degrees of Freedom
1950	1.02	(5.27)	−0.02	(0.15)	−0.08	12
1951	0.96	(3.82)	0.04	(0.27)	−0.08	11
1952	0.92	(3.52)	0.09	(0.53)	−0.06	11
1953	0.90	(3.81)	0.12	(0.69)	−0.04	12
1954	0.96	(3.86)	0.09	(0.50)	−0.06	12
1955	0.87	(3.73)	0.16	(0.87)	−0.02	12
1956	0.90	(3.67)	0.15	(0.75)	−0.03	12
1957	0.96	(3.68)	0.12	(0.54)	−0.06	12
1958	0.89	(3.71)	0.17	(0.80)	−0.03	12
1959	0.86	(3.63)	0.19	(0.90)	−0.02	12
1960	0.90	(3.81)	0.16	(0.70)	−0.04	12
1961	0.86	(3.67)	0.16	(0.69)	−0.04	12
1962	0.87	(4.25)	0.14	(0.71)	−0.04	12
1963	0.92	(4.44)	0.09	(0.45)	−0.07	12
1964	1.02	(4.94)	0.00	(0.00)	−0.08	12
1965	1.01	(5.45)	0.02	(0.10)	−0.08	13
1966	0.96	(5.18)	0.06	(0.34)	−0.07	13
1967	0.86	(4.96)	0.17	(1.04)	0.01	13
1968	0.76	(4.27)	0.27	(1.54)	0.09	13
1969	0.74	(4.11)	0.29	(1.63)	0.11	13
1970	0.70	(3.56)	0.28	(1.38)	0.06	13
1971	0.70	(3.96)	0.26	(1.39)	0.06	13
1972	0.62	(3.95)	0.31	(1.89)	0.16	13
1973	0.58	(3.83)	0.28	(1.79)	0.14	13

Table 3. Regressions of Unadjusted *PPP/R* on *GDP/EMP*, with the Federal Republic of Germany as the Standard Country, 1950–1973

Year	Constant		GDP/EMP		$\bar{R}^2$	Degrees of Freedom
1950	0.95	(3.70)	0.03	(0.20)	−0.12	8
1951	0.75	(1.89)	0.14	(0.68)	−0.08	6
1952	0.68	(1.62)	0.21	(0.91)	−0.03	6
1953	0.60	(2.00)	0.27	(1.51)	0.14	7
1954	0.76	(3.16)	0.20	(1.30)	0.07	8
1955	0.72	(3.31)	0.22	(1.48)	0.11	9
1956	0.77	(3.91)	0.21	(1.51)	0.10	11
1957	0.95	(4.40)	0.11	(0.72)	−0.04	12
1958	0.87	(4.54)	0.16	(1.11)	0.02	12
1959	0.84	(4.39)	0.18	(1.23)	0.04	12
1960	0.86	(4.50)	0.17	(1.10)	0.02	12
1961	0.86	(4.59)	0.15	(0.94)	−0.01	12
1962	0.89	(5.41)	0.11	(0.76)	−0.03	12
1963	0.94	(5.59)	0.06	(0.45)	−0.07	12
1964	1.02	(5.93)	0.00	(0.02)	−0.08	12
1965	1.00	(6.23)	0.02	(0.16)	−0.07	13
1966	0.99	(5.96)	0.04	(0.25)	−0.07	13
1967	0.90	(5.57)	0.13	(0.87)	−0.02	13
1968	0.81	(4.73)	0.21	(1.35)	0.06	13
1969	0.75	(4.14)	0.26	(1.56)	0.09	13
1970	0.70	(3.56)	0.27	(1.40)	0.06	13
1971	0.72	(4.01)	0.23	(1.30)	0.05	13
1972	0.70	(4.06)	0.22	(1.26)	0.04	13
1973	0.74	(4.29)	0.12	(0.68)	−0.04	13

The Statistisches Bundesamt (Statistical Office) publishes exchange rate and PPP data for a number of countries in relation to the Federal Republic of Germany.[21] For many of these countries, the Statistisches Bundesamt provides two PPP computations, one using the weights for the Federal Republic of Germany, the other the domestic country's weights. The PPP concept employed is a cost-of-living level, with the weights referring to household consumption expenditure. Data are provided annually and monthly.[22] For each country, the PPP series are obtained by extrapolation from a base period in which an absolute PPP computation is performed. Consumer price indices in the domestic country and in the Federal Republic of Germany are used in the extrapolation procedure.[23]

The sample selected for the first set of data consists of all members of the Organization for Economic Cooperation and Development for which the Statistisches Bundesamt provides the two PPP series, one with the weighting pattern of the domestic country and the other with the weighting pattern for the Federal Republic of Germany. The Fisher ideal index of the two PPP computations serves as the PPP measure for the variables in Equation (1).[24] The result is a sample consisting essentially of the industrial countries with a market economy: Canada, the United States, Australia, New Zealand, Austria, Belgium, Denmark, Finland, France, Italy, the Netherlands, Norway, Sweden, Switzerland, and the United Kingdom.[25] The standard country, of course, is the Federal Republic of Germany, and Equation (1) is estimated annually for the period 1950–1973. Results are presented in Tables 2, 3, and 4. While the maximum size of the sample is 15, the degrees of freedom can fall below 13 because of missing observations in certain years.

It was mentioned above that the PPP computations of the Statistisches Bundesamt involve extrapolations from a base period. The base period

Table 4.   Regressions of Unadjusted *PPP/R* on *PRODT/PRODNT*, with the Federal Republic of Germany as the Standard Country, 1950–1973

Year	Constant		PRODT/PRODNT		$\bar{R}^2$	Degrees of Freedom
1950	1.84	(1.83)	−0.60	(0.78)	−0.11	3
1951	2.35	(1.78)	−0.97	(0.95)	−0.03	3
1952	2.58	(1.46)	−1.17	(0.82)	−0.09	3
1953	0.74	(0.62)	0.31	(0.30)	−0.22	4
1954	0.98	(2.01)	0.12	(0.27)	−0.15	6
1955	0.89	(1.85)	0.20	(0.44)	−0.13	6
1956	0.89	(1.83)	0.21	(0.45)	−0.13	6
1957	0.86	(1.58)	0.24	(0.46)	−0.13	6
1958	0.78	(1.43)	0.32	(0.61)	−0.10	6
1959	0.69	(1.29)	0.40	(0.76)	−0.06	6
1960	0.73	(1.46)	0.34	(0.68)	−0.07	7
1961	0.61	(1.33)	0.46	(1.01)	0.00	6
1962	0.58	(1.69)	0.46	(1.35)	0.11	6
1963	0.64	(1.93)	0.41	(1.24)	0.07	6
1964	0.85	(2.93)	0.21	(0.70)	−0.07	7
1965	0.91	(3.52)	0.14	(0.54)	−0.09	8
1966	0.81	(2.95)	0.25	(0.89)	−0.03	7
1967	0.76	(2.48)	0.30	(0.99)	−0.00	7
1968	0.80	(2.42)	0.28	(0.83)	−0.04	7
1969	0.75	(2.16)	0.32	(0.90)	−0.02	7
1970	0.65	(1.81)	0.36	(0.99)	−0.00	7
1971	0.70	(2.19)	0.28	(0.91)	−0.02	7
1972	0.59	(2.48)	0.34	(1.50)	0.13	7
1973	0.50	(2.35)	0.34	(1.65)	0.18	7

Table 5. Regressions of Adjusted *PPP/R* on *GDP/POP*, with the Federal Republic of Germany as the Standard Country, 1950–1973

Year	Constant		GDP/POP		$\bar{R}^2$	Degrees of Freedom
1950	0.96	(3.86)	0.00	(0.03)	−0.11	9
1951	0.91	(3.12)	0.06	(0.35)	−0.10	9
1952	0.86	(2.87)	0.11	(0.59)	−0.07	9
1953	0.95	(3.20)	0.08	(0.39)	−0.09	9
1954	1.03	(3.32)	0.04	(0.19)	−0.11	9
1955	0.93	(3.24)	0.12	(0.54)	−0.08	9
1956	0.97	(3.26)	0.10	(0.41)	−0.09	9
1957	1.02	(3.54)	0.08	(0.33)	−0.09	10
1958	0.94	(3.58)	0.14	(0.61)	−0.06	10
1959	0.91	(3.64)	0.16	(0.72)	−0.04	11
1960	0.89	(3.57)	0.17	(0.73)	−0.04	12
1961	0.86	(3.67)	0.16	(0.69)	−0.04	12
1962	0.87	(4.25)	0.14	(0.71)	−0.04	12
1963	0.92	(4.44)	0.09	(0.45)	−0.07	12
1964	1.02	(4.94)	0.00	(0.00)	−0.08	12
1965	1.06	(5.50)	−0.04	(0.19)	−0.07	13
1966	1.02	(5.15)	0.01	(0.05)	−0.08	13
1967	1.00	(4.90)	0.04	(0.22)	−0.07	13
1968	0.89	(3.96)	0.13	(0.62)	−0.05	13
1969	0.86	(3.81)	0.16	(0.70)	−0.04	13
1970	0.85	(3.54)	0.12	(0.49)	−0.06	13
1971	0.84	(3.81)	0.11	(0.47)	−0.06	13
1972	0.88	(4.47)	0.04	(0.18)	−0.07	13
1973	0.81	(4.61)	0.03	(0.19)	−0.07	13

(generally not the same for each country) can change from time to time, giving rise to inconsistencies in a country's PPP series. To facilitate year-to-year comparison of results, the unadjusted PPP series are converted to adjusted PPP series for each country by linking the differently based subperiods by means of a year's overlap or, when a full year is unavailable, by the maximum number of months' overlap available. The base period to which alternatively based subperiods are linked is the one closest to the middle of the time period considered (1950–1973). If a given country's PPP series has an earlier subperiod with no overlap available for linking to a later subperiod, that country is dropped from the sample for the earlier subperiod. The PPP series resulting from this procedure are used to compute a new ideal-index PPP for each country, which is then used in re-estimating Equation (1). The results are presented in Tables 5, 6, and 7.

Table 6. Regressions of Adjusted *PPP/R* on *GDP/EMP*, with the Federal Republic of Germany as the Standard Country, 1950–1973

Year	Constant		GDP/EMP		$\bar{R}^2$	Degrees of Freedom
1950	0.76	(1.78)	0.10	(0.50)	−0.14	5
1951	0.67	(1.36)	0.17	(0.71)	−0.09	5
1952	0.55	(1.07)	0.27	(0.99)	−0.00	5
1953	0.56	(1.19)	0.29	(1.09)	0.03	5
1954	0.82	(2.54)	0.17	(0.86)	−0.04	6
1955	0.77	(2.74)	0.19	(1.04)	0.01	7
1956	0.78	(2.98)	0.19	(1.12)	−0.03	8
1957	1.03	(4.25)	0.06	(0.38)	−0.08	10
1958	0.94	(4.34)	0.12	(0.76)	−0.04	10
1959	0.90	(4.39)	0.14	(0.93)	−0.01	11
1960	0.88	(4.45)	0.15	(0.95)	−0.01	12
1961	0.86	(4.59)	0.15	(0.94)	−0.01	12
1962	0.89	(5.41)	0.11	(0.76)	−0.03	12
1963	0.94	(5.59)	0.06	(0.45)	−0.07	12
1964	1.02	(5.93)	0.00	(0.02)	−0.08	12
1965	1.06	(6.47)	−0.03	(0.24)	−0.07	13
1966	1.05	(6.11)	−0.02	(0.14)	−0.08	13
1967	1.05	(5.76)	−0.01	(0.03)	−0.08	13
1968	0.96	(4.68)	0.06	(0.33)	−0.07	13
1969	0.93	(4.26)	0.09	(0.42)	−0.06	13
1970	0.90	(3.97)	0.06	(0.28)	−0.07	13
1971	0.91	(4.33)	0.04	(0.17)	−0.07	13
1972	0.98	(5.20)	−0.06	(0.34)	−0.07	13
1973	0.96	(5.77)	−0.11	(0.67)	−0.04	13

The results in Tables 2 to 7 have totally negative implications for the existence of a productivity bias. With a total of 144 fitted regressions, not one estimate of β is significant at the 5 percent level. Indeed, in only 30 of the regressions does the productivity variable yield even a positive $\bar{R}^2$.

Gilbert and associates (1958) provide absolute PPP computations (together with corresponding exchange rates) for eight European industrial countries for the years 1950 and 1955, using, alternatively, weights of the domestic country and of the standard country (the United States). The countries considered are Belgium, Denmark, France, the Federal Republic of Germany, Italy, the Netherlands, Norway, and the United Kingdom. The price-level concept used is the GNP, and the 1955 figures are obtained from the 1950 results by means of an extrapolation procedure.[26]

Taking the Fisher ideal index of the domestic-country-weighted and U.S.-weighted PPPs to measure the PPP, Equation (1) was fitted to Gilbert and associates' sample of countries for the years 1950 and 1955, with the results presented in Table 8. One observes that, again, in no case is the coefficient of the productivity variable significant at the 5 percent level, and in only one of six regressions does this variable produce a positive $\bar{R}^2$.

The final set of *PPP/R* data that was considered emanates from Kravis and others (1975). These authors calculate, among other computations, absolute PPP measures for 9 countries for the year 1970, with the United States as the standard country and GDP as the price-level concept. For each country, they present the domestic-country-weighted, U.S.-weighted, and ideal-index PPPs, along with the corresponding exchange rate. Of the 9 countries, 5 are industrial market economies (France, the Federal Republic of Germany, Italy, Japan, and the United Kingdom), and they constitute the sample for fitting Equation (1) to data for 1970.

Table 7. Regressions of Adjusted *PPP/R* on *PRODT/PRODNT*, with the Federal Republic of Germany as the Standard Country, 1950–1973

Year	Constant		PRODT/PRODNT		$\bar{R}^2$	Degrees of Freedom
1950	1.76	(1.87)	−0.52	(0.73)	−0.13	3
1951	2.23	(1.80)	−0.85	(0.89)	−0.05	3
1952	2.42	(1.48)	−1.03	(0.77)	−0.11	3
1953	1.97	(1.25)	−0.66	(0.50)	−0.23	3
1954	1.12	(2.12)	0.05	(0.11)	−0.25	4
1955	1.04	(2.01)	0.12	(0.24)	−0.23	4
1956	1.07	(2.04)	0.09	(0.19)	−0.24	4
1957	1.03	(1.76)	0.15	(0.28)	−0.23	4
1958	0.95	(1.63)	0.23	(0.41)	−0.20	4
1959	0.86	(1.59)	0.28	(0.53)	−0.14	5
1960	0.71	(1.47)	0.37	(0.77)	−0.05	7
1961	0.61	(1.33)	0.46	(1.01)	0.00	6
1962	0.58	(1.69)	0.46	(1.35)	0.11	6
1963	0.64	(1.93)	0.41	(1.24)	0.07	6
1964	0.85	(2.93)	0.21	(0.70)	−0.07	7
1965	0.91	(3.52)	0.14	(0.54)	−0.09	8
1966	0.81	(2.95)	0.25	(0.89)	−0.03	7
1967	0.88	(2.72)	0.19	(0.60)	−0.09	7
1968	0.86	(2.36)	0.23	(0.62)	−0.08	7
1969	0.84	(2.19)	0.24	(0.61)	−0.09	7
1970	0.72	(1.82)	0.29	(0.75)	−0.06	7
1971	0.78	(2.23)	0.21	(0.61)	−0.09	7
1972	0.82	(3.03)	0.13	(0.52)	−0.10	7
1973	0.70	(3.18)	0.16	(0.74)	−0.06	7

Table 8. Regressions of *PPP/R* on Productivity, with the United States as the Standard Country, 1950, 1955, and 1970

Year	Constant		GDP/POP		$\bar{R}^2$	Degrees of Freedom
1950	0.66	(6.63)	0.12	(0.56)	−0.11	6
1955	0.64	(3.12)	0.28	(0.67)	−0.08	6
1970	0.43	(2.42)	0.53	(1.86)	0.38	3

Year	Constant		GDP/EMP		$\bar{R}^2$	Degrees of Freedom
1950	0.66	(2.64)	0.12	(0.21)	−0.24	4
1955	0.71	(3.35)	0.15	(0.30)	−0.15	6
1970	0.35	(2.89)	0.71*	(3.46)	0.73	3

Year	Constant		PRODT/PRODNT		$\bar{R}^2$	Degrees of Freedom
1950	0.93	(5.62)	−0.23	(1.19)	0.12	2
1955	0.67	(3.62)	0.16	(0.73)	−0.10	4
1970	0.61	(2.72)	0.20	(0.77)	−0.16	2

Note:
*The coefficient is significantly different from zero at the 5 percent level.

The ideal-index PPP is used, and the results of estimating Equation (1) are shown in Table 8. In one of the three regressions, the coefficient of the productivity variable (*GDP/EMP*) is significant at the 5 percent level. In the four sets of data to which Equation (1) is fitted, this is the only result lending any credence to the existence of a productivity bias. The overwhelming evidence—from all other regressions of Equation (1)—is that the productivity bias has no operational impact.

It might be objected that the PPP data obtained from the Statistisches Bundesamt and used in Tables 2 to 7 are based on a COL price level and therefore violate point 5 of the experimental design. Nevertheless, these data are used because they alone are available annually over a long time period, allowing conformity with point 11 of the experimental design. The question arises, however, as to how close these PPP measures are to corresponding PPP measures on a GDP (or GNP) price-level basis. The possible direct comparisons are limited to computations for the Federal Republic of Germany and the United States, and ideal indices of PPP are the logical measures to consider. Taking the PPP figures of Gilbert and associates as the norm for 1950 and 1955 and the measure of Kravis and others as the norm for 1970, the percentage deviation of the Statistisches Bundesamt PPP measure from the norm is 2.93 percent in 1950, 1.34 percent in 1955, and 6.58 percent in 1970.

D. Examination of Research Favorable to the Productivity Bias

How can Balassa's positive results regarding the existence of a productivity bias be explained in light of the negative findings developed here? To begin answering this question, one should apply the experimental design of the present study to Balassa's *PPP/R* variable. In particular, this procedure involves dropping the standard country (the United States) from the sample and replacing Balassa's explanatory variable by the three alternative measures of productivity suggested in the experimental design. The results of estimating Equation (1) under these conditions are presented as Equations A1, B1, and C1 in Table 9. Comparison with Balassa's own regressions (Table 1) reveals that the explanatory power of the productivity variable is reduced, but that for the *GDP/POP* and *GDP/EMP* variables the estimate of β remains significant at the 1 percent level.

The effect of dropping the United States from the sample is seen in a

Table 9. Regressions of *PPP/R* on Productivity, with the United States as the Standard Country, 1960[1]

Equation	Constant		GDP/POP	$\bar{R}^2$	Degrees of Freedom
A1	0.47	(8.44)	0.56**(5.71)	0.76	9
A2	0.55	(4.74)	0.39 (1.87)	0.26	6

Equation	Constant		GDP/EMP	$\bar{R}^2$	Degrees of Freedom
B1	0.56	(9.07)	0.43**(3.63)	0.55	9
B2	0.66	(4.45)	0.21 (0.71)	−0.08	6

Equation	Constant		PRODT/PRODNT	$\bar{R}^2$	Degrees of Freedom
C1	0.55	(4.82)	0.28 (2.17)	0.35	6
C2	0.59	(13.26)	0.22**(4.35)	0.75	5

Notes:
**The coefficient is significantly different from zero at the 1 percent level.
[1]The dependent variable is from Balassa (1964). Equations A2, B2, and C2 exclude Canada, Japan, and Sweden.

comparison of Equation A1 (where *GDP/POP* is the explanatory variable) in Table 9 with Balassa's regressions (where *GNP/POP* is the explanatory variable) in Table 1. The reason for the noticeable reduction in the significance of the estimate of β when the United States is excluded from the sample (Equation (A1)) is that, in Balassa's sample (Table 1), the observation for the United States has the highest values for both the dependent and independent variable;[27] it is an extreme observation that biases the results in favor of a more significant coefficient of the productivity variable. One must emphasize, however, that the United States is removed from the sample *not* because it provides an extreme observation but because its inclusion represents an illusory gain in degrees of freedom, as argued earlier in point 6 of the experimental design.

A closer look at the PPP data used by Balassa is warranted. These data fall into two groups:

Group A. Countries for which an ideal index of domestic-weighted and U.S.-weighted PPP measures is used, with the latter measures obtained by extrapolating the 1950 computations of Gilbert and associates (1958). Thus a GNP price-level concept applies for this group. The countries involved are (a) Denmark, France, the Federal Republic of Germany, Italy, the Netherlands, and the United Kingdom, for which the extrapolation is performed by Kravis and others, who use a method described in Pincus (1965, pp. 87–91); and (b) Belgium and Norway, for which the extrapolation is carried out by Balassa himself.[28]

Group B. Countries for which the PPP measure is obtained from unique data sources, and for which an ideal index is not employed. These countries are Canada, Japan, and Sweden. In the case of Canada, Balassa uses the cross-PPP of the domestic-weighted PPPs (as distinct from that weighted for the Federal Republic of Germany) for Canada and the United States published by the Statistisches Bundesamt.[29] It is recalled that the cost of living (rather than GNP) is the price-level concept adopted by the Statistisches Bundesamt. For Japan, the PPP measure is developed by Kravis and Davenport (1963, p. 327), who use PPP calculations of Watanabe and Komiya (1958) and other information. For Sweden, the PPP measure is the cross-PPP between Swedish-U.K. and U.S.-U.K. PPPs computed by the National Institute of Economic and Social Research.[30]

The PPP measures for the countries in Group B not only are of a different nature from those for the countries in Group A but also differ conceptually from each other. Therefore, inclusion of Canada, Japan, and Sweden in the sample violates point 3 of the experimental design, and in four respects:

1. Consider the price-level concepts underlying the PPP measures

for the three countries in Group B. The PPP for Canada is based on a COL concept. The PPP for Japan is founded on an imprecise price-level concept, as the PPP measure is based on retail price comparisons, wholesale price comparisons, and wage comparisons between Japan and the United States.[31] The price-level concept underlying the PPP measure for Sweden is not specified in the data source.[32] In contrast, the PPP measures for the countries in Group A are all based on a GNP price level.

2. The PPP measures for Canada and Sweden are computed from cross parities involving the United States and a standard country (the Federal Republic of Germany for the Canadian PPP, the United Kingdom for the Swedish PPP). For no other country in Balassa's sample is the PPP measure of this nature. Furthermore, the PPP for Japan is derived from a variety of data and a unique method compared to computation of the PPPs for all other countries in the sample. Again, these properties of the PPP measures for the countries in Group B are in contrast to the measures for the countries in Group A. For the latter countries, the PPP measures are all of the same nature (assuming that Balassa's extrapolation procedure for two countries is comparable to that of Kravis for the remaining six countries in the group).

3. The PPP measures for the countries in Group A are Fisher ideal indices of domestic-weighted and U.S.-weighted PPP computations. In contrast, the PPP measures for the countries in Group B are not computed as a Fisher ideal index or any other index that takes into account the weighting patterns of both the domestic and the standard country (thus violating point 4 of the experimental design). Balassa could have taken the Fisher ideal indices of the PPPs for Canada and the Federal Republic of Germany and for the United States and the Federal Republic of Germany to compute the cross-PPP measure, but he chose to use the domestic-weighted PPPs. For Sweden and Japan, Kravis and Davenport (1963, p. 327) specifically state that the Fisher ideal indices are not employed to obtain the PPP measure. Indeed, for Japan, the retail and wholesale price comparisons made by Watanabe and Komiya (1958) are based only on the Japanese weighting pattern.[33]

4. One might mention that, in light of the properties of the PPP measures for the countries in Group B, these measures can be presumed to be less accurate than the PPP measures for the countries in Group A.

For all of the above reasons, it is appropriate to drop Canada, Japan, and Sweden from the sample and to re-estimate Equation (1), again using Balassa's *PPP/R* data and the three alternative productivity variables. Thus the revised sample consists exclusively of the countries in Group A. Results of the regressions are shown as equations A2, B2, and

C2 in Table 9. The coefficients of the *GDP/POP* and *GDP/EMP* variables lose significance at even the 5 percent level. The coefficient of the *PRODT/PRODNT* variable now becomes significant at the 1 percent level, an anomalous result in two respects: (1) the significant/insignificant pattern is opposite to that for the equations (in Table 9) involving GDP/POP and GDP/EMP; and (2) the significant result represents only the second such occurrence out of 156 regressions that are oriented to the experimental design and are estimated here.[34]

The reason why removal of Canada, Japan, and Sweden (along with the United States) from the sample eliminates the significance of the estimated coefficient of a Balassa-type productivity variable (GDP/POP and GDP/EMP) can be seen in the scatter diagram of *PPP/R* and per capita GNP provided by Balassa (1964, p. 590). These four countries constitute extreme observations, which play the dominant role in the least-squares fit of Balassa's regression line. This explanation is reinforced in Table 12, where the rows for 1960 display the coefficient of variation (standard deviation as a percentage of the mean) of each of the variables that appear in the regressions using Balassa's *PPP/R* data (Table 9). It is seen that the exclusion of Canada, Japan, and Sweden from the sample greatly reduces the variability of *PPP/R*, *GDP/POP*, and *GDP/EMP*.

It should also be stated that the countries dropped from Balassa's sample afford no special impetus to the operation of the productivity bias when the observations for these countries conform to the experimental design. The evidence for this statement is clear. Of the four countries removed from Balassa's sample, three (Canada, the United States, and Sweden) are included in the first two sets of data to which Equation (1) is applied in this study—that is, the samples in which the Federal Republic of Germany is the standard country.[35] Thus, samples including three of the four countries dropped from Balassa's sample nevertheless yield uniformly negative results concerning the existence of the productivity bias.

E. Changing Importance of the Productivity Bias

Finally, can one say anything about the changing importance of the productivity bias over time, given that the bias has existence? The regressions displayed in Tables 2 to 9 offer strong evidence that the bias does *not* exist; the general lack of significance of the coefficient of the productivity variable implies that a year-to-year comparison of the magnitude of this coefficient would be wrong.

If the coefficient of the productivity variable were significant in the regressions, the experimental design would have permitted direct comparisons of this coefficient over time for a given set of data. Expressing the domestic country's productivity measure relative to that of the standard country results in a productivity variable without dimension, as is the dependent variable. A generally significant estimate of β would have allowed consideration of its changing magnitude, to aid in determining whether the productivity bias increased or decreased in impact over the period 1950-1973. The lack of significance of the estimate of β effectively closes that approach to assessing changes in the importance of the productivity bias.

An alternative approach is to consider the changing values of the coefficients of variation of the dependent and alternative independent variables used in estimating Equation (1) under the various sets of data. Tables 10 and 11 show, over the time period 1950-1973, the movement

Table 10. Coefficients of Variation of Variables in Unadjusted *PPP/R* Regressions, with the Federal Republic of Germany as the Standard Country, 1950-1973

Year	PPP/R	GDP/POP	GDP/EMP	PRODT/PRODNT
1950	23.62	37.11	38.02	16.84
1951	24.98	31.96	30.92	13.02
1952	24.55	30.71	29.02	10.06
1953	24.62	32.65	33.47	13.89
1954	23.65	30.60	38.34	23.64
1955	21.80	28.92	35.87	22.22
1956	21.83	28.03	32.71	21.28
1957	22.19	27.49	33.52	20.04
1958	20.65	26.91	33.34	19.01
1959	20.61	26.79	32.72	19.35
1960	19.58	25.61	31.22	17.77
1961	18.29	23.08	29.10	17.10
1962	16.33	23.40	29.39	17.68
1963	16.03	22.90	28.69	17.79
1964	15.82	23.13	28.17	17.95
1965	14.12	22.21	25.74	18.18
1966	14.18	22.05	25.03	17.83
1967	13.04	21.19	23.12	16.06
1968	14.21	21.39	22.85	16.46
1969	13.97	20.56	20.56	15.78
1970	14.54	18.81	18.86	15.19
1971	13.19	18.47	18.48	15.96
1972	11.97	17.35	16.84	16.59
1973	12.10	17.06	16.57	16.08

Table 11. Coefficients of Variation of Variables in Adjusted *PPP/R* Regressions, with the Federal Republic of Germany as the Standard Country, 1950–1973

Year	PPP/R	GDP/POP	GDP/EMP	PRODT/PRODNT
1950	27.02	37.21	32.71	16.84
1951	27.74	33.29	29.25	13.02
1952	27.38	32.20	27.56	10.06
1953	26.66	32.98	28.18	13.89
1954	25.74	31.31	37.15	23.64
1955	23.49	30.14	35.28	22.22
1956	23.52	29.49	32.34	21.28
1957	22.35	28.10	34.03	20.04
1958	20.70	27.67	33.86	19.01
1959	19.92	26.30	31.91	19.35
1960	20.08	24.95	31.28	17.77
1961	18.29	23.08	29.10	17.10
1962	16.33	23.40	29.39	17.68
1963	16.03	22.90	28.69	17.79
1964	15.82	23.13	28.17	17.95
1965	15.09	22.73	26.90	18.18
1966	15.21	22.41	25.95	17.83
1967	15.02	21.73	24.50	16.06
1968	16.81	21.41	23.85	16.46
1969	16.45	20.52	21.63	15.78
1970	16.86	18.93	20.16	15.19
1971	15.57	18.56	19.77	15.96
1972	14.29	18.72	19.57	16.59
1973	13.91	18.78	19.71	16.08

of the coefficients of variation of the variables used in the unadjusted *PPP/R* and adjusted *PPP/R* regressions, respectively, with the Federal Republic of Germany as the standard country. There is a strong downward trend of the coefficient for the *PPP/R, GDP/POP,* and *GDP/EMP* variables in each set of data. There is a less strong, but nevertheless distinct, downward trend in the coefficient for the *PRODT/PRODNT* variable, if the years 1950–1953 are eliminated from consideration. For these years there are only five or six observations on this variable (because of missing data), whereas succeeding years have at least eight observations.

The decreasing variability of the *PPP/R* variable implies that PPP is, over time, an ever better measure of the equilibrium exchange rate[36] in a cross-country comparison, leaving ever decreasing scope for operation of the productivity bias—or indeed any bias—in representing the equilibrium exchange rate by the PPP. The decreasing coefficient of variation of the productivity variables means that the countries in the sample are converging over time in their productivity levels. The quantitative impact of a productivity bias—should one exist—thus would be decreasing over time. In other words, a given magnitude of the bias (represented by the value of β) would involve a reduced impact because countries' productivity levels are converging.

For completeness, the coefficients of variation of the variables used in estimating Equation (1) with the United States as the standard country are shown in Table 12. However, as only the data for 1950 and 1955 are comparable, trends in the coefficients cannot be discerned.

In summary, if there is a productivity bias, the available evidence suggests that its impact is steadily decreasing over time. However, the overwhelming conclusion from the findings of this study is that the bias does not exist.

F. Implications for a Bias under Relative PPP

The experimental design was oriented to test for the existence of a productivity bias under *absolute* PPP. Indeed (following point 2 of the experimental design), the use of absolute rather than relative PPP was deliberate. Given that the results are strongly negative regarding the existence of a productivity bias under absolute PPP, are there any implications for the existence and impact of a corresponding bias under relative PPP?

Such a question is highly unusual. When Balassa (1964) estimated Equation (1) and obtained results that supported the existence of a productivity bias for absolute PPP, he noted that the bias would pertain to relative PPP, given a reformulation of his analytical argument in terms

Table 12. Coefficients of Variation of Variables in *PPP/R* Regressions, with the United States as the Standard Country, 1950, 1955, 1960, and 1970

Year	PPP/R	GDP/POP	GDP/EMP	PRODT/PRODNT
1950	8.07	23.59	13.47	18.63
1955	11.65	17.58	17.44	23.76
1960[1]	7.11	15.37	14.49	18.47
1960[2]	11.64	25.99	32.46	17.24
1970	10.00	16.96	16.48	19.83

Notes:
[1]Excluding Canada, Japan, and Sweden.
[2]Including Canada, Japan, and Sweden.

of *increases* (rather than levels) of productivity. Such an approach is the usual one in considering the biases and limitations of the relative PPP theory. A weakness of absolute PPP is established—for example, the existence of trade restrictions or the neglect of the role of income—and the presumption is that this weakness can apply to relative PPP only if the relevant economic condition or variable has *changed* in some manner since the base period. Thus, in the examples cited, only a *change* in the severity of trade restrictions or in the level of income would give rise to a limitation of relative PPP corresponding to that of absolute PPP.[37]

Returning to the productivity-bias hypothesis, as Officer (1976a, p. 22) has noted:

> The Balassa argument of a nonuniform productivity advantage (greater for traded than for nontraded goods) enjoyed by the technologically advanced country involves a bias in absolute PPP. An *increase (decrease) over time* in the advanced country's productivity advantage, as indicated by a higher (lower) rate of growth in per capita income compared with the less advanced country, imparts a similar bias to relative PPP.

In the present study, the opposite situation occurs. The productivity bias has been found to be inapplicable to absolute PPP, but the question remains as to its applicability to relative PPP. In line with the traditional approach to limitations of relative PPP, the answer is that the absence of a bias for absolute PPP provides no basis for a corresponding bias for relative PPP.

Nevertheless, a productivity bias may exist for relative PPP. The impact of productivity *changes* among countries might be significantly stronger than the impact of their productivity *levels*. Such a pattern is certainly possible. It would, however, be anomalous in light of the uniformly negative evidence concerning the existence of a bias under absolute PPP over a 24-year period (1950–73).

The reflections here concerning the existence of a productivity bias under relative PPP are not definitive. In Section II, direct econometric evidence is related to the question.

II. TESTING THE THEORETICAL UNDERPINNING OF THE PRODUCTIVITY BIAS

A necessary condition for the existence of a bias under relative PPP is that *movements* in a country's internal price ratio be determined by the country's productivity *growth*. One notes immediately that since this proposition is stated in terms of changes rather than in terms of levels of variables, it can have relevance only for relative PPP and *not* for absolute PPP.

One should further remark that fulfillment of the proposition is only a necessary condition for the existence of a productivity bias (under relative PPP) and not a sufficient condition. The reason for the latter statement is that the PPP theory, and therefore any impact of the bias, refers to an intercountry comparison. It is quite possible that, for a group of countries that may be considered: (a) there are disparate productivity advances among the countries, and (b) these advances lead to higher internal price ratios in the countries. Yet, the productivity-bias hypothesis might be inapplicable—as the internal price ratios of the countries might be converging while their productivity levels are diverging.

A reason for this result may be that the impact of a given increase in productivity on the internal price ratio might vary from country to country, contrary to the implicit assumption of the proposition. If this *impact* is inversely related to levels of productivity among countries, the convergence of internal price ratios may occur even if advances in productivity among countries are directly related to levels of productivity.[38]

However, the findings described in Section I indicate that both the productivity variables (representing the level of productivity) and the *PPP/R* variable (directly related to the internal price ratio) have converged over time. So, in practice, fulfillment of the proposition relating movements in a country's internal price ratio positively to changes in the country's productivity level *may* constitute both a necessary and a sufficient condition for the productivity-bias hypothesis to apply to relative PPP. How can this proposition be tested?

The approach is to calculate the change in each variable—internal price ratio and level of productivity—as an index number for a given country over a specified time period. The resulting index numbers constitute one observation in a cross-country sample of these index numbers. In other words, a comparative-static time-series computation is made to obtain an index-number observation from each country to be included in the sample. The sample is thus a cross section of these index-number observations, one for each country. Consider the following notation:

PT_i = price index of traded commodities in country i in the current period relative to a base period

PNT_i = price index of nontraded commodities in country i in the current period relative to a base period

$PROD_i$ = productivity index for country i in the current period relative to a base period

Then the hypothesis may be tested by imposing the same base period and the same current period on the three variables defined above and fitting the regression

$$PNT_i/PT_i = \psi + \gamma PROD_i + \omega_i \tag{2}$$

for a sample of N countries, $i = 1, \ldots, N$, where ψ and γ are parameters and the error term ω_i is assumed to be normally, identically, and independently distributed for all i. The theoretical underpinning of the productivity bias is confirmed if the estimate of γ is significantly different from zero. The productivity-bias hypothesis also predicts a positive value for this coefficient.

The preferred numerator of the dependent variable is the price index of nontraded commodities rather than the general price index (which incorporates both traded and nontraded commodities). The reason is explained by the following relationship:[39]

$$\frac{PPP_i}{R_i} \approx \frac{A_i + B_i(PLN_i/PLT_i)}{A_s + B_s(PLN_s/PLT_s)} \tag{3}$$

where

PPP_i = absolute purchasing power parity of country i, number of units of domestic currency per unit of standard currency, where the purchasing power parity is based on the concept of a general price level

R_i = exchange rate of country i, number of units of domestic currency per unit of standard currency

PLN_i = price level of nontraded commodities in country i, with a weight of B_i in the country's general price level

PLT_i = price level of traded commodities in country i, with a weight of A_i in the country's general price level

PLN_s = price level of nontraded commodities in the standard country, with a weight of B_s in the country's general price level

PLT_s = price level of traded commodities in the standard country, with a weight of A_s in the country's general price level

One notes that in relationship (3) the domestic country's PPP/R ratio is directly related to its internal price ratio (that is, the ratio of the price level of nontraded commodities to the price level of traded commodities), indicating that the ideal numerator in the dependent variable in Equation (2) is indeed the price index of nontraded commodities rather than the general price index.

A. Previous Tests of the Theoretical Foundation of the Bias

Only two empirical studies of the theoretical foundation of the productivity bias have appeared in the literature. In both cases the authors specify the less preferred version of the dependent variable—that is, they use a *general* price index for the numerator of the dependent variable in Equation (2).

Balassa (1964) fits Equation (2) to a sample of seven industrial countries (Belgium, France, the Federal Republic of Germany, Italy, Japan, the United Kingdom, and the United States), using base year 1953 and current year 1961 to construct his variables. He uses the GNP deflator as the general price index, the wholesale price index of manufactured goods as the price index of traded commodities, and manufacturing output per man-hour as the measure of productivity. The estimate of γ is positive and significantly different from zero at the 1 percent level.

McKinnon (1971, pp. 221–22) takes 1953 as the base period, the first quarter of 1970 as the current period, the consumer price index (CPI) as the general price index, the wholesale price index (WPI) and export price index (EPI) as alternative measures of the price index of traded commodities, and output per man-hour as the measure of productivity.[40] He calculates the variables specified in Equation (2) for six industrial countries, but he does not fit the regression, nor does he refer to Balassa's earlier study. He does observe that the countries with high productivity growth (the Federal Republic of Germany, Italy, and Japan) have substantially higher *CPI/WPI* and *CPI/EPI* ratios than the countries with low productivity growth (Canada, the United Kingdom, and the United States). The divergence between the two sets of countries is greater for the *CPI/EPI* ratio—an expected result, because the WPI incorporates some nontraded goods.

B. New Evidence on the Theoretical Foundation of the Productivity Bias

Both Balassa and McKinnon used a restricted sample of countries. In contrast, it is appropriate to fit Equation (2) to a sample composed of all the countries (data permitting) included in samples to which Equation (1) was applied in this study. Thus the present sample consists of the following industrial countries with a market economy: Canada, the United States, Japan, Australia, Austria, Belgium, Denmark, Finland, France, the Federal Republic of Germany, Italy, the Netherlands, Norway, Sweden, and the United Kingdom. The base period of 1953, common to both Balassa and McKinnon, is retained, and 1973, the final year of the analysis in Section I of this study, is selected as the current period. It is logical to choose as alternative explanatory variables the productivity measures developed in Section I, expressed as index numbers and without reference to a standard country. GDP is then expressed in constant prices for all three variables. Thus the new variables are as follows:[41]

GDP/POP_i = index of per capita GDP (at constant prices) in country i in 1973, where 1953 = 100

GDP/EMP_i = index of GDP (at constant prices) per employed worker in country i in 1973, where 1953 = 100

$PRODT/PRODNT_i$ = index of the ratio of productivity in the traded sector of the economy of country i to productivity in the nontraded sector of the economy in 1973, where 1953 = 100 and "productivity" is defined as GDP (at constant prices) originating in the sector per employed worker in the sector

If one follows the Balassa-McKinnon procedure of using a general price index in place of the price index of nontraded commodities, it is reasonable to try a variety of alternative measures: CPI, WPI, and PGDP (the GDP price deflator). Correspondingly, either the WPI or the EPI may be used to represent the price index of traded commodities, as the WPI represents a "general" price index only relative to a price index more heavily weighted with traded goods. Then alternative measures of the dependent variable in Equation (2) are CPI/WPI, CPI/EPI, WPI/EPI, $PGDP/WPI$, and $PGDP/EPI$, where the numerator in each case is expressed as a percentage of the denominator.[42]

In light of relationship (3), a direct measure of the internal price ratio as an index number (that is, the ratio of the price index of nontraded commodities to the price index of traded commodities) is a preferred dependent variable, and such a measure is constructed for this study. The price index of traded commodities is obtained as the ratio of GDP at current prices originating in the traded sector of the economy to GDP at constant prices originating in that sector. A similar description applies to the price index of nontraded commodities. The traded and nontraded sectors are defined as in Section I of this study. Thus another alternative dependent variable (PNT/PT) is obtained, where again the numerator is expressed as a percentage of the denominator.[43]

Table 13 presents the results of fitting Equation (2) to the various combinations of the specified dependent and independent variables. Consider, first, the regressions with GDP/POP or GDP/EMP as the ex-

Table 13. Regressions of Price-Index Ratios on the Productivity Index

Dependent Variable	Constant		GDP/POP		$\bar{R}^2$	Degrees of Freedom
CPI/WPI	82.54	(7.32)	0.20**	(4.38)	0.58	12
CPI/EPI	74.48	(3.09)	0.35**	(3.57)	0.46	13
WPI/EPI	99.00	(7.30)	0.08	(1.51)	0.09	12
PGDP/WPI	96.52	(7.47)	0.18**	(3.39)	0.45	12
PGDP/EPI	93.56	(3.47)	0.32*	(2.88)	0.34	13
PNT/PT	122.70	(3.33)	0.12	(0.66)	−0.06	9

Dependent Variable	Constant		GDP/EMP		$\bar{R}^2$	Degrees of Freedom
CPI/WPI	75.79	(6.56)	0.23**	(5.01)	0.73	8
CPI/EPI	67.11	(2.64)	0.39**	(3.80)	0.57	9
WPI/EPI	95.04	(6.05)	0.10	(1.62)	0.15	8
PGDP/WPI	90.83	(6.14)	0.20**	(3.49)	0.55	8
PGDP/EPI	88.07	(2.95)	0.35*	(2.93)	0.43	9
PNT/PT	115.64	(3.36)	0.14	(0.84)	−0.05	5

Dependent Variable	Constant		PRODT/PRODNT		$\bar{R}^2$	Degrees of Freedom
CPI/WPI	168.87	(4.12)	−0.30	(1.18)	0.06	5
CPI/EPI	187.72	(1.59)	−0.29	(0.39)	−0.16	5
WPI/EPI	105.67	(1.46)	0.07	(0.15)	−0.19	5
PGDP/WPI	151.41	(2.77)	−0.14	(0.41)	−0.16	5
PGDP/EPI	168.97	(1.34)	−0.11	(0.14)	−0.20	5
PNT/PT	30.58	(0.57)	0.71	(2.13)	0.37	5

Notes:
*The coefficient is significantly different from zero at the 5 percent level.
**The coefficient is significantly different from zero at the 1 percent level.

planatory variable. Because the WPI is heavily weighted with traded goods, the low significance of the estimate of γ in the regressions involving *WPI/EPI* as the dependent variable is to be expected. The high significance of the estimate of γ in the *CPI/WPI, CPI/EPI,* and *PGDP/ WPI* regressions provides some positive evidence of the real-world existence of the theoretical underpinning of the productivity bias. However, the regressions for *PGDP/EPI* and *PNT/PT* involve a lesser significance (5 percent rather than 1 percent level) and no significance, respectively, of the estimate of γ. Conceptually, the latter variables are the optimal measures of the dependent variable; for *PGDP* is the most extensive general price index, *EPI* is the narrowest price index of traded goods, and *PNT/PT* is a measure especially geared to the theory underlying Equation (2).

If the results for the *GDP/POP* and *GDP/EMP* variables are mixed, with a balance on the side inclined to verify the theoretical basis of the productivity bias, the regressions with *PRODT/PRODNT* as the explanatory variable involve totally negative findings. For none of the dependent variables is the estimate of γ significant at the 5 percent level, and in four out of six cases the explanatory variable yields a negative $\bar{R}^2$. The results for *PRODT/PRODNT* are especially damaging to the productivity-bias hypothesis, as this variable is the productivity measure closest to the concept embodied in the hypothesis.

III. SUMMARY AND CONCLUSIONS

The evidence provided by this study indicates that the productivity-bias hypothesis lacks a firm empirical foundation, suggesting that the general acceptance of the hypothesis is unwarranted. With careful attention paid to the experimental design of the test, the productivity bias was found to have no operational impact on the PPP/exchange-rate relationship, except in extremely rare cases. Furthermore, even if, contrary to these results, the existence of the bias was to be granted, then examination of the changing variability of the variables specified in the productivity-bias hypothesis suggested that the impact of the bias has been steadily decreasing in magnitude over time.

Regarding the theoretical underpinning of the bias—the hypothesis that changes in a country's price ratio are related to changes in the country's productivity—the evidence provided by the study is mixed. The result is contrary to the unambiguous positive findings of the previous studies on the topic. In any event, it should be reiterated that this theoretical underpinning relates only to the relative, and not the absolute, version of PPP.

On balance, the productivity bias does not survive empirical tests of its existence. Should one reject the theory or reject the econometric results? The author has argued elsewhere (Officer, 1974, pp. 873–74) that the productivity-bias hypothesis is questionable on analytical grounds because it ignores quality differences in nontraded commodities (specifically, consumer services) among countries. The more productive country would be expected to have an efficiency advantage in such services as education and medical care, where the labor involved embodies human capital and/or works with physical capital and advanced technology. Thus there exists some analytical support for the empirical findings of this study.

What are the implications for the validity of the PPP theory of exchange rates? An alleged powerful bias—one that overwhelmed the theory and constrained its applicability—has been shown to have little empirical foundation. However, for PPP to be considered an appropriate measure of the equilibrium exchange rate, the PPP theory must pass *positive* tests; it is not sufficient for it to survive negative tests. Elsewhere (Officer, 1976a, pp. 51–54) the author has indicated shortcomings of the positive tests performed to date. There is much scope for improved testing of the PPP theory. The present study implies that avoidance of such testing because of an alleged "productivity bias" is unwarranted.

APPENDIX
DATA FOR TESTING THE PRODUCTIVITY BIAS

The following annual time series were constructed for the time period 1950–1973 (data permitting) for each country considered in the study:

National-Accounts Series

$GDPC$ = GDP at current prices; in millions of units of domestic currency

$GDPK$ = GDP at constant (1970) prices; in millions of units of domestic currency

EAC = GDP excluding flows (such as statistical discrepancy) not allocable to the producing sector of origin, at current prices; in millions of units of domestic currency

EAK = GDP excluding flows (such as statistical discrepancy) not allocable to the producing sector of origin, at constant (1970) prices; in millions of units of domestic currency

AMC = GDP originating in (1) agriculture, hunting, forestry, and fishing, (2) mining and quarrying, and (3) manufacturing, at current prices; in millions of units of domestic currency

AMK = GDP originating in (1) agriculture, hunting, forestry, and fishing, (2) mining and quarrying, and (3) manufacturing, at constant (1970) prices; in millions of units of domestic currency

Labor Series

POP = population; in thousands of persons
$EMPT$ = total civilian employment; in thousands of persons
$EMPA$ = employment in agriculture, hunting, forestry, and fishing; in thousands of persons
$EMPM$ = employment in mining and quarrying and in manufacturing; in thousands of persons
ARM = armed forces; in thousands of persons

For all series, consistent values over time are obtained by linking figures on a former basis to figures on a more recent basis by means of an overlap for the latest available year.[44] In all cases, care is taken to use the most recently published data in preference to unrevised data or data on a former basis.

The basic source of the national-accounts series is the Organization for Economic Cooperation and Development (OECD), *National Accounts of OECD Countries.* A secondary source is the United Nations, *Yearbook of National Accounts Statistics.* The basic problem with the national-accounts data is a switch in concept from a former system to the present system of national accounts.[45] The changeover occurs at different dates for individual OECD member countries, and a few countries have not yet provided data according to the new system. In order to obtain comparable series for all countries, all series are expressed on the former basis. The latest available data are used, as the values of a series under the present system are linked to the values under the former system by using the *earliest* year of overlap. The series at constant prices are then re-expressed in 1970 prices (if necessary) by multiplication by the ratio of the current price to the constant price value for the year 1970.

For the Federal Republic of Germany there is a minor problem of separating GDP originating in the mining and quarrying sector from that originating in the electricity, gas, and water producing sector. As the problem occurs in only a few years, typically the joint output is allocated to the two sectors on the basis of their relative shares in the preceding year.

With respect to the United Kingdom, GDP by industry of origin at constant prices as published by the OECD is based on indices of real output applied to output at current prices in a base year. For 1973, however, only the indices are published. For purposes of this study, the relevant indices are converted to GDP at constant prices, using a technique that approximates the procedure previously followed by the OECD.

The primary source of the labor series is the OECD, *Labour Force Statistics*. A secondary source is the International Labour Office, *Yearbook of Labour Statistics*. For the specific purpose of constructing early years of the ARM series for Australia, New Zealand, and France, the official yearbooks for Australia and New Zealand and *The Statesman's Year-Book* are used.

The principal technique in constructing the series is to use as a basis the figures provided in the general (intercountry) tables on population, total civilian employment, employment in agriculture, and employment in industry (narrowly construed) as published in *Labour Force Statistics*. The OECD makes some attempt to achieve intercountry and intertemporal comparability in these tables. Employment in industry is then allocated to the traded sector ("mining and quarrying" and "manufacturing") and the nontraded sector ("electricity, gas, and water" and "construction") using data published in the individual country tables. Armed-forces data are obtained primarily from the latter tables.

The diverse sources of data are used to provide the maximum length for each series within the 1950–1973 time period where overlaps are available to construct consistent series over time. Owing to data limitations, some gaps remain, principally in the early years.

A general problem in the data concerning the Federal Republic of Germany and the United States is the changes in their geographic boundaries that occurred during the time period of the study. The published national-accounts series for the Federal Republic of Germany exclude West Berlin prior to 1960 and include it thereafter (with an overlap generally unavailable); therefore, the labor series are constructed according to the same principle as are the national-accounts series, the discontinuity in 1960 occurring deliberately.

A slight discontinuity occurs in the national-accounts series for the United States. From 1960 onward, the published series formally include Alaska and Hawaii, with no overlap provided. However, both the U.S. and the OECD authorities state that a portion of Alaskan and Hawaiian output was included in the U.S. national accounts prior to 1960.[46] For this reason, the labor series for the United States are constructed to include Alaska and Hawaii in all years.

Then the following series, used directly to construct variables in the study, are computed for each country annually (data permitting) for the period 1950–1973:

GDPC/POP: per capita GDP in domestic currency at current prices
GDPK/POP: per capita GDP in domestic currency at constant prices

$GDPC/(EMPT + ARM)$: GDP in domestic currency at current prices, per employed person

$GDPK/(EMPT + ARM)$: GDP in domestic currency at constant prices, per employed person

$\dfrac{AMK/(EMPA + EMPM)}{(EAK - AMK)/(EMPT + ARM - EMPA - EMPM)}$: ratio of productivity in the traded sector of the economy to productivity in the nontraded sector

$GDPC/GDPK$: *GDP* price deflator

$\dfrac{(EAC - AMC)/(EAK - AMK)}{AMC/AMK}$: internal price ratio as an index number

A remark is appropriate regarding the inclusion of the armed forces (*ARM*) in the employment measures for the total economy and the non-traded sector. In each case the corresponding measure of output is inclusive of all government production, including defense; therefore, it is incumbent to treat employment in the same manner.

The main limitation of the data concerns the division of the economy into traded and nontraded producing sectors. Allocation of GDP by industry of origin (especially at constant prices) is not available for any year for a number of countries, which explains the relatively small sample in regressions involving the *PRODT/PRODNT* variable (in either of its two versions) and/or the *PNT/PT* variable.

NOTES

1. This chapter appears in the bibliography as Officer (1976b). It is reprinted by permission of the International Monetary Fund.

2. For the concepts of exchange-rate equilibrium underlying the PPP theory, see Officer (1976a, pp. 2–3).

3. For references and discussion, see Officer (1976a, p. 18).

4. For references to their views on the matter, see Officer (1976a, pp. 19, 22).

5. For a summary of their discussion, see Officer (1976a, pp. 19, 36).

6. This test assumes that Equation (1) is the correct specification of the impact of the productivity bias and that omitted variables (representing the effect of other biases), if any, do not affect the value of β.

7. Absolute PPP is the ratio of two countries' price *levels;* relative PPP is the product of the exchange rate in a base period and the ratio of the countries' price *indices* relative to that period.

8. The term "significant" will be used interchangeably with "significantly different from zero."

9. Failure to express per capita GDP relative to the standard country does not affect the significance of the results.

10. However, Grunwald and Salazar-Carrillo indicate that a PPP measure would be a better conversion factor.

11.   Balassa mentions as reasons the differences between DCs and LDCs in the importance of nontraded goods, endowment of natural resources, height of tariffs, and amount of capital inflow.

12.   It is assumed that the variables are based on an annual rather than an intra-annual unit of observation.

13.   For a discussion of this well-known result and references to the literature, see Officer (1976a, pp. 15–16).

14.   Further details on this aspect of Balassa's sample are provided later.

15.   The use of the standard country in constructing the PPP measure (for the dependent variable and the numerator of the productivity variable) is the crucial element here; expression of the productivity variable relative to the standard country does not affect the significance of the results.

16.   The latest element in the literature, which contains references to its predecessors, is Kravis and others (1975). David (1972) provides the most systematic analysis of the bias involved in using exchange rates to convert national-income data from domestic currency to a standard currency. For comments and elaboration on his approach, see Balassa (1973; 1974b), David (1973), and Hulsman-Vejsová (1975).

17.   Actually, their productivity variables are obtained in full from other sources.

18.   This measure of productivity is unambiguously better than the others only if the classification of producing sectors into the traded and nontraded categories is correct. If, based on available data, these sectors do not fall clearly into one category or the other, it *may* be preferable to use a simpler productivity measure.

19.   One notes that both numerator and denominator of the explanatory variable emanating from this measure—the ratio of productivity in the domestic country to productivity in the standard country—are without dimension, thus obviating the need for conversion of data from domestic currency to the standard currency.

20.   In particular, the nontraded sector comprises (1) electricity, gas, and water, (2) construction, (3) wholesale and retail trade, restaurants, and hotels, (4) transport, storage, and communications, (5) finance, insurance, real estate, and business services, (6) community, social, and personal services, (7) government, (8) private nonprofit services to households, and (9) domestic services of households. Construction of the GDP/POP, GDP/EMP, and $PRODT/PRODNT$ variables is described in detail in the Appendix.

21.   The source is Federal Republic of Germany, Statistisches Bundesamt, *Internationaler Vergleich der Preise für die Lebenshaltung*.

22.   The annual PPP data are unweighted averages of the monthly figures; the annual exchange-rate data are weighted averages of the monthly figures, the weights being proportional to the number of days in which the foreign-exchange market is open during the month.

23.   For discussion of the extrapolation procedure and other aspects of the PPP series, see Federal Republic of Germany, Statistisches Bundesamt, *Internationaler Vergleich der Preise für die Lebenshaltung 1974*, pp. 5–11; and *Wirtschaft und Statistik* (November 1954, pp. 516–19; August 1961, pp. 443–49; June 1968, pp. 292–98).

24.   Oddly enough, the Statistisches Bundesamt publishes the arithmetic mean rather than the geometric mean (Fisher ideal index) of its two PPP computations.

25.   Japan is the most important exclusion from the sample.

26.   The extrapolation procedure is described in Gilbert and associates (1958, pp. 157–58). The authors' PPP results at the GNP level are presented in Table 5 (p. 30) of their study; but the 1955 domestic-country-weighted figure for the United Kingdom is listed wrongly as 0.272, whereas it should be 0.242. This reporting error was noticed by Pincus (1965, p. 88).

27. See the scatter diagram provided by Balassa (1964, p. 590) and the table that he presents in his later aritcle (1973, p. 1261).

28. Balassa does not describe his own extrapolation procedure.

29. The data used are from the Federal Republic of Germany, Statistisches Bundesamt, *Wirtschaft und Statistik* (August 1961, p. 445).

30. The PPPs used in the cross computation are published in Needleman (1961, p. 61). Balassa takes the PPP measure for Sweden from Kravis and Davenport (1963, p. 327), who performed the cross computation of PPPs.

31. See the description provided by Kravis and Davenport (1963, p. 327). At best, these authors make a crude attempt to achieve a GNP price-level concept.

32. See Needleman (1961, pp. 60–61). Apparently, Needleman has a COL concept in mind, but the table he provides is in part based on data from Gilbert and associates (1958), where a GNP price-level concept is used.

33. Kravis and Davenport (1963, p. 327) state that both U.S. and Japanese weights are used in their computations, but they could not have done so below the level of aggregation of the product groups studied by Watanabe and Komiya. In any event, a Fisher ideal index or a similar type of index is not employed.

34. These regressions are those listed in Tables 2 to 8, inclusive, together with equations A2, B2, and C2 of Table 9.

35. Japan is excluded from these samples because the Statistisches Bundesamt publishes only a PPP that is weighted for the Federal Republic of Germany, and not a domestic-weighted PPP for that country, preventing the computation of a Fisher ideal index.

36. It is recalled that the equilibrium exchange rate is proxied by the actual rate.

37. For a systematic application of this approach in examining the limitations of absolute and relative PPP, see Officer (1976a, pp. 16-22).

38. A symmetrical argument would apply to the case of diverging internal price ratios with converging productivity levels.

39. This relationship is demonstrated by Officer (1976a, pp. 33-34).

40. McKinnon does not specify how output is defined.

41. One notes that the names of the variables are the same as in Section I but their definitions are different.

42. Data on the CPI, WPI, and EPI are obtained from the International Monetary Fund, *International Financial Statistics* (data tape). Construction of the PGDP variable is described in the Appendix.

43. Construction of the *PNT/PT* variable is described in greater detail in the Appendix.

44. There is one minor exception to this rule, as described below, in connection with the national-accounts series.

45. See references cited in OECD, *National Accounts of OECD Countries, 1962-1973*, Vol. 1, p. 2.

46. See U.S. Department of Commerce, *The National Income and Product Accounts of the United States, 1929-1965*, p. vii; and the Organization for Economic Cooperation and Development, *National Accounts of OECD Countries, 1953-1969*, p. 69.

Chapter XV

The Relationship Between Absolute and Relative Purchasing Power Parity[1]

The absolute purchasing power parity (PPP) theory asserts that the equilibrium exchange rate (number of units of domestic currency per unit of standard currency) is determined by the ratio of the price level of the domestic country to the price level of the standard country.[2] This ratio itself is called the absolute PPP. The relative PPP theory states that the ratio of the equilibrium exchange rate in a current period (t) to the equilibrium exchange rate in a base period (o) is determined by the ratio of the domestic country's price index in period t to the standard country's price index in period t, where both indices are measured relative to period o.

Suppose that the absolute PPP theory is fulfilled in both periods t and o. Then the relative PPP theory may be restated as follows: the ratio of absolute PPP in period t to absolute PPP in period o is determined by the ratio of the domestic country's price index to the standard country's price index, where both indices are measured in period t relative to period o. The question immediately arises, however, whether the relative PPP theory has now become a truism. Is the current/base-period absolute-PPP ratio *identically equal* to the domestic/standard-country price-index ratio? It is the purpose of this article, first, to demonstrate that the restated relative PPP theory is *not* a truism and, second, to provide an empirical test of this interpretation of the PPP hypothesis.

The restatement of the relative PPP theory separates its validity from that of the absolute PPP theory. Relative PPP becomes concerned only with the *movement* from one *potential* exchange-rate equilibrium to another. Whether the exchange rate is actually in equilibrium (à la PPP) at the two end points of the time period becomes the purview of the absolute PPP hypothesis, and is an issue beyond the confines of this paper. But it must be shown that the restated PPP hypothesis is an operational theory rather than a truism.

I. PROOF THAT THE RESTATED PPP THEORY IS NOT A TRUISM

Consider the following notation:

P_j = absolute purchasing power parity in period j, number of units of domestic currency per unit of standard currency
L_j = price level of the domestic country in period j
L_j^s = price level of the standard country in period j
I_j = price index of the domestic country in period j relative to period o
I_j^s = price index of the standard country in period j relative to period o
p_{ij} = price of commodity i in the domestic country in period j
p_{ij}^s = price of commodity i in the standard country in period j
w_{ij} = weight of the price of commodity i in the domestic country's price level in period j
w_{ij}^s = weight of the price of commodity i in the standard country's price level in period j

Then w_{io} (w_{io}^s) is the weight of the price of commodity i in the domestic (standard) country's price *index* for all time periods, in particular, for periods o and t.

By definition,

$$L_j \equiv \sum_i w_{ij} p_{ij} \qquad j = o, t$$

$$L_j^s \equiv \sum_i w_{ij}^s p_{ij}^s \qquad j = o, t$$

$$P_j \equiv L_j/L_j^s \qquad j = o, t$$

$$I_t \equiv \sum_i w_{io} p_{it} / \sum_i w_{io} p_{io}$$

$$I_t^s \equiv \sum_i w_{io}^s p_{it}^s / \sum_i w_{io}^s p_{io}^s$$

The restated PPP theory is a truism if and only if

$$P_t/P_o \equiv I_t/I_t^s \tag{1}$$

i.e., if and only if

$$\frac{\sum_i w_{it}p_{it}/\sum_i w_{it}^s p_{it}^s}{\sum_i w_{io}p_{io}/\sum_i w_{io}^s p_{io}^s} \equiv \frac{\sum_i w_{io}p_{it}/\sum_i w_{io}p_{io}}{\sum_i w_{io}^s p_{it}^s/\sum_i w_{io}^s p_{io}^s}$$

or

$$\frac{\sum_i w_{it}p_{it}}{\sum_i w_{it}^s p_{it}^s} \equiv \frac{\sum_i w_{io}p_{it}}{\sum_i w_{io}^s p_{it}^s}$$

or

$$\left. \begin{array}{l} w_{it} = w_{io} \\ w_{it}^s = w_{io}^s \end{array} \right\} \text{ all } i \tag{2}$$

What is the interpretation of (2)? It states that, for both the domestic and standard country, the weights of the component prices in the *price level* of the country are the same in the current as in the base period. For the country's price *index*, of course, the weighting pattern in the current period is, by definition, equal to that in the base period. But for the price level, equal weighting patterns in the two periods would exist only in a very special case.

Since under the PPP theory a country's price level covers its entire output of commodities, the weights of the price level reflect the production pattern of the country. Assume the absence of money illusion, so that a mere change in units of measurement makes no difference to real economic behavior. Then the only situation in which production would be distributed among all commodities in an unvarying proportion in two time periods would be *the absence of any changes in relative prices* in the economy. Therefore (2) holds if and only if, for both the domestic and standard country, all individual prices in the country in period t are a constant multiple of the prices in period o, i.e.,

$$\left. \begin{array}{l} p_{it} = cp_{io} \\ p_{it}^s = c^s p_{io}^s \end{array} \right\} \text{ all } i \tag{3}$$

where c and c^s are positive constants.

What has been demonstrated? Assuming the absence of money illusion, identity (1) is fulfilled if and only if Equations (3) hold, i.e., there is pure inflation or deflation in both the domestic and standard country. Furthermore, for (1) to hold, the only permissible real change in the economies is an equiproportional increase or decrease in the production of every commodity.

The condition for the restated PPP theory to be a truism is stringent indeed. In practice, prices of individual commodities do not move uniformly with the general price level and therefore the relative production of individual commodities (weights of the individual prices in the price level) also change. So Equation (1) in its identity form cannot be expected to be fulfilled in the real world.

II. ALTERNATIVE PRICE-LEVEL CONCEPTS OF PPP

Let $P \equiv P_t/P_o$ and $D \equiv I_t/I_t^s$. It has been shown that the restated relative PPP theory is not an identity, that is, $P \neq D$. Therefore the theory may legitimately be tested empirically, and it has the general form $P = h(D)$, where h is an increasing function.

Two separate data sets are used to generate samples of observations on P and D.[3] The first data set involves a gross domestic product (GDP) price-level concept for the absolute-PPP computation (P) and, correspondingly, the GDP deflator as the price measure for constructing variable D. The United States is the standard country. The second data set employs a cost-of-living (COL) concept of PPP and the consumer price index as the price measure, with Germany as the standard country.

There are several reasons why the GDP-concept samples are deemed superior to the COL-concept samples for the purpose of testing the PPP theory. An empirical reason is that the United States, as the dominant country in the world economy, can be construed as the optimal standard country for any broad group of domestic countries. There also exist two theoretical arguments in favor of the GDP-concept data set, one on the consumption side, the other on the production side of the economy. To the extent that the PPP theory is justified by the existence of arbitrage and substitutability of commodities in consumption (broadly construed), the price concept underlying PPP should be as comprehensive as possible. Therefore a GDP measure, encompassing all output of the economy, is preferred to a COL measure, which restricts pricing to those commodities purchased by households. On the production side, it can be argued that a unit-factor-cost concept is the most appropriate methodology for absolute PPP (Houthakker, 1962a, pp. 293–294). Now, under certain assumptions, a unit-factor-cost concept of PPP is equivalent to a PPP based on price levels that are production-weighted averages of commodity prices in each country, implying a GDP price-level measure for PPP (Houthakker, 1962a, p. 296; Officer, 1974, pp. 871-872; 1976a, pp. 11-12). However, for equivalence with a COL concept of PPP, i.e, with the use of household consumption weights in the construction of price levels, additional—and more stringent—assumptions are required (Officer, 1976a, pp. 12-13).

On the other hand, the theoretical argument in section I implies that the appropriate price index for the construction of variable D is base-weighted rather than current-weighted. Yet the only available GDP price index is the current-weighted deflator. In contrast, the consumer price

Table 1. Percentage Errors of Strong PPP and Naive Models: GDP Concept

Country	$\dfrac{P-D}{P}$ (%)	$\dfrac{P-1}{P}$ (%)
1950-1955 Period		
Belgium	3.16	0.73
Denmark	-1.15	5.76
France	3.57	21.43
Germany	-6.35	-2.68
Italy	-3.32	3.54
Netherlands	0	7.54
Norway	-2.67	13.19
United Kingdom	-2.52	8.63
Average of Absolute Values	2.84	7.94
1967-1970 Period		
Hungary	-3.68	-7.36
Japan	2.03	3.66
Kenya	-1.10	-7.97
United Kingdom	-2.01	1.01
Average of Absolute Values	2.21	5.00
1950-1970 Period		
France[a]	-0.44	41.46
Germany[a]	-7.52	3.76
Italy[a]	-16.20	5.83
United Kingdom[a]	-14.77	14.77
Average of Absolute Values	9.73	16.46

Note:
[a] Observation excluded from maximum-size sample.

Table 2. Percentage Errors of Strong PPP
and Naive Models: COL Concept

Country	$\dfrac{P-D}{P}$ (%)	$\dfrac{P-1}{P}$ (%)
Computational Period: Less Than 10 Years		
Austria (1954–60)	1.35	2.13
Austria (1960–68)	9.01	15.55
France (1952–58)	7.17	16.33
Israel (1957–61)	25.38	32.34
Israel (1961–69)	4.23	22.87
Italy (1967–72)	−9.17	−7.35
Netherlands (1953–60)	−11.79	−2.97
Netherlands (1960–67)	4.93	10.98
New Zealand (1956–65)	7.04	10.55
Norway (1954–60)	0.31	4.11
Sweden (1952–59)	−16.52	−2.67
Switzerland (1952–57)	5.00	4.82
Switzerland (1957–64)	−7.70	−7.55
United Kingdom (1953–61)	9.30	15.02
Soviet Union (1954–58)	−15.29	−22.73
Average of Absolute Values	8.95	11.86
Computational Period: 10 to 19 Years		
Austria (1954–68)[a]	10.24	17.36
Denmark (1958–75)	12.51	44.97
France (1958–72)	7.83	26.10
Israel (1957–69)[a]	28.54	47.81
Italy (1952–67)	−5.36	12.02
Netherlands (1953–67)[a]	−6.28	8.33
Norway (1960–74)	8.02	27.36
Switzerland (1964–1974/75)	−8.14	4.12
United Kingdom (1961–75)	12.57	43.71
Average of Absolute Values	11.05	25.75
Computational Period: 20 Years or More		
France (1952–72)[a]	14.44	38.17
Italy (1952–72)[a]	−15.02	5.55
Norway (1954–74)[a]	8.31	30.35
Switzerland (1952–1974/75)[a]	−10.63	1.85
United Kingdom (1953–75)[a]	20.70	52.17
United States (1953–73)	−2.31	−5.47
Average of Absolute Values	11.90	22.26

Note:
[a] Observation excluded from maximum-size sample.

index, used in association with the COL-concept PPP, is base-weighted, although there may be changes in the weighting pattern at discrete points in time.

While, on balance, the GDP concept may be construed as the preferred foundation for PPP computation, data availability limits the size of the samples that can be generated on this basis. Observations on P and D are collected for 8 countries in the 1950–1955 period (that is, with 1950 as the base year and 1955 as the current period), 4 countries in the 1967–70 period, and 4 in the 1950–1970 period. Thus there are three distinct samples, and the countries composing each sample are listed in the first column of Table 1.

Use of the COL concept enables the assembling of a much larger data set. Unfortunately, there is no uniformity in base and current periods. So samples are delineated on the basis of the *duration* between base and current period: (i) less than 10 years, a 15-observation sample, (ii) 10 to 19 years, 9 observations, and (iii) 20 years or more, 6 observations. For each sample, the observations are identified by country, base period, and current period in the first column of Table 2.

III. EMPIRICAL ANALYSIS OF THE STRONG PPP AND NAIVE MODELS

The "strong PPP model" is obtained by the inclusion of an error term in Equation (1):

$$P = D + \epsilon_1 \tag{4}$$

In general, an error term is denoted by a subscripted ϵ. The strong PPP model is tested against a corresponding naive model, called the "strong naive model:"

$$P = 1 + \epsilon_2 \tag{5}$$

The strong naive model, in effect, predicts P_t, the absolute PPP in period t, by P_0, the base-period PPP. Price indices in the domestic and standard countries are assigned no role in predicting absolute PPP in the current period relative to the base period.

A comparison of the performance of the strong PPP and strong naive models can be made by calculating their percentage errors in ex post prediction. These errors are $(P - D)/P$ and $(P - 1)/P$, respectively. They are shown in Tables 1 and 2 for the samples based on the GDP and COL concepts, respectively. A positive error implies an underestimate of P, while a negative error implies an overestimate. Then under the GDP concept, the PPP model has a tendency to overestimation, while the naive model has the opposite tendency. With a total of 16 observations over the three samples, the PPP model overpredicts P in 12 cases, with the naive model overpredicting in only 3 cases. The implication is that the relative price level between a domestic and a standard country in a current compared to a base period, tends to be less than that indicated by the corresponding ratio of price indices between the countries. The relative PPP hypothesis tends to predict too great a change in absolute PPP on the basis of changes in price indices.

This result does not carry over to the COL-concept samples. Except for the 20-years-or-more computational period, the PPP model *underestimates* P at double the rate that it overestimates it, while the naive model tends to underpredict P in all samples, and with greater overall frequency. There is no apparent reason for the expected direction of the forecast error to vary with the price-level concept of PPP.

In any event, the direction of a prediction error is less relevant than the amount of the error, especially for comparison with a naive model. Consider the GDP-concept samples first. In terms of *absolute* percentage errors, the PPP model is superior to the naive model (i.e., has a lower percentage error) for 10 of the 16 observations over all samples, it is inferior to the naive model for 5 observations, and there is an equal percentage error for 1 observation. For both shorter time periods (1950–1955 and 1967–1970), the PPP model is superior by a three-to-one margin, under this ordinal criterion. Only for the longer time period (1950–1970) does the naive model outperform the PPP model (by a two-to-one margin, with one tie).

The ordinal superiority of the PPP model is stronger for the COL concept. Over all samples, the PPP model has a lower absolute percentage error than the alternative model in 22 of 30 observations. The PPP model is superior in 8 of 9 observations for the 10-to-19-years sample, and by a two-to-one margin in the other samples.

A cardinal measure of performance of the models is the *average* of the absolute values of the percentage errors. For each sample, this average is shown in Tables 1 and 2. Now the PPP model is superior to the naive model in all samples for both data sets. Especially noticeable in the GDP-concept samples are the low average percentage errors of the PPP model for the shorter time periods, with the average between 2% and 3%. This result is particularly impressive when coupled with the fact that the highest absolute error is below 7% (and the second highest below 4%) for the 1950–1955 period, and below 4% for the 1967–1970 period.

In contrast, an average absolute error of about 9¾% marks a less prominent performance of the PPP model for the 1950–1970 period, even though this result is superior to that of the naive model, which has an average error of nearly 16½%. The inferior result for the 1950–1970 period is not unexpected, because with a longer time period there is greater scope for changes in the price-quantity structure underlying a country's price level, thus reducing the applicability of the PPP model.

Turning to the COL-concept samples, the average absolute error of the PPP model is approximately 9%, 11%, and 12%, respectively, for the three samples in order of duration of the computational period. This performance is superficially inferior to that of the PPP model for the GDP-concept samples. However, the longer duration of the computational periods under the COL data set must be considered. The average computational periods for the COL samples are 6.5, 13.8, and 20.7 years, while the computational periods for the GDP-concept samples are 3, 5, and 20 years. Interestingly enough, for the COL data set, the superiority of the PPP over the naive model increases greatly when the computational period exceeds 10 years.

IV. EMPIRICAL ANALYSIS OF THE WEAK PPP AND NAIVE MODELS

An alternative PPP model, the "weak PPP model," involves a general linear relationship between P and D:

$$P = \alpha + \beta D + \epsilon_3 \tag{6}$$

where α and β are parameters, with β positive. The corresponding naive model, designated as the "weak naive model," again ignores any information on relative price indices in predicting the ratio of absolute PPP in the current period to absolute PPP in the base period. Therefore only the constant and the error term remain in Equation (6). Thus, letting γ be a parameter, the weak naive model is as follows:

$$P = \gamma + \epsilon_4 \tag{7}$$

The weak PPP model allows for a general linear relationship between P and D, with an error term. In contrast, the weak naive model specifies that P is equal to a constant (not necessarily unity) plus an error term. The implication of the naive model is that D can contribute nothing to the explanation of P. A significant correlation coefficient between P and D would indicate a linear association between the two variables and consequently forestall rejection of the weak PPP model.

The correlation coefficient (r) and coefficient of determination (r^2) between P and D for the six samples heretofore discussed are exhibited in Table 3. Because a negative correlation between P and D can be eliminated on theoretical grounds (according to the weak PPP model), a

Table 3. Correlation of *P* with *D*

Sample	Number of Observations	Correlation Coefficient	Coefficient of Determination
GDP Concept			
1950–55	8	.93	.86
1967–70	4	.92	.84
1950–70	4	.98	.96
Maximum Size	12	.95	.90
COL Concept			
Less Than 10 Years	15	.64	.41
10 to 19 Years	9	.88	.77
20 Years or More	6	.96	.93
Maximum Size	22	.90	.81

one-tail test of r is appropriate. Considering first the GDP-concept samples, the correlation coefficient for 1950–1955 is significantly different from zero at the 1% level. With only two degrees of freedom, the test of r for the 1967–1970 and 1950–1970 periods must be viewed with some skepticism. For neither of these samples is r significant at the 1% level; and while r is significant at the 5% level for the 1950–1970 sample, this result is largely due to an extreme observation, that for France.[4]

Results are much better for the COL-concept samples. The correlation coefficient is uniformly significant at the 1% level. Indeed, even for a two-tail test, r continues to be significant at this level for the two longer-period samples and is significant at the 5% level for the less-than-ten-years sample.

With the objective of achieving more powerful tests of r than that provided by the individual samples, for each data set observations are pooled over these samples. While within the individual samples all observations are independent, this is not so between samples. Care must be taken to exclude observations that are dependent on other observations in the data set. The objective is to achieve a maximum-size sample of independent observations for each data set. For the GDP-concept data, this criterion involves excluding the 1950–1970 observations, resulting in a maximum-size sample of 12 observations. For the COL-concept data, 8 observations must be dropped from the longer computational periods, yielding a sample of 22 observations. Excluded observations are identified by superscript a in Tables 1 and 2.

The correlation coefficient and coefficient of determination for the maximum-size samples are presented in Table 3. For both samples, the correlation coefficient is significantly different from zero at the 1% level, even under a two-tail test—a result distinctly favorable for the weak PPP model.

The weak PPP and naive models have been tested against one another using correlation analysis; they may also be tested by means of regression analysis. The weak PPP model is formulated as Equation (6), which can be viewed as a regression model the parameters of which, α and β, can be estimated by ordinary least-squares. The maximum-size samples from the GDP-concept and COL-concept data sets provide sample sizes (n) of 12 and 22 observations, respectively, to which Equation (6) is fitted. The resulting regression lines are as follows:

$$P = -.0666 + 1.0525D$$
$$(.1188) \quad (.1118) \tag{8}$$

$$P = -.4066 + 1.3948D$$
$$(.1699) \quad (.1487) \tag{9}$$

The GDP-concept data yield Equation (8) and the COL-concept data produce Equation (9). Numbers in parentheses are standard errors of the estimated coefficients. The standard error of estimate (s) is 0.0322 in Equation (8) and 0.1145 in Equation (9), while the corrected coefficient of determination is 0.89 in (8) and 0.81 in (9).

The weak naive model is represented by Equation (7), which may be viewed as the following regression model:

$$P = \gamma[1] + \epsilon_4 \tag{10}$$

where [1] is a variable identically equal to unity. Equation (10) is a degenerate regression equation, the parameter of which, γ, may be estimated by ordinary least-squares. The resulting estimate of γ is the mean of the dependent variable ($\bar{P}$). Letting $\hat{\alpha}$, $\hat{\beta}$, and $\hat{\gamma}$ denote the estimates of α, β, and γ, respectively, parameter estimation of the weak PPP and naive models may be summarized as follows:

GDP-concept sample:

$$\hat{\alpha} = -.0666; \hat{\beta} = 1.0525; \hat{\gamma} = \bar{P} = 1.0488$$

COL-concept sample:

$$\hat{\alpha} = -.4066; \hat{\beta} = 1.3948; \hat{\gamma} = \bar{P} = 1.1709$$

Equation (6) may be used to exposit all four models that have been investigated empirically. Each of these models may be identified by the value it assigns to the parameters of Equation (6), as shown in the second

Table 4. Summary of Models

Model	Value of α	Value of β	F-Statistic GDP Concept	F-Statistic COL Concept
Weak PPP	$\hat{\alpha}$	$\hat{\beta}$	—	—
Weak Naive	$\bar{P}$	0	44.24	44.03
Strong PPP	0	1	0.81	4.86
Strong Naive	1	0	58.07	68.51

and third columns of Table 4. For the weak PPP and naive models, where the parameters lack preassigned numerical values, the estimates derived above are used.

The estimated regression Equations (8) and (9), which pertain to the weak PPP model, may be used for statistical testing of the remaining three models. As thus far only the weak PPP model has been subjected to testing with a level of significance (the correlation analysis), it is appropriate to use the estimated versions of this model for econometric testing of the other models.

The weak naive, strong PPP, and strong naive models each involve a joint hypothesis on α and β, the parameters of the weak PPP model. The respective hypotheses are indicated in the second and third columns of Table 4. For joint testing of α and β, the test statistic

$$F = \frac{n(\hat{\alpha} - \alpha)^2 + 2n\bar{D}(\hat{\alpha} - \alpha)(\hat{\beta} - \beta) + \Sigma D^2(\hat{\beta} - \beta)^2}{2s^2}$$

has the F-distribution with $(2, n - 2)$ degrees of freedom (Johnston, 1972, pp. 28–29). The values of F computed for the (α, β) hypotheses implied by the weak naive, strong PPP, and strong naive models, respectively, are listed in the fourth and fifth columns of Table 4.

Results are most striking for the GDP-concept sample. With $(2, 10)$ degrees of freedom, the critical value for the F-distribution at the 0.05% level of significance is 17.9. Both naive models are rejected at this extremely low level of significance. In contrast, the F value for the strong PPP model is such that this model cannot be rejected even at the 40% level of significance.[5] Thus, using the F-test as the criterion, the strong PPP model strongly out-performs both naive models.

For the COL-concept sample, the F-distribution has $(2, 20)$ degrees of freedom; its critical value at the 0.05% level of significance is 11.4. Again the naive models are rejected at this very low level of significance. Indeed, the F-statistics for these models are even further in the tail of the distribution than under the GDP-concept sample. A statement similar in kind applies to the F-statistic of the strong PPP model. With F-distribution critical values of 3.49 and 5.85 at the 5% and 1% levels, respectively, the strong PPP model itself is rejected at the 5% level of significance, though it cannot be rejected at the 1% level. So the strong PPP model survives the F-test more easily under the GDP-concept sample than under the COL-concept sample.

In summary, empirical investigation supports the relative PPP hypothesis in both strong and weak versions. The findings are especially favorable to the relative PPP theory in light of the facts that (i) no secondary variables were used to increase the explanatory power of the PPP model, (ii) complicated functional forms and lagged relationships were not adopted in an effort to increase explanatory power, and (iii) several countries outside the Western industrial mode were included in the samples.

APPENDIX: THE DATA

Absolute PPP

The absolute PPP measure is computed as the geometric mean of the PPPs calculated alternatively using the weighting pattern of the domestic country and that of the standard country. If the weights of only one of the countries are used for the PPP computation, then the calculated PPP will be biased in the direction of an overvalued PPP for that country (Houthakker, 1962a, p. 297; Officer, 1976a, pp. 15–16). Therefore no use is made of PPP measures for which only one of the weighting patterns is available.

Two data sources are used to obtain absolute-PPP measures under the GDP concept: Gilbert and associates (1958), who provide PPP data for the years 1950 and 1955, and Kravis and others (1975), who offer such data for 1967 and 1970. The former authors use a GNP rather than GDP price-level concept. Because the PPP theory concerns prices and production within the boundaries of respective countries, GDP is the preferred concept, as it covers domestic rather than national production. In practice, PPP computations on a GNP basis differ minimally from those on a GDP basis.

The PPP data published by the German Statistical Office (Statistisches Bundesamt) are the source of the COL-concept measures.

GDP Deflator

The data source is OECD national-accounts publications for all countries except Hungary and Kenya, and United Nations (1973) for the latter two countries. For Hungary, GDP data are not available and a less inclusive concept of domestic production, "net material product," must be used.

Consumer Price Index

For all countries except the Soviet Union, the data source is International Monetary Fund (1977). For the Soviet Union, use is made of the "state retail price index," published in International Labour Office (1962).

NOTES

1. This chapter appears in the bibliography as Officer (1978). It is reprinted by permission of the North-Holland Publishing Company.

2. The term "standard" is used in preference to "foreign" currency or country, because this country may serve as the standard of comparison for a group of "domestic" countries.

3. Details on data are provided in the Appendix.

4. See Table 1. With the value of P extremely close to that of D, coupled with by far the highest values of both these variables in the 1950–1970 sample, the observation for France is dominant in the correlation.

5. Critical values for the F-distribution at the 40% level of significance are not published in an accessible source. However, the critical value at this level for the F-distribution with $(2, \infty)$ degrees of freedom is readily obtained as 0.916; for this degrees-of-freedom configuration reduces the F-distribution to a chi-square distribution with 2 degrees of freedom. The corresponding critical value for the F-distribution with $(2, 10)$ degrees of freedom is necessarily greater than 0.916.

Chapter XVI

Effective Exchange Rates and Price Ratios over the Long Run: A Test of the Purchasing-Power-Parity Theory[1]

This study tests the purchasing-power-parity (PPP) theory of exchange rates over a long historical period. The reference here is to the theory in its "relative" rather than "absolute" form. The absolute PPP theory asserts that the exchange value of a country's currency is determined by the ratio of the domestic to the foreign price level. Thus this version of the theory pertains only to a point in time. Of interest in this study, rather, is the relative version, which redefines the exchange rate and price levels so that they are index numbers, ratios of current-period to base-period values. This PPP theory is tested over the long run—a time span ranging from the nineteenth-century gold standard to the managed-float period of the 1970s.

The PPP methodology for this study is described in the first part, followed by multilateral PPP computations. Deviations from PPP are explained next, and longer-run, bilateral PPP computations are provided in the fourth part. Finally, a summary of the findings is presented, followed by a data appendix.

I. METHODOLOGY

Let r_t denote the exchange rate (number of units of foreign currency per unit of domestic currency) in period t, and $p_t^f(p_t^d)$ the foreign (domestic) price index in period t relative to period o, the base period. The exchange-rate index, R_n, and the foreign/domestic price-index ratio, P_n, in the current period, n, are defined as follows:

$$R_n = r_n / r_o \qquad P_n = p_n{}^f / p_n{}^d$$

The closer is R_n to P_n, the stronger is the predictive power of PPP. This computation underlies the comparative-static approach to testing the PPP theory. It tests the predictive power of the PPP hypothesis rather than its fundamental assumption: namely, that monetary changes dominate real changes in the domestic and foreign economies between the base and the current periods.[2] The ideal circumstance under which the PPP theory *exactly* holds ($R_n = P_n$) would be that the two economies be subject to purely monetary changes, and no real changes, during this time interval.[3]

Interestingly enough, only eight published studies have performed comparative-static testing of the PPP theory. And of these, three were performed personally by Gustav Cassel (1916a; 1918; 1919), the greatest proponent of PPP, and pertain to exceedingly short time periods. Yeager (1958), Aliber (1978), Officer (1978), and McKinnon (1979) consider time periods less than a quarter-century in duration. Only the work of Gailliot (1970), with a time span ranging from the pre-World War I gold standard to the post-World War II adjustable-peg system, can be considered long-term in nature, in conformity with the present study.

There are four ingredients in comparative-static testing of PPP: (1) price measure, (2) standard country, (3) base and current periods, and (4) the sample of domestic countries.

Price Measure

The gross-domestic-product (GDP) deflator is selected as the price index in this study because it is the only price concept with a firm analytical foundation in PPP theory.[4] In contrast, the other authors adopt the consumer price index and/or the wholesale price index. Gailliot's exclusive use of the wholesale price index makes his findings (which are favorable to the PPP theory) suspect, because such an index is heavily weighted with traded goods and therefore biases the results in favour of the theory.[5]

Standard Country

The usual standard country in PPP testing is the United States, with the United Kingdom or West Germany playing the role on occasion. Yeager, Gailliot, Aliber, and McKinnon use the United States, while Officer adopts the United States and Germany as the standard country for alternative samples. Selection of *any* unique standard country has the disadvantage of permitting tests of PPP in which price movements and the exchange rate pertain only to the domestic vis-à-vis the standard country. Such bilateral tests are relatively weak, because they do not incorporate the full range of economies involved in the domestic country's trade and payments.

For a given domestic country, the optimal standard country is the one with which the former country's trade and payments links are strongest. This suggests that the concept of the "effective exchange rate" (ER) be applied to PPP, so that in effect the standard country's currency (rather, its exchange-rate index with respect to the domestic currency) and price index are replaced by appropriately weighted averages of the currencies (rather, their exchange-rate indices with respect to the domestic currency) and price indices of the domestic country's main partners in trade and payments. The definition and method of construction of the ER and of the corresponding price variable follow.[6]

Building on previous notation, let

ER_{in} = effective exchange rate for currency i in period n relative to period o, number of units of foreign currency per unit of domestic currency

R_{ijn} = exchange-rate index between currency i and currency j in period n relative to period o, number of units of currency j per unit of currency i

w_{ij} = weight of currency j in the effective exchange rate for currency i

Then, by definition,

$$ER_{in} = \Pi_j R_{ijn}{}^{w_{ij}}, \qquad \text{where } \Sigma_j w_{ij} = 1 \text{ and } w_{ii} = 0$$

A geometric rather than arithmetic average is used to construct the ER because of the former's properties of reversibility (interchangeability of periods o and n) and symmetry (interchangeability of currencies i and j).[7] Assuming orderly cross rates involving the U.S. dollar (denoted by the subscript $\$$),

$$ER_{in} = \Pi_j (R_{i\$n}/R_{j\$n})^{w_{ij}} = e \cdot exp(lnR_{i\$n} - \Sigma_j w_{ij}lnR_{j\$n})$$

Thus the ER may be calculated from exchange-rate data involving the U.S. dollar alone. This is the way the computation is performed in the present study.

Analogously, one defines the "effective price-index ratio" (EP) using the following additional notation:

EP_{in} = effective price-index ratio for country i in period n, foreign price index divided by domestic price index

P_{kn} = price index of country k in period n relative to period o

By definition,

$$EP_{in} = \Pi_j(P_{jn}/P_{in})^{w_{ij}} = e \cdot exp(\Sigma_j w_{ij} \ln P_{jn} - \ln P_{in})$$

The comparative-static test of PPP then proceeds exactly as for the analogous bilateral variables, R_n and P_n. The theory postulates, under ideal conditions, that ER_{in} is equal to EP_{in}. So the closer ER_{in} is to EP_{in}, the greater is the predictive power of the theory.

An advantage in using the ER concept is that there is no standard country which perforce does not receive a PPP test for itself as the domestic country. The numeraire currency, the dollar for the computations here, is treated symmetrically with the other currencies. The United States is the subject of its own ER computations. The formulas become:

$$ER_{\$n} = e \cdot exp(-\Sigma_j w_{\$j} \ln R_{j\$n})$$
$$EP_{\$n} = e \cdot exp(\Sigma_j w_{\$j} \ln P_{jn} - \ln P_{\$n})$$

The ER concept used here has the weight w_{ij} proportional to the value of merchandise trade (exports plus imports) of country j with country i.[8] Existing computations of ERs are for short time periods, with the weight base at the beginning of (or even preceding) the period of calculation. For the long-term computations of the present study, it is preferable to let the beginning and ending periods (the base and current periods, o and n) play equal roles in determining the weights. Letting w_{ijt} denote the proportion of country i's trade with country j in period t, w_{ij} is the unweighted arithmetic average of w_{ijo} and w_{ijn}.

Time Periods and Selection of Samples

In order to perform comparative-static testing of PPP, another decision must be made: the determination of the base and current periods of the analysis. The base and current periods should involve exchange-market stability, so that PPP computations under the ideal condition of purely monetary changes between base and current period would neither perpetuate a genuine disequilibrium nor give rise to an apparent one. Exchange control and severe trade restrictions should be absent. If exchange rates are floating, they should be relatively stable during the period. If fixed or managed floating, balance-of-payments deficits or surpluses should be neither large nor persistent. Perhaps most important, expectations of major changes in domestic and foreign economies should either be absent or occur under a situation in which such changes are deemed not to affect the foreign-exchange market. In sum, there should be a reasonable approximation to ongoing exchange-market equilibrium in the base and current periods.

Three sets of data are required in order to compute the variables ER_{in} and EP_{in} and thereby test the PPP theory: (1) exchange rates, (2) trade flows, and (3) GDP at both current and constant prices, thereby permitting construction of the GDP deflator, the selected price measure. It happens that the effective constraint in determining base periods and the associated country samples is availability of the national-accounts data. Table 13 in the data appendix lists the countries and associated years or annual averages for which data are available permitting the construction of a consistent GDP-deflator series over time. Countries are included in the table only if a GDP-deflator series may be constructed beginning prior to World War I.

In view of non-uniform availability of the GDP deflator among countries over time, several base periods and associated country samples are used. All samples share the same current period and "intervening periods." The current period selected is 1975, the three-quarter point of the twentieth century. This year was one in which currencies floated in the exchange market, though with varying degrees of management. An alternative current period would be one during which exchange rates were fixed. The period 1963–1966, during the adjustable-peg system, was a time of complete exchange-market stability in the sense that there were no changes in the par values of the countries listed in Table 13. However, the British pound and French franc were clearly overvalued, at least during the latter part of this period, and the mark was undervalued. Probably no time interval in the post-World War II era is fully satisfactory as a current period.[9]

The years 1963–1966 are used not as a current period, but rather as an "intervening period" between base and current period (n). Intervening periods (say, period m) are similar to the current period in the sense that ER_{im} and EP_{im} are computed and compared, thus testing the PPP theory. However, the weights, w_{ij}, are not recalculated using trade flows in period m in conjunction with the flows in period o. Rather, the weights are identical to those employed in calculating ER_{in} and EP_{in}: that is, they are based on trade flows in periods o and n. This procedure has the advantage that ER_{in} and ER_{im}, as well as EP_{in} and EP_{im}, are consistent index numbers for all m and the given n.

Also desirable would be an intervening year for the interwar period. Unfortunately, it is impossible to find a subperiod of 1919–1939 which

Table 1. Weighting Patterns for Effective Exchange Rates[a]

Country	Base Period	Weighting Pattern[b]						Coverage[c]
Austria	1913	0.6723GER	0.1348ITA	0.1130UK	0.0800US			(0.62, 0.47)
Canada	1910	0.7681US	0.2319UK					(0.85, 0.71)
Denmark	1879–88	0.3453GER	0.3033UK	0.2059SWE	0.0730US	0.0726NOR		(0.98[d], 0.57)
Denmark	1905–13	0.3215UK	0.3191GER	0.1668SWE	0.0961US	0.0590NOR	0.0376FRA	(1.02[d], 0.60)
Denmark	1913	0.3451GER	0.3374UK	0.1696SWE	0.0873US	0.0606NOR		(0.91[d], 0.57)
France	1905–13	0.3505GER	0.2645UK	0.1698US	0.1546ITA	0.0606SPA		(0.45, 0.41)
Germany	1879–88	0.4083UK	0.2573US	0.2403ITA	0.0941SWE			(0.24, 0.22)
Germany	1905–13	0.2216US	0.2055FRA	0.1910UK	0.1880NET	0.1338ITA	0.0601SWE	(0.40, 0.46)
Germany	1913	0.2268US	0.2162NET	0.1861UK	0.1539AUS	0.1505ITA	0.0665SWE	(0.43, 0.37)
Italy	1879–88	0.4417GER	0.3381UK	0.2203US				(0.29, 0.30)
Italy	1905–13	0.3603GER	0.2512FRA	0.2123US	0.1762UK			(0.52, 0.43)
Italy	1913	0.4008GER	0.2278US	0.1820UK	0.0976AUS	0.0918SWI		(0.56, 0.34)
Japan	1905–13	0.6039US	0.1748UK	0.1075GER	0.0688FRA	0.0282ITA	0.0168NET	(0.50, 0.27)
Japan	1910	0.5932US	0.1856UK	0.1113GER	0.0613CAN	0.0324ITA	0.0162NET	(0.43, 0.29)
Japan	1913	0.6529US	0.1736UK	0.1180GER	0.0383ITA	0.0172NET		(0.42, 0.26)
Netherlands	1905–13	0.6450GER	0.2155UK	0.1395US				(0.59, 0.42)
Netherlands	1913	0.6448GER	0.2110UK	0.1443US				(0.60, 0.42)
Norway	1879–88	0.3348UK	0.2624GER	0.2293SWE	0.1040DEN	0.0696US		(0.72, 0.60)

							Coverage[c]
Norway	1905–13	0.2987_{UK} / 0.0594_{NET}	0.2539_{GER} / 0.0463_{FRA}	0.1777_{SWE}	0.0864_{US}	0.0776_{DEN}	(0.79, 0.67)
Norway	1910	0.3020_{UK} / 0.0550_{NET}	0.2716_{GER} / 0.0124_{CAN}	0.1821_{SWE}	0.1017_{US}	0.0753_{DEN}	(0.75, 0.65)
Norway	1913	0.2968_{UK} / 0.0592_{NET}	0.2760_{GER}	0.1908_{SWE}	0.1005_{US}	0.0768_{DEN}	(0.75, 0.64)
Spain	1906–13	0.2946_{FRA}	0.2522_{UK}	0.2521_{US}	0.2011_{GER}		(0.63, 0.41)
Spain	1913	0.3568_{US}	0.3384_{UK}	0.3048_{GER}			(0.41, 0.30)
Sweden	1879–88	0.3484_{UK}	0.2759_{GER}	0.1749_{DEN}	0.1284_{NOR}	0.0724_{US}	(0.78, 0.48)
Sweden	1905–13	0.2992_{GER} / 0.0717_{FRA}	0.2634_{UK}	0.1168_{DEN}	0.1040_{NOR}	0.0879_{US}	(0.84, 0.57)
Sweden	1913	0.3240_{GER} / 0.0587_{NET}	0.2788_{UK} / 0.0569_{NET}	0.1235_{DEN}	0.1153_{NOR}	0.0997_{US}	(0.76, 0.53)
Switzerland	1913	0.4545_{GER}	0.1610_{ITA}		0.1364_{US}	0.0974_{AUS}	(0.61, 0.48)
U.K.	1879–88	0.6452_{US}	0.3548_{GER}				(0.24, 0.17)
U.K.	1905–13	0.3754_{US}	0.2649_{GER}	0.2029_{FRA}	0.1568_{NET}		(0.30, 0.30)
U.K.	1910	0.4025_{US}	0.2920_{GER}	0.1757_{NET}	0.1297_{CAN}		(0.27, 0.26)
U.K.	1913	0.4559_{US}	0.3419_{GER}	0.2023_{NET}			(0.24, 0.23)
U.S.	1879–88	0.6311_{UK}	0.3689_{GER}				(0.49, 0.09)
U.S.	1905–13	0.3479_{UK}	0.2683_{JAP}	0.2517_{GER}	0.1321_{FRA}		(0.47, 0.22)
U.S.	1910	0.3595_{CAN}	0.2931_{UK}	0.1946_{GER}	0.1528_{JAP}		(0.48, 0.41)
U.S.	1913	0.3895_{UK}	0.3110_{JAP}	0.2995_{GER}			(0.37, 0.19)

Notes:

[a] The same weighting patterns are used for the corresponding price-index ratios.

[b] Obvious symbols are used to represent component countries (i.e., bilateral exchange rates) in the effective exchange rate.

[c] Trade with countries included in weighting pattern as a proportion of the domestic country's total trade. First entry refers to base period, second entry to 1975.

[d] Coverage in the base period is overestimated.

involves exchange-rate stability.[10] The year 1938 is chosen as the intervening period for two reasons. It is the last year prior to the outbreak of World War II, marking the end of the interwar period; it is also the year most often used by the OECD statisticians to carry back national accounts prior to World War II (see Table 13). Data limitations require that 1937 serve as the intervening year for Austria and 1935 for Spain.

Having selected the current and intervening periods, the base periods and associated samples remain to be determined. It is desired to have any base period antedate World War I, when the old gold standard existed. Only in 1879, with resumption of specie payments by the U.S. Treasury at the pre-Civil War parity, could the gold standard be deemed to exist on a worldwide basis.[11] Therefore the earliest acceptable base year is 1879.

For whatever reasons, the mint parity under the international gold standard had good characteristics of an equilibrium exchange rate.[12] Expectations that even major changes in economies would seriously affect the foreign-exchange market were minimal. Therefore, at least for countries that adhered to the gold standard, virtually any of the years from 1879 to 1913 are acceptable base periods. In order to maximize country coverage given data availability, four alternative base periods are selected: 1879–1888, 1905–1913, 1910, and 1913.[13]

Table 1 describes the weighting pattern of ER and EP for each country in each of the four samples (corresponding to the base periods). A measure of the quality of the ER and EP indices for a given country and base period is the proportion of the country's total trade accounted for by the countries with positive weight in the indices. This measure is called the "coverage" of the indices and is listed in the final column of Table 1. The first entry in the coverage vector refers to the base period, the second entry to the current period (always 1975).[14]

II. MULTILATERAL PPP COMPUTATIONS

Effective exchange rates and price-index ratios are reported for the 1879–1888, 1910, 1905–1913, and 1913 samples in Tables 2–5, respectively. Dropping the country subscript (i), the PPP theory predicts, under ideal conditions, that ER_t/EP_t equals unity for any period t. The computations pertain to selected intervening periods ($t = 1938$, 1963–1966) and the current period ($t = 1975$).

A measure of the predictive power of the PPP theory for a given domestic country and given period t is $ln(ER_t/EP_t) = ln[(ER_t/EP_t)/1]$, the proportionate deviation of ER_t/EP_t from unity (its predicted value), that is, the proportionate forecasting error of PPP. Also, by definition,

Table 2. Effective Exchange Rates and Price-Index Ratios

Base period: 1879–88

Country	Variable	1938	1963–1966	1975
Denmark	ER	0.6918	0.7035	0.7173
	EP	0.8718	0.6594	0.5861
	ln(ER/EP)	−0.2312	0.0647	0.2021
Germany	ER	2.3037	4.2859	7.5567
	EP	1.5824	4.2185	5.2677
	ln(ER/EP)	0.3755	0.0158	0.3608
Italy	ER	0.2205	0.0100	0.0083
	EP	0.3101	0.0102	0.0091
	ln(ER/EP)	−0.3408	−0.0168	−0.0826
Norway	ER	0.8266	0.7120	0.8645
	EP	0.9185	0.7706	0.7916
	ln(ER/EP)	−0.1054	−0.0792	0.0882
Sweden	ER	0.8516	1.0446	1.1473
	EP	0.9371	0.9935	1.0570
	ln(ER/EP)	−0.0956	0.0502	0.0820
United Kingdom	ER	0.8345	0.5639	0.3776
	EP	0.8175	0.5967	0.4236
	ln(ER/EP)	0.0205	−0.0565	−0.1149
United States	ER	0.8220	1.3919	1.3464
	EP	1.0772	1.3273	1.6256
	ln(ER/EP)	−0.2703	0.0475	−0.1885

Notes:
ER = effective exchange rate: number of units of foreign currency per unit of domestic currency.
EP = effective price-index ratio: foreign price index divided by domestic price index.

$ER_0 = EP_0 = 1$. Therefore $ln(ER_t/EP_t) = \Delta \, ln(ER_t/EP_t) \equiv ln(ER_t/EP_t)$ − $ln(ER_0/EP_0)$ is also the proportionate change in ER_t/EP_t since the base period. The measure $ln(ER_t/EP_t)$ has the property of being unbounded in both directions. The closer it is to zero, the higher is the predictive power of the PPP theory. If $ln(ER_t/EP_t)$ is greater (less) than zero, the domestic currency is overvalued (undervalued) according to the PPP theory by $100 \, |ln(ER_t/EP_t)|$ percent. For example, with base period 1879–1888, Denmark's currency is overvalued by 20.21 percent in 1975, a magnitude that is interpreted as the percentage forecasting error of PPP. The Danish krone exchanges for 20.21 percent more units of foreign currency in the current period than is justified by the price-level movements in Denmark and abroad since the base period.[15] For a given domestic country and given *t*, ER_t and EP_t may differ across base

Table 3. Effective Exchange Rates and Price-Index Ratios

Base period: 1910

Country	Variable	1938	1963–1966	1975
Canada	ER	0.9931	1.2262	1.2200
	EP	1.0718	1.1828	1.1808
	ln(ER/EP)	−0.0763	0.0360	0.0327
Japan	ER	0.5585	0.0071	0.0086
	EP	0.6266	0.0047	0.0042
	ln(ER/EP)	−0.1151	0.4131	0.7118
Norway	ER	0.8017	0.6894	0.8245
	EP	0.9211	0.7719	0.7828
	ln(ER/EP)	−0.1389	−0.1131	0.0520
United Kingdom	ER	0.8167	0.5981	0.3908
	EP	0.7359	0.5905	0.4371
	ln(ER/EP)	0.1042	0.0127	−0.1120
United States	ER	0.9847	2.5069	2.4183
	EP	1.1029	2.6155	3.0407
	ln(ER/EP)	−0.1134	−0.0424	−0.2290

Notes:

ER = effective exchange rate: number of units of foreign currency per unit of domestic currency.

EP = effective price-index ratio: foreign price index divided by domestic price index.

periods not only because of the varying time base, but also because of different weighting patterns of trading partners' series in the indices.

There are some distinct country differences in the results. The PPP theory works best for Canada—the only country for which the absolute forecast error, $|ln(ER_t/EP_t)|$, is below 10 percent in all periods—Italy (except for 1938), Norway, and Sweden. The theory's performance is worst for Austria, Japan, and Switzerland. The question arises as to whether such country differences in results are due to systematic factors, that is, whether deviations from the PPP theory can be explained. Hypotheses of this nature are tested below.

As an indicator of the overall predictive performance of the PPP theory, the average of the absolute percentage errors, $100 |ln(ER_t/EP_t)|$, is presented in Table 6 for each sample and each period t. A total of fourteen countries are examined, but the maximum sample size is twelve, for the 1913 base period. Therefore the computations are made for two additional samples, each including all fourteen countries. The "extended 1913 sample" adds Canada (base 1910) and France (base 1905–1913) to the 1913 sample. A second comprehensive sample selects the

Table 4. Effective Exchange Rates and Price-Index Ratios

Base period: 1905–1913

Country	Variable	1938ᵃ	1963–1966	1975
Denmark	ER	0.7506	0.8263	0.8635
	EP	0.8284	0.6916	0.6180
	ln(ER/EP)	−0.0986	0.1780	0.3346
France	ER	0.1539	0.0291	0.0300
	EP	0.1987	0.0253	0.0256
	ln(ER/EP)	−0.2556	0.1376	0.1585
Germany	ER	2.8070	6.1934	9.4774
	EP	1.9543	6.5631	7.8579
	ln(ER/EP)	0.3621	−0.0580	0.1874
Italy	ER	0.3638	0.0282	0.0228
	EP	0.4993	0.0314	0.0274
	ln(ER/EP)	−0.3167	−0.1088	−0.1848
Japan	ER	0.6341	0.0096	0.0114
	EP	0.7746	0.0070	0.0062
	ln(ER/EP)	−0.2001	0.3164	0.6019
Netherlands	ER	0.9754	0.7515	0.8247
	EP	1.2160	0.7496	0.6686
	ln(ER/EP)	−0.2205	0.0025	0.2098
Norway	ER	0.8826	0.8524	1.0194
	EP	1.0206	0.9756	0.9941
	ln(ER/EP)	−0.1454	−0.1349	0.0251
Spainᵇ	ER	1.2211	0.4111	0.3972
	EP	1.5281	0.6176	0.5126
	ln(ER/EP)	−0.2243	−0.4071	−0.2550
Sweden	ER	0.9344	1.3378	1.4086
	EP	1.0405	1.3092	1.3548
	ln(ER/EP)	−0.1075	0.0216	0.0389
United Kingdom	ER	1.2251	1.5119	0.9731
	EP	1.1054	1.5562	1.1658
	ln(ER/EP)	0.1028	−0.0288	−0.1807
United States	ER	1.3080	8.7990	7.8618
	EP	1.4453	9.1682	10.9432
	ln(ER/EP)	−0.0998	−0.0411	−0.3307

Notes:

ER = effective exchange rate: number of units of foreign currency per unit of domestic currency.

EP = effective price-index ratio: foreign price index divided by domestic price index.

ᵃ 1935 for Spain.

ᵇ Base period: 1906–1913.

Table 5. Effective Exchange Rates and Price-Index Ratios

Base period: 1913

Country	Variable	1938ᵃ	1963–1966	1975
Austria	ER	0.7731	0.3738	0.4139
	EP	1.4299	0.5901	0.6078
	ln(ER/EP)	−0.6150	−0.4567	−0.3842
Denmark	ER	0.6895	0.7030	0.7310
	EP	0.7622	0.5763	0.5153
	ln(ER/EP)	−0.1003	0.1986	0.3497
Germany	ER	1.9472	3.4328	5.0226
	EP	1.3010	3.2891	3.8821
	ln(ER/EP)	0.4033	0.0428	0.2576
Italy	ER	0.2191	0.0104	0.0078
	EP	0.3176	0.0114	0.0097
	ln(ER/EP)	−0.3715	−0.0916	−0.2183
Japan	ER	0.5605	0.0073	0.0088
	EP	0.7606	0.0058	0.0052
	ln(ER/EP)	−0.3052	0.2265	0.5231
Netherlands	ER	0.9755	0.7497	0.8218
	EP	1.2140	0.7474	0.6656
	ln(ER/EP)	−0.2187	0.0030	0.2108
Norway	ER	0.7994	0.6915	0.8208
	EP	1.0026	0.8430	0.8542
	ln(ER/EP)	−0.2265	−0.1981	−0.0399
Spain	ER	0.6483	0.1103	0.1076
	EP	0.8681	0.1595	0.1311
	ln(ER/EP)	−0.2920	−0.3690	−0.1978
Sweden	ER	0.8061	0.9843	1.0320
	EP	0.9123	0.9515	0.9839
	ln(ER/EP)	−0.1237	0.0339	0.0478
Switzerland	ER	1.1597	3.2334	4.3636
	EP	1.1808	2.4581	2.4315
	ln(ER/EP)	−0.0181	0.2742	0.5848
United Kingdom	ER	0.7885	0.6084	0.3815
	EP	0.7441	0.6087	0.4475
	ln(ER/EP)	0.0579	−0.0005	−0.1596
United States	ER	1.0160	6.1469	5.4692
	EP	1.1339	6.2508	7.4950
	ln(ER/EP)	−0.1098	−0.0168	−0.3151

Notes:
ER = effective exchange rate: number of units of foreign currency per unit of domestic currency.
EP = effective price-index ratio: foreign price index divided by domestic price index.
ᵃ 1937 for Austria, 1935 for Spain.

Table 6. Average Absolute Percentage Errors

Sample	Sample Size	1938[a]	1963–1966	1975
1879–88	7	20.56	4.72	15.99
1905–13[b]	11	19.39	13.04	22.79
1910	5	10.96	12.35	22.75
1913	12	23.68	15.93	27.41
extended 1913[c]	14	22.67	14.90	24.86
maximum coverage[d]	14	20.39	15.74	24.35

Notes:
[a] 1937 for Austria, 1935 for Spain.
[b] 1906–1913 for Spain.
[c] 1913 sample plus Canada (1910) and France (1905–1913).
[d] Canada and U.S.: 1910; Austria, Netherlands, and Switzerland: 1913; Spain: 1906–1913; all other countries: 1905–1913.

base period for each country by maximizing the coverage of the ER and EP indices (thus presumably obtaining highest-quality indices) for each country among the alternative base periods. The resulting sample involves base period 1910 for Canada and the United States; 1913 for Austria, Netherlands, and Switzerland; 1906–1913 for Spain; and 1905–1913 for all other countries.

For any sample and time period (*t*), the average absolute percentage error is less than 30 percent. For 1963–1966, this average forecasting error is below 16 percent in each sample, a better performance than for 1938 and 1975. The implication (for a believer in the PPP theory) is that the unchanging par values of the mid-1960s yielded an exchange-rate configuration closer to equilibrium than did the managed-float regime of the mid-1970s. The fourteen-country samples follow the general pattern of the results, with the average forecasting error for 1975 slightly below 25 percent and that for 1963–1966 in the order of 15 percent.

Previous writers have been content merely to compute purchasing power parities, subjectively noting (where seemingly appropriate) that the errors are "close to zero."[16] But only statistical analysis can indicate "how close is close" and whether deviations from PPP are systematic. In this analysis four samples are used: the forecast-error vectors, $1n$(ER/EP), for the maximum-coverage (*M*) and extended 1913 (*E*) samples, alternatively with respect to two current periods, 1963–1966 and 1975.

First, the random property of these deviations from PPP is investigated. Shapiro and Wilk (1965) provide a test that a sample emanates from a normal distribution with unknown parameter values. Shapiro, Wilk, and Chen (1968) show that this test is generally superior to alterna-

Table 7. Shapiro-Wilk *W* Statistic

Sample	W Statistic
M, 1963–1966	0.938
M, 1975	0.945
E, 1963–1966	0.922
E, 1975	0.964

tive procedures and is sensitive to non-normality even for small samples. The computed Shapiro-Wilk *W* statistic for the four samples is exhibited in Table 7. For fourteen observations, given normality, the probabilities that *W* is less than 0.895 and 0.947 are 0.10 and 0.50, respectively (see Shapiro and Wilk, 1965, p. 605). So for the 1963–1966 samples normality cannot be rejected at a level of significance greater than 10 percent, and for the 1975 samples it cannot be rejected at (or almost at) the 50 percent level.

Second, the hypothesis that the mean deviation from PPP is zero can be tested. Table 8 exhibits the equations obtained by regressing $\ln(\text{ER}/\text{EP})$ on a vector identically equal to unity. The estimated coefficient and its *t*-value (in parentheses) are in the "constant" column and *S* in the standard error of estimate. The regression coefficient is the mean value of $\ln(\text{ER}/\text{EP})$, which in every case is not significantly different from zero.

This result is not too surprising. It follows from the fact that the forecast errors are relatively symmetric around zero. The *absolute* errors, summarized in Table 6, are of greater importance. Repeating the regression analysis for the corresponding $|\ln(\text{ER}/\text{EP})|$ vectors (Table 9), the coefficient (mean of $|\ln(\text{ER}/\text{EP})|$) is significant at the 1 percent level (two-tail test) in all cases. This result suggests that deviations from long-run PPP might be explainable in terms of economic variables. Since elements of the error vectors pertain to mutually exclusive domestic countries, the specified explanatory variables have each observation similarly construed.

Table 8. Regressions of $\ln(\text{ER}/\text{EP})$ on Constant

Sample	Constant		S
M, 1963–1966	−0.0193	(0.33)	0.22
M, 1975	0.0672	(0.83)	0.30
E, 1963–1966	−0.0129	(0.23)	0.21
E, 1975	0.0607	(0.75)	0.30

Table 9. Regressions of $|ln(\text{ER/EP})|$ on Constant

Sample	Constant		S
M, 1963–1966	0.1574	(3.93)	0.15
M, 1975	0.2435	(5.03)	0.18
E, 1963–1966	0.1490	(3.86)	0.14
E, 1975	0.2486	(5.49)	0.17

III. EXPLAINING DEVIATIONS FROM PPP

Algebraic Deviations

In explaning deviations from PPP, algebraic and absolute deviations are considered separately, with different sets of explanatory variables. The reason is that the corresponding sets of hypotheses cannot be mixed. Certain variables are postulated to explain *algebraic* deviations from PPP; other variables are hypothesized to influence *absolute* deviations from PPP.

Considering first the algebraic values of the forecast-error vectors, $ln(\text{ER/EP})$, there are two potential explanatory variables. The first, denoted as PR, is the ratio of productivity in the current period to productivity in the base period. The underlying proposition is best expressed initially in terms of the absolute PPP theory: the ratio of the exchange rate (price of the domestic currency in terms of foreign currency) to the foreign/domestic price level is an increasing function of the ratio of productivity in the domestic country to that abroad.[17] Re-expressing all variables in terms of indices with respect to the same base period, the hypothesis can be reformulated to pertain to the relative PPP theory: the (logarithm of the) ratio of the exchange-rate index to the foreign/domestic price-index ratio (i.e., $ln(\text{ER/EP})$) is an increasing function of the ratio of the productivity index in the domestic country to that abroad. However, the productivity index (PR) of the domestic country alone is used because of data limitations. Data on productivity in the base periods (prior to World War I) are non-uniform across countries, both conceptually and in terms of the period for which the data are available. It would be incongruous to generate an "effective" productivity measure by taking a weighted average of trading partners' productivity indices that are subject to varying base periods.

The second explanatory variable is the change in the country's terms of trade from the base period to the current period. Letting TT denote the ratio of the country's terms of trade in the current period to that in the

Table 10. Regressions of ln(ER/EP) on Explanatory Variables

No.	Sample	Constant		PR		$ln(TT)$		N	S	$\bar{R}^2$
1	M, 1963–1966	−0.30	(1.31)	0.099	(1.27)			14	0.22	0.0
2	M, 1975	−0.23	(1.09)	0.071	(1.50)			14	0.29	0.0*
3	E, 1963–1966	−0.22	(0.87)	0.077	(0.84)			14	0.21	−0.0*
4	E, 1975	−0.20	(0.89)	0.066	(1.24)			14	0.30	0.0
5	M, 1963–1966	0.10	(2.02)			−0.21	(1.32)	9	0.13	0.0
6	M, 1975	−0.35	(1.36)	0.12*	(2.11)	0.26	(0.87)	9	0.25	0.2*
7	E, 1963–1966	−0.27	(1.46)	0.12	(1.83)	0.21	(1.30)	10	0.11	0.1
8	E, 1975	−0.56	(2.62)	0.17**	(3.30)	0.62*	(2.60)	10	0.21	0.5

Notes:
*Significant at 5 percent level (one-tail test).
**Significant at 1 percent level (one-tail test).

base period, the variable used is $ln(TT)$[18] and it is expected to have a positive effect on ln(ER/EP). If a country's terms of trade improve, this in itself enhances the value of its currency. The terms-of-trade movement is a change in relative prices within the general price level that is expected to increase the exchange rate beyond PPP.

The PR variable is available for all fourteen countries in all samples, but $ln(TT)$ has missing observations. So two regressions are run for each sample, with results reported in Table 10, where $\bar{R}^2$ denotes R^2 corrected for degrees of freedom. Equations 1–4 involve PR as the sole explanatory variable, with the full number of observations. In these equations the slope coefficient is not significant at the 5 percent level. Equations 5–8 potentially have both PR and $ln(TT)$ as independent variables (but with sample size restricted by the data availability of $ln(TT)$); for each sample, the regression shown is the one that maximizes $\bar{R}^2$ (minimizes S) among the regressions involving all combinations of the explanatory variables (PR alone, $ln(TT)$ alone, both included). In Equation 6 the coefficient of PR is significant at the 5 percent level, but the presence of $ln(TT)$ reduces $\bar{R}^2$ (increases S). Dropping $ln(TT)$ and increasing the number of observations brings one to Equation 2, in which PR no longer has a significant coefficient. However, Equation 8 provides a satisfactory explanation of algebraic deviations from PPP. Both PR and $ln(TT)$ have significant coefficients with the correct sign, and the regression explains fully half the variation in ln(ER/EP) even after correcting for degrees of freedom.

Absolute Deviations

Turning to absolute deviations from PPP, $|ln$(ER/EP)$|$, there exists a larger number of potential explanatory variables. One hypothesis is that the absolute prediction error of PPP is positively related to the amount of inflation at home, $1nG$, where G (denoted in Section 1 as p_n^d) is the GDP deflator in the current relative to the base period. An alternative hypothesis involves replacing $1nG$ by $|1n(\text{EP})|$, the foreign/domestic inflation differential in absolute value.[19] The rationale for these hypotheses is that large monetary changes in economies may carry with them large structural changes and therefore large deviations from PPP.

A change in relative prices within the general price level would be another indicator of structural changes. The wholesale price index is heavily weighted with traded goods; so changes in its relationship to a general price index are a particularly suitable measure of relative-price changes for the purpose at hand. Letting WPI denote the wholesale price index in the current relative to the base period, it is expected that $|1n(\text{WPI}/G)|$ has a positive effect on $|1n(\text{ER}/\text{EP})|$.

It may be that the absolute forecast error of PPP is greater, the poorer is the quality of the data in the PPP computation. "Quality of the data" is measured by the average coverage of the ER and EP indices in the current and base periods. The hypothesis is that $|1n(\text{ER}/\text{EP})|$ is negatively related to $(C_{75} + C_o)/2$, where C denotes coverage, 75 represents the year 1975, and o is the base period.

Another hypothesis is that absolute deviations from PPP are positively affected by the change in the trade structure of the country. This change could be measured by the absolute value of the change in coverage between the base and current periods. However, the percentage change in trade structure is a superior measure, as it corrects for country differences in the coverage level of their indices. The level is defined as the average coverage in the base and current periods. Therefore $|C_{75} - C_o|/((C_{75} + C_o)/2)$ is expected to have a positive effect on $|1n(\text{ER}/\text{EP})|$.

The weight, W, of a country's main trading partner (in its ER and EP indices) is expected to have a negative effect on $|1n(\text{ER}/\text{EP})|$. The underlying hypothesis is that the absolute deviation from PPP is negatively affected by the country's trade concentration. The PPP theory should come closer to fulfilment, the greater the ties of the country to its main trading partner.

Finally, the ratio of domestic fixed investment to GDP in the current relative to the base period—this variable denoted by INV—is yet another measure of structural change in the economy (possibly as indicating changes in the real rate of interest). Therefore INV should have a positive effect on $|1n(\text{ER}/\text{EP})|$.

For each sample, three sets of regressions are run, with results reported in Table 11. The regression shown is the one that maximizes $\bar{R}^2$ (minimizes S) among the regressions involving all combinations of the explanatory variables defining the set. Equations 1–4 are based on var-

Table 11. Regressions of $|ln(\text{ER/EP})|$ on Explanatory Variables

No.	Sample	Equation	N	S	$\bar{R}^2$
1	M, 1963–1966	$0.091 + 0.024 lnG$ $(1.32) \quad (1.16)$	14	0.15	0.03
2	M, 1975	$0.18 + 0.044\|ln(\text{EP})\|$ $(2.98) \quad (1.46)$	14	0.17	0.08
3	E, 1963–1966	$0.15 - 0.33\|ln(\text{WPI}/G)\| + 0.025 lnG$ $(1.93) \quad (1.13) \qquad (1.14)$	14	0.15	−0.01
4	E, 1975	$-0.067 + 0.27W + 0.62^*\|ln(\text{WPI}/G)\|$ $(0.53) \quad (1.25) \quad (3.22)$	14	0.13	0.41
5	M, 1963–1966	$0.044 + 0.46 \dfrac{\|C_{75} - C_0\|}{\dfrac{C_{75} + C_0}{2}}$ $(0.59) \quad (1.79)$	13	0.14	0.15
6	M, 1975	$-0.040 + 0.57^*\|ln(\text{WPI}/G)\| + 0.41 \dfrac{\|C_{75} - C_0\|}{\dfrac{C_{75} + C_0}{2}}$ $(0.50) \quad (3.06) \qquad (1.75)$	13	0.13	0.53
7	E, 1963–1966	$0.17 - 0.48\|ln(\text{WPI}/G)\| + 0.033 lnG - 0.064 \dfrac{\|C_{75} - C_0\|}{\dfrac{C_{75} + C_0}{2}}$ $(1.65) \quad (1.41) \qquad (1.34) \qquad (0.25)$	13	0.15	−0.03
8	E, 1975	$-0.15 + 0.22W + 0.64^*\|ln(\text{WPI}/G)\| + 0.36 \dfrac{\|C_{75} - C_0\|}{\dfrac{C_{75} + C_0}{2}}$ $(1.12) \quad (1.03) \quad (3.25) \qquad (1.68)$	13	0.13	0.48

Note:
*Significant at 1 percent level (one-tail test).

Table 12. Bilateral Exchange-Rate Indices and Price-Index Ratios

Countries	Base Period	Variable	1913[a]	1938	1963–1966	1975
France/U.K.	1835–1844	R	1.0000	6.7346	54.35	37.75
		P	0.8110	4.0394	48.63	39.36
		ln(R/P)	0.2095	0.5112	0.1112	−0.0416
U.S./U.K.	1839	R	0.9823	0.9869	0.5643	0.4485
		P	1.0224	0.8471	0.6146	0.4398
		ln(R/P)	−0.0400	0.1527	−0.0854	0.0195
U.S./U.K.	(1839, 1844, 1849)[b]	R	0.9914	0.9960	0.5695	0.4526
		P	1.0561	0.8750	0.6348	0.4543
		ln(R/P)	−0.0632	0.1295	−0.1086	−0.0037

Notes:
R = exchange-rate index: number of units of currency of numerator country per unit of currency of denominator country.
P = price-index ratio: price index of numerator country divided by price index of denominator country.
[a] 1905–1913 for France/U.K.
[b] Three-year base period.

iables for which all fourteen observations are available: $\ln G$, $|\ln(\mathrm{EP})|$, W, and $|\ln(\mathrm{WPI}/G)|$, the last variable only for the extended 1913 samples. Equations 5–8, with thirteen observations, involve the four preceding variables together with variables where Denmark (the excluded observation) has either a missing observation ($|\ln(\mathrm{WPI}/G)|$, for the maximum-coverage samples) or a biased observation (variables involving the coverage measure—see data appendix). The third set of regressions, not shown, includes all preceding explanatory variables plus INV, for which fewer observations are available. Since INV makes a positive contribution to $\bar{R}^2$ in no case, regressions involving that variable are not shown.

Equation 6 provides the best explanation of deviations from PPP, with a $\bar{R}^2$ of over 0.50. The equation's two explanatory variables depict structural change and have the theoretically expected sign. Equations 4 and 8 also have relatively high $\bar{R}^2$; but in each case the coefficient of W has the incorrect sign. It is not surprising that deviations from PPP, whether algebraic or absolute, are more susceptible of explanation for the 1975 samples than the 1963–1966 samples. The reason is the generally larger deviations when 1975 is used as the current period (see Table 6).

IV. BILATERAL PPP COMPUTATIONS

In this section the effective-exchange-rate concept is replaced by the usual bilateral exchange rate, but in every other respect the methodol-

Table 13. Availability of National-Accounts Data

Country	European Statistics[a]/Other[b]	OECD National Accounts[c]
Austria	1913, 1924-37	1937, 1948-50[d]/1950-75
Canada	1867, 1870, 1880, 1890, 1900, 1910, 1920, 1929[e]/1929-50[f]	1950-75
Denmark	1870-1914, 1921-38	1938, 1947-50[d]/1950-75
France	1781-90, 1803-12, 1815-24, 1825-34, 1835-44, 1845-54, 1855-64, 1865-74, 1875-84, 1885-94, 1895-1904, 1905-13, 1920-24, 1925-34, 1935-38[g] 1901-13, 1920-38[h]	
Germany	1850-1913, 1925-38[j]	1938, 1947-50[d]/1950-51[i]/1951-75
Italy	1861-1938	1938, 1949-50[d]/1950-51[i]/1951-75
Japan	1905-52[l]	1938, 1947-50[d]/1950-51[k]/1951-75
Netherlands	1900-38	1952-75
Norway	1865-1938[m]	1938, 1947-50[d]/1950-51[i]/1951-75
Spain	1906-35, 1939-54	1954-75
Sweden	1861-1947	1947-50[d]/1950-75
Switzerland	1913, 1924, 1929-38	1938, 1947-50[d]/1950-51[i]/1951-75
U.K.	1830-1938	1938, 1947-50[d]/1950-52[i]/1953-60[n]/1960-75
U.S.	1839, 1844, 1849, 1854, 1859, 1869-78[o]/1869-78, 1879-88, 1889-1950[p]	1950-75

Notes and Sources:

[a] Source: Mitchell (1975).
[b] Other sources identified in footnotes.
[c] Source: OECD (1975). *National Accounts of OECD Countries*, Volume I. Earlier source issues identified in footnotes.
[d] OEEC, *Statistics of National Product and Expenditure, No. 2, 1938 and 1947 to 1955*.
[e] Firestone (1958).
[f] Statistics Canada (1976).
[g] Annual averages of periods listed.
[h] Data available at constant prices but not at current prices.
[i] 1950-68 issue.
[j] Data pertain to Germany of the era as distinct from the post-World War II Federal Republic.
[k] 1950-61 issue.
[l] Ohkawa and Rosovsky (1973).
[m] Datum at constant prices for 1930 obtained from original source: Statistisk Sentralbyra (1966).
[n] 1953-69 issue.
[o] Gallman (1966). Annual average for 1869-78 period.

ogy of the first section is retained. The objective is to examine the predictive power of the PPP theory over a lengthened time span. As Table 13 shows, only three countries possess national-accounts data that enable construction of a GDP-deflator series extending back to the first half of the nineteenth century: France, the United Kingdom, and the United States. Data availability limits the bilateral computations to the United Kingdom vis-à-vis France and the United States, respectively.

The earliest possible base period for the U.S./U.K. computation is the year 1839. Because a multi-year base period might yield more reliable results, the years 1839, 1844, and 1849 are chosen to provide an alternative, three-year discrete, base period. For the France/U.K. relationship, the earliest base period is the 1835–1844 decade. For the base periods chosen, all three countries had pegged exchange rates and convertible currencies.[20] In addition to the intervening periods (1938, 1963–1966) used above, a third such period is adopted: the end of the gold standard. For the U.S./U.K. computation, the year 1913 serves as this period. For the U.K./France relationship, the decade average 1905–1913 is used.

Table 12 presents the relevant computations: the exchange-rate index (R), price-index ratio (P), and forecast error of the PPP theory ($1n(R/P)$), calculated for the three intervening periods and the current period (1975). Over a period of more than one and one-third centuries, the forecast error of the PPP theory is barely over 4 percent for the France/U.K. exchange rate and either 2 percent or less than 1/2 of 1 percent for the U.S./U.K. rate.[21]

V. SUMMARY

In this study the predictive power of the PPP theory was tested over long time periods spanning the pre-World War I gold standard to the managed-float regime of the 1970s. A comparative-static test of the theory was devised using a general price concept, the GDP deflator, and a multilateral exchange-rate concept, that of effective exchange rates. The main results of the study are as follows:

1. In multilateral computations, the average forecast error of the theory is in the order of 5–15 percent for 1963–1966 as the terminating period, and 15–25 percent for 1975 in that role.

2. Considering bilateral computations and a longer time span, one of well over a century, the average forecast error is in the order of 10 percent and 1–4 percent for the 1963–1966 and 1975 periods, respectively.

3. The hypothesis that deviations from PPP follow a normal distribution cannot be rejected.

4. Regression analysis suggests that deviations from PPP can be explained in terms of structural changes in economies.

APPENDIX:
THE DATA

National-Accounts Data

A GDP deflator for a given country over time is obtained by creating consistent series of GDP at current and constant prices, and then dividing the one by the other. The GDP series are constructed by taking OECD, *National Accounts of OECD Countries* (1975) as the basic source, and working back in time to incorporate series published earlier, using overlapping years to generate consistent series. Table 13 provides a complete account of the data sources for each country, showing the time period for which each published source is used and the common years for which overlapping factors are computed. While OECD publications provide GDP data, other sources offer GDP, GNP, or NNP series, as the case may be. Table 13 also shows the sources for calculating the ratio of investment to GDP.

Exchange Rates

Prior to World War I. Dollar/domestic-currency mint parities are obtained largely from Bloomfield (1963). Other sources are Davis and Hughes (1960) for the United Kingdom and Bank of Japan (undated) for Japan. The US/Canada parity is cited by Gailliot (1970). The franc/pound mint parity is obtained from Morgenstern (1959). The dollar/pound exchange rate (incorporating deviations from the mint parity) during 1839–1849 is taken from Davis and Hughes (1960).

For Spain in 1906–1913, the dollar/peseta exchange rate is computed as the ratio of the dollar/pound mint parity to the peseta/pound rate (the latter obtained from *The Economist*). A similar technique is used to obtain the dollar/lira exchange rate for Italy in 1879–1881.

1935–1938. For all currencies, market exchange rates with respect to the dollar are obtained from Board of Governors (1943).

1963–1966 and 1975. Market exchange rates with respect to the dollar are taken from IMF (May 1976).

Trade Flows

Base Periods. The data source for European countries and the United Kingdom is Mitchell (1975). Statistics for Canada, Japan, and the United

States are from Urquhart and Buckley (1965), Bank of Japan (1966), and U.S. Bureau of the Census (1975), respectively.

For Denmark, total-trade figures appear to be inconsistent with the country distribution of trade. Either the former data are underestimated or the latter overestimated in the Mitchell volume. A comparison of bilateral trade between Denmark and its partner countries in the Scandinavian Monetary Union is instructive. For all the base periods (1879–1888, 1905–1913, and 1913) Danish statistics on total bilateral trade are never greater in magnitude than those of Norway and Sweden. This result suggests that the data for the country allocation of Danish trade are not overestimated, and therefore the weights of its ER and EP indices are correct. Only the coverage of the indices is incorrect, biased upward.

1975. The primary source is United Nations (1976), supplemented by IMF, *Direction of Trade*.

Productivity

Productivity is defined here as the ratio of constant-priced GDP to employment. For 1963–1966 and 1975, employment data are obtained from OECD, *Labour Force Statistics*. For the 1905–1913 period, the data on "economically active population" compiled by Deldycke, Gelders, and Limbor (1968) are used.

Wholesale Price Indices

For European countries, data through 1952 are taken from Mitchell (1975). For Canada, the United States, and Japan, the sources are Urquhart and Buckley (1965), U.S. Bureau of the Census (1975), and Bank of Japan (1966), respectively. These data are linked to series in IMF (various issues).

Terms of Trade

For European countries, data through 1952 are obtained from Kindleberger (1956). For Canada, the United States, and Japan, the sources are Urquhart and Buckley (1965), U.S. Bureau of the Census (1975), and Ohkawa and Rosovsky (1973), respectively. These data are linked to series in IMF (1979).

NOTES

1. This chapter appears in the bibliography as Officer (1980a). It is reprinted by permission of the Canadian Economics Association.
2. The only existing test of this assumption is in Officer (1978).

3. This proposition, which assumes the absence of money illusion, is well established. For references to the literature, see Officer (1976a, pp. 8-9).

4. See Officer (1978, pp. 563-64).

5. This point, which is often ignored even in the modern literature, was first made by Keynes (1930, pp. 72-74), an early proponent of Cassel's theory, who later became a critic.

6. Multilateral computations, though with a different methodology, are also made by McKinnon; but his data are confined to the post-World War II period.

7. For details, see Allen (1975, pp. 15-18) and Morgan Guaranty Trust Company (1976, p. 10).

8. Ideally, ER_{in} is the hypothetical *uniform* proportionate change in the value of currency i vis-à-vis all other currencies (all j) from period o to n that would have the same effect on country i's balance of payments as did the *actual* set of exchange-rate changes, R_{jn} for all j. This viewpoint leads Rhomberg (1976) to argue that for optimal computation of ERs, the weights should be derived from a model in which parameters portray the effects of changes in the relative values of the currencies of all other countries on each country's balance of payments. Econometric modelling of this kind can yield weights that enable construction of ERs closest in accordance with the ideal concept. However, such modelling is unfeasible for the long time span of the present study, in view of the many structural changes in the economies concerned and severe data limitations in the earlier part of the period. A trade-weighted concept of ER provides a weighting pattern inferior to one derived from a correctly specified and appropriately estimated macro-econometric model; but for a long-run study it is probably the best of the feasible alternative schemes.

9. A contrary view is offered by Gailliot (1970), who argues that 1963-1967 is without qualification a suitable time period for PPP computations.

10. A reading of Brown (1940) and Nurkse (1944), the standard works on the international monetary system in the interwar period, confirms the conclusion that no year in that period comes close to exhibiting exchange-market equilibrium. See also Yeager (1976, chapters 16-18) and Einzig (1970, chapter 20).

11. Bloomfield (1963, p. 4) lists 15 major countries as adhering to gold in 1880, and deems the worldwide gold standard to exist as of that date. Yeager (1976, p. 299) sees the origin as no earlier than the 1870s. Morgenstern (1959) chooses 1870 as the beginning date for his study, while Condliffe (1950, p. 362) considers the international gold standard as beginning in the 1870s.

12. Explanations for the smoothly functioning adjustment process under the gold standard are provided by Anderson (1949, pp. 3-7), Ellsworth (1950, pp. 338-40), Morgenstern (1959, pp. 17-21) and Yeager (1976, p. 308).

13. Two countries are included in the samples for time periods when they were not on the gold standard: Italy in 1879-1881 and Spain in 1906-1913. (The year 1905 is lost owing to data limitations.) The exchange-rate data show that both the peseta and lira were relatively stable during these floating periods, suggesting that the criterion of exchange-market stability is not seriously violated. In 1905-1913, though nominally off gold, Italy kept the exchange value of the lira close to its mint parity.

14. The coverage is almost always lower in 1975 than in the base period. A principal reason is the high expenditures on oil imports and consequent large exports to the oil-producing countries in 1975. This trade does not bias the weighting patterns, because only "relative trade" among the sample countries is relevant. Since all countries in the sample are industrial, the oil crisis of the 1970s could not have affected their *relative* trade significantly.

15. An alternative measure of the forecasting error is $(ER_t/EP_t - 1)$. It suffers from the defect that while there is no upper bound for currency overvaluation, there is a lower

bound (100 percent) for undervaluation. It is also an asymmetric measure, in the sense that $|ER_t/EP_t - 1| \neq |EP_t/ER_t - 1|$. In contrast, $ln(ER_t/EP_t)$ is unbounded in both directions, and $ln(ER_t/EP_t) = -ln(EP_t/ER_t)$.

16.   The present author escaped this practice thanks to the gentle prodding of the Managing Editor and referees.

17.   The mechanism underlying this hypothesis was developed most fully by Balassa (1964).

18.   All explanatory variables of a price nature are expressed as logarithms of current-to-base-period ratios, in conformity with the dependent variable.

19.   It is redundant to express lnG in absolute value because G is always greater than unity, i.e., the countries in the sample experienced long-run inflation rather than deflation.

20.   Only Britain was on a legal and effective gold standard. The United States was legally on a bimetallic standard; but by 1839 was effectively on a gold standard, because the U.S. relative price of gold with respect to silver was higher than the world price. France was both legally and effectively on a bimetallic standard, and in fact was the dominant bimetallic country. So, for the France/U.K. exchange market, France could be construed as a gold-standard country in the sense that the franc/pound gold parity was applicable.

21.   A possible explanation why the PPP theory performs better for these longer-run bilateral computations than for the multilateral computations is that the base periods for the bilateral computations antedate the international gold standard and so do not necessarily involve exchange-market stability. For example, Davis and Hughes (1960) provide convincing evidence that gold-point stability in the U.S./U.K. exchange market was much weaker in the earlier 1870s than afterwards. It is possible that the superior performance of PPP in the bilateral computations involves perpetuating exchange-market disequilibria.

Part V

CONCLUSIONS

Chapter XVII

Concluding Comments

"The purchasing-power-parity doctrine, incomplete though it may be, comes closer than any of its rivals to having a specific content." (Leland B. Yeager, 1976, p. 211)

The PPP theory is not the oldest theory of exchange rates; that distinction belongs to the demand-and-supply theory. Further, it isn't the newest theory; that honor belongs to the asset-market approach. PPP isn't the model that provides maximum scope for policy determination of a floating rate; the monetary theory of exchange-rate determination has that property. Yet it isn't the explanation that best permits policy-makers to excuse themselves from responsibility for the exchange value of their country's currency; that function is ideally served by the balance-of-payments theory. Finally, the PPP theory is not the approach most oriented to the current managed-float system of exchange rates; the exchange-market-pressure model takes that honor.

Nevertheless, the PPP theory has three interrelated properties that put it in the forefront of exchange-rate theories and make it the most useful and used of all such theories. First, it is a simple and intuitively appealing theory. Second, there is an inherent concreteness to the PPP approach. The ingredients of the theory are minimal and basic: price levels and exchange rates (for absolute PPP), inflation and exchange-rate changes (for relative PPP). Third, *whether or not the strict PPP theory holds,* that theory is of interest. It is useful to know *to what extent* the PPP theory is valid, for example, what proportion of relative-price changes between countries is likely to be offset by exchange-rate changes. So even if the PPP theory is invalid, one would be interested in measuring the amount of deviation from PPP. One cannot make this third claim for any other exchange-rate theory. Indeed, the abstractness of the other theories means that it is difficult even to envisage a measure of the deviation from the theory's predicted value of the exchange rate.

Whenever the economic situation involves inflation and floating exchange rates, there is a resurgence of interest in the PPP approach. The first instance of this was 16th-century Spain; the latest is the industrial market economies since the mid-1970s . While Spanish economists of the first episode developed the PPP approach, it was Gustav Cassel who refined the approach during and after World War I.

Then perhaps the most salient result of this volume is that Cassel's theory *qua* theory has stood the test of time. There is little in the current state of PPP theory that was not embodied in Cassel's writings. The failure of the theory to develop along sophisticated lines is in an important respect a favorable feature. Other models of exchange-rate determination have become increasingly complex. It is the principal virtue of the PPP approach that computations of equilibrium exchange rates can be performed "on the back of an envelope" without the need of sophisticated econometric or mathematical techniques. Such simple calculations may provide checks on the results of high-powered models that seek to explain the movement of the exchange rate or to find its equilibrium value.

It is a virtue of PPP theory to be simple; but the theory would have to be rejected if it were simple-minded. The theory does have limitations, and the many criticisms leveled at the theory over the years reflect these limitations. Crucial to survival of the PPP approach is the ability to allow scope for the imperfections noticed by critics (and by proponents). These imperfections are of three kinds. Some refer to the fact that the PPP theory, like any theory, cannot make exact predictions, that is, results are subject to random error. While the distribution of this random error is of importance in empirical work, of course; for theoretical purposes acknowledgement of the approximate nature of PPP computations suffices.

A second kind of limitation is one that can be corrected by a simple alteration or extension of the theory. For example, one way to incorporate income movements in exchange-rate determination is to let the PPP itself represent the role of income in addition to that of prices; thus, only the interpretation (and possibly the lag specification) of the theory is affected. Another approach is to include an income variable in addition to the PPP as determinants of the actual exchange rate. If the PPP remains the more important explanatory variable, the PPP theory has been amended but not eclipsed. Such techniques may be used to incorporate speculation, trade restrictions, and other influences on a floating exchange rate.

The third kind of limitation is the existence of a systematic bias in the PPP computation of the (long-run) *equilibrium* exchange rate. Fundamental alterations in the theory are required to cope with such a limitation, and the result might be a theory of the exchange rate that is no longer recognized as in the PPP tradition.

However, the existence of systematic biases need not destroy the empirical applicability of the theory. It might turn out that in practice PPP is a robust theory that predicts movements of floating exchange rates and estimates long-run equilibrium rates to a high degree of accuracy. In other words, systematic biases might exist but have only a small quantitative impact. In this respect, empirical testing of the theory for various countries and diverse time periods is essential; for a bias may show itself to be significant only in certain circumstances.

Even if a systematic bias does exist and is substantial, the PPP approach need not be abandoned; for the bias might be predictable in its effect. A relationship between the exchange rate, the PPP, and variables representing the impact of the bias may be used to determine equilibrium exchange rates, evaluate existing rates, and predict the movements of floating rates. As a *theory* such an approach is haphazard; as a practical technique, it may have value.

The renewed interest in the PPP theory in the mid-1970s involved distinct improvements in empirical investigations of the theory. A multilateral approach, involving effective exchange rates, is occasionally taken. Also, the price measures used to compute PPP are now sometimes selected with some attention paid to advantages and disadvantages of the alternative measures available. Much testing of the theories now concerns the floating exchange rates of the 1970s and beyond instead of periods in the distant past. Further, the real exchange rate, a useful summary measure, is often employed. Moreover, some researchers extend the theory's applicability by adopting an augmented-PPP approach to explain deviations of the nominal exchange rate from PPP (or the real rate from unity). Finally, one must mention the ongoing excellent work on international comparisons of income and purchasing power by Irving B. Kravis and his associates. The data developed by this group will be increasingly used by other researchers on PPP.

Yet empirical work on PPP can still be improved. Some testing of the theory continues to refer to periods in the distant past. Thomas (1973b, p. 182) seems to be alone in warning against an unqualified projection of results based on historical periods to the current situation. Considering studies of the floating exchange rates that followed World War I, he notes that expectations of a return to the old mint parities, greater flexibility of wages and prices, and a small role for government macroeconomic policy are all elements that are not present in the current situation. Hyperinflation cases, such as Germany after World War I, are another set of experiences that should not be examined from the standpoint of naive extrapolation to present circumstances.

The nature of the testing of PPP theory also requires examination. One basic test that has yet to be documented involves a comparison of the theory's forecasting ability with that of other exchange-rate models, both sophisticated and naive. Furthermore, a prerequisite for usable results from research on PPP is careful attention to the basic components of the approach. For example, the base period for relative PPP must be chosen with care. In this respect it is unfortunate that the rationale of selecting a period in which the exchange rate is in long-run equilibrium is generally ignored. In particular, no researcher has used balance-of-payments data (or apparently any quantitative data) to determine an optimal base period. Also, some authors still use the WPI, whether general or for manufactures, as the price measure for relative PPP. Such indices are particularly deficient for this purpose. A praiseworthy few, but very few, researchers adopt the optimal price measure: the GDP deflator.

Still, when all is said and done, what have we learned from the existing empirical investigations of the PPP theory? In the long run, the PPP theory tends to hold. In the very short run, however, other influences can make for substantial divergences from the strict PPP prediction.[1] Research can perhaps be most fruitful in examing the applicability of PPP to intermediate time spans—longer than month-to-month, or perhaps even quarter-to-quarter, but certainly shorter than a decade permitted for adjustment.

Irrespective of the outcome of this and other research on PPP, the theory will continue to be in the tool kit of those examining exchange rates. Gustav Cassel rescued the PPP theory from near oblivion. The tradition, simplicity, concreteness, and adaptability of the theory will keep it in the domain of economics.

NOTE

1. These are also the assessments of Kohlhagen (1978, p. 4) and Mussa (1979, pp. 22-23). The former author, however, sees the evidence for short periods as conflicting regarding the existence of significant deviations from PPP.

Bibliography

Aldrich, Mark. "Flexible Exchange Rates, Northern Expansion, and the Market for Southern Cotton: 1866-1879." *Journal of Economic History* 33(June 1973):399-416.

Aliber, Robert Z. "Speculation in the Foreign Exchanges: The European Experience, 1919-1926." *Yale Economic Essays* 2(Spring 1962):171-245.

_____. "Speculation in the Flexible Exchange Revisited." *Kyklos* 23(Fasc. 2, 1970):303-313.

_____. "Speculation in the Flexible Exchange Re-revisited—Reply." *Kyklos* 26(Fasc. 3, 1973):619-620.

_____ (1976a). "Equilibrium and Disequilibrium in the International Money Market." *Weltwirtschaftliches Archiv* 112(No. 1, 1976):73-90.

_____ (1976b). "The Firm Under Pegged and Floating Exchange Rates." *Scandinavian Journal of Economics* 78(No. 2, 1976):309-326.

_____. *Exchange Risk and Corporate International Finance.* London: Macmillan, 1978.

Aliber, Robert Z., and Clyde P. Stickney. "Accounting Measures of Foreign Exchange Exposure: The Long and Short of It." *Accounting Review* 50(January 1975):44-57.

Allen, R. G. D. *Index Numbers in Theory and Practice.* Chicago: Aldine, 1975.

Allen, William R. "Discussion." In Robert V. Eagly (ed.), *Events, Ideology and Eonomic Theory.* Detroit: Wayne State University Press, 1968, pp. 32-36, 40-43.

Amacher, Ryan C., and John S. Hodgson. "Purchasing-Power Parity Theory and Economic Reform in Yugoslavia." *Journal of Political Economy* 82(July/August 1974):809-816.

Anderson, Benjamin M. *Economics and the Public Welfare.* New York: D. Van Nostrand, 1949.

Andréadès, A. *History of the Bank of England 1640 to 1903.* London: Frank Cass, fourth edition, 1966.

Angell, James W. "Monetary Theory and Monetary Policy: Some Recent Discussions." *Quarterly Journal of Economics* 39(February 1925):267-299.

_____. *The Theory of International Prices: History, Criticism and Restatement.* Cambridge, Mass.: Harvard University Press, 1926.

Anonymous. "Is the Swedish Exchange Overvalued Abroad?" Skandinaviska Kreditaktiebolaget *Quarterly Report* (September 1921):36-37.

293

Arrow, K. J., H. B. Chenery, B. S. Minhas, and R. M. Solow. "Capital-Labor Substitution and Economic Efficiency." *Review of Economics and Statistics* 43(August 1961):225–250.

Artus, Jacques R. "Methods of Assessing the Long-run Equilibrium Value of an Exchange Rate." *Journal of International Economics* 8(May 1978):277–299.

Aukrust, Odd. "PRIM I: A Model of the Price and Income Distribution Mechanism of an Open Economy." *Review of Income and Wealth* 16(March 1970):51–78.

Australia, Commonwealth Bureau of Census and Statistics. *Official Year Book of the Commonwealth of Australia.* Canberra, various years.

———. *Pocket Compendium of Australian Statistics.* No. 53. Canberra, 1968.

Bacha, Edmar, and Lance Taylor. "Foreign Exchange Shadow Prices: A Critical Review of Current Theories." *Quarterly Journal of Economics* 85(May 1971):197–224.

Balassa, Bela. "Patterns of Industrial Growth: Comment," *American Economic Review* 51 (June 1961):394–397.

———. "The Purchasing-Power Parity Doctrine: A Reappraisal," *Journal of Political Economy* 72(December 1964):584–596.

———. "Just How Misleading Are Official Exchange Rate Conversions? A Comment." *Economic Journal* 83(December 1973):1258–67.

——— (1974a). "Purchasing Power Parity and Factor Price Equalization: Comment." *Kyklos* 27(Fasc. 4, 1974):879–883.

——— (1974b). "The Rule of Four-Ninths: A Rejoinder." *Economic Journal* 84(September 1974):609–614.

Balassa, Bela, and Daniel M. Schydlowsky. "Effective Tariffs, Domestic Cost of Foreign Exchange, and the Equilibrium Exchange Rate." *Journal of Political Economy* 76(May/June 1968):348–360.

Bank of Japan. *Hundred-Year Statistics of the Japanese Economy.* 1966.

———. *Supplement to Hundred-Year Statistics of the Japanese Economy: English Translation of Explanatory Notes.* Undated.

Barlow, Robin. "A Test of Alternative Methods of Making GNP Comparisons." *Economic Journal* 87(September 1977):450–459.

Batchelor, R. A. "Sterling Exchange Rates 1951–1976: A Casselian Analysis." *National Institute Economic Review* 81(August 1977):45–66.

Basevi, Giorgio, and Paul De Grauwe. "Vicious and Virtuous Circles: A Theoretical Analysis and a Policy Proposal for Managing Exchange Rates." *European Economic Review* 10(December 1977):277–301.

Baumol, William J. "Macroeconomics of Unbalanced Growth: The Anatomy of Urban Crisis." *American Economic Review* 57(June 1967):415–426.

———. "Macroeconomics of Unbalanced Growth: Comment." *American Economic Review* 58(September 1968):896–897.

———. "Comment on the Comment." *American Economic Review* 59(September 1969):632.

———. "Macroeconomics of Unbalanced Growth: Reply." *American Economic Review* 62(March 1972):150.

Beckerman, Wilfred. *International Comparisons of Real Incomes.* Paris: Organisation for Economic Co-operation and Development, 1966.

Berkman, Neil G. "A Rational View of Rational Expectations." *New England Economic Review* (January/February 1980):18–29.

Bhagwati, Jagdish. *Trade, Tariffs and Growth.* Cambridge, Mass.: The M.I.T. Press, 1969.

Bilson, John F. O. (1978a). "Rational Expectations and the Exchange Rate." In Jacob A. Frenkel and Harry G. Johnson (eds.), *The Economics of Exchange Rates: Selected Studies.* Reading, Mass.: Addison-Wesley, 1978, pp. 75–96.

_____ (1978b). "The Monetary Approach to the Exchange Rate: Some Empirical Evidence." International Monetary Fund *Staff Papers* 25(March 1978):48–75.

Birch, J. W., and C. A. Cramer. "Macroeconomics of Unbalanced Growth: Comment." *American Economic Review* 58(September 1968):893–896.

Blake, William. *Observations on the Principles Which Regulate the Course of Exchange.* London: Edmund Lloyd, 1810.

Bloomfield, Arthur I. "Foreign Exchange Rate Theory and Policy." In Seymour E. Harris (ed.), *The New Economics.* New York: Alfred A. Knopf, 1947, pp. 293–314.

_____. *Short-term Capital Movements Under the Pre-1914 Gold Standard.* Princeton Studies in International Finance No. 11. Princeton, N.J.: International Finance Section, Princeton University, 1963.

Board of Governors of the Federal Reserve System. *Banking and Monetary Statistics 1914–1941.* Washington, D.C., 1943.

Bond, M. E., and D. P. Haroz. "Is the Dollar Overvalued? A Test of a Past Devaluation." *Review of Business and Economic Research* 11(Spring 1976):1–14.

Bresciani-Turroni, Constantino. "The 'Purchasing Power Parity' Doctrine." *L'Egypte Contemporaine* 25(1934):433–464.

_____. *The Economics of Inflation.* London: George Allen & Unwin, 1937.

Brillembourg, Arturo. "Purchasing Power Parity and the Balance of Payments: Some Empirical Evidence." International Monetary Fund *Staff Papers* 24(March 1977):77–99.

Brisman, Sven. "Some Reflections on the Theory of Foreign Exchange." In *Economic Essays in Honour of Gustav Cassel*, pp. 69–74. London: George Allen & Unwin, 1933.

Brown, William Adams, Jr. *The International Gold Standard Reinterpreted, 1914–1934.* New York: National Bureau of Economic Research, 1940.

Bunting, Frederick H. "The Purchasing Power Parity Theory Reexamined." *Southern Economic Journal* 5(January 1939):282–301.

Burns, A. R. *Money and Monetary Policy in Early Times.* London: Kegan, Paul, Trench, Trubner, 1927.

Cannan, Edwin. "Introduction." In *The Paper Pound of 1797–1821. A Reprint of the Bullion Report*, pp. vii–xlix. London: P. S. King & Son, second edition, 1925.

Cassel, Gustav (1916a). "The Present Situation of the Foreign Exchanges." *Economic Journal* 26(March 1916):62–65.

_____ (1916b). "The Present Situation of the Foreign Exchanges." *Economic Journal* 26 (September 1916):319–323.

_____ (1916c). *Germany's Economic Power of Resistance.* New York: Jackson, 1916.

_____. "The Depreciation of Gold." *Economic Journal* 27(September 1917):346–354.

_____. "Abnormal Deviations in International Exchanges." *Economic Journal* 28(December 1918):413–415.

_____. "The Depreciation of the German Mark." *Economic Journal* 29(December 1919):492–496.

_____ (1920a). "Further Observations on the World's Monetary Problem." *Economic Journal* 30(March 1920):39–45.

_____ (1920b). "Some Leading Propositions for an International Discussion of the World's Monetary Problem." *Annals of the American Academy* 89(May 1920):259–267.

_____. *The World's Monetary Problems.* London: Constable, 1921.

_____. *Money and Foreign Exchange After 1914.* London: Constable, 1922.

_____ (1923a). "The Problem of the Undervalued Currencies." Skandinaviska Kreditaktiebolaget *Quarterly Report* (January 1923):1–5.

———— (1923b). "The Restoration of the Gold Standard." *Economica* 3(November 1923):171–185.

————. "The Purchasing-Power Parity." Skandinaviska Kreditaktiebolaget *Quarterly Report* (October 1924):68–70.

———— (1925a). *Fundamental Thoughts in Economics.* New York: Harcourt, Brace, 1925.

———— (1925b). "Sweden's Experiences of the Gold Standard." Skandinaviska Kreditaktiebolaget *Quarterly Report* (January 1925):5–9.

———— (1925c). "Rates of Exchange and Purchasing-Power Parity." Skandinaviska Kreditaktiebolaget *Quarterly Report* (April 1925):17–21.

———— (1925d). "Some Recent Experiences of Monetary Policy." Skandinaviska Kreditaktiebolaget *Quarterly Report* (October 1925):55–58.

———— (1925e). "The Restoration of Gold as a Universal Monetary Standard." In *European Currency and Finance*, pp. 205–206. By John Parke Young. Commission of Gold and Silver Inquiry, United States Senate, Foreign Currency and Exchange Investigation, Serial 9, Volume I. Washington: Government Printing Office, 1925.

————. "Exchanges, Foreign." In *Encyclopedia Britannica.* Supplementary Volume I, 13th edition, 1926, pp. 1086–1089.

———— (1928a). *Post-War Monetary Stabilization.* New York: Columbia University Press, 1928.

———— (1928b). "The International Movements of Capital." In *Foreign Investments.* Chicago: University of Chicago Press, 1928, pp. 1–93.

———— (1928c). "The Treatment of Price Problems." *Economic Journal* 38(December 1928):589–592.

———— (1932a). *The Crisis in the World's Monetary System.* Oxford: Oxford University Press, 1932.

———— (1932b). *The Theory of Social Economy.* New York: Harcourt, Brace, revised edition, 1932.

————. *The Downfall of the Gold Standard.* Oxford: Oxford University Press, 1936.

Caves, Richard E., and Ronald W. Jones. *World Trade and Payments: An Introduction.* Boston: Little Brown, 1973.

Chacholiades, Miltiades. *International Monetary Theory and Policy.* New York: McGraw-Hill, 1978.

Christiernin, Pehr Niclas. *Summary of Lectures on the High Price of Foreign Exchange in Sweden.* Stockholm: Tryckt hos Directör Lars Salvius, 1761. Printed in English in *The Swedish Bullionist Controversy*, pp. 41–99, By Robert V. Eagly. Philadelphia: American Philosophical Society, 1971.

Clague, Christopher, and Vito Tanzi. "Human Capital, Natural Resources and the Purchasing-Power Parity Doctrine: Some Empirical Results." *Economia Internazionale* 25(February 1972):3–18.

Commission of the European Communities. *Inflation and Exchange Rates: Evidence and Guidelines for the European Community.* OPTICA REPORT 1976. Brussels, 1977.

Condliffe, J. B. *The Commerce of Nations.* New York: W. W. Norton, 1950.

Connolly, Michael, and José Dantas da Silveira. "Exchange Market Pressure in Postwar Brazil: An Application of the Girton-Roper Monetary Model." *American Economic Review* 69(June 1979):448–454.

Council on Prices, Productivity and Incomes. *First Report.* London: Her Majesty's Stationery Office, 1958.

Cournot, Augustin. *Recherches sur les principes mathématiques de la théorie des richesse.* Paris: L. Hachette, 1838. Printed in English as *Researches into the Mathematical Principles of the Theory of Wealth.* New York: The Macmillan Company, 1927.

Crump, Norman. "The New York Exchange: A Reply to Professor Cassel." *Journal of the Royal Statistical Society* 88(May 1925):428–432.

Culbertson, William Patton, Jr. "Purchasing Power Parity and Black-Market Exchange Rates." *Economic Inquiry* 13(June 1975):287–296.

David, Paul A. "Just How Misleading Are Official Exchange Rate Conversions?" *Economic Journal* 82(September 1972):979–990.

_____. "A Reply to Professor Balassa." *Economic Journal* 83(December 1973):1267–1276.

Davis, L. E., and J. R. T. Hughes. "A Dollar-Sterling Exchange, 1803–1895." *Economic History Review* 13(August 1960):52–78.

Delahaut, J. P., and E. S. Kirschen. "Les revenus nationaux du monde non communiste." *Cahiers Economiques de Bruxelles*, No. 10 (April 1961):145–175.

Deldycke, T., H. Gelders, and J.-M. Limbor. *The Working Population and Its Structure.* Brussels: l'Institut de Sociologie de l'Université Libre de Bruxelles, 1968.

De Roover, Raymond. *Money, Banking and Credit in Mediaeval Bruges.* Cambridge, Mass.: The Mediaeval Academy of America, 1948.

de Vries, Margaret G. "Exchange Depreciation in Developing Countries." International Monetary Fund *Staff Papers* 15(November 1968):560–578.

Dino, Richard N. *An Econometric Test of the Purchasing Power Parity Theory: Canada 1870–1975.* Unpublished Ph.D. dissertation, State University of New York at Buffalo, 1976.

Dornbusch, Rudiger. "Monetary Policy under Exchange-Rate Flexibility." In *Managed Exchange-Rate Flexibility: The Recent Experience.* Federal Reserve Bank of Boston, 1978, pp. 90–122.

_____. "Issues in International Finance: Who or What Controls the Dollar?" *Data Resources World Economic Bulletin* (Spring 1979):96–111.

_____. "Exchange Rate Economics: Where Do We Stand?" *Brookings Papers on Economic Activity* (No. 1, 1980):143–185.

Dornbusch, Rudiger, and Dwight Jaffee. "Purchasing Power Parity and Exchange Rate Problems: Introduction." *Journal of International Economics* 8(May 1978):157–161.

Dornbusch, Rudiger, and Paul Krugman. "Flexible Exchange Rates in the Short Run." *Brookings Papers on Economic Activity* (No. 3, 1976):537–575.

Duffy, Gunter, and Ian H. Giddy. "Forecasting Exchange Rates in a Floating World." *Euromoney* (November 1975):28–35.

Dupriez, Leon H. "Postwar Exchange-Rate Parities: Comment." *Quarterly Journal of Economics* 60(February 1946):299–308.

Eagly, Robert V. "Money, Employment and Prices: A Swedish View, 1761." *Quarterly Journal of Economics* 77(November 1963):626–636.

_____. "The Swedish and English Bullionist Controversies." In Robert V. Eagly (ed.), *Events, Ideology and Economic Theory.* Detroit: Wayne State University Press, 1968, pp. 13–31.

_____. "Part One: Introductory Essay." In Robert V. Eagly (ed.), *The Swedish Bullionist Controversy.* Philadelphia: American Philosophical Society, 1971, pp. 1–37.

Economic Commission for Latin America. "The Measurement of Latin American Real Income in U.S. Dollars." *Economic Bulletin for Latin America* 12(October 1967):107–142.

Economics Department, First National City Bank. "Purchasing Power: A Polestar for Drifting Exchange Rates." First National City Bank *Monthly Economic Letter* (November 1973):13–15.

The Economist. London, various issues.

Einzig, Paul. *A Dynamic Theory of Forward Exchange.* London: Macmillan, 1962.

———. *The History of Foreign Exchange*. London: Macmillan, second edition, 1970.

Ellis, Howard S. *German Monetary Theory, 1905-1933*. Cambridge, Mass.: Harvard University Press, 1934.

———. "The Equilibrium Rate of Exchange." In *Explorations in Economics*, New York: McGraw-Hill, 1936, pp. 26-34.

Ellsworth, P. T. *International Economics*. New York: Macmillan, 1938.

———. *The International Economy*. New York: Macmillan, 1950.

Evelyn, Sir George Shuckburgh. "An Account of Some Endeavours to Ascertain a Standard of Weight and Measure." *Philosophical Transactions of the Royal Society of London* (Part I, 1798):133-182.

Farag, Attiat A., and David J. Ott. "Exchange Rate Determination under Fluctuating Exchange Rates: Some Empirical Evidence." In J. Carter Murphy (ed.), *Money in the International Order*. Dallas: Southern Methodist University Press, 1964, pp. 84-105.

Fetter, Frank Whitson. "Introduction." In *The Irish Pound 1797-1826*. Evanston, Ill.: Northwestern University Press, 1955, pp. 7-62.

———. "Introduction." In Frank Whitson Fetter (ed.), *The Economic Writings of Francis Horner*. London: London School of Economics and Political Science, 1957, pp. 1-22.

———. *Development of British Monetary Orthodoxy 1797-1875*. Cambridge, Mass.: Harvard University Press, 1965.

Firestone, O. J. *Canada's Economic Development 1867-1953*. London: Bowes & Bowes, 1958.

Fisher, Irving. *The Rate of Interest*. New York: Macmillan, 1907.

———. *The Theory of Interest*. New York: Macmillan, 1930.

Floyd, John E. "The Overvaluation of the Dollar: A Note on the International Price Mechanism." *American Economic Review* 55(March 1965):95-107.

Flux, A. W. *The Foreign Exchanges*. London: P. S. King, 1924.

Foster, John Leslie. *An Essay on the Principle of Commercial Exchanges*. London: J. Hatchard, 1804.

Frenkel, Jacob A. "A Monetary Approach to the Exchange Rate: Doctrinal Aspects and Empirical Evidence." *Scandinavian Journal of Economics* 78(No. 2, 1976):200-224.

———. "Purchasing Power Parity: Doctrinal Perspective and Evidence from the 1920s." *Journal of International Economics* 8(May 1978):169-191.

———. "Exchange Rates, Prices, and Money: Lessons from the 1920's." *American Economic Review* 70(May 1980):235-242.

———. "The Collapse of Purchasing Power Parities During the 1970's." *European Economic Review* 15(March 1981):1-21.

Frenkel, Jacob A., and Michael L. Mussa. "The Efficiency of Foreign Exchange Markets and Measures of Turbulence." *American Economic Review* 70(May 1980):374-381.

Friedman, Milton, and Anna Jacobson Schwartz. *A Monetary History of the United States, 1867-1960*. Princeton: Princeton University Press, 1963.

Fry, Maxwell J. "A Monetary Approach to Afghanistan's Flexible Exchange Rate." *Journal of Money, Credit and Banking* 8(May 1976):219-225.

Furniss, Edgar S. *Foreign Exchange*. Boston: Houghton Mifflin, 1922.

Gailliot, Henry J. "Purchasing Power Parity as an Explanation of Long-Term Changes in Exchange Rates." *Journal of Money, Credit and Banking* 2(August 1970):348-357.

Gallman, Robert E. "Gross National Product in the United States, 1834-1909." In *Output, Employment, and Productivity in the United States After 1800*. New York: Columbia University Press, 1966, pp. 3-76.

Gandolfo, Giancarlo. "The Equilibrium Exchange Rate: Theory and Empirical Evidence." In Marshall Sarnat and Giorgio P. Szegö (eds.), *International Finance and Trade*, Volume 1. Cambridge, Mass.: Ballinger, 1979, pp. 99-130.

Garnsey, Morris E. "Postwar Exchange-Rate Parities." *Quarterly Journal of Economics* 60 (November 1945):113-135.

———. "Reply." *Quarterly Journal of Economics* 60(August 1946):624-630.

Germany, Federal Republic of, Statistisches Bundesamt. *Preise, Löhne, Wirtschaftsrechungen, Reiche 10: Inernationaler Vergleich der Preise für die Lebenshaltung.* Stuttgart, various issues.

———. *Statistisches Jahrbuch für die Bundesrepublik Deutschland.* Various issues.

———. *Wirtschaft und Statistik.* Various issues.

Genberg, Hans. "Purchasing Power Parity under Fixed and Flexible Exchange Rates." *Journal of International Economics* 8(May 1978):247-276.

Gibbon, Edward. *The History of the Decline and Fall of the Roman Empire.* Volume I. Edited by J. B. Bury. London: Methuen, 1900.

Giddy, Ian H. "An Integrated Theory of Exchange Rate Equilibrium." *Journal of Financial and Quantitative Analysis* 11(December 1976):883-892.

Gilbert, Milton, and associates. *Comparative National Products and Price Levels.* Paris: Organisation for European Economic Co-operation, 1958.

Gilbert, Milton, and Irving B. Kravis. *An International Comparison of National Products and the Purchasing Power of Currencies.* Paris: Organisation for European Economic Co-operation, 1954.

Girton, Lance, and Dan Roper. "The Evolution of Exchange Rate Policy." In Bluford H. Putnam and D. Sykes Wilford (eds.), *The Monetary Approach to International Adjustment.* New York: Praeger, 1978, pp. 215-228.

Goldstein, Henry N. "Floating Exchange Rates and Modified Purchasing Power Parity: Evidence from Recent Experience Using an Index of Effective Exchange Rates." In *Proceedings of 1978 West Coast Academic/Federal Reserve Economic Research Seminar.* Federal Reserve Bank of San Francisco, 1979, pp. 166-183.

Goldstein, Morris, Mohsin S. Khan, and Lawrence H. Officer. "Prices of Tradable and Nontradable Goods in the Demand for Total Imports." *Review of Economics and Statistics* 62(May 1980):190-199.

Goldstein, Morris, and Lawrence H. Officer. "New Measures of Prices and Productivity for Tradable and Nontradable Goods." *Review of Income and Wealth* 25(December 1979):413-427.

Goodman, Stephen H. "Foreign Exchange Rate Forecasting Techniques: Implications for Business and Policy." *Journal of Finance* 34(May 1979): 415-427.

Goschen, Viscount. *The Theory of the Foreign Exchanges.* London: Isaac Pitman & Sons, fourth edition, 1932. Reprint of third edition, 1864.

Graham, Frank D. "International Trade under Depreciated Paper: The United States, 1862-79." *Quarterly Journal of Economics* 36(February 1922):220-273.

———. *Exchange, Prices, and Production in Hyper-Inflation: Germany, 1920-1923.* Princeton: Princeton University Press, 1930.

Gregory, T. E. *Foreign Exchange Before, During and After the War.* London: Oxford University Press, 1925.

———. *The First Year of the Gold Standard.* London: Ernest Benn, 1926.

Grice-Hutchinson, Marjorie. *The School of Salamanca.* Oxford: The Clarendon Press, 1952.

———. *Early Economic Thought in Spain 1177-1740.* London: George Allen & Unwin, 1978.

Grunwald, Joseph, and Jorge Salazar-Carrillo. "Economic Integration, Rates of Exchange, and Value Comparisons in Latin America." In D. J. Daly (ed.), *International Comparisons of Prices and Output.* New York: Columbia University Press, 1972, pp. 227-280.

Gudin, Eugenio, and Jorge Kingston. "The Equilibrium Exchange Rate of the Cruzeiro." *Economia Internazionale* 4(February 1951):60-81.

Gupta, Suraj B. "Some Tests of the International Comparisons of Factor Efficiency with the CES Production Function." *Review of Economics and Statistics* 50(November 1968):470-476.

Haberler, Gottfried. *The Theory of International Trade.* London: William Hodge, 1936.

———— (1944a). "Currency Depreciation and the International Monetary Fund." *Review of Economic Statistics* 26(November 1944):178-181.

———— (1944b). "Some Comments on Professor Hansen's Note." *Review of Economic Statistics* 26 (November 1944):191-193.

————. "The Choice of Exchange Rates After the War." *American Economic Review* 35(June 1945):308-318.

————. "Comments on 'National Central Banking and the International Economy.' " In *International Monetary Policies.* Postwar Economic Studies, No. 7. Washington: Board of Governors of the Federal Reserve System, 1947, pp. 82-102.

————. *A Survey of International Trade Theory.* Special Papers in International Economics, No. 1. International Finance Section, Princeton University, revised edition, 1961.

————. "International Aspects of U.S. Inflation." In *A New Look at Inflation: Economic Policy in the Early 1970s.* Washington, D.C.: American Enterprise Institute for Public Policy Research, 1973, pp. 79-105.

————. "Inflation as a Worldwide Phenomenon—An Overview." In David I. Meiselman and Arthur B. Laffer (eds.), *The Phenomenon of Worldwide Inflation.* Washington, D.C.: American Enterprise Institute for Public Policy Research, 1975, pp. 13-25.

————. "Some Currently Suggested Explanations and Cures for Inflation." In Karl Brunner and Allan H. Meltzer (eds.), *Institutional Arrangements and the Inflation Problem.* Carnegie-Rochester Conference Series on Public Policy, Volume 3. Amsterdam: North-Holland Publishing Company, 1976, pp. 143-177.

Hagen, Everett E. "Comment." In *Problems in the International Comparsion of Economic Accounts.* Princeton: Princeton University Press, 1957, pp. 377-388.

————. "Some Facts About Income Levels and Economic Growth." *Review of Economics and Statistics* 42(February 1960):62-67.

Hansen, Alvin H. "A Brief Note on 'Fundamental Disequilibrium.' " *Review of Economic Statistics* 26(November 1944):182-184.

Harris, S. E. *The Assignats.* Cambridge, Mass.: Harvard University Press, 1930.

————. "Measures of Currency Overvaluation and Stabilization." In *Explorations in Economics.* New York: McGraw-Hill, 1936, pp. 35-45.

Harrod, R. F. *International Economics.* London: Nisbet, 1939.

Haugh, Larry D. "Checking the Independence of Two Covariance Stationary Time Series: A Univariate Residual Cross-Correlation Approach." *Journal of the American Statistical Association* 71(June 1976):378-385.

Hawtrey, R. G. *Currency and Credit.* London: Longmans, Green, 1950.

Hayek, F. A. V. "Introduction." In Henry Thornton, *An Enquiry into the Nature and Effects of the Paper Credit of Great Britain.* Edited by F. A. v. Hayek. New York: Farrar & Rinehart, 1939, pp. 11-63.

Heckscher, Eli F. "Sweden in the World War, Part III. Monetary History, 1914- 1925, in Its Relations to Foreign Trade and Shipping." In Eli F. Heckscher and others, *Sweden, Norway, Denmark and Iceland in the World War.* New Haven: Yale University Press, 1930, pp. 125-277.

Hekman, Christine Ries. *Structural Change and Purchasing Power Parity.* Unpublished Ph.D. dissertation, University of Chicago, 1977.

Helliwell, John F. "Policy Modeling of Foreign Exchange Rates." *Journal of Policy Modeling* 1(September 1979):425-444.

Hicks, J. R. *Essays in World Economics*. London: Oxford University Press, 1959.

Hodgson, John S. "An Analysis of Floating Exchange Rates: The Dollar-Sterling Rate, 1919-1925." *Southern Economic Journal* 39(October 1972):249-257.

Hodgson, John S., and Patricia Phelps. "The Distributed Impact of Price-Level Variation on Floating Exchange Rates." *Review of Economics and Statistics* 57(February 1975):58-64.

Hollander, Jacob H. "The Development of the Theory of Money from Adam Smith to David Ricardo." *Quarterly Journal of Economics* 25(May 1911):429-470.

Holmes, James M. (1967a). *An Econometric Test of Some Modern International Trade Theories: Canada, 1870-1960*. Institute for Research in the Behavioral, Economic, and Management Sciences. Herman C. Krannert Graduate School of Industrial Administration. Purdue University. Lafayette, Indiana, April 1967.

_____ (1967b). "The Purchasing-Power-Parity Theory: In Defense of Gustav Cassel as a Modern Theorist." *Journal of Political Economy* 75(October 1967):686-695.

Holzman, Franklyn D. (1968a). "The Ruble Exchange Rate and Soviet Foreign Trade Pricing Policies, 1929-1961." *American Economic Review* 58(September 1968):803-825.

_____ (1968b). "Soviet Central Planning and Its Impact on Foreign Trade Behavior and Adjustment Mechanisms." In Alan A. Brown and Egon Neuberger (eds.), *International Trade and Central Planning: An Analysis of Economic Interactions*. Berkeley and Los Angeles: University of California Press, 1968, pp. 280-305.

Horner, Francis. Review of *An Inquiry into the Nature and Effects of the Paper Credit of Great Britain*, by Henry Thornton. *Edinburgh Review* 1(October 1802), pp. 172-201. Reprinted in *The Economic Writings of Francis Horner*, pp. 28-56. Edited by Frank Whitson Fetter. London: London School of Economics and Political Science, 1957.

Houthakker, Hendrik S. (1962a). "Exchange Rate Adjustment." In *Factors Affecting the United States Balance of Payments*, pp. 287-304. Compilation of studies prepared for the Subcommittee on International Exchange and Payments, Joint Economic Committee, 87th Congress, 2nd Session, Washington, D.C.: U.S. Government Printing Office, 1962.

_____ (1962b). "Should We Devalue the Dollar" *Challenge* 11(October 1962):10-12.

_____. "Problems of International Finance." *Agricultural Policy Review* 3(July/September 1963):12-13.

_____. "Purchasing Power Parity as an Approximation to the Equilibrium Exchange Ratio." *Economics Letters* 1(No. 1, 1978):71-75.

Hsiao, Cheng (1978a). *Autoregressive Modelling of Canadian Money and Income Data*. Working Paper No. 7812. Toronto: Institute for Policy Analysis, University of Toronto, 1978.

_____ (1978b). *Autoregressive Modelling and Money-Income Causality Detection*. Technical Report No. 262. Palo Alto: Institute for Mathematical Studies in the Social Sciences, Stanford University, 1978.

Hulsman-Vejsová, Marie. "Misleading Official Exchange-Rate Conversions." *Economic Journal* 85(March 1975):140-147.

Hume, David. *Essays* (1742). Oxford: Oxford University Press, 1963.

Humphrey, Thomas M. "The Monetary Approach to Exchange Rates: Its Historical Evolution and Role in Policy Debates." In Bluford H. Putnam and D. Sykes Wilford (eds.), *The Monetary Approach to International Adjustment*. New York: Praeger, 1978, pp. 147-161.

_____. "The Purchasing Power Parity Doctrine." *Federal Reserve Bank of Richmond Economic Review* 65(May/June 1979):3-13.

————. "Bullionists' Exchange Rate Doctrines and Current Policy Debates." *Federal Reserve Bank of Richmond Economic Review* 66(January/February 1980):19–22.

Ingram, James C. "The Canadian Exchange Rate, 1950–57." *Southern Economic Journal* 26(January 1960):207–218.

International Labour Office. *Bulletin of Labour Statistics.* Various issues.

————. *Yearbook of Labour Statistics.* 1962 and other issues.

International Monetary Fund. *Direction of Trade, Annual 1970–76.* 1977.

———— (IMF). *International Financial Statistics.* Various issues and data tape.

————. *International Financial Statistics.* 1977 Supplement.

Isard, Peter. *Exchange-Rate Determination: A Survey of Popular Views and Recent Models.* Princeton Studies in International Finance No. 42. International Finance Section, Princeton University, 1978.

Isenman, Paul. *Inter-Country Comparison of "Real" (PPP) Incomes: Revised Estimates and Unresolved Questions.* World Bank Staff Working Paper No. 358. Washington, D.C.: The World Bank, 1979.

Jacque, Laurent L. *Management of Foreign Exchange Risk.* Lexington, Massachusetts: D. C. Heath, 1978.

Johnson, Harry G. "International Trade: I. Theory." In *International Encyclopedia of the Social Sciences,* Volume 8, pp. 83–96. New York, Macmillan & The Free Press, 1968.

————. "Secular Inflation and the International Monetary System." *Journal of Money, Credit and Banking* 5(February 1973, Part 2):509–519.

Johnson, Paul R. "Balance of Payments 'Pressure': The Colombian Case." *Southern Economic Journal* 37(October 1970):163–173.

Johnston, J. *Econometric Methods.* New York: McGraw-Hill, 1972.

Kalamotousakis, George J. "Exchange Rates and Prices: The Historical Evidence." *Journal of International Economics* 8(May 1978):163–167.

Katano, Hikoji. "Econometric Determination of Foreign Exchange Rate of Japan for 1926–1935." *Kobe Economic and Business Review* 3(1956):9–25.

————. "Reconstruction of the Theory of Purchasing Power Parity." *Kobe Economic and Business Review* 4(1957):125–148.

Kato, Hirotaka. "Statistical Analysis of the Gap between Consumer Price and Wholesale Price Movements in Japan, 1960–1964." *Sho-Kei Ronso* 2(No. 4, 1967):1–25.

Katseli-Papaefstratiou, Louka T. *The Reemergence of the Purchasing Power Parity Doctrine in the 1970s.* Special Papers in International Economics No. 13. International Finance Section, Princeton University, 1979.

Kawai, Masahiro. "Exchange Rate—Price Causality in the Recent Floating Period." In David Bigman and Teizo Taya (eds.), *The Functioning of Floating Exchange Rates.* Cambridge, Mass. Ballinger, 1980, pp. 197–219.

Keleher, Robert E. "Of Money and Prices: Some Historical Perspectives." In Bluford H. Putnam and D. Sykes Wilford (eds), *The Monetary Approach to International Adjustment.* New York: Praeger, 1978, pp. 19–48.

Kemp, Donald S. "The U.S. Dollar in International Markets: Mid-1970 to Mid-1976." *Federal Reserve Bank of St. Louis Review* 58(August 1976):7–14.

Keren, Michael. "Macroeconomics of Unbalanced Growth: Comment." *American Economic Review* 62(March 1972):149.

Kern, David. "Inflation Implications in Foreign Exchange Rate Forecasting." *Euromoney* (April 1976):62–69.

Kershaw, Joseph A. "Postwar Brazilian Economic Problems." *American Economic Review* 38(June 1948):328–340.

Keynes, John Maynard. "Official Figures Relating to Inflation." *Economic Journal* 29 (December 1919):504–506.

_____. *A Tract on Monetary Reform.* London: Macmillan, 1923.

_____. *The Economic Consequences of Mr. Churchill.* London: L. and V. Woolf, 1925. Reprinted in *Essays in Persuasion,* pp. 244–270. New York: Harcourt Brace, 1932.

_____. "The Stabilisation of the Franc." *The Nation and Athenaeum* (June 30, 1928). Reprinted in *Essays in Persuasion,* pp. 113–117. New York: Harcourt, Brace, 1932.

_____. *A Treatise on Money.* Volume I. London: Macmillan, 1930.

_____. "The Future of the Foreign Exchanges." Lloyds Bank Limited *Monthly Review* 6(October 1935):527–535.

Kindahl, James K. "Economic Factors in Specie Resumption: The United States, 1865–79." *Journal of Political Economy* 69(February 1961):30–48.

Kindleberger, Charles P. *The Terms of Trade: A European Case Study.* New York: The Technology Press and John Wiley, 1956.

_____. "Measuring Equilibrium in the Balance of Payments." *Journal of Political Economy* 77(November/December 1969):873–891.

_____. *International Economics.* Homewood, Ill.: Richard D. Irwin, fifth edition, 1973.

King, David T. "The Performance of Exchange Rates in the Recent Period of Floating: Exchange Rates and Relative Rates of Inflation." *Southern Economic Journal* 43(April 1977):1582–1587.

Kohlhagen, Steven W. *The Behavior of Foreign Exchange Markets—A Critical Survey of the Empirical Literature.* Monograph Series in Finance and Economics. Monograph 1978-3. Solomon Brothers Center for the Study of Financial Institutions, New York University, 1978.

Komiya, Ryutaro, and Yoshio Suzuki. "Inflation in Japan." In Lawrence B. Krause and Walter S. Salant (eds.), *Worldwide Inflation: Theory and Recent Experience.* Washington, D.C.: The Brookings Institution, 1977, pp. 303–348.

Kravis, Irving B. "A Survey of International Comparisons of Productivity." *Economic Journal* 86(March 1976):1–44.

Kravis, Irving B., and Michael W. S. Davenport. "The Political Arithmetic of International Burden-Sharing." *Journal of Political Economy* 71(August 1963):309–330.

Kravis, Irving, B., Zoltan Kennessey, Alan Heston, and Robert Summers. *A System of International Comparisons of Gross Product and Purchasing Power.* Baltimore: Johns Hopkins University Press, 1975.

Kravis, Irving B., and Robert E. Lipsey. "Price Behavior in the Light of Balance of Payments Theories." *Journal of International Economics* 8(May 1978):193–246.

Kravis, Irving B., Alan Heston, and Robert Summers (1978a). *International Comparisons of Real Product and Purchasing Power.* Baltimore: Johns Hopkins University Press, 1978.

Kravis, Irving B., Alan W. Heston, and Robert Summers (1978b). "Real GDP *Per Capita* for More Than One Hundred Countries." *Economic Journal* 88(June 1978):215–242.

Krugman, Paul R. "Purchasing Power Parity and Exchange Rates: Another Look at the Evidence." *Journal of International Economics* 8(August 1978):397–407.

Launhardt, Wilhelm. *Mark, Rubel und Rupie.* Berlin: Ernst & Korn, 1894.

League of Nations, *Monetary Review.* Money and Banking, 1935/36, Volume I. Geneva, 1936.

Lee, Moon H. *Purchasing Power Parity.* New York: Marcel Dekker, 1976.

Lester, Richard A. *Monetary Experiments.* Princeton: Princeton University Press, 1939.

Levich, Richard M. *The International Money Market.* Greenwich, Connecticut: JAI Press, 1979.

Lutz, F. A. *The Problem of International Economic Equilibrium*. Amsterdam: North-Holland, 1966.

Machlup, Fritz. *International Payments, Debts, and Gold*. New York: Charles Scribner's Sons, 1964.

Maddison, Angus. "Comparative Productivity Levels in the Developed Countries." Banca Nazionale del Lavoro *Quarterly Reivew* (December 1967):295–315.

Malynes, Gerrard D. *A Treatise of the Canker of England's Commonwealth*. London: R. Field for W. Iohnes, 1601. Excerpts reprinted in *Tudor Economic Documents*, Volume III, pp. 386–404. Edited by R. H. Tawney and Eileen Power. London: Longmans, Green, 1924.

Marshall, Alfred. "Memoranda and Evidence Before the Gold and Silver Commission" (1888). In *Official Papers*, pp. 17–195. London: Macmillan, 1926.

———. "Evidence Before the Indian Currency Commission" (1899). In *Official Papers*, pp. 263–326. London: Macmillan, 1926.

———. *Money, Credit & Commerce*. London: Macmillan, 1923.

McKinnon, Ronald I. *Monetary Theory and Controlled Flexibility in the Foreign Exchanges*. Essays in International Finance, No. 84. International Finance Section, Princeton University, 1971.

———. *Money and Capital in Economic Development*. Washington, D.C.: The Brookings Institution, 1973.

———. *Money in International Exchange: The Convertible Currency System*. New York: Oxford University Press, 1979.

McLeod, A. N. *A Critique of the Fluctuating-Exchange-Rate Policy in Canada*. The Bulletin, No. 34–35. C. J. Devine Institute of Finance, New York University, 1965.

Meade, J. E. *The Balance of Payments*. London: Oxford University Press, 1951.

Meier, Gerald M. *International Economics: The Theory of Policy*. New York: Oxford University Press, 1980.

Meinich, Per. *A Monetary General Equilibrium Theory for an International Economy*. Oslo: The Norwegian Research Council for Science and the Humanities, 1968.

Metzler, Lloyd A. "Exchange Rates and the International Monetary Fund." In *International Monetary Policies*, pp. 1–45. Postwar Economic Studies, No. 7. Washington: Board of Governors of the Federal Reserve System, 1947.

———. "The Theory of International Trade." In Howard S. Ellis (ed.), *A Survey of Contemporary Economics*. Philadelphia: Blakiston, 1948, pp. 210–254.

Michaely, Michael. "Analyses of Devaluation: Purchasing Power Parity, Elasticities, and Absorption." In David Bigman and Tetzo Taya (eds.), *The Functioning of Floating Exchange Rates*. Cambridge, Mass.: Ballinger, 1980, pp. 33–54.

Mikesell, Raymond F. "The Determination of Postwar Exchange Rates." *Southern Economic Journal* 13(January 1947):263–275.

Mill, John Stuart. *Principles of Political Economy* (1848). Edited by Sir W. J. Ashley. London: Longmans, Green, 1929.

Minhas, Bagicha Singh. *An International Comparison of Factor Costs and Factor Use*. Amsterdam: North-Holland, 1963.

Minsol, Archen. "Some Tests of the International Comparisons of Factor Efficiency with the CES Production Fucntion: A Reply." *Review of Economics and Statistics* 50 (November 1968):477–479.

Mints, Lloyd W. *A History of Banking Theory*. Chicago: University of Chicago Press, 1945.

Mises, Ludwig von. *Theorie des Geldes und der Umlaufsmittel*. Munich: Verlag von Duncker & Humblot, 1912.

_____. *The Theory of Money and Credit.* New York: Harcourt Brace, 1936.

_____. *On the Manipulation of Money and Credit.* Translated by Bettina Bien Greaves and edited by Percy L. Greaves, Jr. Dobbs Ferry, New York: Free Market Books, 1978.

Mitchell, B. R. *European Historical Statistics 1750-1970.* New York: Columbia University Press, 1975.

Mitchell, Wesley Clair. *A History of the Greenbacks.* Chicago: University of Chicago Press, 1903.

Moggridge, Donald E. *British Monetary Policy, 1924-1931: The Norman Conquest of $4.86.* Cambridge: Cambridge University Press, 1972.

Morgenstern, Oskar. *International Financial Transactions and Business Cycles.* Princeton, N.J.: Princeton University Press, 1959.

Mudd, Douglas R. "Movements in the Foreign Exchange Value of the Dollar During the Current U.S. Expansion." Federal Reserve Bank of St. Louis *Review* 60(November 1978):2-7.

Mussa, Michael. "Empirical Regularities in the Behavior of Exchange Rates and Theories of the Foreign Exchange Market." In Karl Brunner and Allan H. Meltzer (eds.), *Policies for Employment, Prices, and Exchange Rates.* Carnegie-Rochester Conference Series on Public Policy, Volume 11. Amsterdam: North-Holland, 1979, pp. 9-57.

Myhrman, Johan. "Experiences of Flexible Exchange Rates in Earlier Periods: Theories, Evidence and a New View." *Scandinavian Journal of Economics* 78(No. 2, 1976):169-196.

Needleman, L. "The Burden of Taxation: An International Comparison." *National Institute Economic Review* (March 1961):55-61.

Neuberger, Egon. "Central Planning and its Legacies: Implications for Foreign Trade." *In* Alan A. Brown and Egon Neuberger (eds.), *International Trade and Central Planning: An Analysis of Economic Interactions.* Berkeley and Los Angeles: University of California Press, 1968, pp. 349-377.

New Zealand, Department of Statistics. *The New Zealand Official Year Book.* Wellington, various years.

Nurkse, Ragnar. *International Currency Experience.* League of Nations. Princeton, N.J.: Princeton University Press, 1944.

_____. *Conditions of International Monetary Equilibrium.* Essays in International Finance, No. 4. International Finance Section, Princeton University, 1945. Reprinted in *Readings in the Theory of International Trade,* pp. 3-34. Edited by Howard S. Ellis and Lloyd A. Metzler. Philadelphia: Blakiston, 1950.

O'Brien, D. P. *The Classical Economists.* Oxford: Oxford University Press, 1975.

Officer, Lawrence H. "Purchasing Power Parity and Factor Price Equalization." *Kyklos* 27(Fasc. 4, 1974):868-878.

_____ (1976a). "The Purchasing-Power-Parity Theory of Exchange Rates: A Review Article." International Monetary Fund *Staff Papers* 23(March 1976):1-60.

_____ (1976b). "The Productivity Bias in Purchasing Power Parity: An Econometric Investigation." International Monetary Fund *Staff Papers* 23(November 1976):545-579.

_____. "The Relationship Between Absolute and Relative Purchasing Power Parity." *Review of Economics and Statistics* 60(November 1978):562-568.

_____ (1980a). "Effective Exchange Rates and Price Ratios Over the Long Run: A Test of the Purchasing-Power-Parity Theory." *Canadian Journal of Economics* 13(May 1980):206-230.

_____ (1980b). Review of *Money in International Exchanges: The Convertible Currency System,* by Ronald I. McKinnon. *Journal of Money, Credit and Banking* 12(August 1980):562-564.

Ohkawa, Kazushi, and Henry Rosovsky. *Japanese Economic Growth*. Stanford, California: Stanford University Press, 1973.

Organization for Economic Co-operation and Development (OECD). *Labour Force Statistics 1964–1975*. 1977.

————. *Labour Force Statistics*. Various issues.

————. *National Accounts of OECD Countries*. Various issues.

Organization for European Economic Co-operation (OEEC). *Statistics of National Product and Expenditure, No. 2, 1938 and 1947 to 1955*. 1957.

Paige, Deborah, and Gottfried Bombach. *A Comparison of National Output and Productivity of the United Kingdom and the United States*. Paris: Organisation for European Economic Co-operation, 1959.

Paxton, John (ed.). *The Statesman's Year-Book*. New York: St. Martin's Press, various years.

Pearce, I. F. *International Trade*. New York: W. W. Norton, 1970.

Perkins, Edwin J. "Foreign Interest Rates in American Financial Markets: A Revised Series of Dollar-Sterling Exchange Rates, 1835–1900." *Journal of Economic History* 38(June 1978):392–417.

Pigou, A. C. "The Foreign Exchanges." *Quarterly Journal of Economics* 37(November 1922):52–74.

Pincus, John A. *Economic Aid and International Cost Sharing*. Baltimore: Johns Hopkins University Press, 1965.

Pippenger, John E. "Spot Rates, Forward Rates, and Interest-Rate Differentials. *Journal of Money, Credit and Banking* 4(May 1972):375–383.

————. "Speculation in the Flexible Exchange Re-revisited." *Kyklos* 26(Fasc. 3, 1973):613–618.

Polak, J. J. *The National Income of the Netherlands Indies, 1921–1939*. New York: Netherlands and Netherlands Indies Council of the Institute of Pacific Relations, c. 1943.

Poole, William. "The Stability of the Canadian Flexible Exchange Rate, 1950–1962." *Canadian Journal of Economics and Political Science* 33(May 1967):205–217.

Porzecanski, Arturo C. "A Comparative Study of Exchange Rate Policy under Inflation." *Journal of Developing Areas* 12(January 1978):133–151.

Pryor, Frederic L. "Comparable GNPs per Capita: An Addendum." *Economic Journal* 89 (September 1979):666–668.

Quirk, Peter J. "Exchange Rate Policy in Japan: Leaning Against the Wind." International Monetary Fund *Staff Papers* 24(November 1977):642–664.

Report from the Committee on the Circulating Paper, the Specie, and the Current Coin of Ireland; and also, on the Exchange between that Part of the United Kingdom and Great Britain. House of Commons, May and June 1804. Reprinted in *The Irish Pound 1797–1826*. By Frank Whitson Fetter. Evanston, Illinois: Northwestern University Press, 1955.

Report from the Select Committee on the High Price of Bullion. House of Commons, 1810. Reprinted in *The Paper Pound of 1797–1821. A Reprint of the Bullion Report*. By Edwin Cannan. London: P. S. King & Son, second edition, 1925.

Rhomberg, Rudolf R. "The Canadian Exchange Rate, 1950–57: Comment." *Southern Economic Journal* 27(October 1960):141–143.

————. "Indices of Effective Exchange Rates." International Monetary Fund *Staff Papers* 23(March 1976):88–112.

Ricardo, David. *The High Price of Bullion* (1810–11). Reprinted in Sraffa (1951), Volume III, pp. 47–127.

———— (1811a). *Reply to Mr. Bosanquet's Practical Observations on the Report of the Bullion Committee* (1811). Reprinted in Sraffa (1951), Volume III, pp. 157–256.

_____ (1811b). *Letter to [Malthus?], 23ᵈ June 1811.* Printed in Sraffa (1952), Volume VI, pp. 29-30.

_____ (1811c). *Letter to Malthus, 17 July 1811.* Printed in Sraffa (1952), Volume VI, pp. 35-40.

_____. *Letter to Horner, 4 Jan. 1812.* Printed in Sraffa (1952), Volume VI, pp. 78-81.

_____. *Proposals for an Economical and Scarce Currency* (1816). Reprinted in Sraffa (1951), Volume IV, pp. 49-141.

_____. *On the Principles of Political Economy and Taxation* (1817-21). Reprinted in Sraffa (1951), Volume I, pp. 1-442.

_____ (1819a). *Evidence on the Resumption of Cash Payments* (1819). Reprinted in Sraffa (1952), Volume V, pp. 349-457.

_____ (1819b). *Letter to McCulloch, 2 Oct. 1819.* Printed in Sraffa (1952), Volume VIII, pp. 85-93.

Robertson, D. H. *Money.* London: Nisbet, 1922.

Robinson, Joan. "The Foreign Exchanges." In *Essays in the Theory of Employment.* New York: Macmillan, 1937, pp. 183-209.

_____. "Macroeconomics of Unbalanced Growth: A Belated Comment." *American Economic Review* 59(September 1969):632.

Rogalski, Richard J., and Joseph D. Vinso. "Price Level Variations as Predictors of Flexible Exchange Rates." *Journal of International Business Studies* 8(Spring/Summer 1977):71-81.

Rogers, James Harvey. *The Process of Inflation in France 1914-1927.* New York: Columbia University Press, 1929.

Roll, Richard. "Violations of Purchasing Power Parity and Their Implications for Efficient International Commodity Markets." In Marshall Sarnat and Giorgio P. Szegö (eds.), *International Finance and Trade,* Volume I. Cambridge, Massachusetts: Ballinger, 1979, pp. 133-176.

Rothschild, K. "Actual and Implied Exchange Rates." *Scottish Journal of Political Economy* 5(October 1958):229-235.

Sadie, J. L. "Further Observations on Foreign Exchange Rates." *South African Journal of Economics* 16(June 1948):194-201.

Sakakibara, Eisuke. "Purchasing Power Parity and Currency Substitution." *Economic Studies Quarterly* 30(December 1979):202-218.

Salazar-Carrillo, Jorge. "Latin American Real Product Comparisons." *Economic Journal* 87 (December 1977):761-764.

Samuelson, Paul A. "Disparity in Postwar Exchange Rates." In Seymour Harris (ed.), *Foreign Economic Policy for the United States.* Cambridge, Mass.: Harvard University Press, 1948, pp. 397-412.

_____. "Theoretical Notes on Trade Problems." *Review of Economics and Statistics* 46(May 1964):145-154.

_____. "An Exact Hume-Ricardo-Marshall Model of International Trade." *Journal of International Economics* 1(February 1971):1-18.

_____. "Analytical Notes on International Real-Income Measures." *Economic Journal* 84 (September 1974):595-608.

Sayers, R. S. "Ricardo's Views on Monetary Questions." *Quarterly Journal of Economics* 67(February 1953), pp. 30-49.

_____. "The Return to Gold, 1925." In L. S. Pressnell (ed.), *Studies in the Industrial Revolution,* London: The Athlone Press, 1960, pp. 313-327.

Scammell, W. M. *International Monetary Policy.* London: Macmillan, second edition, 1961.

Schumpeter, Joseph A. *History of Economic Analysis.* New York: Oxford University Press, 1954.

Shapiro, S. S., and M. B. Wilk. "An Analysis of Variance Test for Normality (Complete Samples)." *Biometrika* 52(December 1965):591–611.

Shapiro, S. S., M. B. Wilk, and H. J. Chen. "A Comparative Study of Various Tests for Normality." *Journal of the American Statistical Association* 63(December 1968):1343–1372.

Silberling, Norman J. "Financial and Monetary Policy of Great Britain During the Napoleonic Wars." *Quarterly Journal of Economics* 38(May 1924):397–439.

Sims, Christopher A. "Money, Income and Causality." *American Economic Review* 62 (September 1972):540–552.

Solnik, Bruno. "International Parity Conditions and Exchange Risk." In Marshall Sarnat and Giorgio P. Szegö (eds.), *International Finance and Trade,* Volume I. Cambridge, Mass.: Ballinger, 1979, pp. 83–97.

Sraffa, Piero (ed.). *The Works and Correspondence of David Ricardo.* Volumes I-VIII. Cambridge: Cambridge University Press, 1951 and 1952.

Statistics Canada. *National Income and Expenditure Accounts.* Volume I. The Annual Estimates 1926–1974. Ottawa: Information Canada, 1976.

Statistisches Bundesamt. See Germany, Federal Republic of.

Statistisk Sentralbyra. *Langtidslinjer I Norsk Økonomi 1865–1960.* Oslo, 1966.

Stern, Robert M. *The Balance of Payments: Theory and Economic Policy.* Chicago: Aldine, 1973.

Stockman, Alan C. "On Explaining the Behavior of Exchange Rates: A Comment on Papers by Mussa and Bilson." In Karl Brunner and Allan H. Meltzer (eds.), *Policies for Employment, Prices, and Exchange Rates.* Carnegie-Rochester Conference Series on Public Policy, Volume 11. Amsterdam: North-Holland, 1979, pp. 123–130.

―――. "A Theory of Exchange Rate Determination." *Journal of Political Economy* 88 (August 1980):673–698.

Stolper, W. F. "Purchasing Power Parity and the Pound Sterling from 1919–1925." *Kyklos* 2(Fasc. 3, 1948):240–269.

Subercaseux, Guillermo. *El Papel Moneda.* Santiago, Chile: Imprenta Cervantes, 1912.

Summers, Robert, Irving B. Kravis, and Alan Heston. "International Comparisons of Real Product and Its Composition: 1950-77." *Review of Income and Wealth* 26(March 1980):19–66.

Syrett, W. W. "A Revision of the Theory of Forward Exchanges." *The Banker* (June 1936):202–206.

Tamagna, Frank M. "The Fixing of Foreign Exchange Rates." *Journal of Political Economy* 53(March 1945):57–72.

Terborgh, G. W. "The Purchasing-Power Parity Theory." *Journal of Political Economy* 34 (April 1926):197–208.

Thomas, Lloyd B. "Some Evidence on International Currency Experience, 1919–25." *Nebraska Journal of Economics and Business* 2(Autumn 1972):145–155.

―――― (1973a). "Speculation in the Flexible Exchange Revisited—Another View." *Kyklos* 26(Fasc. 1, 1973):143–150.

―――― (1973b). "Behavior of Flexible Exchange Rates: Additional Tests from the Post-World War I Episode." *Southern Economic Journal* 40(October 1973):167–182.

Thompson, Gerald Richard. *Expectations and the Greenback Rate, 1862–1878.* Unpublished Ph.D. dissertation, University of Virginia, 1972.

Thornton, Henry. *An Enquiry into the Nature and Effects of the Paper Credit of Great Britain.*

London: J. Hatchard and F. and C. Rivington, 1802. Reprinted, edited by F. A. v. Hayek. New York: Farrar & Rinehart, 1939.

_____. *Parliamentary Speech, May 7, 1811.* In Henry Thornton, *An Enquiry into the Nature and Effects of the Paper Credit of Great Britain,* pp. 327–346. Edited by F. A. v. Hayek. New York: Farrar & Rinehart, 1939.

Thygesen, Niels. "Inflation and Exchange Rates: Evidence and Policy Guidelines for the European Community." *Journal of International Economics* 8(May 1978):301–317.

Triffin, Robert. "La théorie de la surévaluation monétaire de la dévaluation belge." *Bulletin de L'Institut de Recherches Economiques* 9(November 1937):19–52.

_____. "National Central Banking and the International Economy." In *International Monetary Policies.* Postwar Economic Studies, No. 7. Washington: Board of Governors of the Federal Reserve System, 1947, pp. 46–81.

Tsiang, S. C. "Fluctuating Exchange Rates in Countries with Relatively Stable Economies: Some European Experiences After World War I." International Monetary Fund *Staff Papers* 7(October 1959):244–273.

Tyler, William G. "Exchange Rate Flexibility under Conditions of Endemic Inflation: A Case Study of the Recent Brazilian Experience." In C. Fred Bergsten and William G. Tyler (eds.), *Leading Issues in International Economic Policy.* Lexington, Mass.: D. C. Heath, 1973, pp. 19–49.

United Nations. *Yearbook of International Trade Statistics, 1975.* Volume I. Trade by Country. New York, 1976.

_____. *Yearbook of National Accounts Statistics.* Volume I. New York, 1973.

_____. *Yearbook of National Accounts Statistics.* New York, various years.

Urquhart, M. C., and K. A. H. Buckley, eds. *Historical Statistics of Canada.* Toronto: Macmillan, 1965.

U.S. Bureau of the Census. *Historical Statistics of the United States, Colonial Times to 1970.* Bicentennial Edition. Washington, D.C.: U.S. Government Printing Office, 1975.

U.S. Department of Commerce, Office of Business Economics. *The National Income and Products Accounts of the United States, 1929–1965.* Washington, D.C.: U.S. Government Printing Office, 1966.

United States Tariff Commission. *Depreciated Exchange and International Trade.* Washington: Government Printing Office, 1922.

Vanek, Jaroslav. *International Trade: Theory and Economic Policy.* Homewood, Ill.: Richard D. Irwin, 1962.

Vaubel, Roland. "Real Exchange-Rate Changes in the European Community: The Empirical Evidence and Its Implications for European Currency Unification." *Weltwirtschaftliches Archiv* 112(No. 3, 1976):429–470.

_____. "Real Exchange-Rate Changes in the European Community: A New Approach to the Determination of Optimum Currency Areas." *Journal of International Economics* 8(May 1978):319–339.

Viner, Jacob. *Studies in the Theory of International Trade.* New York: Harper and Brothers, 1937.

Wasserman, Max J. "The Compression of French Wholesale Prices During Inflation, 1919–1926." *American Economic Review* 26(March 1936):62–73.

Wasserman, Max J., Charles W. Hultman, and Roy M. Ware. *Modern International Economics.* Cambridge, Massachusetts: Schenkman, revised edition, 1971.

Watanabe, Tsunehiko, and Ryutaro Komiya. "Findings from Price Comparisons Principally Japan vs. the United States." *Weltwirtschaftliches Archiv* 81(I, 1958):81–96.

Wheatley, John. *Remarks on Currency and Commerce.* London: Cadell and Davies, 1803.

————. *An Essay on the Theory of Money and Principles of Commerce.* London: T. Cadell and W. Davies, 1807.

————. *Report on the Reports of the Bank Committees.* London: Longman, Hurst, Rees, Orme, and Brown, 1819.

Whitaker, John K., and Maxwell W. Hudgins, Jr. "The Floating Pound Sterling of the Nineteen-Thirties: An Econometric Study." *Southern Economic Journal* 43(April 1977):1478–1485.

White, Horace G., Jr. "Foreign Exchange Rates and Internal Prices under Inconvertible Paper Currencies." *American Economic Review* 25(June 1935):259–272.

Whittaker, Edmund. *A History of Economic Ideas.* New York: Longmans, Green, 1940.

Wihlborg, Clas. *Currency Risks in International Financial Markets.* Princeton Studies in International Finance No. 44. International Finance Section, Princeton University, 1978.

————. "Flexible Exchange Rates, Currency Risks and the Integration of Capital Markets." In Assar Lindbeck (ed.), *Inflation and Employment in Open Economies,* Amsterdam: North-Holland, 1979, pp. 169–187.

Wijnholds, H. W. J. "Some Observations on Foreign Exchange Rates in Theory and Practice." *South African Journal of Economics* 15(December 1947):235–247.

Wiles, P. J. D. *Communist International Economics.* New York: Frederick A. Praeger, 1969.

Willett, Thomas D. "Floating Exchange Rates and Modified Purchasing Power Parity: Discussion Comments." In *Proceedings of 1978 West Coast Academic/Federal Reserve Economic Research Seminar.* Federal Reserve Bank of San Francisco, 1979, pp. 184–189.

Williams, John H. "Foreign Exchange under Depreciated Paper." *Journal of the American Bankers Association* 14(January 1922):492–494.

Wu, Chi-Yuen. *An Outline of International Price Theories.* London: George Routeledge & Sons, 1939.

Yeager, Leland B. "A Rehabilitation of Purchasing-Power Parity." *Journal of Political Economy* 66(December 1958):516–530.

————. *The International Monetary Mechanism.* New York: Holt, Rinehart and Winston, 1968.

————. "Fluctuating Exchange Rates in the Nineteenth Century: The Experiences of Austria and Russia." In Robert A. Mundell and Alexander K. Swoboda (eds.), *Monetary Problems of the International Economy.* Chicago: University of Chicago Press, 1969, pp. 61–89.

————. *International Monetary Relations: Theory, History, and Policy.* New York: Harper & Row, 1976.

Young, John Parke. *European Currency and Finance.* Commission of Gold and Silver Inquiry, United States Senate, Foreign Currency and Exchange Investigation, Serial 9, Volumes I and II. Washington: Government Printing Office, 1925.

————. *International Trade and Finance.* New York: The Ronald Press, 1938.

————. "Exchange Rate Determination." *American Economic Review* 37(June 1947):589–603.

Author Index

316 / *Purchasing Power Parity and Exchange Rates*

Foster, John Leslie
  member of bullionist committees, 69, 70
  modern assessments of, 72 n.18
  PPP theory, 61
  quantity theory of money, 61-62
Frenkel, Jacob A.
  price measure for PPP, 121
  PPP/floating-exchange-rate contemporaneous comparisons, 179-180, 182, 194 n.18
  Ricardo, 53, 72 n.24
  tests of causality, 184-185
  validity of PPP theory, 135
  Wheatley, 53
Friedman, Milton
  GDP price level or deflator, 122
  PPP theory, 113
  real-exchange-rate investigations, 191
Fry, Maxwell J.
  productivity-bias hypothesis, 131
Furniss, Edgar S.
  PPP/floating-exchange-rate contemporaneous comparisons, 175

Gailliot, Henry J.
  comparative-static PPP/exchange-rate comparisons, 187, 262, 284 n.9
  mint-parity data, 282
Gallman, Robert E.
  national-accounts data, 280
Gandolfo, Giancarlo
  equilibrium exchange rate, 14-15
Garnsey, Morris E.
  depreciation of Belgian franc in 1935, 144
  overvalued Belgian franc in 1935, 143, 144, 158 n.10
Gelders, H.
  labor data, 283
Genberg, Hans
  price index required for PPP, 121
  productivity-bias hypothesis, 172 n.12
  PPP/floating-exchange-rate: contemporaneous comparisons, 181; lagged relationships, 184
  real-exchange-rate investigations, 192
  validity of PPP theory, 135
Gibbon, Edward
  imports of Roman Empire, 26, 36 n.1

Nero's role in Roman international trade, 26
  price difference between Rome and its trading partners, 27
  profit in Rome's international trade, 26-27
  Roman international trade route, 26
  Roman oceanic fleet, 26
  self-sufficiency of ancient Arabia and India, 27
Giddy, Ian H.
  exchange-rate forecasting, 154
  interest-rate theory of exchange-rate expectations, 115
  relative PPP theory, 117 ns.15-16
Gilbert, Milton
  absolute-PPP data, 163, 164, 172 n.4, 224, 226, 228, 245 n.26, 246 n.32, 259
Girton, Lance
  neutrality hypothesis, 108
Goldstein, Henry N.
  augmented PPP theory, 189
  effective exchange rate, 22 n.13
Goldstein, Morris
  tradable/nontradable price-ratio investigations, 195 n.30
  tradable/nontradable productivity ratio, 172 n.11
Goodman, Stephen H.
  exchange-rate forecasting, 152-153
Goschen, Viscount
  balance-of-payments theory, 76, 77, 82, 84
  Cassel on, 88, 89
  Einzig on, 82
  floating exchange rate, 76-77
  neutrality hypothesis, 76-77
  price-level concept, 76
  quantity theory of money, 76
  real/nominal exchange-rate distinction, 76-77
  relative PPP theory, 76-77, 82, 86
Graham, Frank D.
  augmented PPP theory, 194 n.26
  PPP/floating-exchange-rate contemporaneous comparisons, 176-177
  WPI for domestic commodities, 189
Gregory, T. E.
  overvaluation of British pound in 1925, 142, 158 n.5

318 / *Purchasing Power Parity and Exchange Rates*

Hodgson, John S.
augmented PPP theory, 189
PPP/floating-exchange-rate: contem-
poraneous comparisons, 178–179,
194 n.16; lagged relationships, 184
exchange-rate policy of Yugoslavia,
150–151
Hollander, Jacob H.
1804 bullionist committee report, 72 n.27
English bullionist debate, 71 n.2
Horner, 71 n.7
Thornton, 71 n.4
Wheatley, 71 n.11
Holmes, James M.
augmented PPP theory, 189–190
Cassel, 90, 98, 99, 102 n.7
Holzman, Franklyn D.
exchange-rate systems of STEs, 158 n.15
overvaluation of Russian rouble, 151–152
Horner, Francis
Blake on, 62, 72 n.20
market/real/nominal exchange-rate concepts, 51–53
member of 1810 bullionist committee,
69, 70
modern assessments of, 71 n.7
neutrality hypothesis, 53
price-level measure, 51, 52
PPP theory, 51–53
review of Thornton's work, 51, 53, 71 n.7
Ricardo on, 67
tradable/nontradable price ratio, 52
Houthakker, Hendrik S.
COL level, 112–113
factor-price equalization, 199
Fisher ideal index, 136 n.8, 205
GDP deflator or price level, 112, 113,
122, 250–251
index-number problems in PPP theory
of, 112–113, 210
long-term capital movements, 111, 124,
210 n.2
overvaluation of U.S. dollar: in 1957,
146–147, 158 n.12, 199; in 1962,
146, 158 n.12, 171, 199
unilateral transfers, 111, 124, 210 n.2
ULC (and implied price) parity, 110–113,
117 n.13, 132, 200–203, 209, 210,
210 n.2, 250
validity of PPP theory, 119, 139, 199

weighting pattern of price level, 112, 136
n.7, 203–205, 259
Hsiao, Cheng
tests of causality, 194 n.21
Hudgins, Maxwell W., Jr.
augmented PPP theory, 194–195 n.27
Hughes, J. R. T.
mint-parity data, 282
19th-century gold standard, 83, 285 n.21
Hulsman-Vejsová, Marie
international comparison of output, 245
n.16
productivity-bias hypothesis, 172 n.6
Hultman, Charles W.
Thornton, 48
Hume, David
law of one price, 60, 72 n.17
transport costs, 72 n.17
Wheatley on, 72 n.17
Humphrey, Thomas M.
absolute PPP theory, 117 n.4
asset-market approach, 136 n.3
Blake, 72 n.19
Christiernin, 41
English bullionist position, 71 n.2
general price indices and classical
economists, 71 n.10
Mises, 84 n.6
neutrality hypothesis, 108
Ricardo, 72 ns.24 *and* 26
Thornton, 48, 53, 71 n.4
Wheatley, 48, 53, 58, 72 n.14
Huskisson, William
member of 1810 bullionist committee, 70

Ingram, James C.
augmented PPP theory, 188
PPP/floating-exchange-rate lagged relationships, 183
Isard, Peter
comparative-static PPP/exchange-rate
comparisons, 187
criterion for PPP theory, 22 n.12
productivity-bias hypothesis, 172 n.12
relative PPP theory, 117 n.14
Salamancans, 36 n.5
tradable/nontradable price ratio, 107
Isenman, Paul
alternative to productivity-bias
hypothesis, 170–171

Tanzi, Vito
  alternative to productivity-bias
    hypothesis, 169–170, 172 n.19
  productivity-bias hypothesis, 165, 166,
    168–169, 170, 172 n.9, 214–219 *scattered*
Taussig, F. W.
  productivity-bias hypothesis, 127, 136
    n.14
Taylor, Lance
  base period, 128
  neutrality hypothesis, 129
Terborgh, G. W.
  absolute PPP theory, 117 n.2
  role of PPP theory, 22 n.11
Thomas, Lloyd B.
  augmented PPP theory, 189
  exchange-market speculation in French
    franc after World War I, 148
  extrapolating historical results on PPP to
    current situation, 291–292
  PPP/floating-exchange-rate: contem-
    poraneous comparisons, 178, 194
    ns.13–15; lagged relationships,
    183–184
Thompson, Gerald Richard
  augmented PPP theory, 188–189
Thornton, Henry
  member of bullionist committees, 69, 70
  modern assessments of, 47–48, 53, 71 n.4
  neutrality hypothesis, 50–51
  price-level concept, 48, 54, 58
  PPP theory, 49–51
  quantity theory of money, 48–49, 50
  work reviewed by Horner, 51, 53, 71 n.7
Thygesen, Niels
  exchange-market intervention policy,
    155, 156, 159 n.24
  GDP deflator, 159 n.24
  PPP/floating-exchange-rate contem-
    poraneous comparisons, 194 n.19
  WPI, 121
Triffin, Robert
  depreciation of Belgian franc in 1935,
    143–144
  equilibrium exchange rate, 12
  overvalued Belgian franc in 1932–35,
    143–144, 158 n.9
Tsiang, S. C.
  exchange-market speculation after
    World War I, 148, 158 n.13

Tyler, William G.
  real exchange rate for Brazilian cruzeiro,
    149

Urquhart, M. C.
  terms-of-trade data, 283
  trade data, 282–283
  WPI data, 283
Usher, Dan
  productivity-bias hypothesis, 127, 136
    n.14
Uzzano, Giovanni di Antonio da
  money-supply theory of foreign ex-
    change, 29

Vanek, Jaroslav
  national income, 136 n.19
  neutrality hypothesis, 108
  structural conditions, 136 n.20
  weighting pattern of price level or index,
    120
Vaubel, Roland
  real exchange rate: for countries of EC,
    150; for regions of Germany, Italy
    and United States, 150
Viner, Jacob
  English bullionist debate, 71 n.2
  English bullionist period, 71 n.1
  Evelyn, 55, 72 n.12
  neutrality hypothesis, 108
  price-level concept lacked by classical
    economists, 54–55, 65
  productivity-bias hypothesis, 127, 136
    n.14
  Ricardo, 65, 66, 67, 72 n.23
  weighting pattern of price level or index,
    120
  Wheatley, 71 n.11
Vinso, Joseph D.
  tests of causality, 184

Ware, Roy W.
  Thornton, 48
Wasserman, Max J.
  Thornton, 48
  PPP/floating-exchange-rate contem-
    poraneous comparisons, 177
Watanabe, Tsunehiko
  absolute-PPP data, 228, 229, 246 n.33
Wheatley, John
  absolute PPP theory, 57–61

Subject Index

Balance of Payments, *cont'd.*
current-account balance, 7–8, 9, 11, 14, 15, 92
monetary gold, 8, 10, 22 ns.3–4
official-settlements balance, 8, 15
trade balance, 9, 14, 92
inhibiting relative PPP theory, 191
motivational concept of, 10, 13
potential disequilibrium in, 12–13, 14, 22 n.6
(*see also* Balance-of-payments theory of exchange rate; Balance of trade; Capital movements; Current account)
Balance-of-payments theory of exchange rate
of Bank of England, 69
of Bank of Ireland, 69
of Blake, 62, 64
confirmed by Crump, 175
convenient for policy-makers, 289
denied by Wheatley, 58, 64, 72 n.15
in 18th-century Sweden, 39
in English bullionist period, 46–47
of Goschen, 76, 77, 82, 84
of Marshall, 78
rejected by Cassel, 95–96, 101, 175
of Ricardo, 68
Balance of trade
in augmented PPP theory, 188, 191, 192, 194–195 n.27
in definition of equilibrium exchange rate, 9, 14, 92
determined by current PPP, 183
inhibiting relative PPP theory, 175, 177, 191
theory of exchange rate. (*See* Balance-of-payments theory of exchange rate)
Balance on goods and services (*See* Current account)
Bank of England (*See* Bullionist period, English; United Kingdom)
Bank of Ireland (*See* Bullionist period, Irish)
Bank Restriction Period (*See* Bullionist period, English)
Base period
actual exchange rate versus absolute PPP in, 136 n.15
Cassel, 97

in definition of exchange-rate index, 17
in definition of relative PPP concept, 5–6, 6–7
conflicting criteria in selecting, 130
difficult to find normal or equilibrium, 128
exchange rate may not be in equilibrium in, 128, 285 n.21
rationale for, generally ignored, 292
requirements for, in comparative-static PPP/exchange-rate comparisons, 185, 264–265
used in PPP computations
prior to 1913, 187, 281, 285 n.20
1913, 141, 145, 148, 174, 175, 185, 188
1920s, 144, 147, 183
1930s, 143–147 *scattered*, 158 ns.8–9, 177, 186
1940s, 147, 148–149
1950s, 147–151 *scattered*, 214
1960s, 149, 181
1970s, 181
Basic balance
in definition of equilibrium exchange rate, 9, 10, 11, 14, 15, 22 ns. 3–4, 96
Belgium
deflation and unemployment in 1932–35, 143
subject in comparative-static PPP/exchange-rate comparison, 251
subject in testing of productivity-bias hypothesis for absolute PPP, 222, 224, 228
subject in tradable/nontradable price-ratio investigation, 237
(*See also* Franc, Belgian)
Borrowing or lending abroad. (*See* Capital movements)
Brazil
overvalued currency in 1946, 145–146
real exchange rate of cruzeiro, over 1957–72 and 1963–71, 149
subject in PPP/floating-exchange-rate contemporaneous comparison, 182
Britain (*See* United Kingdom)
Bullion, price of
proxy for price level, 51, 71 n.10
Bullionist Committee (of 1804)
creation of, 69
membership of, 69, 70

Investment income (*See* Interest and dividends)

Ireland (*See* Bullionist period, Irish; Depreciation, exchange-market; Inflation)

Israel
subject in comparative-static PPP/exchange-rate comparison, 252

Italy
real exchange rate for regions over 1959–76, 150
subject in comparative-static PPP/exchange-rate comparison, 251, 252, 269, 270
subject in PPP/floating-exchange-rate contemporaneous comparison, 175
subject in test of equivalence of ULC and price parities, 208–209, 210 n.6
subject in testing of productivity-bias hypothesis for absolute PPP, 163, 222, 224, 225, 228
subject in tradable/nontradable price-ratio investigation, 237
(*see also* Lira, Italian)

Japan
subject in comparative-static PPP/exchange-rate comparison, 187, 251, 270
subject in PPP/floating-exchange-rate contemporaneous comparison, 177–178, 180–181, 194 ns.11 *and* 13–14
subject in real-exchange-rate investigation, 192
subject in testing of productivity-bias hypothesis for absolute PPP, 217, 225, 228, 245 ns.25 *and* 35
subject in tradable/nontradable price-ratio investigation, 193, 195 n.29, 237
(*see also* Yen, Japanese)

Kenya
subject in comparative-static PPP/exchange-rate comparison, 251

Krona (crown), Swedish
floating during World War I, 175, 176, 185, 186
floating in 1923–24, 144

floating in 1930s, 147–148, 183
overvalued in 1924, 144–145
foreign or standard currency in PPP computations, 147, 185, 186

Latin America
absolute-PPP data of Economic Commission for, 172 n.9
countries of, subjects in testing of alternative to productivity-bias hypothesis for absolute PPP, 170
countries of, subjects in testing of productivity-bias hypothesis for absolute PPP, 165–166, 169, 170, 172 n.9, 214–215
international comparison of output in, 140
(*see also names of individual countries*)

Law of one interest rate (*See* Law of one price, for real interest rates)

Law of one price
for general price levels
accounting for international transmission of inflation, 108
Cassel, 96–97
expression of, 60
in form of augmented PPP theory, 189–190
Hume, 60, 72 n.17
Marshall, 77, 79, 84 n.5
Mill, 73–74
permits use of PPP theory in forecasting, 154
in recent literature, 107–108, 117 n.7
relationship to absolute PPP theory, 60, 107–108, 117 n.7
Ricardo, 66–67, 73
test of PPP theory in form of, 184
Wheatley, 59–61, 66, 72 n.17, 73, 74
for tradable commodities, 67, 107, 112, 162, 203, 205
Artus, 110
Cassel, 91
empirical testing of, 168, 172 n.16
Marshall, 78–79, 84 n.5
Mill, 74, 84 n.2
for individual commodities (Cournot), 82, 173
for nontraded commodities, 112, 203–204, 205, 210

List of Symbols

Symbol	Brief Description	Pages where Defined
abs (superscript)	absolute	6
AMC	GDP originating in tradable sector, at current prices	241
AMK	GDP originating in tradable sector, at constant prices	241
ARM	armed forces	242
C	coverage of effective exchange rate	277
CES	constant elasticity of substitution	207[a]
COL	cost of living	18
CPI	consumer price index	18
D	price-index ratio	250
DC	developed country	167
E	exchange rate[b]	18, 151, 178
E	extended 1913 (sample)[b]	273

Notes:
[a]Not defined.
[b]Identical symbol has two alternative meanings.
[c]Identical symbol has five alternative meanings.
[d]Identical symbol has three alternative meanings.

Notes:
[a]Not defined.
[b]Identical symbol has two alternative meanings.
[c]Identical symbol has five alternative meanings.
[d]Identical symbol has three alternative meanings.

L	price level	6, 248
LDC	less developed country	165
l*n*	logarithm	264[a]
log	logarithm	20
M	maximum-coverage (sample)	273
MPL	marginal product of labor	111, 200
N	sample size	276[a]
NNP	net national product	282[a]
o (subscript)	base period	6
OECD	Organization for Economic Co-operation and Development	164
OEEC	Organization for European Economic Co-operation	280[a]
OPTICA	OPTImum Currency Area	155
p	price index[b]	261
p	price (of individual commodity)[b]	248
P	price index[c]	3
P	price-index ratio[c]	262, 264
P	price level[c]	111, 190, 200
P	purchasing power parity[c]	18, 151, 178, 179, 248
P	ratio of purchasing power parities[c]	250
PGDP	GDP price deflator	238
PL	general price level	162
PLN	price level of nontraded commodities	236
PLT	price level of traded commodities	236
PN	price level of nontraded commodities	162
PNT	price index of nontraded commodities	235

Notes:
[a]Not defined.
[b]Identical symbol has two alternative meanings.
[c]Identical symbol has five alternative meanings.
[d]Identical symbol has three alternative meanings.

Notes:
[a]Not defined.
[b]Identical symbol has two alternative meanings.
[c]Identical symbol has five alternative meanings.
[d]Identical symbol has three alternative meanings.

UFC	unit factor cost	18
ULC	unit labor cost	18
UN	United Nations	208[a]
w	weight of commodity in price level[b]	248
w	weight of currency in effective exchange rate[b]	263
W	wage rate[b]	111, 200
W	weight of main trading partner in effective exchange rate[b]	277
WPI	wholesale price index	18
π	rate of inflation	114
ϵ	error term	253

Notes:
[a]Not defined.
[b]Identical symbol has two alternative meanings.
[c]Identical symbol has five alternative meanings.
[d]Identical symbol has three alternative meanings.